The Final Countdown Vol. 3

FIRST PRINTING

Billy Crone

Copyright © 2018
All Rights Reserved

Cover Design:
Chris Taylor

To my wife, Brandie.

*Thank you for being so patient
with a man full of dreams.
You truly are my gift from God.
It is an honor to have you as my wife
and I'm still amazed that you willingly chose
to join me in this challenging yet exhilarating
roller coaster ride called the Christian life.
God has truly done exceedingly abundantly above all
that we could have ever asked or even thought of.
Who ever said that living for the Lord was boring?!
One day our ride together will be over here on earth,
yet it will continue on in eternity forever.
I love you.*

Contents

Preface...................................vii

1. *The Jewish People............................. 9*
2. *Modern Technology............................ 23*
3. *Worldwide Upheaval...........................37*
4. *The Rise of Falsehood......................... 87*
5. *The Rise of Wickedness....................... 125*
6. *The Rise of Apostasy......................... 167*
7. *One World Religion...........................207*
8. *One World Government........................245*
9. *One World Economy...........................319*
10. *The Mark of the Beast........................345*

How to Receive Jesus Christ............... 399
Notes......................................401

Preface

Unfortunately, in the Church today, the study of prophecy has been forsaken under the assumption that one can't really know for sure what it all means and therefore we should refrain from teaching it. Yet, when you think about it, this is actually a slap in the face to God; for a majority of the Holy Scriptures deal directly or indirectly with prophetic issues. Why would God put prophecy in the Bible if it wasn't meant to be understood? Do we dare say that He is playing cat and mouse with us? In addition, how can one say that they are being faithful to present the whole counsel of God when they leave a major portion of it, prophecy, out of the picture?

Bible prophecy has a wonderful way of bringing home two crucial truths that seem to be long forgotten in the American Church. One truth is that this world is not going to last forever. A flood destroyed it the first time and the next time it will be by fire. This forces you and I, the Christian, to stop living merely for the temporary things of this world, thus wasting our lives, and instead to get busy storing up treasures in heaven which last forever. Is that not needed today? Additionally, Bible prophecy drives home the second truth of God being absolutely sovereign. He is in full control of all things at all times. So much so that God has already mapped out mankind's history. Therefore, only the student of Bible prophecy can rightly discern the times in which we live. Best of all, because God is sovereign, no matter how uncomfortable things may get, we can still be at peace knowing that our Lord reigns and that He will soon return to take us to be with Him.

What you are about to read will most assuredly shock you and certainly push you out of your comfort zone. If it doesn't, then you might want to check your pulse. Lest you think I'm making this material up, I invite you to check it out for yourself. This is why everything has been meticulously documented. This is not a time to react in fear but in faith. Our hope is not to be here, but in Heaven. Remember, God is sovereign! One last piece of advice; when you are through reading this book will you please *READ YOUR BIBLE*? I mean that in the nicest possible way. Enjoy, and I'm looking forward to seeing you someday!

Billy Crone
Las Vegas, Nevada
2018

Chapter One

The Jewish People

"Last week, Bill was in line at Burger King and he was in a hurry during his lunch break. This teenager was in front of him and he was holding up the line, ranting and raving to the Manager about how cold his french fries were, you know, acting like a spoiled brat.

Well, Bill couldn't take it anymore, and he decided to set him straight.

He said, 'Excuse me? You think you've got it bad? Hey, in my day we never even went out to eat. The only time we went out to eat was when somebody died! It was called a potluck!

And we had no such thing as microwaves to heat up your french fries! If we wanted to heat something up, we had to use the stove or build a fire. And then if we wanted popcorn, we had to use that stupid Jiffy POP thing and shake it over the stove forever like an idiot and it still burned it black!

And this Internet thing you guys have got, we didn't have that! If we wanted to know something, we had to go to the library and look it up ourselves in the card catalog!

And there was no email stuff either! We had to actually write somebody a letter, with a pen in cursive! And then you had to walk all the way across the street and put it in the mailbox and it would take like a whole week to get there!

And there were no MP3s or free downloads stuff! If you wanted free music, you had to wait around all day to tape it off the radio and the DJ would usually talk over the beginning of it and mess the whole thing up!

And you want to hear about hardship? We didn't have all this fancy stuff like Call Waiting! If you were on the phone and somebody else called, they got a busy signal, just like everybody else!

And we didn't have Caller ID Boxes either! When the phone rang, you had no idea who it was, it could be your boss, your Mom, a collections agent, you didn't know!!! You just had to pick it up and take your chances!

And as far as those fancy PlayStation games with 3D graphics! All we had was the Atari 2600! With games like Space Invaders and Asteroids! Your guy was a little square! You had to use your imagination, you know what I'm saying!

And there were no multiple screens or levels, it was just one screen forever! And you could never win; the game just kept getting harder and harder and faster and faster until you died! Just like in real LIFE, buddy!

And you want to talk about dangerous! There was no such thing as car seats! Mom just threw you in the front seat and you just hung on for your life! And there were no airbags either!

If a car was coming your way, at the last minute you'd get the safety arm across the chest, and if you hit your head on the dashboard it was still all your fault because you called shotgun in the first place!"

I'm sorry, is my order ready yet?'"[1]

  How many of you would say Bill was having a bad day, you know what I'm saying? Time to switch to decaf or something.
  But seriously, believe it or not, I think I've discovered a day that's even worse than that one! It goes something like this. You're driving down the road in heavy traffic, and suddenly your whole family disappears right there in the car! And then you notice it's happened to the other drivers around you too. You're still reeling from the shock of it all when cars start to collide with each other as driverless vehicles start slamming into other vehicles. So you swerve to avoid one yourself but you land in the ditch just as a plane is flying overhead without a

pilot and smashes into a high rise and catches it on fire. Then your radio comes on a with a national news reporter declaring that millions of people all over the planet are suddenly missing.

That's when you see your spouse's Bible sitting on the front seat and it suddenly dawns on you that your family was right after all when they kept telling you about the rapture of the Church. And at that moment, to your horror, you realize that you've been left behind and you're about to be catapulted into the 7-year Tribulation that's coming upon the entire world. The time of the Tribulation is not a party. It's an outpouring of God's wrath on a wicked and rebellious planet.

Jesus said in Matthew 24 that it would be a "time of greater horror than anything the world has ever seen or will ever see again." And that "unless God shortened that time frame, the entire human race would be destroyed!"

But praise God, God's not only a God of wrath, He's a God of love as well. And because He loves you and me, as we saw before, He's given us many warning signs to wake us up so we'd know when the Tribulation is near and His 2nd Coming is rapidly approaching. And that is why we went through our previous study called The Final Countdown. It was 10 signs given by God to wake us up so we'd give our lives to Him before it's too late, if we're not saved. Or, if we are saved, to get motivated before it's too late. Even though that was a long study that we recently finished, so much has happened recently concerning Bible Prophecy, I thought I'd better give you an update! There's no time to waste, so let's get started!

The 1st update on The Final Countdown study is none other than **The Jewish People.**

As we saw before, one of the first and foremost important prophetic events on God's end time calendar is concerning the Jewish people. If you want to know how close we are to the end, then pay attention to the Jewish people. Why? Because from God's point of view, Jerusalem is the center of the earth! This is where the line of the Messiah started! King David ruled from there. This is where Jesus (the actual Messiah) died on a cross.

This is where the End Times culminate with the Battle of Armageddon outside of Jerusalem. This is where Jesus returns at His 2nd Coming. And this is where Jesus reigns after His 2nd Coming. It's all in Jerusalem! As we saw before, Jerusalem is also where the Jewish people will rebuild their last days temple into which the actual Antichrist will go, halfway into the 7-year Tribulation, and declare himself to be god! But don't take my word for it. Let's listen to God's.

2 Thessalonians 2:1-4. "Concerning the coming of our Lord Jesus Christ and our being gathered to Him, we ask you, brothers, not to become easily unsettled or alarmed by some prophecy, report or letter supposed to have come from us, saying that the day of the Lord has already come. Don't let anyone deceive you in any way, for that day will not come until the rebellion occurs and the man of lawlessness is revealed, the man doomed to destruction. He will oppose and will exalt himself over everything that is called God or is worshiped, so that he sets himself up in God's temple, proclaiming himself to be God."

As we saw before, this text tells us that in the last days, the Antichrist is going to go up into the rebuilt Jewish Temple, halfway into the 7-year Tribulation, and declare himself to be god. Do we see any signs of the Jewish people getting ready to rebuild this last days temple that the actual Antichrist will be going up into and declaring himself to be god?

As we saw before, the plans are already made, the priests have been trained, the sacrifices have been instituted again, the stone altar and the articles have been reproduced, and even the ashes of a red heifer needed to cleanse the temple, it's all here. In fact, they're inviting us to go check it out! Let's take a look.

TV Commercial:

"Jerusalem, eternal city of God. The very word is a symphony to the ear to all to whom the Bible is precious. At the heart of Jerusalem lies its secret, the Holy Temple on Mt. Moriah, place of the Sheenah, a divine presence, called by Isaiah The House of Prayer for all nations. For two thousand years the Jewish people have prayed to return to the land of Israel, to Jerusalem, and to rebuild the Holy Temple.

Today we have returned. The city of Jerusalem is built up, a thriving, vibrant city. But what of Jerusalem's secret, what of the dream? For over two decades the Temple Institute has been recreating the biblically appointed vessels to be used in the Holy Temple in preparation for its rebuilding. Tins of sacred vessels have been completed. These vessels of priestly garments on exhibit in the Temple Institutes, Treasures of the Holy Temple Exhibition, in Jerusalem's old city are now copies or replicas that are fit to be used according to strict biblical standards in the new Holy Temple. Original source materials such as gold, silver, and copper, and the original sizes and measurements are used exclusively.

Each year 100,000 visitors come to see, learn about, and experience the promise of the Holy Temple.

A visit to the Temple Institute is the highlight of a trip to Israel, for in the presence of these vessels one can feel that the time of the redemption is indeed drawing close. The golden menorah, the golden table of the showbread, the incense altar, and tins of other sacred vessels have been painstakingly and precisely recreated. Silver trumpets, rabbinical harps and lyres are ready to be heard once again in the streets of Jerusalem.

The priestly garments, including the uniform of the high priest, the ephod, the breastplate and the golden crown, the results of years of intense research and the efforts of Israel's finest artisan craftsmen, are on display for all to see. The Temple Institute provides specially trained guides who explain the history of the Holy Temple, the nature of the divine service, and the significance of the Holy Temple for all mankind.[2]

Don't you want to check it out? See how close we are to building the last days temple that the actual Antichrist is going to go into and declare himself to be god? Folks, it's getting that close! In fact, the Minister of Housing & Construction in Israel is right now calling for the construction of the third temple and Landlords are even preparing contracts for the arrival of the Messiah who they believe will rebuild the temple.

"Many Jerusalem rental contracts are including the unusual stipulation that when the Messiah arrives, tenants must move out so the landlord can move in and enjoy the ensuing paradise."

"Many of Jerusalem's residents believe not only that the Messiah will return, but that his arrival is imminent – so imminent they have taken legal precautions to ensure they can return to Jerusalem immediately upon his return."

The owners, generally religious Jews living abroad, are concerned that he will arrive, build a third temple, turn Israel into paradise and they will be stuck waiting for their apartment tenants' contracts to run out before they can move back. That's how close they think it is for this temple to be rebuilt! They're even preparing the contracts to make sure they don't miss it! But that's still not all

Rabbi Friedman, the Director of the School that is right now training the hundreds of Priests for the services in the Temple said, *"There are 10 studies about the location of the Ark of the Covenant. We read them and studied all of them, and reached the conclusion that it's buried in the tunnels under the Temple Mount. When the day comes, we will get to it."*

In other words, nobody is going to stop us! That's how close we're getting! In fact, they're even working on the financing as we speak!

An Ethiopian Jew is suing Israel's major banks because they're trying to deny him the loans to build the Third Holy Temple. When he arrived in the country in 1991, 'We had tears in our eyes and we kissed the land when we arrived. But we later learned that the Temple was not yet rebuilt.'

"God has revealed Himself to me and placed upon me the responsibility to rebuild the Temple. I have been collecting donations for this purpose, but I have been facing opposition to this plan from authorities."

"The banks are not allowing me to open accounts to receive donations, much less provide loans." *So, he is seeking damages in the amount of $35 million which he said would go to rebuild the Temple.*[3]

Either way, they'll get the money for it! In fact, they're getting so close they're airing commercials saying, "They're ready to rebuild!"

TV Commercial:

What a beautiful day for dad to take his two kids to the beach to enjoy the sun and sand. The sea of Galilee is a wonderful place to enjoy the peace and watch the kids play while he reads his newspaper. They are close by, running through the water, laughing and playing.

When they grow tired of the water they decide to play in the sand with their bucket. After diligently working on their project, they are so proud of what they have accomplished, they run back to their dad to ask him to come and see what they have just finished.

At first, he just wants to continue reading his paper but after a few more tugs on his pant leg he decides he better get up and go see what they have built. He closes his eyes so they can lead him to the spot. When he gets there, he stands in awe of what they have built in the sand. He drops his paper to the ground and stares in disbelief.

They have built the new Temple out of sand. A beautiful, perfect, new Temple made by his daughter and his son on the beach. He is so proud of his children and he knows THE CHILDREN ARE READY.[4]

The children are ready! Let's get that temple built now, shall we? Can you believe how close it's getting? And here's the point. This is the Temple that the Antichrist will go into and put an end to the sacrifices and declare himself to be god! If that happens during the 7-year Tribulation, the mid-way point, and it's almost here, then how much closer is the rapture of the Church which takes place prior to the 7-year tribulation? We're getting close. Time to get motivated!

But speaking of the Antichrist, the **2nd update** on *The Final Countdown* is none other than **The Antichrist Himself.**

The **1st thing** we know about the Antichrist according to the Bible is **He'll Slaughter 2/3rd of the Jewish People**.

As horrible as that is, that's what we see in the Book of Zechariah.

Zechariah 13:8-9 "In the whole land," declares the LORD, "two-thirds will be struck down and perish; yet one-third will be left in it. This third I will bring into the fire; I will refine them like silver and test them like gold. They will call on my name and I will answer them; I will say, 'They are my people,' and they will say, 'The LORD is our God.'"

This passage tells us that one day, the good news is that the Jewish people will eventually lose their blindness, as Paul tells us in Romans 11, and they will get right with God. The bad news is, two-thirds of them are going to be struck down by the Antichrist. Which, as we saw before, if it were to happen today, would be about 5 million people. It's horrible!

Again, this is the question, are there any signs of this horrible event? Is another Jewish Holocaust ever happening again in our lifetime, especially when WWII wasn't that long ago, with all the evils that Hitler did? Unfortunately, yes. Anti-Semitism is not just on the rise it's approaching an all-time high around the world!

Antisemitism is not only on the rise, but it is approaching an all-time high around the planet once again.

Holocaust Global Awareness and Denial Global Awareness Group:

Nearly 70 years after the end of World War II, awareness of the Holocaust is alarmingly low in many parts of the world. Even more disturbing is the percentage of people who have heard of the Holocaust but think it is either a myth or that the number of Jews who died has been greatly exaggerated. The percentage of people around the world who have heard of the Holocaust is 54%.

You know what that means? Now flip that figure around, 46% of the people have never heard of the Holocaust. Nearly half of the planet has never even heard of the Holocaust. The percentage of people around the world who have heard about the Holocaust but think it is either a myth or has been greatly exaggerated is 32%. But it gets even worse.

Over 1/4th of the planet now holds Anti-Semitic views. Another 35% believe that "Jews have too much power in the business world". It's the same lie that is being repeated that happened in Germany. 75% in the worst areas say that "People hate the Jews because of the way they behave."

One guy said, *"It's hard to believe that so much of the world is Anti-Semitic." That is truly horrible, but it shouldn't be too much of a shock because the Bible clearly says it's going to happen again in the last days. And, "Some Jews see shocking similarities between Pre-WWII Europe and today." They admit, it is being repeated. In fact, in one country, Greece of all places, 69% of the population admits to Anti-Jewish bias." And, "This renewed hatred of the Jews seems to stem from the severe economic crisis."*

The Golden Dome party in Greece places the blame squarely on the shoulders of the Jewish People, and it's expected this year that Greece will elect its first neo-Nazi politician, a member of the Golden Dome party, to sit on the European Union Parliament. I wonder if we have just seen if that is the party, the Golden Dome party that the Antichrist is going to come out of. And, he is also preparing the next generation for what is to come. [5]

Now, wait a second. The Antichrist comes out of the Revived Roman Empire, you know like the European Union, and he hates the Jewish people and wants to kill 2/3^{rds} of them. I wonder if he'll be a part of the Golden Dome Party? Can you believe this? It's all happening right now! The Bible said in the last days, the Antichrist will arise and seek to kill 2/3^{rds} of the Jewish people, and it looks like the planet is ripe for it once again, in our lifetime, even after what Hitler did!! In fact, it also looks like the Antichrist is preparing the next generation of kids to pull the trigger.

This is a children's program brainwashing the kids to kill all the Jews when they grow up here real soon!

A normal Saturday morning TV show for kids comes on. The kids are all sitting in front of the TV, watching a person dressed up like a bumble bee. This should be a fun show for the kids to watch, but as you start listening to what is being said it's a whole different situation.

Three little girls about 5 years old are sitting on the couch talking to the bumble bee. They love being with the bumble bee and they have big smiles on their faces. They are so happy to be on the TV show and get to talk to the bee. He asks the first little girl, "My friend Qays, do you have Jews in Jenin?" Qays answers, "Not now". The bumble bee waves at the camera like he is having so much fun. He says, "I heard that they go over there every day." She replies, "Yes, but they don't live there now, they come from the refugee camp".

The bumble bee shakes his fist and says, "Listen my friend, make a fist. The next time they come, punch them. Turn their faces into tomatoes, to liberate Palestine, Allah willing." Then he turns to the other little girl. "Rawan, I want to tell you to pick up a stone, and when the Jews come, to take it and throw it. That's right, if your neighbors are Jewish, we should beat them up".

The little girls are watching this bumble bee with wide eyes as they are taking in what he is saying. The one adult that is there with them replies, "If his neighbors are Jewish or Zionist, that goes without saying". Now a question is asked of a third little girl. "Tulin, why do you want to become a policewoman? Like who?" She answers, "Like my uncle". "Who is your uncle?" the bee asked. "His name is Ahmad, he is a policeman" was her reply. "Oh, what do policemen do?" he asked.

After a second or two to think about her answer she said, "They catch thieves and trouble makers." "And they shoot Jews, right?" he asked. "Right!" she answered. "You want to be like him, Allah willing, when you grow up?" He asked. "Yes, I will shoot the Jews. All of them!"[6]

Go shoot all the Jews? Wow! I thought Barney, the kids character, was bad. That bee's in a class all its own! Can you believe that? A children's program telling kids to grow up to kill all the Jews. Wow! In fact, if you think about it, maybe we just saw one of the kids who is going to grow up and become a part of the Antichrist slaughter of 2/3rds of the Jewish people. Again, here's the point. If this all happens during the 7-year Tribulation, then how much closer is the rapture of the Church which takes place prior to the 7-year tribulation? We're getting so close it's time to start doing that rapture practice!

The **2nd thing** we know about the Antichrist is **He'll Cause People to Worship His Image.**

Revelation 13:14-15 "Because of the signs he was given power to do on behalf of the first beast, he deceived the inhabitants of the earth. He ordered them to set up an image in honor of the beast who was wounded by the sword and yet lived. He was given power to give breath to the image of the first beast, so that it could speak and cause all who refused to worship the image to be killed."

We saw in this passage that the False Prophet is going to use his deception around the world to get people to what? To specifically worship the Antichrist image or be killed, right? And apparently, it has something to do with his death, or "appearing" to die and so you honor his great power by worshiping his image.

That's the question. Do we see any technology on the planet that could help create not only an image of the Antichrist, but one that could talk with and interact with people, and even cause their death if they don't do what he says? You know, like worship him? As we saw before, it's called 3-D Holograms. That's just one technology. And as we saw before, they're not only used in news broadcasts, concerts, and concerts of dead singers, Tupac was the one we saw, but even recently Michael Jackson came "back to life" on stage.

Justin Timberlake may have taken home top honors, but Jennifer Lopez and Michael Jackson stole the show last night at the Billboard Awards in Las Vegas. The big show stopper was this, Michael Jackson, or a hologram of Michael Jackson, brought down the house. The late king of pop, or the hologram of the king of pop, performing 'Slave' with the rhythm of a 5-piece band and 16 live dancers. That hologram took half a year to plan, choreograph and put out.[7]

That looked real, didn't it? Remember his funeral? It was like people were worshiping him or something. But now, he comes "back to life" and people interact with him, and maybe "worship" him, again. But our passage says it is going to come to pass that this technology will not only be used by entertainers, but political leaders, right? That's who the Antichrist is, a satanically inspired political leader. So, the question is, "Are there any world political leaders who are using this technology around the world?" Yes, in fact, they're all the rage! We saw before Prince Charles has already used them, and recently even the Prime Minister of Turkey used a huge one!

The sky is black. All eyes are watching the sky as the flood lights are bright and swiping across the sky in anticipation of something big. But what could it be? Suddenly a man appears in the sky and the crowd starts clapping. It is their Turkish leader standing before them in the sky giving his speech.[8]

Wow! It's almost like they're worshiping that political guy or something. But that's not the half of it. As we saw before, the Antichrist has a cohort who helps trick the world into worshiping the image and he's called the False Prophet. A world religious leader who deceives the people into worshiping the Antichrist, right? Wonder of wonders, can anyone guess what the new Pope is doing? He's not only going around the world forming a One World Religion, and Lord willing we'll get to that later, but he's also using the same technology, even in 3D!

On the 27th of April, the entire world will meet in Rome in St Peter's Square to canonize the most beloved Pope of the twentieth century. The Vatican television center in partnership with Skype presents an unprecedented event in 3D, televised on Skype and distributed to cinemas around the world by Nexo Digital.

It will be like being there. Thanks to the force of the 3D pictures. The canonization ceremony of Pope John the 23rd and Pope John Paul 2nd officiated by Pope Francis will be on Sunday the 27th of April in cinemas around the world in 3D with free admittance.[9]

Well, that's nice. They made it so you could watch it for free. I mean, at least they're not charging for it, or making a penalty for it, like the Antichrist when he does it, if you don't worship him you die! Seriously, can you believe that? What's going on here? A major world religious event is being broadcast by a world religious leader, in Rome, in 3D, for the entire world to watch and partake in at the same time. Who would have thought the Vatican would use the same technology in our lifetime? Or as one guy put it, "Could it be we're seeing the Vatican testing the actual equipment that will be used for the Antichrist's arrival?" It's getting that close!

By the way, they just came out with another technology, called The Leia Display, named after Princess Leia of Star Wars. That technology can beam 3D holographic images literally in thin air, onto a cloud of water vapor. If the Antichrist wants to make a big splash around the world, maybe he can just use that technology to shoot that image up into the sky for the whole world to see, in the clouds, at the same time, to worship him. It's all coming together and it's all happening right now! Time to get motivated!

Maybe the Antichrist wants to take a more personal approach with this image. You know, you're supposed to worship him. It's a private thing. Maybe we'll each have our own robot with his image on it, or robots with his image on them stationed around the world in public places to ensure we don't miss out on worshiping him at the appropriate time.

If you think that's crazy, believe it or not, we've got the technology for that too! They're called Socibots. They can not only interact with you intelligently, in real time, carry on a conversation, and monitor your mood, but you can customize them with any face you want to put on them, including the Antichrist!

This embodied robot can identify you in a crowd, mimic human emotions, and follow you around the room with its eyes, plus it's programmable to display any face, even your own. Expressions and features are easy to modify and control with voice recognition, facial tracking, lip syncing and speech synthesis in more than 20 languages. Anyone can converse freely with our chattiest robot.

Socibot has applications at airports, malls, science museums and theme parks. Engineers hope that potential clients will see its possibilities as the ultimate telepresence device, thanks to its ability to recognize people and their moods, as well as convey subtle humanlike expressions using any face the client wants to program it to display.[10]

It's the Antichrist, isn't it? Hey Bob! Guess we better start worshiping him or he's going to kill us, out here in public! Did you catch all the features on that robot? It not only has any face or image you want, but it can recognize your face, follow you around the room, even detect what kind of mood you're in, just in case you're trying to fake your worship! And they want to put them where? Not only in your home, but in malls, in airports and in banks. I wonder if you'll have to worship the Socibot's image before you can take money out of the bank to buy and sell.

What's weird about this is, it sounds eerily like what the early Church went through with worshiping Caesar. They had to make a public acknowledgement of worship to a man's statue and image as god, or they would die! Caesar worship was made universal and compulsory in the early Church for every race and nation in the Empire, with an exception for the Jews. On a certain day in the year, every Roman citizen had to come to the Temple of Caesar and had to burn a pinch of incense to Caesar's statue or image and say, 'Caesar is Lord.' He's god. When the person did that, he was given a certificate to guarantee that he had done so and could continue living as a Roman citizen with its benefits. Those that didn't were sentenced to be tortured and die, and became food for lions in the gladiatorial games. You know, the early Church.

Now here's my point. For the first time in mankind's history, we've got all the bases covered, whether it's an image of the Antichrist on a global scale, in 3D, in the sky, or a public statue /robot that comes around and ensures you pass the test of worship. If you do, you can continue to buy and sell. If you don't, you die! This is all happening right now! And again, here's the point. If all this happens during the 7-year Tribulation, then how much closer is the rapture of the Church which takes place prior to the 7-year tribulation? Are you ready for that rapture practice yet? We're getting close!

That's precisely why, out of love, God has given us this update on The Final Countdown concerning the Jewish People & the Antichrist. To show us that the Tribulation is near and the 2nd Coming of Jesus Christ is rapidly approaching. That's why Jesus Himself said…

Luke 21:28 "When these things begin to take place, stand up and lift up your heads, because your redemption is drawing near."

People of God, like it or not, we are headed for *The Final Countdown*. The point is this. If you're a Christian today and you're not doing anything for the Lord, shame on you! Get busy doing something for Jesus now! We need you! Don't sit on the sidelines! Get on the front line and help us! Let's get busy working together doing something splendid for Jesus with what time is left! If you're not a Christian, then I beg you, please, heed the signs, heed the warnings, give your life to Jesus today, because as Jesus says;

Matthew 7:13 "Enter through the narrow gate. For wide is the gate and broad is the road that leads to destruction, and many enter through it. But small is the gate and narrow the road that leads to life, and only a few find it."

You see, according to Jesus, the bulk of the planet is unfortunately going to wait until it's too late. They are going to continue on the broad road that leads to destruction. They're going to think that going to church services saves them, or trying to be a good person. But only a few escapes that lie and truly surrender to Jesus, and show it with their lives, like these guys share.

"There is no hope this generation will fill Heaven any quicker than any other generation, we are so corrupt, unless God in His mercy fills us." When He speaks about few finding eternal life, he's talking about those who profess His name. Among those who call Jesus, Lord, few of them will find eternal life. Nobody's purpose is to go to Hell.

They all think they will get right with God before the end and most men shipwreck. Few there be that find it. You mean all those many people, they just live life all Hell bent, they don't expect to go to Hell, and most go. We already know these people consider themselves disciples, and they call Jesus "Lord, Lord", but their life is not marked by the will of God. So, to sum this up, this is what is being said, "Depart from me, those of you who considered yourselves my disciples, and even emphatically declared me to be Lord, but you did not commune with me and you lived as though I never gave you a law to obey." I just described American Christianity.

Even though they said Lord, Lord, we did many mighty works in your name and we went to church every Sunday, He dismisses them as evil doers because they did not have the holiness without which no one would receive the Lord. It also means that there are many church going people who believe that they are saved because they once prayed to receive Jesus, not realizing that the proof of the genuineness of that prayer is perseverance in faith and holiness. He who endures to the end, will be saved not those who endure half way to the end and then abort. I believe my ministry would be a failure if you came to this church 5 years, 10 years, 20 years or 30 years and then went to Hell for all eternity."[11]

Chapter Two

Modern Technology

"One day this woman was playing golf and she hit a ball into the woods. So, she went into the woods to look for it and found a frog in a trap. Believe it or not, the frog said to her, 'If you release me from this trap, I will grant you three wishes.'

The woman freed the frog, and the frog said, 'Thank you, but I failed to mention that there was a condition to your wishes. Whatever you wish for, your husband will get times ten!'

So, the woman said, 'That's okay.' And so, for her first wish, she wanted to be the most beautiful woman in the world.

The frog warned her, 'You do realize that this wish will also make your husband the most handsome man in the world, an Adonis to whom women will flock?'

The woman replied, 'That's okay, because I will be the most beautiful woman and he will have eyes only for me.'

So, KAZAM -- she's the most beautiful woman in the world!

For her second wish, she wanted to be the richest woman in the world. So, the frog said, 'That will make your husband the richest man in the world. And he will be ten times richer than you.'

And the woman said, 'That's okay, because what's mine is his and what's his is mine.'

So, KAZAM -- she's the richest woman in the world!

Well finally, the frog inquired about her third wish, and she answered, 'I'd like a mild heart attack.'

Moral of the story: Women are clever. Don't mess with them.[1]

    That's right, the very fact that the women could laugh over that one, means we're in big trouble, how many of you would agree? But that's right, as troubling as that is, believe it or not, I think I've found something even worse!
    It goes like this. You wake up one day, to discover that millions of people have suddenly disappeared all over the planet, and your family is gone, and it suddenly dawns on you that you have been left behind! You will be catapulted into the 7-year Tribulation and that's not a joke! The Bible says it's an outpouring of God's wrath on a wicked and rebellious planet.
    The Jewish people really are literally on the verge of rebuilding the last days temple that the actual Antichrist is going to go into and declare himself to be god. We're getting that close! Then we read how the Antichrist himself isn't going to have much of a problem slaughtering $2/3^{rd}$ of the Jewish people, like Zechariah says, because there's a massive rise of global hatred towards the Jewish people all over the planet. Like never before!
    We even have the technology for people to worship the Antichrist image all over the world, even in public, around the globe, and force them to do it or they will die, exactly like the Bible said, when you are living in the last days!

The 3rd update is none other than Modern Technology.

    Modern Technology is a huge sign that we're living in the last days! But don't take my word for it. Let's listen to God's.

Daniel 12:1-4. "At that time Michael, the great prince who protects your people, will arise. There will be a time of distress such as has not happened from the beginning of nations until then. But at that time your people—everyone whose name is found written in the book—will be delivered. Multitudes who sleep in the dust of the earth will awake: some to everlasting life, others to shame and everlasting contempt. Those who are wise will shine like the brightness of the heavens, and those who lead many to righteousness, like the stars for ever and ever. But you, Daniel, close up and seal the words of the scroll until the time of the end. Many will go here and there to increase knowledge."

As we saw before with this passage, God gives Daniel two signs to be an indicator that we're in the end of times. And notice what they were. Not just the activity of the Archangel Michael, but what? People would be traveling here and there all over the earth and there would be an explosion of knowledge like never before, right?

So, here's the point. Can anybody guess what in the world is happening all around us right now? We are travelling all over the earth and there's an incredible explosion of knowledge, exponentially so! Which means, this very passage is being fulfilled before our very eyes! We are living in the end times, according to Daniel!

The 1st way that **Modern Technology** reveals this, that we're really living in the last days, is by the **Increase of Travel.**

When Daniel wrote down the words of this prophecy, the mode of travel was basically the same for 1,000's of years. It's only in this last century alone that we see a major change in transportation.

For instance, the fastest that mankind could travel for thousands of years was about 30 mph via horseback. From Adam to Alexander the Great to Abraham Lincoln, transportation pretty much stayed the same, until now. We need to wake up! All in the last century alone, we have gone from the horse to the horseless carriage, the car. We've gone from a top speed of 30 mph to literally 100's of mph. And in just a few decades, we now rush here and there an average of 15,000 miles per year (used to be 14,000 - it's now gone up).

We used to have an estimation that 1 billion cars would be on the road by 2025, but we've already surpassed that and they're now estimating we're going to have 1.7 billion cars on the road by 2035. It's speeding up! We all need to drive here and there! Then, believe it or not, we won't even have to drive our own car to get us to rush from here to there, it's going to do it for us, like this video shows! Once again, Google to the rescue!

A beautiful morning to take a drive. The gentleman walks out of his house into a gentle breeze and his wind chimes are ringing. He walks out to his driveway and wipes his hand across his little blue car sitting in the driveway. He walks around to the door, opens it and gets in. His friend is already in the car and asks "Hi, how are you doing today?" He replies, "Just great! Let's eat!" He pulls out onto the residential street and says, "Let's go!" Then he lets go of the steering wheel and cries "Look Ma, no hands" and they both laugh as they raise their hands up to touch the roof.

He drives a block or so and comes to a stop. "We're at a stop sign," he says. His friend tells him that the car has its own radar and laser that tells it when to stop and if anything is coming from either direction. He gives a little nervous chuckle about trusting the car to make the right decisions. His friend tells him "Old habits die hard, and some old habits don't die; anyone up for a taco?" His friend says, sure and suggests that they go through the drive through. They pull into the parking lot to get to the drive through lane. He asks, "Does anyone have any money?" His friend says, "I do. I have my wallet right here. You can just roll down your window and order a burrito." The order taker asks, "How are you?" He replies, "Very well, how are you doing?" and places his order.

They pull up to the window and she hands them their food. He then pulls out onto the street and proceeds to the highway, eating as they go. His friend tells him, "There are some places you can't go and some things you cannot do with this car". But he realizes that this is just what he needs as he is driving back to his house. He says, "This can change my life and give me back my independence and flexibility to be able to go places I want to go and need to go." He pulls into this driveway and gets out of his car while still eating his burrito. Steve Mahan, self-driving car user.[2]

  Can you imagine if we get one of those, we can go back to using our cell phones and eating while we drive? Why, everyone is going to want one of these driverless vehicles! What did Daniel say? In the last days, you're going to be seeing people rush around here and there, anywhere we want, anytime we want, including that guy, who by the way is legally blind! Isn't that wild?
  Oh, but that's just transportation on land. Thanks to the invention of the airplane, which also occurred during the last century, the world has become a much smaller place. We can now drive not only anywhere we want, but we can fly anywhere we want, anywhere in the world, at any time. In fact, it's getting so advanced as we saw before, that for the first time in mankind's history, soon, we can even fly out of the world. Not just if you become an astronaut, but as we saw last time, Virgin Airlines, has come out with Virgin Galactic so that the average Joe can now fly into space! And they just completed their first official test flight!

Three pilots are walking out to the air strip where the Virgin Galactic aircraft sits to be taken out for a test flight. It's just about sunup and it's a good day for a test flight. The date is January 10, 2014. "Okay guys, have a good flight," is called out to them from another pilot who had been walking with them. They shook hands and he turned around to go back. The plane looks like there are three planes that are somehow all linked together.

After they take off and are flying you can hear 9-8-7-6-5-4-3-2-1 and the center spaceplane is released to fall back down towards earth, but the combustion of its engine causes it to take flight on its own. This suborbital spaceplane is designed to carry six passengers and two pilots to an altitude of about 62 miles (100 kilometers). George Whitesides, former NASA staff chief, said expectations for commercial flights in 2018 are realistic.[3]

Wow! Can you believe the days we're living in? Pretty soon, the average Joe can fly into space! Oh, but that's still not all! For those of you who want to go even further than Virgin Galactic can take you, for the first time in mankind's history, we now have people working on getting the average Joe to Mars! I'm not kidding you. They now have a modern technology called the VASIMR rocket and it will speed up a trip to mars from about 2 years to just a matter of days!

"Hello, my name is Franklin Chang Diaz. I am a physicist and engineer. I was also a NASA astronaut for 25 years and had the opportunity to fly on 7 space shuttle missions. We are developing a new type of rocket engine. We call it the Vasimr engine. It is a rocket like no other rocket you might have seen in the past. It is a plasma rocket.

There are 6 basic missions that we are currently considering for the use of the technology. These are asteroid retrieval, orbital debris mitigation, space station reboots, lunar cargo, deep space and asteroid deflection. Our goal: we intend to use our technology to transform space transportation.[4]

Which includes getting a person to Mars in a matter of days instead of years. Can you believe that? And keep in mind, this is all occurring in our lifetime! What did Daniel say? When you see people rushing here and there wherever and whenever they want all over the world, even out of the world, it's not just cool, it's a sign you're living in the last days!

The **2nd way** Modern Technology reveals that we are living in the last days is by the **Death of the Two Witnesses.**

Revelation 11:3-9 "And I will give power to my two witnesses, and they will prophesy for 1,260 days, clothed in sackcloth.' These are the two olive trees and the two lampstands that stand before the Lord of the earth. If anyone tries to harm them, fire comes from their mouths and devours their enemies. This is how anyone who wants to harm them must die. These men have power to shut up the sky so that it will not rain during the time they are prophesying; and they have power to turn the waters into blood and to strike the earth with every kind of plague as often as they want. Now when they have finished their testimony, the beast that comes up from the Abyss will attack them, and overpower and kill them. Their bodies will lie in the street of the great city, which is figuratively called Sodom and Egypt, where also their Lord was crucified. For three and a half days men from every people, tribe, language and nation will gaze on their bodies and refuse them burial."

Once again, we're looking at the classic passage where we see the death of the Two Witnesses. If we are going to get the prophetic significance of what's going on here with Modern Technology, we have to first look at this in its historical setting. Imagine what it must have been like when the Apostle John was writing this down nearly 2,000 years ago. It must have seemed like an incredible fantasy for the whole planet to simultaneously watch two dead bodies and rejoice over their deaths, right? That's what the text says! But guess what? As we all know, it's not fantasy anymore! It's commonplace!

Due to the advent of television and global satellite technology, you and I can simultaneously watch anything we want, anywhere we want, around the world, can't we? It happens every day! Which means, this passage can be fulfilled before our very eyes today! We have the technology right now to do this, to watch the deaths of the Two Witnesses for 3½ days for the first time in the history of mankind! But that's still not all. The text says one more thing. As they were watching this event, notice what they did. Let's go back to the text.

Revelation 11:10 "The inhabitants of the earth will gloat over them and will celebrate by sending each other gifts, because these two prophets had tormented those who live on the earth."

What's amazing about this is when you look at this from the Apostle John's perspective 2,000 years ago. This must have totally blown his mind! How could people not only watch the deaths of two guys from around the world simultaneously for 3½ days, but how in the world are they going to be able to celebrate and send each other gifts around the world within 3½ days? Because that's the time-frame there. I mean, they didn't even have the Pony Express back then! Well guess what? As we all know, it's not a surprise anymore! For the first time in man's history we now have a global distribution network! Thanks to this rise of Modern Technology we now have a global transportation system that's hooked up to a global communications system, that's linked to a global supply chain system that's overseen by a global trade and commerce system that allows us to go down to our local store and get fresh crabmeat shipped to us from Thailand, or have a thoroughbred horse shipped from New Zealand. Or get fresh flowers all the way from South America, or have a New York City pizza delivered anywhere in the world, or send a package from Japan in the afternoon and have it arrive in Washington the next morning. Including a celebratory package sent by someone who's gloating over the deaths of Two Witnesses, within 3½ days, for the first time in man's history. That's right, soon we're going to have the technology to do it in even less than 3½ days!

Believe it or not, Amazon and eBay are looking at offering customers same day delivery service with a fleet of drones!

"Next year, behemoths like Amazon and eBay will be stepping up their efforts to deliver goods on the same day they're bought, even if that day's a Sunday. Eventually, Amazon founder Jeff Bezos envisions unmanned drones bringing products to our doors within half-an-hour. In the meantime, he's increasing his number of warehouses and overhauling his partnerships with couriers to get us what we want as quickly as possible."

Including that celebratory gift over the death of the Two Witnesses.

Amazon Prime Air is a service that will deliver packages up to five pounds in 30 minutes or less using small drones. You will be able to order what you want on your tablet, it goes directly to the Amazon warehouse, the item goes into a box and immediately set on the conveyor belt to be launched back to you via the Amazon Prime Air Drone. It looks like science fiction but one day it will be as common as the mail truck.[5]

Can you believe how close we are to the last days? Think about this. Did we just read about the delivery service that people will use to send a celebratory gift to anyone anywhere in the world over the death of the Two Witnesses within

3½ days? It's getting that close! And it's escalating! They are also working on another modern technology that can speed it up even faster! It's called 3-D printers. And they can not only print anything you want right before your very eyes, but it's getting so cheap that just about anyone can own one.

What do you think of when you think of traditional printing? We went to a fair where 2D printing is a thing of the past. 3D printers read blue prints of an object that users download to a computer. The reason they are getting a lot of attention is called Form One. It's a 3D printer that raised more than a million dollars in 3 days on a crowd hunting site call Kick Starter. The thing people are excited about Form-One is the detail.

The technology really allows us to get much higher resolution. The Form One uses a different process than most 3D printers. Light as opposed to heat to harden plastic. Technology that was previously too costly. The printer built support structures around detailed shapes that users can break off after it dries. Like the way people do desk top publishing now, people are going to be designing things and printing them. Here's a sign that 3D printing may be the coming main stream.

MakerBot's just opened a store recently in New York City devoted to selling these printers. To be able to go into a retail store and see it in action and touch the things it can make, it really opens people's minds to the possibilities. MakerBot's just released its replicator too. It's a faster model that releases higher resolution products. Industrial 3D printers have been around for decades. They've been used for everything from printing prosthetic limbs to food.[6]

Maybe they're going to send a celebratory cake as well! Can you believe that? George Jetson eat your heart out! What did the Bible say? Whenever you see people having the ability to gloat over two dead bodies simultaneously anywhere in the world and even send gifts anywhere to anyone in the world within 3½ days or even faster, including that 3-D printer, it's a sign you're living in the last days! That's going to happen during the 7-year Tribulation. Therefore, the point for you and I is, how much closer is the rapture of the Church which takes place prior to that?

The 3rd way Modern Technology reveals that we are living in the last days is by the **Increase of Knowledge.**

Daniel 12:4 "But you, Daniel, close up and seal the words of the scroll until the time of the end. Many will go here and there to increase knowledge."

When Daniel wrote down the words of this prophecy, the amount of retrieving and sharing knowledge was severely limited. We didn't even see the invention of the printing press until a few centuries ago. Oh, but look at us today! All in our lifetime, just like the Bible said, we are experiencing nothing short of an information explosion! As we saw before, a weekday edition of any major newspaper has more information than the average person living in the 17th century would have come across in a lifetime.

Thanks to the Internet, thousands of international papers are at your fingertips. There's over 100 Billion searches on Google every month. If Facebook were a country, it would be the largest in the world. It is estimated that 4 exabytes of unique information will be generated this year, which is more than the previous 5,000 years.

As we saw before, all this is leading to a serious danger that they're calling singularity. This describes the point where the technology grows so fast that it spawns a type of super intelligence that far exceeds any kind of human intelligence and then it begins to take over, which, at this point, "The human era will be ended, and machines will take over." Experts are saying it could happen very soon. Here's what all this explosion of knowledge is leading to!

Humans have had an interest in artificial intelligence even before the term was coined in the 1950's. The modern concept is part of a tradition that extends through myth and legend all the way back to the ancient Greeks. It's been a source of hopes and fears, dreams and nightmares.

Will our creations be our allies or our mortal or immortal enemies? Until recently it didn't really matter. The ability to create intelligent machines was impossibly out of reach. But Ray Kurzweil believes it is not only possible but inevitable and coming sooner than you think.

The inventor and author has become the most outspoken advocate of the coming technological singularity. "By the time we get to the 2040's and 2045 we'll be able to multiply you in intelligence a billion-fold. That will be a profound change that is singular in nature, so we use this term." It's a label first used in 1993 by computer scientist and science fiction writer Vernor Vinge. Vinge predicted that within 30 years we would create a super human intelligence and shortly after that the human era would be over.[7]

Daniel calls it the time of the end! By the way, Ray Kurzweil is one of the top men at Google, the ones gathering all this information. What did Daniel say? Whenever you see an explosion of knowledge all over the world, even to the point where it starts to threaten to take over the world, Google and all, it's a sign you're living in the last days!

The 4th way that Modern Technology reveals that we really are living in the last days is by the **Death of the Antichrist.**

You see, all this explosion of information and technology and even printing technology is leading to the possible fulfillment of this passage of Scripture dealing with the death of the Antichrist.

Revelation 13:2-4 "The dragon gave the beast his power and his throne and great authority. One of the heads of the beast seemed to have had a fatal wound, but the fatal wound had been healed. The whole world was astonished and followed the beast. Men worshiped the dragon because he had given authority to the beast, and they also worshiped the beast and asked, 'Who is like the beast? Who can make war against him?'"

In other words, this person is seemingly invincible! I mean, you kill him, he gets this fatal head wound, and he "seemingly" comes back to life. Who can make war against him, right? So that's the question. How do we know we're getting close to this? Do we see any technology on the planet now that could "give the appearance" of somebody coming back to life, including the Antichrist? The fact is, believe it or not, for the first time in man's history, we now have the technology to "seemingly" "give the appearance" of somebody coming back to life, including printing them new body parts. Here's the other side to 3-D printers. Here is what else they can print!

It may be the most eye-catching development in printing since Guttenberg invented the printing press 600 years ago. A machine that can make copies of almost anything, but this time in 3D. It seems like science fiction, but 3D printing is already in use building hearing aids, jewelry, even parts for NASA.

Now the technology is becoming available to anyone. You can turn your garage into a small factory. So, what would you build if you could create anything? An ear is being printed as layer upon layer of tiny droplets are deposited building up the structure. "So, this is someone's ear?" Mia Sheldon asks. "This would be printed to be someone's ear," he replies. "Oh, my goodness!" The project is a type of 3D printing called Bio-printing led by Doctor Anthony Atalla at the Wake Forest Institute for Regenerative Medicine in North Carolina.

"Same technology you have in your very own home but instead of printing sheets of paper with ink you're actually printing tissue with cells," says Dr. Atalla. The premise is simple. Send a scanned image of a body part to the printer and the machine starts building ears, noses and, fingers. Dr. Atalla's goal is to transplant the parts directly into patients.[8]

Which would include the Antichrist if he needs a new body part like a part of his head that suffered a fatal wound, or any other organ for that matter. Can you believe that? For the first time in mankind's history, we can print body parts for people! Just in time for that "fatal wound" of the Antichrist! But that's right, speaking of fatal wounds, we now have the technology to make body parts "come back to life." For the first time in man's history we have an actual movement called Transhumanism that has plans to "bring people back from the dead" and achieve "man-made immortality." As wild as that is, they have not only succeeded in already getting FDA approval of "human suspended animation trials," to preserve somebody's body when it dies, like the Antichrist, to keep them alive until you provide an alternative body, print it up, clone it up, whatever.

But the ultimate goal is to "preserve the human brain and transform it, hence that term Transhumanism, into a computer image inside of a computer, to seemingly extend their lives forever! Hollywood just came out with a propaganda movie starring Johnny Depp called Transcendence, which is all about promoting Transhumanism. These people are so serious that they've created a timeline for when they plan to pull this off. This isn't make believe. This is really what they're working on. This is where all this information technology is leading to. And according to them, it's coming really soon!

2013-2014, new centers working on cybernetic technology for the development of radical life extension. The race for immortality starts. 2015-2020, The Avatar is created, a robotic human copy controlled by thought of a brain computer interface. It becomes as popular as a car. In Russia and in the world, appear in testing mode several breakthrough projects: android robots to replace people in manufacturing tasks, android robot servants for every home, thought control avatars to provide telepresence in any place in the world and abolish the need for business trips, flying cars, thought driven mobile communications built into their bodies or sprayed onto their skin. 2020-2025, an autonomous system providing life support for the brain and allowing it interaction with the environment is created. The brain is transplanted into an Avatar being.

With that, Avatar man receives new expanded life. 2025 the new generation of Avatars provide complete transmission of sensations from all 5 sensory robot organs to the operator. 2030-2035, re-brain, the colossal project of brain reverse engineering is implemented. World science comes very close to understanding the principals of consciousness. 2035, the first successful attempt to transfer one's personality to an alternative carrier.

The evolution of cybernetic immortality begins. 2040-2050, bodies made of nano-robots that can take any shape arise beside hologram bodies. The main priority of its development is spiritual self-improvement. A new era dawns. The era of Neo humanity.[9]

The Era of New Humanity, where you can become your own god and live forever, as well as resurrect the Antichrist. What did Daniel say? When you see all this explosion of information across the planet, it's a sign you're living in the last days! You think these people aren't serious? They're deadly serious. Dr. Richard Seed, a Transhumanist actually said this, *"You don't like it? We'll take you out!"*

Richard Seed:

Physicist, human cloning researcher states: "We are going to become gods, period. If you don't like it, get off. You don't have to contribute or participate. But if you are going to interfere with me becoming a god, we'll have big trouble and we'll have warfare"[10]

In other words, we'll kill you if you try to stop us from becoming our own gods. It's the same lie that Satan used to cause the fall of man the first time!

Genesis 3:4-5 "You will not surely die, the serpent said to the woman. For God knows that when you eat of it your eyes will be opened, and you will be like God, knowing good and evil."

In the beginning of creation, Satan caused the fall of mankind with the lie that you can "be like god," and in the last days, he's doing the exact same lie and men are falling for it as well. Just in time for the Antichrist's arrival with his "seemingly coming back to life" and demanding worship as a god. You know, it's almost like we're living in the last days! And again, the point is this. If that happens during the 7-year Tribulation, and we have the technology now, then how much closer is the rapture of the Church which takes place prior to the 7-year tribulation?

Out of love, God has given us this update on *The Final Countdown* concerning the Modern Technology to show us that the Tribulation is near, and the Rapture is right around the corner! That's why Jesus Himself said:

Luke 21:28 "When these things begin to take place, stand up and lift up your heads, because your redemption is drawing near."

The point is this. If you're reading this today and you are a Christian, then what in the world are you doing for Jesus? Let's get busy working together fulfilling the Great Commission doing something splendid for Jesus, amen? But if you're not a Christian, then I beg you, please, heed the signs, heed the warnings, give your life to Jesus today, because tomorrow may be too late! You are going to live forever, but it won't be in a computer, or in some man-made alternate body. It will be Heaven or hell. And if you don't accept Jesus Christ as your Savior right now, it's going to be hell. No technology can save you from that reality…only Jesus can! So, accept Him now!

Chapter Three

Worldwide Upheaval

"One time there was this lady named Mildred and she was this church gossip. And she was the self-appointed monitor of the church's morals so she kept sticking her nose into other people's business.

Not a good thing to do.

Well, several members did not approve of her extra-curricular activities, but they feared her enough to maintain their silence. She kept control of them.

Well, one afternoon she made the mistake of accusing this new member named Frank of being an alcoholic after she saw his old pickup parked out in front of the town's only bar.

So, she emphatically told Frank (and several others) that everyone seeing it there would know what he was doing!

Well, Frank was a man of few words and he stared at her for a moment and then just turned and walked away. He didn't explain, he didn't defend, he didn't even deny it. He just simply said nothing and walked away!

But later that night, Frank quietly parked his pickup truck in front of Mildred's house, walked home... and left it there all night.

You got to love Frank!

Moral of the story: Don't mess with men either, ladies. They're clever too![1]

And that's right! That's for all you ladies who laughed last time at the joke "Don't mess with Women!" Turnabout's fair play! And we don't even need a frog to help us out! But seriously, how many of you would say Mildred learned her lesson the hard way? Did you know she's not the only one learning lessons the hard way? The Bible says one day the whole planet's going to learn a hard lesson and it's going to go like this. One day, they're going to wake up and not only see Frank's pickup parked out there, but they're going to see that Frank is gone! And so are millions of other Christians around the planet. They'll discover the hard way that they have been left behind. And they will be catapulted into the 7-year Tribulation and that's not a joke!

The 4th update on The Final Countdown is none other than **Worldwide Upheaval.**

That's right, the planet's going to get seriously messed up, right before Jesus comes back!

The 1st sign to indicate that we are headed for this Worldwide Upheaval and we are living in the last days, is that there would be an **Increase of Wars.**

But don't take my word for it. Let's listen to God's word.

Matthew 24:3-8 "As Jesus was sitting on the Mount of Olives, the disciples came to Him privately. Tell us, they said, when will this happen, and what will be the sign of Your coming and of the end of the age? Jesus answered: Watch out that no one deceives you. For many will come in My name, claiming, I am the Christ, and will deceive many. You will hear of wars and rumors of wars, but see to it that you are not alarmed. Such things must happen, but the end is still to come. Nation will rise against nation, and kingdom against kingdom. There will be famines and earthquakes in various places. All of these are the beginning of birth pains."

According to our text, as we've seen before, right after the first warning of deceit from Jesus, what was the very next thing He told us was going to be a sign we're living in the last days? Wars and rumors of wars, right? Nations would rise against nations and kingdoms against kingdoms, right?

The scoffer is going to look at this passage and say something sarcastic like, "Wars are no big deal, we've always had wars." But as we saw before, not like we see today! In the last century alone, we have seen nothing short of an explosion of worldwide wars like never before. In fact, more people have been killed by wars in the previous century then at any other time of mankind's history. It's clearly on the rise exactly like Jesus said! The rise of wars and the armies that go along with them is also giving rise to the fulfillment of several other passages of Scripture concerning Bible Prophecy.

The **1st passage** of Scripture that's coming alive due to the **Increase of Wars** is **The Creation of a Super War or The Gog & Magog Prophecy.**

Ezekiel 38:1-6 "The word of the LORD came to me: "Son of man, set your face against Gog, of the land of Magog, the chief prince of Meshach and Tubal; prophesy against him and say: 'This is what the Sovereign LORD says: I am against you, O Gog, chief prince of Meshach and Tubal. I will turn you around, put hooks in your jaws and bring you out with your whole army – your horses, your horsemen fully armed, and a great horde with large and small shields, all of them brandishing their swords. Persia, Cush and Put will be with them, all with shields and helmets, also Gomer with all its troops, and Beth Togarmah from the far north with all its troops – the many nations with you."

This is just a teaser of what's going on with the Gog & Magog prophecy. It continues throughout Chapter 38 and Chapter 39. But as we saw before, it deals with a confederation of nations that God's not too pleased with. The reason He's not too pleased is because they're trying to come against Israel and destroy it! Not a good thing to do! The key to understanding just how close we are to fulfilling this passage of Scripture, that many believe will be WWIII, is figuring out who in the world these nations are that are coming against Israel. How many of you took your last vacation in Put, or Beth Togarmah? You need to do your homework. These nations today are Russia, (Magog), Turkey, Iran, Sudan, Libya, and apparently other nations with them, and according to Ezekiel, all are going to try to destroy Israel in the last days. Whew! Man! I'm just so glad that we see absolutely no sign of that prophecy coming to pass anytime soon, excuse me? What's in the news?

Russia (or Magog) is the one right now arming these nations with weapons to go against Israel. Russia is on the move in the North again with this Ukraine issue, and many believe it's starting to fulfill this passage of Scripture.

CBN reports:

The crisis in the Ukraine and Russia's aggressive actions may have greater implications than security in Europe. Many believe Vladimir Putin has global ambitions and they point to the role Russia plays in Biblical Prophecy. "President Vladimir Putin, back in 2008 invades Georgia and now he has taken control of Crimea and made it part of the Russian map. What is his ultimate goal?" the reporter asks.

Joel Rosenberg responds with this, "One thing that is sure about Vladimir Putin, when you go back into his life, he doesn't see himself simply as the President of Russia. He sees himself as a czar. He wants to rebuild the glory of mother Russia. My family were Orthodox Jews that escaped under a czar, Nicholas the second. We have a bad history with the czars. Czars are imperialists. They want to expand.

Putin has not been stopped in any of these excursions. I think he is probing and I think he will take more the moment he thinks he can get it." Reporter: "Let's talk about Biblical Prophecy. I know you have written so much on this and it's a part of the things that you keep a very close eye on.

What does the Bible say about Israel and Russia?" Joel Rosenberg answers, "Well, it's very interesting. The main prophecy is Ezekiel 38,39, what's known as the war of Gog and Magog. A Russian dictator rises in what's known as Magog and teams up with Persia, which we know as Iran. Now people ask me, do you think Vladimir Putin is this evil dictator Gog of which the Bible speaks? It's too early to make a conclusion like that. Is Putin 'Gogesque'? Yes, I think that is a fair statement. He is a dictator that is rising, he is building an alliance with Iran. Putin is selling arms to Iran. He is selling nuclear technology to Iran. He is defending Iran at the UN amidst this whole scenario".

Reporter: "Many Jews in Ukraine are fearful of the growing Russian intrusion. Clearly there are some questions about some of the groups that are involved in the uprising, the protests in Ukraine, but do they have a reason to be concerned? Like the Crimeans?" Joel Rosenberg: "They are concerned, should be concerned, and in many ways, I think they should be on planes heading to Israel".[2]

Why? Because in the last days, Ezekiel prophesied 2,600 years ago that Russia would help the Islamic nations of Turkey, Iran, Sudan, and Libya try to destroy Israel. What in the world is in the news right now? The first three are already in Syria, right on Israel's border! We better get motivated! Some would say this war takes place right after the 7-year Tribulation starts and some would say it takes place just prior to the 7-year Tribulation. Either way, it's getting close and we better get ready! Jesus is coming back to get us!

The **2nd passage** that's coming alive due to the Increase of Wars is **The Creation of a Super Hideout.**

Revelation 6:12-17 "I watched as he opened the sixth seal. There was a great earthquake. The sun turned black like sackcloth made of goat hair, the whole moon turned blood red, and the stars in the sky fell to earth, as late figs drop from a fig tree when shaken by a strong wind. The sky receded like a scroll, rolling up, and every mountain and island was removed from its place. Then the kings of the earth, the princes, the generals, the rich, the mighty, and every slave and every free man hid in caves and among the rocks of the mountains. They called to the mountains and the rocks, "Fall on us and hide us from the face of him who sits on the throne and from the wrath of the Lamb! For the great day of their wrath has come, and who can stand?"

According to our text, we see that the people in the 7-year Tribulation are going to try to hide from the wrath of God, which isn't going to happen because there's only one way to escape it, and that's though Jesus. Where of all places are they going to try to hide? In the mountains, in the caves, or in other words, in the holes in the ground! Thanks to the rise of wars and the various military inventions that come along with them, for the first time in mankind's history, governments are doing just that! They're trying to hide away from the Wrath of God in the mountains or caves or holes in the ground, with these things called D.U.M.B.'s or Deep Underground Military Bases. They're trying to protect themselves from some horrible catastrophe that they believe is coming!

It is dumb to try to hide away from God's wrath, because again, you're not going to; the only way out is through Jesus Christ, take the smart way out. The point is, it's not just the military doing this now, it's the average Joe. That's exactly what the text says! Not just the kings, and the princes, and the generals.

Not just the rich and the mighty, but every slave, every free man, in other words, the average Joe, would hide in the ground to escape God's wrath!

Believe it or not, that's happening right now! The average person can now get your hands on what's called a Luxury Bunker! And the price is very economical!

CBN Reports:

Preparing for the worst by setting yourself up with only the best. We're talking about luxurious kitchens, swimming pools, even a gym. These are bunkers built just in case of an emergency. Bomb shelters were a common sight in back yards during the cold war in the 1950's.

Today's back yard survival bunkers look more like a 5-star resort equipped with everything from an indoor pool, state of the art movie theatre, a dog run and even an interactive classroom, all underground. Logic Integrations specialists: "They can live here and enjoy the facility and not just survive."

Survive whatever may come in comfort whether it's a natural disaster or future terror attack. It was part of the selling point that a future owner paid to reserve space in this underground luxury bunker for his family, his wife and 3 kids. The cost, $50,000 per adult and $35,000 for children under the age of 16. That's nearly $200,000 for the average family of 4.

Leather sofas, high end kitchens, comfortable bedrooms. Several companies have designed and built these high-end shelters. Some are privately made for individual families, but this buyer chose a community shelter created by Vivos with dozens of other people.

It's like an apartment complex that can hold up to 80 people. It's fully stocked with a year's worth of food, toiletries, linens, medical supplies, ATV's and so much more. The massive 10,000 square foot shelter has all the comforts of home but built 65 feet below ground with reinforced concrete and steel.[3]

Huh? That should do it! And what did the Bible say? In the last days, you're going to see a strange trend on the planet. Kings, princes, general, rich, mighty, slave, free, the average Joe, will build holes in the ground to try to escape something horrible coming! That all comes to fruition during the 7-year

Tribulation. And if we're seeing that trend happen now, then how much closer is the rapture of the Church which takes place prior to the 7-year tribulation?

The **3rd passage** that's coming alive due to the increase of wars is **The Creation of a Super Beast.**

Revelation 6:7-8 "When the Lamb opened the fourth seal, I heard the voice of the fourth living creature say, 'Come!' I looked, and there before me was a pale horse! Its rider was named Death, and Hades was following close behind him. They were given power over a fourth of the earth to kill by sword, famine and plague, and by the wild beasts of the earth."

So again, here we see that the Apostle John predicted nearly 2,000 years ago that 1/4th of the earth is going to die during the first half of the 7-year Tribulation by means of sword, famine, plague and wild beasts. Here's the point, I can see the sword, famine, and plague, but who in the world is concerned about wild beasts nowadays, right? I mean they're all in zoos and protected areas. What's the big deal? Not if the environmental movement gets their way! They want to turn the United States into one big giant animal preserve with the Biodiversity Treaty, remember that? When that famine hits, not only will people be hungry, but so will all these wild animals all over the place! They'll be looking for food too! Maybe that's what John saw. Maybe those are the wild beasts.

But it just so happens for the first time in mankind's history, thanks to the rise of wars and the various military inventions that come along with them, maybe John saw something much more technological than that! You see, it just so happens that one of the biggest developers for Modern Technology and weaponry for the military, is an organization called D.A.R.P.A. or Defense Advanced Research Project Agency. They are the ones who have been coming up with all kinds of wild futuristic and even science fiction-like weaponry for today's soldiers. One of their latest developments just happens to be a robotic pack animal they call Big Dog designed to carry all the gear for the soldiers.

We're walking thru the woods and we hear a loud sound like a lawn mower behind the trees. We look up and see a large metal object laying on the ground but as we get closer this object stands up on 4 legs. It looks like a large dog. A robotic dog. It has the words Boston Dynamics written across its side and it has white feet. The robotic dog climbs the hill and heads out to the dirt road. It runs to catch up with a man already walking down the road.[4]

Okay, kind of cool, kind of creepy. I think I'll stick to my wiener dogs! But seriously, that's the tip of the iceberg. There's all kinds of animals and various critters being designed by the military and other entities for various purposes. Let's look at a few of them.

A bug that looks like a roach is walking on 4 legs across a pile of white rocks. It makes it over the rocks like its feet are grabbing hold to keep its balance. When you take a closer look, it is made of metal, it is a robotic bug. Above is a fly buzzing around and it is a robotic fly. The wings and legs look so real but then you realize that the fly is getting instructions from a computer to the chip in its back to fly to the right or to the left.

The robotic spider is furry and black with 8 legs. It moves like a spider does. It has a platform using 26 super micro high-tech servos, 3 in each leg, 2 in the tail and a controller who has preprogrammed a whole bunch of walking and reverse kinetic sequences, so it is an incredible mover in terms of distributing its forward motion across its legs.

Their basic technology is the controller board and algorithms to coordinate all the leg movements. But, algorithms that control the leg movements are not just walking forward or walking backwards, turn left turn right, its far more advanced than that.[5]

Hmmm. Okay, Big Dog, Little Dog, Big Bug, Little Bug! Giant nasty looking spider, that's kind of creepy. Remember what John said. Put all this together. He saw wild beasts taking part in killing 1/4th of the earth's population during the 7-year Tribulation. All these robotic versions are now leading up to the latest version. A robotic cheetah, you know, a wild animal, that can hunt you down and take you out!

First, start with who oversees technology development for the military. That is the US Defense Advanced Research Projects Agency or DARPA. An agency that is the stuff of mystery novels and recently we have noticed that they have been beefing up on robots.

Most recently they have contracted with Boston Dynamics to create a cheetah robot. It's a 4-legged robot that reportedly runs faster than the fastest human. It will be able to zigzag and take tight turns to chase and evade and it will also be able to make sudden stops and could end up with a tail.[6]

Or maybe a gun, and who knows what else they're going to put on there to take you out. Did you catch that? Not just evade, but chase you. What did John say? 1/4th of the earth is going to die during the first half of the 7-year Tribulation, after this global war, by means of sword, famine, plague, and wild beasts? Not going to say, "Thus saith the Lord," but could it be that maybe we just saw the prototype, for the first time in mankind's history, the wild beasts that John saw in his vision nearly 2,000 years ago? Could be. But either way, here's the point. That all happens during the 7-year Tribulation, and we have the technology for it now. So therefore, how much closer is the rapture of the Church which takes place prior to that?

The **4th passage** that is coming alive due to the increase of wars is **The Creation of a Super Soldier.**

That's right! Iron Man eat your heart out! Let's look at what people do during the 7-year Tribulation.

Revelation 16:13-14,16 "Then I saw three evil spirits that looked like frogs; they came out of the mouth of the dragon, out of the mouth of the beast and out of the mouth of the false prophet. They are spirits of demons performing miraculous signs, and they go out to the kings of the whole world, to gather them for the battle on the great day of God Almighty. Then they gathered the kings together to the place that in Hebrew is called Armageddon."

In other words, at the end of the 7-year Tribulation, Satan, the Antichrist and the False Prophet are going to trick the world into trying to take on God at the Battle of Armageddon. It's the ultimate suicide mission. I don't know about you, but how many of you would say it's totally insane to try to take on God, as if you could ever defeat Him? Seriously, if ever there was a lesson in futility, it's got to be this. How in the world is Satan and the Antichrist and the False Prophet going to convince anybody, let alone, the whole world to engage in this ridiculous plan, trying to take on God? Can you say, "D.A.R.P.A. to the rescue? They're not only working on creating super beasts for the soldiers, but they're working on creating Super Soldiers themselves. They will have super human capabilities to take on any foreign power, no matter how big, maybe even God Himself! The first thing they're doing is they're building these exoskeletons for the soldiers to make them into a literal HULK. In fact, that's what it's called, the HULC.

The HULC is an antihomophobic exoskeleton which mimics the human form. It provides extra support that enables the person to carry more weight than they normally could. Exoskeleton technology is considered part of the robotics field.

If you want to think about them as wearable robots, that would be accurate. This technology could be a real benefit to the military. Just imagine you are a soldier operating at 6,000 feet in the Afghan mountains and being asked to take 120 lbs. up in that level of thin air.

How exhausted you would be once you got there? An Exoskeleton provides the ability to carry that weight the same distance but have energy left to execute the mission once you are there.[7]

That's just the beginning. They're also working on not just super human strength, but even super human protection with this invention called TALOS.

A new type of suit being manufactured for the US Army will not only help keep troops safer but also make them look like something straight out of a movie. How much more awesome does it get than to look like a real-life Ironman.

The Army has commissioned a tactical assault light operated suit that would provide super human abilities like night vision, enhanced strength, and protection from gunfire. Each suit would have an onboard computer. TALOS can ward off explosions, seal wound, and is climate controlled to withstand extreme heat or cold.

According to the Army's official website, scientists at the Massachusetts Institute of Technology are currently developing liquid body armor that transforms from liquid to solid in milliseconds when a magnetic field or electrical current is applied. Though still in development this technology will likely be submitted to support Talos.[8]

Iron Man eat your heart out! Whoa! I mean, think of this! Why, with this new kind of technology, I could take on any huge entity, any foreign power, no matter how big they were, maybe even God. Now, speaking of Iron Man and Hollywood, has anybody noticed all the massive amount of super hero movies out there now? I mean, week after week, here comes another one! It's almost like they're preparing us for something. Maybe a reality where Super Soldiers are really to become Super Heroes to save the day from some sort of global catastrophe. If you think that's crazy and far out there, even this guy gets it.

Since we were kids we have been told by our parents that what we see in comics isn't real. When I was six I tried climbing on a second story building bannister and my mom yelled at me, "Do you think you are Spider Man or something? Get off that, Spider Man is not real."

But, today I'm going to talk about DARPA, the Defense Advanced Research Projects Agency and how they're working on making soldiers into pretty much real-life superheroes, so take that, parents. Like I just mentioned the Defense Advanced Research Projects Agency is working on a super-soldier program, a three-billion-dollar super soldier program to be exact.

The project got started to help make a metabolically dominant soldier, so in layman's terms, the military is studying on how to use technology and biology to combine man-machine and science to transcend the limits of the human body. They are working on gears, gadgets, and suits that are things that Tony Stark would make.

The wearer would be able to run at a 100-meter Olympic sprinter speed for hours on end along with being the person jumping the 7ft vertical leap. The capability of wall climbing and being the huge Spider Man fan, I say Heck yeah to that one. Also, flight and enhanced strength are probably the two top things people would want and have asked what superpowers they could have, not to mention invisibility and being able to carry huge weapons on your back, kind of like a war machine.

But I did say this was a super soldier program meaning they are trying to alter the genes within our bodies to make humans stronger and superhuman without the help of gadgets. I meant what I said because I don't lie and because they're doing just that. They are working on drugs and genetic enhancements and some technology that would allow for regeneration just like Lizard from Spider Man, faster and healing just like Wolverine, enhanced strength just like Captain America, and even something that would make you like the god of thunder, Thor, where you can operate without sleep for days without lack of performance.

Also, a major focus is helping soldiers' bodies to deal better with trauma and physical injury. One idea in development is a pain vaccine. Researchers are hopeful that these vaccines will be able to block the senses of pain for almost a month. It would block the pain in less than 10 seconds. Let's say you are in war and you are stabbed, you will only feel the pain for less than 10 seconds before the vaccine kicks in and then boom, no more pain. DARPA says they have already hit their first milestone with animal testing and are preparing reports for scientific conferences.[9]

Which means, they're getting ready to unleash it. And you might think, "Well, that's cool. But where are you going with all this?" Well, let's put it all together and go back to our text. We now can make a person have super human strength, super human endurance, super human protection, super human flight, and super human pain tolerance. Just like Iron man, Spiderman, Captain America, Wolverine, and War Machine. How in the world are you ever going to convince people to take on God at the Battle of Armageddon? Well, if you're Satan, and the Antichrist, and the False Prophet, and you had a little help from Hollywood, you could tell people, this foreign entity from the sky, coming to earth, isn't God, but some dangerous alien threat from another world. If you give them this super human strength, super human endurance, super human protection, super human flight, and super human pain tolerance, just like a Super Hero, you'd probably have a whole lot of people lining up! And once again, Hollywood is helping us to envision this battle!

Anybody see the Super Hero movie The Avengers? Did you notice the last scene there? How these super human heroes with these super human capabilities could defeat a danger from outer space? Let's look at that, is this propaganda for a future event?

The Movie Avengers:

Everyone is stationed at their computers trying to figure out how to save the world. The missile is on its way to earth.

Then we see Iron Man flying to the craft in the sky. He has caught the missile and is taking it back to where it came from. All eyes are on him. He flies straight up and into the craft, everyone on earth cheers. He has saved the day.

As he is flying into the void with the missile, he remembers what he has left behind on earth, sad that he may not see them again.

He lets go of the missile and starts to slow down while the missile is about to make contact with the alien ship. He watches intently while it hits the mother ship and explodes.

He has succeeded in his journey. It is completely destroyed, but not only that, the alien soldiers that have been on earth are falling over. Their power is gone.

Captain America and Thor see that the earth is now safe, thanks to Iron Man sacrificing himself to destroy the Alien Ship.

As Iron Man starts to fall to earth he is starting to pick up speed. His powers are gone, and he can't help himself. The Heroes on earth have to close the hole that allowed Iron man to get through space to the alien ship.

But just as it closes you see Iron Man just fall through it, going faster towards earth. Now they know that if he can't be stopped or slowed down he will die. They realize that he is not slowing down and is falling like a rag doll.

As he comes closer and closer and faster and faster, you see the Hulk fly up to catch him and shield him as he falls to earth. They run over to see if he is still alive.

They listen for a heartbeat. There is no sign of life. They stand there; what can they do? Hulk gets so frustrated that he growls at Iron Man, how can he be dead after what the Hulk did to save him. Upon hearing the loud growl, Iron Man suddenly awakes with a jolt.

He asks, "What just happened? Please tell me no body kissed me."

Captain America says, "We won." Iron man says, "Ok, good job, guys".

Captain America says, "We're not done yet." And we see the villain trying to pull himself up. But just as he does, he turns around to see all the Super Heroes standing over him with an arrow pointed straight at him.[10]

Well, don't you know? You just saved the day with all your technology! From an alien threat from another world, but we won! We won! So is it farfetched to say that maybe Satan, the Antichrist, and the False Prophet are going to dupe the world into taking on God at the Battle of Armageddon, by not only having this actual technology on the planet to create Super Heroes, but spin the Second Coming like this; That's not God coming from the sky from another dimension called the spirit realm, that's an alien entity from another world and we better rise up one last time as humanity and throw all our technology at this threat and "save the day", just like The Avengers did.

If you think that's crazy, other prophecy teachers are coming to the same conclusion. At the end of the 7-year Tribulation, Satan gathers together the remaining forces of the ungodly world, and heads for the land of Israel. They gather together to fight or perish. Right now, he tells them, it's fight or die. The executioner is on the brink, Jesus Christ is rising from the throne and gathering all His holy angels, and they are about to descend upon the earth and bring a devastating judgment on the whole planet.

So, the world, under Satan's deception, comes armed to the teeth. And you can believe that whatever nuclear capability they have, whatever warheads, whatever exotic, sophisticated kinds of powers they may be able to amass on the level of weaponry, which includes whatever 'Star Wars' kind of operations they can pull off from satellites, they're going to have it all. They're going to 'aim it all at God,' at the Battle of Armageddon and lose in horrible fashion. Why? Because here's how the Bible says that battle's going to go. God doesn't lose!

Revelation 19:11-21 "I saw heaven standing open and there before me was a white horse, whose rider is called Faithful and True. With justice He judges and makes war. His eyes are like blazing fire, and on His head, is many crowns. He has a name written on Him that no one knows but He Himself. He is dressed in a robe dipped in blood, and His Name is the Word of God. The armies of heaven were following Him, riding on white horses and dressed in fine linen, white and clean. Out of His mouth comes a sharp sword with which to strike down the nations. 'He will rule them with an iron scepter.' He treads the winepress of the fury of the wrath of God Almighty. On His robe and on His thigh, He has this name written: KING OF KINGS AND LORD OF LORDS. And I saw an angel standing in the sun, who cried in a loud voice to all the birds flying in midair, 'Come, gather together for the great supper of God, so that you may eat the flesh of kings, generals, and mighty men, of horses and their riders, and the flesh of all people, free and slave, small and great.' Then I saw the beast and the kings of the earth and their armies gathered together to make war against the rider on the horse and His army. But the beast was captured, and with him the false prophet who had performed the miraculous signs on his behalf. With these signs he had deluded those who had received the mark of the beast and worshiped his image. The two of them were thrown alive into the fiery lake of burning sulfur. The rest of them were killed with the sword that came out of the mouth of the rider on the horse, and all the birds gorged themselves on their flesh."

Revelation 14:20 "They were trampled in the winepress outside the city, and blood flowed out of the press, rising as high as the horses' bridles for 1,600 stadia."

In other words, that's 4 feet deep for 200 miles! So much for your technological deception! Tony Stark. LOSER! You talk about deceit! No wonder the Bible calls Satan "The Great Deceiver" and "A Murderer." He knows he can't win, but dupes mankind one more time, and leads them to a horrible slaughter! This is all happening in our lifetime. What more does God need to do? We need to wake up!

When our Lord was on earth the first time, He told His disciples of a great feast to which all men were invited to come freely. Love set the table and compassion was there to serve. Grace sat as host and joy poured the wine. For almost two thousand years the Lord has sent out His servants, crying out the invitation to one and all, and for almost two thousand years, men for the most part have rejected the love that invited them and despised the grace that pleaded with them. The Lord **is** the God of patience, but patience will not be mocked forever. The day of wrath will come. And those who have refused the call of grace to the banquet of love must themselves be the victims at another great supper, where their flesh will be picked clean by the fowls of the air.

In other words, you can "sup" with Jesus now, and escape this whole mess, or you can continue to reject him and "sup with Satan" at the Battle of Armageddon, where the birds will eat your flesh! Choose to be there with Jesus now!

The 2nd sign to indicate that we are headed for Worldwide Upheaval, that the planet is going to get messed up, like Jesus says, right before He comes back, is that there would be an **Increase of Famines**.

Don't take my word for it. Let's listen to God's word.

Matthew 24:3-8 "As Jesus was sitting on the Mount of Olives, the disciples came to Him privately. Tell us, they said, when will this happen, and what will be the sign of Your coming and of the end of the age? Jesus answered: Watch out that no one deceives you. For many will come in My name, claiming, I am the Christ, and will deceive many. You will hear of wars and rumors of wars, but see to it that you are not alarmed. Such things must happen, but the end is still to come. Nation will rise against nation, and kingdom against kingdom. There will be famines and earthquakes in various places. All these are the beginning of birth pains."

As we saw before, right after the first warning of deceit, wars and rumors of wars, as told by Jesus, is a sign we're living in the last days. What was the very next thing He told us there was going to be, another sign that we're living in the last days? You'd also see an Increase of Famines, right? Again, the scoffer would look at this passage and sarcastically state, "Famines are no big deal, we've always had famines." And granted, yes, that is true, but not like we see today! In the last century alone, we have seen nothing short of an explosion of worldwide famines and it's about to get incredibly worse!

The World Health Organization estimates that while 1/3 of the world is well-fed, another 1/3 are under-fed and the final 1/3 is starving to death right now. Why? Because 12,000 square miles of Africa per year is now turning into desert. In two of their countries, Sudan and Somalia, they are facing some of their worst droughts ever!

Al Jazeera Reports:

There is a lot of hunger here in Sudan and if the rains aren't good this year it's going to really be bad. The biggest problem is death rates and the disease rates are simply out of hand. If they understand that there is no water for them here, they will have to look for water.

Because of the drought this is now the reality of the meaning of famine.

We discuss the terminology, the numbers, the figures, statistics, and this is what the reality is. When we say famine, we look at these families and this is famine reality in the flesh.

The situation is very, very desperate for them to have walked, traveled 320 kilometers across the arid desert in the heat, leaving everything that they know; it must have been shear desperation to make that arduous journey.

We'd like to think that this family is the fortunate ones. It's difficult to say I'm looking at a fortunate family. It's a real failure of humanity and I think this is how we are going to be judged in the future.[11]

That's what the Bible says. And we get upset over cold french fries? This is just the tip of the iceberg. Africa is not the only country with this problem. As we saw before, so are the Chinese. Today as we speak, China is losing 4,000 square miles of land mass to deserts each year. About 1/3 of their total land is now covered in the form of massive drifting sand dunes.

And throughout the world, a land area bigger than the state of Texas is becoming desert every single year. No matter what they try to do, the deserts just keep on coming and so will the famine.

This is one of those Bible Prophecy signs that I don't think we get here in the West. I mean, it doesn't seem to hit us with much seriousness, because we're cushioned from it. But not anymore! You better get ready! It's about to come here to America? Why? Because number one, the context of our passage is global, which means, like it or not, it must come to America! It's already started. "Drought is spreading across 14 states from Florida to Arizona and The U.S. Department of Agriculture designated all 254 counties in Texas as natural disaster areas." Here's the photo we saw last time…let's remind ourselves of that!

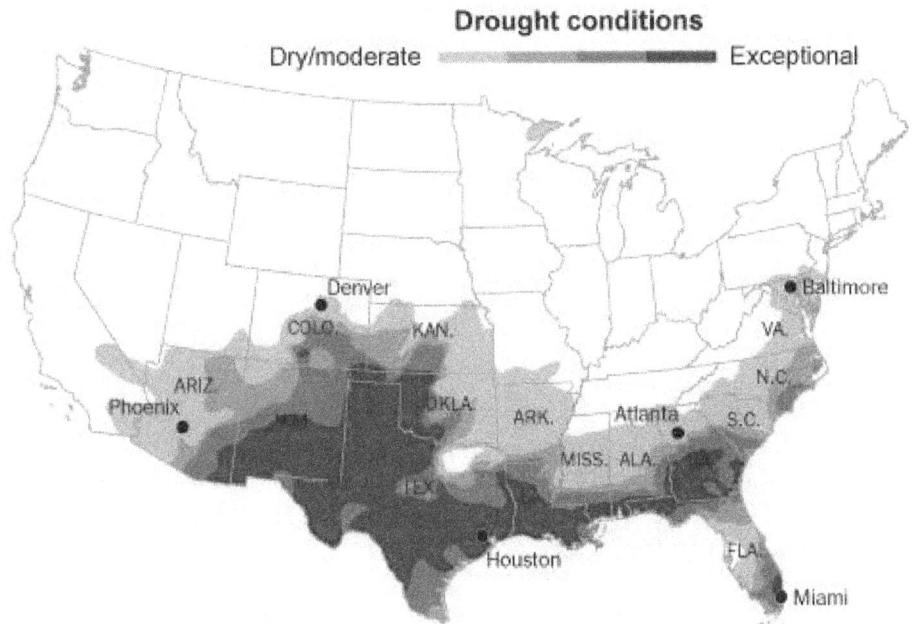

On the following page is how much it has changed in just about 8 months.

U.S. Drought Monitor
Total U.S.

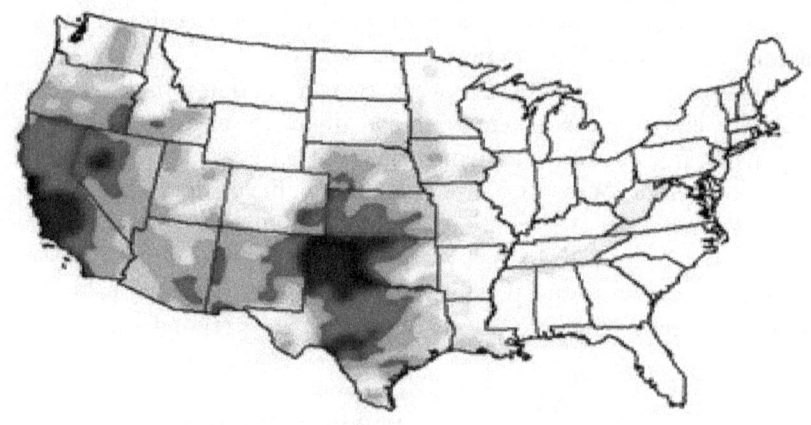

Notice it's all over the state of California? Right now, half of the United States is in a drought and its spreading! In fact, it's being called "The New Dust Bowl" with conditions "drier than they were during the worst times in the 1930's" and just like the old Dust Bowl, dust storms are once again on the rise! This is one of them in Lubbock Texas.

NBC Reports:

The folks in West Texas say it's the worst storm in decades and it swept through Lubbock yesterday (10/17/11) in a way that reminded some of the veterans, the old timers, of the dust bowl storms back in the 1930's. Home video captured this scene in west Texas. The horizon looked like something from a science fiction thriller. "That is terrifying".

To the residents in Lubbock Texas it was no movie. "It was horrible, scary really. Just that big old black cloud of dust." That 8000-foot-high wall dust washed across the high plains with hurricane force winds. They had wind gusts of 74 miles per hour.

Video shows the wall of dust. Winds bent power poles and ripped buildings apart. "We saw a third of our roof blown off across the back-parking lot and landed on several cars and some of it ended up about 100 yards away", One resident had to say. "Look at all the dust!" I've never seen anything this severe in West Texas. As the seasons change and the drought continues, Texas runs the risk of seeing more scenes like this, when dust turns day into night.[12]

Believe it or not, that was just a baby one! One dust storm was so big that it, "covered most of Kansas, Western Oklahoma, the Texas Panhandle, and Eastern Colorado," all at the same time. That's massive! One guy said, "This is a recipe for disaster." Why? Because it's become so bad that some towns in Texas are now being forced to drink their own toilet water!

NBC Reports:

Inside the Wichita Falls city water treatment plant, officials insist that the process is not only safe but necessary because of the drought, but some residents think "It's just plain gross". In bone dry Texas, desperate times are calling for desperate measures. "It makes me nervous, I'm concerned about my kid's health," one resident had to say. In Wichita Falls, population 100,000, years of sizzling drought has prompted sprinkler and car wash restrictions. But the city fears it will run out of water in just 2 years, so its fishing for answers down the toilet. "We don't have any other options and drinking your own waste water is never comforting".[13]

How many of you would agree? Disgusting! But you have got to do what you have got to do! It's not just Texas. California is being thrashed at the same time. Which not only causes concerns for us in America, but the whole planet. Why? Because California feeds a whole lot of people! And we'll get to that in a second. Right now, California is experiencing its worst drought in 1,250 years. A federal agency just came out and said, "Some California farmers will receive no irrigation water this year". "It's the first time the State Water Project has turned off its spigot in its 54-year history." Why? Because there simply isn't enough water to go around. In fact, they are gearing up to "truck in drinking water to parched communities." Here's how bad it is!

"It's dry, nothing can grow in there," says a farmer in Riverside County. This field usually produces wheat which ends up as bread. This year's historic

California drought may doom most of his harvest. "We grow about 3000 acres of wheat and we'll probably not harvest any of it," he says.

California is considered the bread basket of the world and produces half of all the fruit, vegetables, and nuts consumed in the U.S. "Everybody is going to feel it not only in food prices but in water prices too." The state is also warning that 17 small water systems could run out of water within weeks. California isn't alone in its water troubles.

The U.S. Department of Agriculture has declared drought disaster areas in parts of 11 states. Water managers throughout the region are being forced to tap other depleting water sources. "We are relying on ground water to make up as much surface water shortages as we can. That means our ground water level is going to decrease," says Jim Beck of the Kern County Water District.[14]

Not just decreased, it may never come back! You talk about a Divine Appointment. In January while on vacation, I had a conversation with a drought expert, a hydrologist, in Coloma, California. My kids and I went there to meet him at a blacksmith shop, where he was a volunteer. What he told me was that it was worse off than even the news was reporting. He said it's not only the worst drought in 1,250 years, but the average well depth in Texas used to be 5-7 feet and now its 500 feet. The underground aquifer is depleting! And the current answer to the problem is to just drill more wells, which will only make it deplete faster. He said even if you stop the wells it can't be replenished because the soil that used to hold water has now collapsed in on itself because it's so dry. So even if it rains a bunch, it can't hold it, it's gone! In fact, I found a news broadcast that admitted it.

The Weather Channel Reports

America relies on its Central Valley for most of its fruits and vegetables, and the Central Valley relies on the San Joaquin river to grow those crops. That river is running dry. And the consequences could change California and the country forever. "The salmon are gone, the steelhead are gone, there just is no water for anything. Agriculture, fish, recreation, or anything.

To keep farms and cities alive, holes have been drilled to tap the ground water, but those aquifers are over used. When you take the water out of those spaces, then the space collapses a little bit and now you have subsidence of the land surface. The major impact of the withdrawing is the impact of what is happening to the land. An area the size of Rhode Island right in the middle of California sinking. It's a disaster evolving into a catastrophe.[15]

Why? Because you're losing your ability to store the water! I asked the hydrologist the "proverbial question" What about desalination plants? He said not even those are a quick fix. He said there are several problems with that idea. First of all, there's the cost. Do you have a billion dollars to build one? They're not cheap, you know? In fact, one plant that was supposed to go online in 2016 in the San Diego area costs just that, $1 billion dollars! And when it goes online, listen to this. It will produce "50 million gallons per day" which is enough to offset only 7 percent of the county's water usage. As one guy put it, "That's a huge bill for not very much additional water." It's not a quick fix, okay? That's not all. Then you have a power problem, the hydrologist said. Do you want a nuclear power plant next to each one? Even if you could, you still have a massive plumbing problem. Even if you have a plant say in San Francisco, how do you get it to the rest of California or the rest of the internal U.S? How much is this going to cost? How much time is that going to take? There simply isn't enough time! He said he believes we are 4-8 years away from the tipping point, in other words, the point of no return!

Experts are saying that we need to "brace ourselves for a mega-drought, one that could last for 200 years or more. And that's precisely why they're also saying, "We are headed for a serious food crisis." In fact, it's already begun. Right now, here in the U.S., 49 million Americans are facing "food scarcity." Experts are saying this is a "threat that should not be taken lightly." Why? Because California, is the "Breadbasket of America!" Let's look at just what California produces for us.

44% of asparagus
50% of bell peppers
66% of carrots
83% of fresh spinach
89% of cauliflower
90% of the leaf lettuce we consume
94% of broccoli
95% of celery
A third of total fresh tomatoes consumed in the U.S. & 95% of ones destined for cans and other processing purposes

99% of the artichokes grown in the US

As for fruit...
25% of oranges
84% of peaches
86% of lemons
88% of fresh strawberries
97% of fresh plums[16]

    In other words, if California goes down, we all go down, right? Not just fruits and vegetables, but meat. Have you noticed the prices of meat going up in the store? And you want to know why? California and other states not only don't have the water to grow plants, but that means they don't have the plants to feed the animals that end up producing the meat. It all spills downhill! In fact, right now, farmers are having to get rid of cattle because there is no grass to feed them. The cattle supply in America is at a 61-year low and some ranchers are reporting that their herds are 90% smaller than what they used to be.
    Which is why one guy said, "It will be catastrophic and there will be repercussions at the supermarket." Prices are going to go nuts, even worse than what they are now. Not just us, but around the entire world. California and America feed the planet. Everybody feels the pinch! Which is why they are now saying, "We are headed for a global food crisis." What happens here affects the world! In fact, it's already begun! Food riots have already occurred in Tunisia, Egypt, Yemen, Somalia, Cameroon, Mozambique, Sudan, Haiti, India, Syria, Iraq, Oman, Saudi Arabia, Bahrain, Libya, Uganda, Mauritania, Algeria, Argentina, Brazil, Bangladesh, China, Kyrgyzstan, South Africa, Colombia, Libya, Sweden, Bulgaria, Chile, Thailand, Bangladesh, Ukraine, Bosnia, and so on and so forth - it's happening now! Africa, China, and America are not the only ones experiencing a water crisis. So is the whole planet right now, and it's about to get astronomically worse!

Right now, 1.6 billion people live in areas of the world that are facing "absolute water scarcity."

Global water usage has quadrupled over the past 100 years and continues to rise rapidly.

One third of the global corn crops are facing "water stress."

A child dies from a water-related disease every 15 seconds.

By 2025, two-thirds of the population of Earth will be "living under water stressed conditions."

The amount of water that China imports is greater than the amount of oil that the United States imports.

Approximately 80% of the major rivers in China have become so polluted that they no longer support any aquatic life at all.

The Great Lakes here in America hold about 21% of the total supply of fresh water in the entire world, but Barack Obama is allowing water from those lakes to "be drained, bottled, and shipped to China" "at a frightening pace."

It is being projected that India will essentially run out of water by 2050.

It has been estimated that 75% of all surface water in India has been heavily contaminated by human or agricultural waste.

The global demand for water will exceed the global supply of water by 40% by 2030.

As one person said, "For generations, we have been able to take our seemingly endless supplies of fresh water completely for granted, but things have now changed. We are heading into a horrendous water crisis unlike anything that the world has ever experienced before, and right now there do not seem to be any large-scale solutions capable of addressing this crisis. If nothing is done, the lack of fresh water will eventually be deeply felt by nearly everyone on the entire planet. But this is just the beginning."[17]

Jesus says, You ain't seen nothing yet! This is the beginning of birth pains! It's going to get even worse during the 7-year Tribulation and you don't want to be there! Yes, we may have always had famines since the fall of man, but nothing like we see today. And that's exactly what Jesus said would happen, right before He came back!

The **3rd sign** to indicate we are headed for this Worldwide Upheaval, and we are living in the last days, is that there would be an **Increase of Earthquakes.**

Matthew 24:3,7,8 "As Jesus was sitting on the Mount of Olives, the disciples came to him privately. Tell us, they said, when will this happen, and what will be the sign of your coming and of the end of the age? There will be famines and earthquakes in various places. All these are the beginning of birth pains."

The scoffer would look at this passage and sarcastically state, "Earthquakes are no big deal, we've always had earthquakes." And granted, yes, that is true. We've always had earthquakes, but not like what we see today. In the last century alone, we have seen nothing short of an explosion of worldwide earthquakes like never before. The ground is literally cracking up all over the planet! "Scientists are now sounding the alarm that 'mysterious cracks' are appearing across the planet!" right now! Which has caused them to say, "we are entering a new period of great seismic disturbances." Where have I heard that before? They are not only saying, "Something is seriously wrong," but they're acknowledging that the earthquakes are getting bigger and more numerous all over the planet! Let's look at some of that proof again.

Back in 2006 there were 454 earthquakes in just one week in the United States. Two years later in one week there were 1,100 earthquakes. If you don't think that is a trend, the USGS shows the magnitudes of 6 going up to 8. This is serious.[18]

They're acknowledging that earthquakes are on the rise, just like Jesus said would happen, in the last days. But not only that, it's also starting to happen in various places! In places you'd never think would have earthquake problems, like Oklahoma! And I quote, "Oklahoma had 20 earthquakes hit in one day, and 2,611 of them just last year alone!" And for the first few months of this year, Oklahoma was outpacing California for the number of earthquakes! This is a place you'd never expect to have a problem with earthquakes! And that's why people are sounding the alarm that something strange is happening, like this news broadcast shows.

CBS Reports:

Earthquakes in Oklahoma. It is in our thought that the Sooner State is not exactly earthquake country. Yet just this week there were 150 Oklahoma quakes and this year, less than 2 months into 2014, the number is nearly 800.

Jeffrey Kluger with Time Magazine is here with more. "Jeffrey, good morning". "Good morning," He replies. "This is a pretty stunning number, isn't it?" asked the interviewer. "It is a very stunning number, especially when you consider the fact that from 1975 to 2008 there was precisely one quake per year with a magnitude of 3.0 or over in Oklahoma. There were 2600 quakes under 3.5 last year alone."

He replied. "Could these earthquakes get a lot bigger?" The interviewer asked. "Yes, and the analogy I like best is a 3.0 quake causing a shaking that is equivalent to a carton of milk falling off your counter onto the kitchen floor." He responds. "That's not too much, but Oklahoma had a 5.6 Richter quake in 2011 which broke a 60-year record; that was a 5.5 back in 1952, so they are getting bigger and that could mean trouble," states the interviewer.[19]

Sounds like there's no safe place to hide anymore. And it's not just Oklahoma. Hundreds of earthquakes are now happening in other odd "various places" like Idaho, Ohio, and even Alabama. Because as we all know, for years, our families have warned us. "Don't move to Alabama! There's earthquakes there, you'll die!" Yeah right! Now, some say this increase of earthquakes in these areas is due to "fracking" or a new way they have for drilling oil, but if you think about it, that doesn't change the prophetic significance of what Jesus said.

Whether an earthquake is caused by "natural means," or by "fracking," who cares? What is the point? Earthquakes, regardless, however are on the rise exactly like Jesus said they'd be before He came back. In fact, one of the big ones they're really concerned about is called the New Madrid Fault Line in an area that most of us would say should be perfectly safe from earthquakes, and that's in America's Heartland and if that baby goes off again, folks we're in a heap of trouble.

The biggest earthquake ever to hit the lower 48 states was not the 6.7 Northridge quake in 1994, or the 6.9 Loma Prieto quake in 1989, or even the 7.8 San Francisco quake of 1906, but the series of three quakes which struck near St Louis in 1811 and 1812.

The earth didn't just shake, it discharged bazaar sand geysers, spewed strange vapors, made the Mississippi River run backward, and sucked lakes dry. "Suddenly the hand of God comes down and strikes right where you're at." For many it seems to be the end of the world. "These people were scared to death."

But it wasn't over. Thousands of aftershocks rattled the continent for 5 more months. They rang church bells in Boston, they rattled china in New York, they were felt in Detroit, they were felt in Washington DC. What if that same earthquake were to strike the Midwest today? The lives of at least 11 million Americans would be in peril. The problem today is that what was an unpopulated area in America is now very populated. It happened before, and it will happen again.[20]

How does he know that? Maybe he's been reading the Bible and that it tells us it will happen again! Here's the proof!

Revelation 6:12-14 "I watched as he opened the sixth seal. There was a great earthquake. The sun turned black like sackcloth made of goat hair, the whole moon turned blood red, and the stars in the sky fell to earth, as late figs drop from a fig tree when shaken by a strong wind. The sky receded like a scroll, rolling up, and every mountain and island was removed from its place."

That would include the New Madrid Fault Line, which means, it is going off again soon. You can laugh and scoff all you want, but if you continue to reject Jesus as your Lord and Savior, you are headed for that reality! The last time the New Madrid Fault Line went off, it was felt across 1 million square miles. To put it into perspective, the Great San Francisco Earthquake was felt only 6,200 square miles.

The 4th sign to indicate that we are headed for Worldwide Upheaval is an **Increase of Pestilence, Disease, and literally Plagues**.

Let's go to the parallel passages of **Matthew 24**, and **Luke 21**, and let's discover another couple of nuggets that Jesus mentions about some signs you can expect in the Last days.

Luke 21:7-11 "Teacher, they asked, when will these things happen? And what will be the sign that they are about to take place? He replied: Watch out that you are not deceived. For many will come in My Name, claiming, I am he, and, the time is near. Do not follow them. When you hear of wars and revolutions, do not be frightened. These things must happen first, but the end will not come right away. Then He said to them: Nation will rise against nation, and kingdom against kingdom. There will be great earthquakes, famines and pestilences in various places, and fearful events and great signs from heaven."

As we can clearly see, right after Jesus warned about the rise of deceit, wars, famines, and earthquakes, what was the very next thing He said was going to be a sign you're in the last days? You'd see a rise of pestilence or disease, right? Once again, the scoffer would look at this passage and sarcastically state, "Pestilence is no big deal; we've always had outbreaks of diseases." And once again, that is true. But not like we see today! In the last century alone, we have seen nothing short of an explosion of worldwide pestilence like never before. And yet, in total arrogance, as recently as 1979, the U.S. Surgeon General said, "It is time to close the books on infectious diseases." We've whooped them! Really? Are you kidding me? By the 1990's, instead of fading out of existence, infectious diseases have gone ballistic and they continue to do so right up to today!

Diseases that were once considered conquered such as Tuberculosis, are coming back like wildfire! In fact, they're projecting that 10 million people might die of it by next year, Tuberculosis, I thought we had that whipped. But that's not the only one that's coming back. So is Whooping Cough.
And I quote, "The Whooping Cough has reached epidemic levels and epidemic proportions with 800 new cases being reported in just two weeks, just in California." But don't take my word for it; lets read this news report.

CBS News Reports:

Health officials in California this morning, are alerting the state's population about an alarming number of cases of whooping cough. The disease is particularly dangerous for young children causing bouts of violent coughing and gasping for air. Carter Evens reports it is officially at epidemic levels. "More than 800 cases of whooping cough have been reported in California during the past two weeks, leading the state's department of public health to declare an epidemic on Friday.

There have already been more than 3400 cases in the state so far this year. Whooping cough usually starts with cold like symptoms and progresses into severe coughing fits that leave those infected gasping for air. It's a very unpleasant disease. Although California is the only state to declare an epidemic, there has been a 24% increase in whooping cough cases nationally from this time last year.[21]

Sounds to me like it's spreading. Interesting. I thought we had that one under control. Guess not. Another disease that's coming back is Polio. I couldn't believe this one! Get this! "Polio was one of the most dreaded childhood diseases of the 20th century and provided the impetus for the "Great Race" to develop vaccines." That's what started the whole vaccine movement! So surely, we beat that one, right? No! "For the first time ever, the World Health Organization declared the spread of polio an international public health emergency that could grow in the next few months and unravel the decades effort to eradicate the crippling disease. The agency described current polio outbreaks across at least 10 countries as an 'extraordinary event' that required a coordinated international response. In other words, we better get serious, it's starting to spread! Unless it is eradicated, it will continue to spread internationally. Polio is making a comeback! Can you believe that?

Another disease that we thought we had conquered is Measles. Measles are coming back and are epidemic! Measles cases in the United States hit a 20-year high, according to the Center for Disease Control, and one guy said, "This is not the kind of record we want to break; it should be a wake-up call for us." Uh, yeah, I'd say so! By the way, so is mumps and even smallpox! Get this! And I quote, "A new smallpox related virus raises alarms. Smallpox was a disfiguring scourge that killed an estimated 300 million to 500 million people in the 20th century alone, and had been eradicated worldwide. But now, the Center for Disease Control has announced that a new smallpox virus has been discovered in Western Asia, and they're concerned it could spread or be used as a bioterrorism agent." Hey, wait a second, is that where some of these diseases are coming from? They wouldn't do that, would they? Unfortunately, yes!

We live in the days when man now uses "diseases" to kill each other, just in time for the increase of diseases that Jesus said would happen in the last days! I'm sure it's just a coincidence though. Yeah right! It's all coming to pass!

But that's still not all. Another disease we'd thought we once conquered is syphilis! What? Come on! That's not coming back, is it? Uh, yeah! And you want to know why? Because we didn't want to listen to God!

1 Corinthians 6:18 "Flee from sexual immorality. All other sins a man commits are outside his body, but he who sins sexually sins against his own body."

You're going to pay the price for it in your own body! The Bible says that any sex outside of marriage is dangerous to your health. But we didn't want to listen to God, and we reap what we sow! And I quote, "Syphilis is making a worrying comeback in the United States, with cases nearly doubling since 2005." Why? Because "more than 90% of the cases are among men who are mostly gay or bisexual." Good thing we're not promoting that behavior in America. You reap what you sow! "After being on the verge of elimination in 2000, the United States syphilis cases have rebounded." I wonder why? That's still not all.

Another disease we thought we'd once conquered that's coming back is Cholera! And you're thinking, "Well, what's that?" Oh, just one of the worst diseases ever!

HX News Reports:

Throughout history, mankind's biggest killer in the 14th century, the Plague, sweeps through Asia and Europe killing 1/5th of all the people on the planet. The city becomes a threat to the survival of mankind. 1854, London, the largest city in the Industrial World, population 2.5 million. A third living in slums, up to eight to a room, 40 to a house, twice as crowded as Mumbai in India today.

The entire city of London, the most advanced metropolitan area in the world was really an open sewer. Number 40 Broad Street, the first victim, Sara Lewis's five-month-old daughter dying of cholera. Vibrio Cholerine, a strain of bacteria that doubles in number every 13 minutes, attacking the stomach and intestines, killing a healthy adult in hours. In just three days 127 dead in London.[22]

It's making a comeback and we're worried about the economy! And I quote, "Despite efforts to corral the outbreak of cholera in the world, the sheer number of rising cases paints a worrisome picture for health officials." In other words, we better wake up and take this seriously! You might be thinking, "Well, wait a second. How can there be such an increase of worldwide pestilence like never before when we're living in the most medically advanced era ever?"

The **1st reason** why diseases are spreading all over the world, just like Jesus said they would, is from **Mosquitoes**.

Diseases typically are spread by viruses or tiny parasites, but mosquitoes can transmit those same viruses when they bite animals or people and then pass them along to other people they bite. It's like a flying syringe. And that's been the method for recent outbreaks of Malaria and other diseases like the West Nile Virus and Yellow Fever, etc. The latest concern is that mosquitoes are transferring new viruses as well. The latest one is a virus called the Chikungunya Virus and it started spreading primarily in the Caribbean from mosquitoes. Guess what has flown over here? Mosquitoes! And now the Chikungunya Virus is in 15 states and its spreading.

Joseph Alton, M.D. aka Dr. Bones reports:

Now health officials are warning about another virus carried by mosquitos. This one has infected tens of thousands of people throughout the Caribbean and now Americans are coming down with it too.

The chikungunya virus, or the chick v, as it's known, is a mosquito borne virus which has been confirmed in 15 states including New York. According to the Center for Disease Control and Prevention, 25 cases have been reported in Florida alone.

So far, all the infected Americans have contracted the virus in parts of the world where it is most common, but researchers are worried that mosquitos in the U.S. could pick up the disease by biting infected people. There's a concern that people from the United States who go to the Caribbean might be bitten by an infected mosquito and then bring this illness, this virus, back to the United States.

We have the kind of mosquito that will transmit this virus here in the United States. Prior outbreaks have occurred in Africa, Asia, and Europe. Late last year the virus was found for the first time on the Caribbean islands where more than 100,000 have been sickened.[23]

Now it's here in the United States, thanks to mosquitoes! But that's not all. Mosquitoes are also spreading another virus here in America called the Dengue (Dengee) Fever, which is worse than the Chikungunya Virus, which caused one health official to say, "The threat is greater than I have seen in my lifetime." from mosquitoes. And I quote, "If there's public apathy towards this, we're going to have a problem." In other words, you better take it seriously!

The 2nd reason why diseases are spreading all over the world like never before is from **Chickens.**

And I quote, "Superbug bacteria is widespread in U.S. chicken. About half of the raw chicken breasts in a nationwide sampling, carried antibiotic-resistant 'superbug' bacteria." The group said it tested for six types of bacteria in 316 raw chicken breasts purchased from retailers nationwide. Almost all the samples of chicken contained harmful bacteria.

The 3rd reason why diseases are spreading all over the world just like Jesus said, is from **Border Problems.**

Because we apparently can't seem to get a grip on our border problem, people aren't just waiting for mosquitoes or chickens to transfer diseases to them; we're doing it ourselves!

And I quote, "Health Experts Warn Diseases Crossing the Border are Becoming a Crisis." Well, what diseases? Things like TB, measles, scabies, lice, dengue fever, and leprosy, just to name a few, right now, are crossing the border! Why? Because, "President Obama's non-enforcement immigration doctrine has invited illegal border crossings, which brings with it a wave of illnesses and diseases that have long been stamped out in America." But not anymore! Because the previous administration basically said, "Come on over one and all; it's brought with them diseases one and all!" like this report shows.

ABC 15 Reports:

This news reporter is now reaching out to the Federal Homeland Security Director for answers and she says that the president isn't giving any. In Texas, where we are learning exclusively about a new health threat coming from illegal border crossers, the Border Patrol is now worried about a virus outbreak.

ABC 15 Navideh Forghani has that story in Texas. "They are seeing crossers with contagious infections. Sources tell me right now all that is separating the sick from the healthy is yellow caution tape, and agents tell me that's not enough." Agent Chris Cabrera says, "We are seeing people everywhere and the average citizen doesn't realize what's going on down here."

His concerns go way past the hundreds of women and children that cross the Rio Grande River every day in Southern Texas. "We are having an outbreak of scabies, it's been going on for a month or so now." "The illegals that come across and jump that fence," says Texas resident, Jorge Garcia, "a border patrol agent comes and checks with us almost daily here and they tell us about the outbreak of scabies here at the McAllen station."

And that's not all. We are starting to see chicken pox, staph infections, we are starting to see different viruses. Jorge Garcia feels that the viruses are not confined to the detention center. Not long ago a group of border crossers came knocking on his door. "There was a 7-month-old baby and the baby was cold and shaking, and it had a high fever." Jorge Garcia continues. We are told that the Dept. of Homeland called in the Coast Guard Medics. This trailer is just one of many used to treat the sick.

They are all contagious, so now we are transporting people to various parts of the state, various parts of the country, and some of these viruses are asymptomatic at this point. They are not showing the symptoms.[24]

Which means, later after they arrive in your state they "look healthy" but soon enough the disease pops up! Sounds to me like we need to take the border crisis a little more serious, how about you?

The 4th reason why diseases are spreading all over the world, just like Jesus said, is from **Modern Transportation.**

Now as we saw before, one of the most horrific outbreaks of disease was the infamous Influenza Outbreak of 1918 that killed anywhere from 50-130 million people worldwide, or about 3% of the world's population. We saw the reason it spread so fast was, it just so happens, that we have for the first time in mankind's history, a global transportation system that helped transport the disease like never before. It's still a big problem even today. Dr. Diana Bensyl of the CDC said, "With today's patterns of global travel and trade, disease can spread nearly anywhere on the planet within 24 hours."
Our modern travel technology is helping to spread diseases across the planet! Just in time for Jesus' prediction to be fulfilled for diseases to spread across the planet in the last days! I'm sure that's just a coincidence! Yeah right! Because of modern travel technology, one of the biggest ones they are concerned about right now is MERS. It stands for Middle East Respiratory Syndrome and it first started in Saudi Arabia, with no known treatment or cure, by the way, and it is extremely contagious. It carries a 30% death rate, and it's spreading! Why? Because our traveling habits are helping it to spread, even here in America, like this report shows.

The MERS virus was first reported in 2012 in Saudi Arabia. There are 401 known cases worldwide with 93 deaths. All the cases can be traced back to the Arabian Peninsula.

The second case of the deadly MERS virus has been confirmed in the Netherlands as the World Health Organization issues a new warning calling the spread of this virus more urgent. 570 cases of MERS have been identified since 2012 with nearly one third of them fatal. That's a disturbing fatality rate. A deadly disease has appeared for the first time in the U.S. It's called Middle East Respiratory Syndrome, the MERS virus for short. The Center for Disease Control says MERS turned up in Indiana where one patient, recently returned from Saudi Arabia is being treated.

Until now the MERS virus has been seen only in the Middle East and Europe, a dozen countries in all, and about 100 people have died from it. Dr. John Lapuke says, "The unidentified patient was a health care worker in Saudi Arabia. On April 24th he flew from Riyadh to London and on to Chicago, then took a bus to Indiana. Three days later, fever, cough, and shortness of breath developed. The next day he was admitted to Community Hospital in Munster, Indiana.

The patient's travel history led the Health Department to test for MERS." The MERS outbreak is spreading in the U.S.A. The second case has been identified by officials, but now there is no specific anti-viral drug that we have available to treat these patients.[25]

  Looks to me like its spreading! And by the way, the second person who contracted it from the U.S. was, "Traveling from Saudi Arabia to London, to Boston, to Atlanta, and to then on to Florida, where they reported as feeling unwell with a fever, chills, and a slight cough." Hmmm. I wonder how many people they coughed on that we don't even know about yet? That's still not all. Another disease they're really worried about, thanks to modern travel technology, is the Ebola Virus. And this baby is deadly! Check this out! The Ebola Virus is one of the most lethal infectious diseases on the whole planet and it's spreading right now! One person stated, "We are facing an epidemic of a magnitude never before seen," of Ebola! It has a fatality rate of 90%, the other one had 30%, and it kills you very quickly with uncontrollable internal and external bleeding. Nine out of 10 people who get this die, and there is no cure! That's right, thanks to modern travel technology, it's spreading right now out of control. I didn't say that. These people did.

In Africa, medical teams, are scrambling to contain a deadly outbreak of Ebola. A highly contagious, often fatal virus with no known treatment or vaccine. American specialists have been deployed to Uganda to try and stop this regional emergency from spreading into a global pandemic.

"I have to say there are few things I have done in medicine that are as nerve racking as going into this place. Ebola is untreatable." The president of Guinea has urged the people not to panic as his government deals with the outbreak of

the deadly Ebola virus. The medical team says the country is facing an unprecedented epidemic of Ebola.

So far, 78 have died from the disease in Guinea. It causes severe bleeding. The country has 122 cases of suspected Ebola since January. The strain can kill up to 90% of its victims that suffer excessive internal and external bleeding. Now 4 deaths are being reported in neighboring Liberia.

The news agency reports suggest that the fever outbreak may have crossed the border into neighboring Sierra Leon. NBC reports that many of the worlds medical professionals especially in the field of infectious disease and public health are focused on what is feared to be a major outbreak of one of the deadliest diseases known to the planet, the Ebola virus.

In recent weeks, it has spread quickly in West Africa killing more than 100 people, raising concerns that it could move quickly beyond there and pose an even broader threat. Dr. Tim Jagatic, of Doctors Without Borders, works with the infected there and spoke to us today by phone. "The urban area has more possibilities of more contact with people moving around various parts of the city, leaving the city, going to various parts of the country, and possibly even leaving the country." FOX reports an Ebola breakout in West Africa is totally out of control. That is according to an official of Doctors Without Borders.[26]

It's now the greatest Outbreak of Ebola in history! You know, it's almost like we're living in the last days, because we're seeing a massive rise of diseases all over the planet that are out of control. Where have I heard that before? Oh yeah, that's right, it's Jesus!

The 5th reason why diseases are spreading all over the world just like Jesus said they would is from **Laboratories.**

Believe it or not, we're not even waiting for the diseases to come back any longer or be transported by the planes or mosquitos or anything like that. We're reproducing them in the laboratory ourselves! Isn't that wonderful? They're working on making the Bird Flu even more contagious, so they can "understand it better" in case it jumps to humans. They're even recreating the Black Plague!

Most of the time when doctors find something in your teeth it's a cavity, but now researchers have found DNA in the teeth of two Germans killed 1500 years ago by the Justinian plague and used those scrapings to recreate the bacteria and what do they find, but the very same bacteria that caused the Justinian plague also caused the famous black death plague.

But in recreating the strains of the plague the scientists did something very similar to what researchers attempted during the film 28 Days Later and Hendrick Poner who led the research told the AP that as the plague becomes airborne people could die within 24 hours of being infected and that's very scary.[27]

But don't worry, the government can be trusted. Hey, I wonder if that has anything to do with the recent reports of 32 people dying from the Black Plague in Madagascar recently? How did that get there? If you think that's not possible, let's look at the government's track record when it comes to handling these diseases in the laboratory. How well do they keep them contained?

- *The Human H1N1 virus escaped from a lab in Russia.*

- *A Smallpox Virus escaped in Great Britain three different times from two different Smallpox Laboratories.*

- *The Foot and Mouth disease was released in the UK when construction vehicles from a Biosafety Laboratory in Pirbright carried mud contaminated with the FMD disease from a defective wastewater line to the first farm.*

- *A Venezuelan Equine Encephalitis virus was released in Venezuela and Columbia either from an unrecognizable infection of a lab worker or visitor, or an infected laboratory animal or mosquito.*

- *The SARS virus has had six escapes from virology labs, one each in Singapore, and Taiwan, and four separate escapes in from the same laboratory in Beijing.*

- *And even recently, even here in America, 86 Atlanta CDC workers were exposed to Anthrax.*[28]

We have nothing to worry about. These people know exactly what they're doing. Therefore, the experts are saying, "The public health danger, posed by potentially pandemic causing viruses escaping from laboratories has become the subject of considerable discussion. The danger of a manmade pandemic sparked by a laboratory escape is not hypothetical. Ironically, these laboratories that are working with pathogens to "prevent" outbreaks might very well be the "cause" of these outbreaks." Just in time for the spread of diseases Jesus warned about in the last days!

The 6th reason why diseases are spreading all over the world just like Jesus said they would is from **Antibiotics.**

You might be thinking, "Well hey, there's nothing to worry about! We've got modern medicine! This is mankind you're talking about here! We always win! Haven't you watched Hollywood? We always find some way to win!"

Not anymore. Listen to this, because we have over-saturated ourselves with so many antibiotics, the diseases are now mutating and becoming resistant to all known medication. That's why the experts are now saying, "The emergence of bacteria strains that cannot be killed by the current arsenal of antibiotics could become a public health threat worse than AIDS." Other reports are saying we're getting ready to head back to the Dark Ages medically, like this report shows.

The CDC dropped this scary truth bomb on us this week. The U.S. will soon be in a post antibiotic era. But don't panic, well, actually do panic, we are all going to die. The days of using antibiotics to handle common bacterial infections are numbered.

Many of the bacteria that make us sick are rapidly developing defenses against the treatments that we must have to kill them off, which leaves us with a lot of sick people and no way to cure them. Why is this happening? Antibiotics are way over prescribed. 4 out of 5 Americans are prescribed antibiotics every year, which is a rate the CDC describes as excessive.

Some doctors hand them out like candy because it's a quick fix or because patients insist on it. It's prescribed without any medical necessity or benefit. For instance, the cold is the most common condition that antibiotics are prescribed for, yet it does literally nothing to cure a cold.

Plus, every time you take an antibiotic the organisms in your body are at a greater risk of resisting the antibiotic for over a year. Then we can make super, super, super, mega bugs. But wait, these freak me out as antibiotic resistance has the power to return us to a time when it was common for people to die from ordinary infections.[29]

Not to mention that we are recreating the Black Plague and making the Bird Flu even more contagious, and who knows what else! Therefore, the medical community is saying that "Modern medicine has failed when it comes to managing infectious diseases and newer strains of bacteria have out-witted us." "The age of antibiotics is coming to an end," In other words, we are headed for, "a medical disaster." Yes, we may have always had pestilence or disease since the Fall of Man, but nothing like we see today. Exactly like Jesus said would happen, when you are living in the last days.

The 5th sign to indicate that we are headed for Worldwide Upheaval is an Increase of **Signs in the Sky.**

Luke 21:7-11 "Teacher, they asked, when will these things happen? And what will be the sign that they are about to take place? He replied: Watch out that you are not deceived. For many will come in My Name, claiming I am he, and the time is near. Do not follow them. When you hear of wars and revolutions, do not be frightened. These things must happen first, but the end will not come right away. Then He said to them: Nation will rise against nation, and kingdom against kingdom. There will be great earthquakes, famines and pestilences in various places, and fearful events and great signs from heaven."

We can clearly see, right after Jesus warned about the rise of deceit, wars, famines, earthquakes, and pestilence, what did He say was going to be the next thing to happen? He lets us know we are in the last days when He said you'd also see this rise of great signs from the heavens, right? It's "ouranos" in the Greek. It means sky, atmosphere, or space. Do we see any weird signs or things going on in the sky, atmosphere, or space, letting us know Jesus is getting ready to come back? Just a few!

The 1st sign from the sky letting us know Jesus is right around the corner is the rise of **Solar Activity.**

Revelation 16:1,8-9 "Then I heard a loud voice from the temple saying to the seven angels, "Go, pour out the seven bowls of God's wrath on the earth." The fourth angel poured out his bowl on the sun and the sun was given power to scorch people with fire. They were seared by the intense heat and they cursed the name of God who had control over these plagues, but they refused to repent and glorify Him."

That's how hard man's heart is! But as you can see, the Bible says that during the 7-year Tribulation the sun is going to get cranked up so that people are getting seared, literally, across the planet. So that's the question, do we see any sign of the sun getting cranked up and hotter so to speak? Yeah! In fact, as we saw before, all kinds of weird things are going on with the sun, right now! There's been massive mega solar flares, huge massive sunspots, a solar tornado on the sun's surface that was 125,000 miles high, which is about half the distance between the earth and the moon. That's how big it was. These solar storms can, "Hit the earth with the force of 100 million hydrogen bombs." How many of you would say that would mess things up? In fact, the news is even starting to pick up on this danger and they're saying that if it happens, it will radically disrupt everything on the planet, beyond belief.

Imagine if the lights just went out across the entire country. "The power went out and everybody was panicking, and they didn't know what to do, there's reports that blackouts are happening all over the East Coast," says one resident.

They announce on the radio, "Blackouts may run along the entire whole Northwest quarter." If the electric grid goes it will be absolute catastrophe for society. Every major city in America, how would it get its water supply, where do we get our medication, what happens to our transportation for our food supply and hospitals?

Again, the radio announces, "The lights are out, people are without water!"

John Kappenman, principal investigator of the NSA Severe Space Weather Study and U.S. Congress EMP Commission says, "One violent active region on the sun can cause planetary scale impacts to our critical infrastructure. The power grid is gravely threatened by an electromagnetic pulse blast from the sun. We don't have any planning on how to deal with that. We could lose our whole grid. We're talking water, power plant, we're talking nuclear power plants, we're talking fuel, we're talking transportation and computers, to order parts for people to communicate, all of that would be gone.

It's so traumatic that I don't think people can even fathom how bad it would be. It would literally paralyze all the United States, not for just a day or an hour, but for months to years. We're talking about the loss of all electricity and all satellite activity. We would be thrown a hundred years back into the past.

We didn't realize the potential about the geomagnetic storms as being a source of power grid outages to nuclear plants and we could have hundreds like Fukushima at the same time. Essentially, we are playing a game of Russian Roulette with the sun," John Kappenman, reports. "The likelihood of a severe geomagnetic event crippling our electro grid is 100%." Says Congresswoman Yvette Clarke (D-NY)[30]

In other words, they're saying it's going to happen. You better get ready! The sun is getting ready to do something horrible to the planet. Where have I heard that before? You might be thinking, "Well, yeah, I agree, the sun is heating up and that would really mess things up, but curse God? The text said these people will curse God because of the sun. I mean, those things are bad, but why do they curse God?" Jesus said all these things we're seeing now is just the beginning of birth pains! Which means it's going to get worse than what we just saw! When the sun gets heated up to its full extent during the 7-year Tribulation, it's going to look like chump change. In fact, maybe the "searing of the flesh" will look something like this, maybe this is why they curse God unfortunately!

Clip from the Movie Knowing:

He drives as fast as he can to get home. When he looks through his rear-view mirror he sees fire coming down from the sky and destroying everything that it touches. Everyone is off the streets, trying to take shelter. The radio is telling him, "We are going to stay on the air as long as possible. All we can say is take shelter underground." He turns the radio off and keeps driving. The fire is getting closer. He finally makes it to his parents' home. He looks at his dad, mom and sister. They know this is the end of life. As they all come together in a final hug the sun flares finally reach their part of the town and disintegrates their building. The fire continues through the city, through the state, through the country. The sun has destroyed most of the earth.[31]

What did the text say? Towards the end of the 7-year Tribulation, "They were seared by the intense heat and they cursed the name of God." I can see why. Don't recommend it, but I understand it! You can laugh and scoff all you want. But if you continue to reject Jesus as your Lord and Savior and do not receive His free gift of salvation, you are headed for that reality! Don't kid yourself! It's really coming! I didn't say that, God did!

The **2nd sign** from the sky letting us know Jesus is coming back real soon is the rise of an **Asteroid Impact**.

Revelation 8:2,8-9 "And I saw the seven angels who stand before God, and to them were given seven trumpets. The second angel sounded his trumpet, and something like a huge mountain, all ablaze, was thrown into the sea. A third of the sea turned into blood, a third of the living creatures in the sea died, and a third of the ships were destroyed."

Now as we saw before, if it wasn't bad enough that the sun was going to get cranked up, now we see another event in the sky that's going to take place in the 7-year Tribulation. That's from an asteroid being thrown into the sea, right? Do we see any sign in the skies that we're under any threat of a giant asteroid smashing into the earth any time soon? As we saw before, there's been all kinds of warnings for many years! In fact, in Hollywood, it's commonplace. For several years all kinds of movies have been made warning us about it. Scientists are now saying, "It's not just a matter of 'if' but 'when' we get struck by an asteroid." 100% it's going to happen! And the damage they say is going to be inconceivable.

"The loss of human, animal, and plant life would take place on a grand scale like never before. The shockwaves from that event would create huge tsunami waves, destroying both coastlines and inland areas." Not to mention a whole bunch of ships exactly like the Bible says! 1/3rd of the world's ships are going to be destroyed! In fact, the experts are now saying, *"It might be a whole lot sooner than you think."*

ABC News Reports:

All of us on this planet are on the brink of a close encounter. A big asteroid is hurdling through space and it's supposed to miss us by a cosmic edge, just

17,000 miles. That's closer than some of our weather satellites. In fact, it's so close that scientists are springing into action.

ABC's Neal Karlinsky reports, "Right now as you are reading this, a space rock big enough to level a city is hurdling towards our planet 8 times faster than a speeding bullet. The good news is, scientists say it will miss. The scary news is, the 130,000-metric ton asteroid, called TA14 is the size of half a football field and it will be much closer than the moon. In fact, it will thread the needle between earth and the roughly 600 satellites around us. The ones that your cell phones rely on. Possibly even smashing one to smithereens, on its way by. But if you are still thinking it's a long, long way away from us, way down here walking the streets, you may want to think again. The last close call turned out to be a direct hit. It was 1908 and luckily it hit the middle of nowhere in Siberia, decimating 1,000 miles of trees but no people. Amazingly, no one knew TA14 was headed our way until a Spanish dentist and amateur astronomer randomly discovered it a year ago. NASA doesn't have the resources to look for asteroids.[32]

Well gee, it's a good thing somebody cut their budget, we'll still be safe! An amateur found it! How's that for an early warning system? The Bible says an asteroid will slam into the earth. Mankind will not stop it, and it's so big it's like a huge mountain on fire and the effects are going to be unbelievable! In fact, as we saw, the Bible says this asteroid in the 7-year Tribulation will, "Cause the sea to turn into blood." You might be thinking, "Well, what's that all about?"

Some would say that the 'blood' here is actual 'real blood' and God supernaturally causes the sea to turn into it and it could be. God created the entire world just like that, He could do this, no problem. But others would say, it speaks more symbolically of death, since the Bible says that "the life is in the blood." And I kind of lean that way more myself. It still fits the text because what's the result? Not only 1/3rd of the ships were destroyed, but "a third of the living creatures in the sea died." So, the question is, "What kind of death causing agent could be released by an asteroid smacking into the ocean killing 1/3rd of the fish or sea creatures?

For the first time in mankind's history it just so happens, thanks to Modern Technology, we now know that if you crack open the earth too deep in the ocean, for oil drilling, it releases a death causing liquid. We saw that with the Gulf oil spill a few years ago. That was America's worst oil spill in history. It killed many of the sea creatures in the area. Some aerial shots were taken of the oil that rose to the surface. You tell me what this oil pictured on the next page looks like to you from above.

Gulf Oil Spill Photos

Gulf Oil Spill Photos

So, put it all together, some asteroid slams into the earth, cracks the mantle of the earth, and that stuff comes to the surface. It floats to the top, looks just like blood, and probably kills 1/3rd of the ocean life. Where have I heard that before! I'm not going to say, "Thus saith the Lord," that for the first time in mankind's history we can see what John saw in his vision. 1/3rd of the ocean turning to blood, killing 1/3rd of the sea creatures. Makes you kind of wonder, doesn't it?

The 3rd sign from the sky letting us know Jesus is coming back real soon is the rise of **Volcanoes**.

Revelation 6:12-14 "I watched as he opened the sixth seal. There was a great earthquake. The sun turned black like sackcloth made of goat hair, the whole moon turned blood red, and the stars in the sky fell to earth, as late figs drop from a fig tree when shaken by a strong wind. The sky receded like a scroll, rolling up, and every mountain and island was removed from its place."

As we saw before, this text clearly tells us that during the first half of the 7-year Tribulation, a great earthquake will occur and will what? Turn the sun black like sackcloth and the moon turned blood red, right? In other words, after this earthquake, the sun is going to become darkened during the daytime and at night the moon is going to take on a reddish hue. Most experts believe this passage is to be taken literally because for the first time in mankind's history, thanks to the science of seismology, we now know this fits the perfect description of an after-effect of an earthquake. It's called **Volcanic Eruption**! That's what earthquakes trigger! And we now know, it's common sense today, when a volcano erupts it spews forth massive tons of volcanic ash into the air. And guess what it does? It darkens the sunlight, almost like something's covering it, like maybe sackcloth and at night the moon takes on a reddish color. It fits the text perfectly! Mystery solved!

Do we see any signs of volcanic activity increasing on the planet showing us we're getting closer to this giant one going off in the 7-year Tribulation? Just a few! Right now, there's one going off in Russia, one of their largest ones, and that's just the tip of the iceberg. Go to this website, I invite you, *www.volcanodiscovery.com* and see for yourself just how many volcanoes are going off right now, all over the planet at the same time.

In Italy, Hawaii, Papua New Guinea, Vanuatu, Mexico, Guatemala, Tanzania, Congo, Indian Ocean, Indonesia, Japan, Ecuador, and even Antarctica, just to name a few, volcanoes are all going off right now. In fact, they're occurring in record numbers! The Alaskan Volcano Observatory said, "The Aleutian Volcanoes are waking up. In the last few months it's the most activity they've seen in 26 years!" Last year the experts said worldwide, "This year will go down on record as seeing the most volcanic eruptions recorded in Modern History." It's almost like volcanoes are on the rise all over the world! Where have I heard that before? In fact, one of the one's they're really concerned about is the Yellowstone Caldera. Experts are now saying it's not a matter of "if" but "when" it goes off and 3/4^{ths} of the United States will be annihilated. There's nothing you can do about it.

At Yellowstone, we might be on the edge of a precipice. The question is not if it will erupt but how and when it will erupt. There's nothing you can do about a volcano, if it's going to go off it's going to go off. And the effects on civilization are going to be drastic.

The first indications of a Yellowstone eruption will be rumblings heard under foot as dozens of small earthquakes begin. The ground begins to rise from the pressure of the expanding hot water, gases and surging magma. Lava first appears oozing out of cracks on the surface, then steam and ash explode hundreds of feet into the air. From 5 miles below the surface, molten rock is heated to 1200 degrees. It bursts into the air like a hurricane of ash. Pyroclastic flows grip along the ground at 100 miles per hour.

For those who left the park in the past half hour their luck has run out. Fifty miles away the 30,000 residence of Bosman, Montana watch in horror as the plum of ash and rock reaches into the sky. If they know anything about Yellowstone's past, they'll know they have little time before their city is devastated.

The pyroclastic flows may go out as far as 50 to 100 miles away from the volcano. So, you will see the flows coming across ridge after ridge after ridge and then finally hitting where you are. So locally it's absolutely devastating. Everything will be killed. Wave after wave of burning ash and debris would destroy everything in their paths. With so little warning nearly 400,000 people are at risk and it gets worse.

The weight of the falling ash collapses roofs across the states of Wyoming, Utah, and Idaho killing thousands while a cloud of lighter ash, a 1000 time larger than the ones produced by Mt. St. Helens, drifts eastward with the wind. And then the deadliest part of the Yellowstone eruption begins.

There's lots of ways you can die in a pyroclastic eruption. One way is to inhale the stuff and inhale sharp pieces of glass. They attack the lungs, they attack the bones, they kill you from the inside. Farm animals have no protection. Within weeks vast numbers of the countries livestock die.

Much of the volcanic ash will cover much of the Midwest farmlands. They can't grow anything in that ash. Fresh volcanic ash is sterile. So, it wipes out the bread basket of the world, bread basket of Canada, bread basket of the United States.[33]

It will not only mess up the U.S., it will mess up the world! And that's just one Volcano! When that *Great Earthquake* in **Revelation 6** goes off, the one that removes every mountain and island from their place, it's going to trigger the rest of the world's active volcanoes because they're on top of the fault lines on the earth. That's what we see in this map.

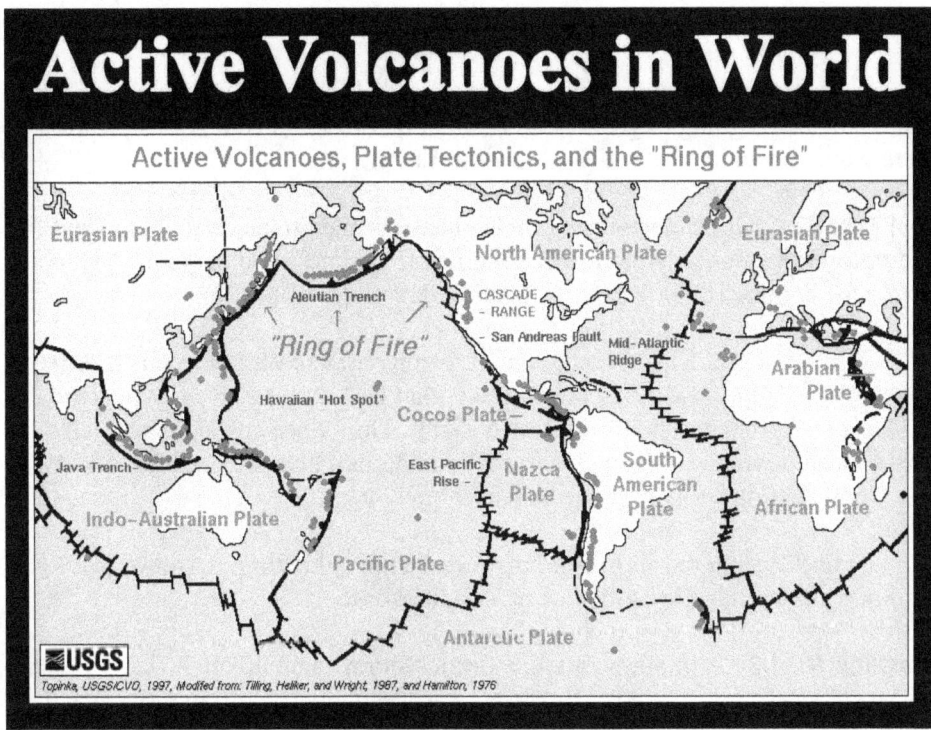

When the **Revelation 6** earthquake goes off that will trigger all those fault lines, all those volcanoes, to go off all at the same time all over the world! And what would that do? I think it'll cause, "The sun to turn black like sackcloth and the moon turn blood red," all over the planet! In fact, a recent article shared about the Ring of Fire, "Ten major volcanoes have erupted along the Ring of Fire during the past few months, and the mainstream media in the United States has been strangely silent about this." In fact, speaking of the U.S. being silent, I learned this interesting tidbit from a news outlet in South Africa.

"If the Yellowstone super volcano erupts then millions of U.S. citizens could end up in Brazil, Australia, or Argentina. The African National Congress was offered $10 billion a year for 10 years if it would build temporary housing for Americans in case of an eruption."

Why are you making plans to relocate us if nothing is going on? In fact, Yellowstone just had its largest earthquake in 34 years. It's almost like something's going on and nobody's telling us. I wonder why? Could it be it's a sign we're living in the last days?

The 6th sign to indicate that we are headed for this worldwide upheaval that the planet is going to get messed up right before Jesus comes back, is that there would be an increase of **Signs on the Earth.**

Joel 2:30-31 "I will show wonders in the heavens and on the earth, blood and fire and billows of smoke. The sun will be turned to darkness and the moon to blood before the coming of the great and dreadful day of the LORD."

In other words, you don't want to be there! Here we see in this text that God will not only show us signs in the sky, that He's getting ready to judge us, but He's also going to do it on the earth, right? Do we see any signs that the earth is also going to go through some weird aberrant behavior, letting us know that God's getting ready to judge us real soon?

The 1st sign the earth's getting messed up and letting us know God is getting ready to judge us is the rise of **Weird Weather.**

Matthew 8:24-27 Without warning, a furious storm came up on the lake, so that the waves swept over the boat. But Jesus was sleeping. The disciples went and woke Him, saying, "Lord, save us! We're going to drown!" He replied, "You of little faith, why are you so afraid?" Then He got up and rebuked the winds and the waves, and it was completely calm. The men were amazed and asked, "What kind of man is this? Even the winds and the waves obey Him!"

Here we see why Jesus wasn't afraid of the weather. Why? He obviously controlled the weather, what's there to worry about, right? The reason I bring this up again, is because most people, even Christians, think that when it comes to the weather, it's just some naturalistic explanation. Yet, they have no idea it might be a wakeup call from God! God, as we saw, controls the weather! In fact, sometimes He uses it for judgment! Do we see any signs of weird wacky weather on the planet that very well could be a wakeup call from God, letting us know His Judgment is just around the corner? Uh, yeah! Just a little bit!

We already saw that scientists are saying right now, "We are warning the world to prepare for extreme weather, earthquakes, heat waves, floods, super typhoons, blizzards, landslides, and droughts". These have killed at least ¼ million people in one year alone. And that, "More people have been killed worldwide by natural disasters in one year than have been killed by terrorism attacks in the past 40 years combined." And that's the tip of the iceberg. Recently, Britain experienced its worst hailstorms since 1843. The Mid-West in the U.S. is experiencing weather so bad that they are calling it land hurricanes or **Derecho** and it brings with it, massive hail, giant winds, and tornadoes, all at the same time.

ABC News Reports:

There is a severe storm rolling across the nation right now. The weather experts are putting out an all-points bulletin. One in five Americans are in the path of what could become a weather phenomenon called a Derecho. It is 240 miles stretch of wicked wind. ABC meteorologist, Ginger Zee reports, as she is standing watch with the people of Chicago.

"Tonight, the atmosphere is fully charged, tornadoes already touching down in Iowa and Illinois. And we are right here. Chaos in the atmosphere could produce a dangerous weather phenomenon known as a Derecho. Its calling card, often amanous shelf clouds. A Derecho is a powerful line of storms that can expand hundreds of miles long with wind blasting 100 miles per hour. It starts to take on a bow shape because air rises in the storms, cools and falls behind them, then pushes the front of the line out.

They can be deadly and certainly as damaging as weak tornadoes. Last year's big Derecho tore through twelve states, with its blinding down pours from Illinois to D.C. Winds gusting to over 100 miles per hour and a huge part of the nation peppered with lightning. Trees were plucked and chucked into homes and cars. *This street in Ohio blanketed in power lines. It left one billion dollars in damage and killed 13 people.*[34]

All that from a land hurricane! Land hurricanes! Maybe it's just me, but I kind of think God's trying to get our attention or something, how about you? We now have land hurricanes! What more does He have to do?

The **2nd sign** the earth is letting us know God's judgment is just around the corner is the **Rise of Plagues.**

The **1st plague** that could very well be a sign of God's coming judgment is the rise of **Locusts.**

Exodus 10:3-6 "So Moses and Aaron went to Pharaoh and said to him, 'This is what the LORD, the God of the Hebrews, says: 'How long will you refuse to humble yourself before Me? Let My people go, so that they may worship Me. If you refuse to let them go, I will bring locusts into your country tomorrow. They will cover the face of the ground so that it cannot be seen. They will devour what little you have left after the hail, including every tree that is growing in your fields. They will fill your houses and those of all your officials and all the Egyptians – something neither your fathers nor your forefathers have ever seen from the day they settled in this land till now."

It's the biggest most mind-blowing thing, you have ever seen anything like it! Here we see when God wants to judge a nation, like Egypt, He'll not only take down their livestock, send a bunch of hail and various other things, but He'll also send them a bunch of insects, specifically locusts, right? Do we see any signs of a massive locust invasions letting us know that God could be getting ready to judge us like He did with Egypt? Just a little bit! In fact, the locust invasions are getting so big, as the text said, something you can't believe, they're starting to appear on radar.

ABC News Reports:

Meteorologists have been confused. They called in a radar professional who was equally baffled. What was the green blob that was showing on the radar map over Albuquerque, New Mexico? The radar professional says, "We really thought that the radar was broken. So, we had our technicians go out there a couple times, but we couldn't find anything wrong.

We had to call our National Radar Depot in Oklahoma." Well, the experts in Oklahoma answered the question. They wanted to know if the Albuquerque region had an insect problem. And as it turns out, they did. That green radar patch was radar spotting thousands of grasshoppers flying a thousand feet high above the towns tallest buildings. It was the city's worst insect invasion in 20 years.[35]

It's almost like God's trying to get our attention. Our locust invasions are getting so big, they're now appearing on radar! What did the text say? "It would be something neither your fathers nor your forefathers have ever seen from the day they settled in this land till now." Locust invasions so big, they're appearing on radar! It's almost like we're living in the last days and God's getting ready to judge us!

The **2nd plague** that very well could be a sign of God's coming judgment is the rise of **Frogs**.

What? Even that one's starting to happen!

Exodus 8:1-2 "Then the LORD said to Moses, 'Go to Pharaoh and say to him, 'This is what the LORD says: Let My people go, so that they may worship Me. If you refuse to let them go, I will plague your whole country with frogs."

You might be thinking, "I can see the bugs and the hail, but come on, there's no way we're seeing frog invasions like back in Egypt!" Really? Well, you might want to tell that to the people in Greece! They're having in their own words, quote, *"A Biblical Plague of Frogs."*

We've had the skies closed due to volcanic ash but now we have more travel cares due to the act of God. This time roads are closed due to a Biblical plague of a hoard of frogs closing the highways in Greece. The local police chief putting the number of frogs in the millions.[36]

Frog invasions, just like in Egypt. What more does God have to do to get our attention? Are we really going to remain as stubborn as Pharaoh? This is precisely why, out of love, God has given us all these signs of worldwide upheaval, the rise of wars and rumors of wars, famines, earthquakes, pestilence, signs from the sky, and signs from the earth to show us that the Tribulation is near, and the Rapture is right around the corner! That's why Jesus Himself said,

Luke 21:28 "When these things begin to take place, stand up and lift up your heads, because your redemption is drawing near."

The point is this. If you're reading this today and you are a Christian, then what in the world are you doing for Jesus? Let's get busy working together fulfilling the Great Commission doing something splendid for Jesus, amen? But if you're not a Christian, then I beg you, please, heed the signs, heed the warnings, give your life to Jesus today, because tomorrow may be too late!

Chapter Four

The Rise of Falsehood

"In the beginning, God created the heavens and the earth, and He populated the earth with broccoli, cauliflower, spinach, and green and yellow vegetables of all kinds, so Man and Woman could live long healthy lives.

But Satan used God's gifts to create Ben and Jerry's Ice Cream and Krispy Creme Donuts. And Satan said, "You want chocolate with that?"

And Man said "Yes!" and Woman said, "Hey, as long as you're at it, add some sprinkles." And they gained ten pounds. And Satan smiled.

Then God created healthy yogurt and fresh green salad. But Satan brought forth Thousand-Island dressing, buttery croutons and garlic toast on the side. So, man unfastened his belt and the woman went from size 6 to size 14.

Then God created a light, fluffy wonderful white cake, and He named it Angel Food, and said. "It is good." But Satan created chocolate cake and named it, Devil's Food. And Man gained more weight, and his cholesterol went through the roof.

So finally, God brought forth running shoes so that his children might lose those extra pounds. But Satan gave them cable TV with a remote so man would not have to get up off the couch to change the channels. So, Man and Woman gained even more pounds.

So finally, God gave Man lean beef so that he might consume fewer calories and still satisfy his appetite. But Satan created Kentucky Fried Chicken and said, 'You want fries with that?' And Man replied, "Yes! And super-size them!" And Satan said, "It is good." And Man went into cardiac arrest.

But finally, God, out of mercy, created for man the quadruple bypass surgery.

But Satan created the Obama Health Care System and we're all doomed! Amen.[1]

Does that sound familiar, or what? Did you know I think I've found something even more doomed than the Obama Health Care System? Believe it or not, it's called planet earth! Those who continue to reject God's one and only healthy provision through Jesus Christ, as the only way out of this mess, will be doomed! They will be left behind at the rapture of the Church and they will be catapulted into the 7-year Tribulation. And that's not a joke! The Bible says it's an outpouring of God's wrath on a wicked and rebellious planet.

The Bible clearly tells us when you see these signs in the sky of a rise of solar activity, asteroid impacts, and volcanic eruptions as well as signs on the earth with weird weather, locust plagues, and even frog plagues, it's a sign you're living in the last days. It very well could be a sign that God's getting ready to judge us, just like he did with Egypt! We better not harden our hearts like Pharaoh!

The 5th update on The Final Countdown study is **The Rise of Falsehood.**

The **1st sign of falsehood**, letting us know we're living in the last days is **The Rise of False Messiahs**.

But don't take my word for it. Let's listen to God's.

Matthew 24:1-5 "Jesus left the temple and was walking away when His disciples came up to Him to call His attention to its buildings. 'Do you see all these things?' He asked. 'I tell you the truth, not one stone here will be left on another; everyone will be thrown down.' As Jesus was sitting on the Mount of Olives, the disciples came to Him privately. 'Tell us,' they said, 'when will this happen, and what will be the sign of Your coming and of the end of the age?' Jesus answered: 'Watch out that no one deceives you. For many will come in My Name, claiming, 'I am the Christ,' and will deceive many."

According to our text, the very first sign that Jesus mentions, to indicate when we are in the last days, is there would be an increase of deceit specifically from False Messiahs saying, "I am He! I'm Jesus! I am the Christ!" Throughout history we've had a few people here and there claiming to be Jesus. That's commonplace. But what's not common is how in the last century alone, there has been an explosion of people claiming to be the Messiah.

Reverend Sun Myung Moon of the Moonies who has tons of followers. He not only claimed to be the "messiah" and the "lord of the universe" but he has even stated that Jesus follows him. But he recently died, so I guess He's not the "lord of the universe" after all!

Jesus of Siberia, has thousands of his own disciples who think he is Jesus. After all, he walks around in a crimson robe and has long brown hair. His devotees say that he "radiates incredible love and speaking to him is like an electric shock or like bells ringing."

"What's Your Name." This false messiah in Pennsylvania is called "What's Your Name" because when people ask him, "What's your name," he will only reply, "What's Your name?" Sounds like an annoying version of the messiah to me? Yet he has thousands of people visiting him who state, "I was in his presence for an hour and felt unbelievable."

David Shayler, the self-proclaimed MI5 Messiah, a former MI5 British Secret Agent, said, "I started meditating, then I learned how to channel the 'light' and the more research I did into Freemasonry, the Knights Templar, Kabbalah the more convinced I became that I was the Christ." Then in June a psychic channeled the spirit of Mary Magdalene and anointed him the messiah. "Finally," he said, "my whole life made sense."

John Miller of Australia, a former I.T. worker from Queensland's Bible Belt. He claims he's Jesus Christ back from the dead to spread a message he calls "the divine truth." He's is currently on a worldwide tour with his girlfriend Mary. Not any Mary, but Mary Magdalene who witnessed the crucifixion. She also heads up his video ministry.

Lord Maitreya of whom thousands of people all over the world consider him to be Jesus. His appearance is supposed to have spawned "healing springs," "weeping and bleeding statues," and even "divine messages inscribed by the seeds within fruit and vegetables." And now his cohort, Benjamin Crème, is saying all these signs in the sky we're seeing is not heralding the return of Jesus Christ, but Lord Maitreya, who will bring peace to the world.

According to British author, Benjamin Crème, Maitreya, a teacher of extraordinary stature is here in the world to inspire us and make the fundamental changes that will usher in an unprecedented golden age of brotherhood and justice. "Maitreya is emerging into the open beginning public work on television and radio throughout the world beginning in America and Japan and then other nations.

Maitreya and his group have created hundreds and hundreds of signs for humanity to show that something tremendous is afoot. These are known throughout the world as extraordinary and seemingly impossible happenings, but are happenings which do happen. The latest of these signs pointing to act against a herald of Maitreya is a new star like object which has appeared all over the world. It looks like a star only bigger, brighter and nearer, with tremendous brilliance and changing color, and moving.

When Jesus was born 2000 years ago, a star appeared in the heavens. It was a space craft sent by the spiritual hierarchy to guide the three wise men and act like a sign. This has been repeated today. The first crop circle created this year, many weeks ahead of the usual date that they appear as a star and is to remind those who need to know that this is the star, the herald of Maitreya, who is entering public work. This is indeed a unique time in the whole history of the world."[2]

Jose Miranda who not only says he is Jesus Christ, but he encouraged his followers to tattoo 666 on their bodies as a sign of allegiance to him and that 666 is actually a blessing. He taught that heaven can be found here on earth, simply by following him.

Bill Maher: Who are you Biblically? Jose Miranda: I am Jesus Christ 'man'. The second coming of Christ, I am. The Old Testament speaks of me, clearly, and the New Testament also. Bill Maher: About you personally? Not just because you share the name Jesus? Jose Miranda: No, No.

Bill Maher: Because you shared the name Miranda, maybe you are the second coming of Carmen Miranda, you should have fruit on your head instead of in your head. 'Laughing.' Why do you think God chose you? Jose Miranda: Jesus of Nazareth had a wife so after they killed him his seed kept going, maybe through France, Spain and then from Spain to Puerto Rico.

The bloodline came from Abraham to David to Jesus of Nazareth, from Jesus of Nazareth to me. Bill Maher: I thought the second coming was Christ himself, not a descendent of Jose Miranda: No, not a descendent. Bill Maher: You don't believe in Hell or the Devil or even Sin, right? Jose Miranda: No there's not a sin any longer. Bill Maher: So, what you teach is that Jesus died for our sins and so there's not really any sinning any more. Jose Miranda: No, there is no more sin.

Bill Maher: This is like a diet doctor saying eat anything you want, you won't lose weight, but it is easy to stick to. 'Laughing' Jose Miranda: That's what I believe, Bill. Bill Maher: Oh, I know you do. Jose Miranda: Now many people believe in this. Bill Maher: And yet you have a little twinkle in your eye when you say it. 'Laughing' Jose Miranda: I believe it, I believe.[3]

There is no sin and there is no hell, but he recently found that out the hard way because he too recently died and yet, believe it or not, his followers are saying he will be resurrected any day now.

HE PROMISED TO RETURN…THEREFORE IN THAT DAY MY PEOPLE SHALL KNOW MY NAME. SOON WE WILL SEE HIS TRANSFORMATION. THE MAN CHRIST JESUS IS HERE. Via a medium, Jose Miranda speaks to a cheering congregation. "A greeting for all of you, what joy today to return to the cameras and be with you, it's a joy to be with you again. Soon I will talk about the death they celebrated about me August 8th for you. Well, they buried me and there my life ended, however the word says that the years of that one that was coming would not end. So then, I feel better than ever, healthier than ever. My thoughts are more organized than ever. So then, I feel perfectly fine.[4]

Yahweh ben Yahweh, born as Hulon Mitchell, Jr., a black nationalist and separatist who created the Nation of Yahweh, proclaimed himself the living Messiah of the Nation of Yahweh, and allegedly orchestrated the murder of dozens of persons. In fact, the mayor of Miami Florida declared on October 7, 1990, "Yahweh ben Yahweh Day", a month before his indictment for alleged crimes.

Laszlo Toth claimed he was Jesus Christ as he battered Michelangelo's Pieta (a statue of Jesus being held in the arms of Mary after the crucifixion) in the Vatican with a geologist hammer. He initially worked at a soap factory and later his skull was fractured in a fight. He then moved to Rome and sent letters to the Pope in an unsuccessful attempt to meet him.

Wayne Bent also known as Michael Travesser of the Lord Our Righteousness Church, also known as the "Strong City Cult", convicted in 2008 for criminal sexual contact of a minor and two counts of contributing to the delinquency of a minor. He's a former Seventh Day Adventist pastor who left his congregation claiming that, during an experience in his living room in June 2000, God told him, "You are the Messiah." And later Bent agreed saying, "I am the embodiment of God. I am divinity and humanity combined."

Iesu Matayoshi, a Japanese political activist, who not only established the World Economic Community Party based on his conviction that he is God and the Christ, but he calls himself either "The only god Matayoshi Mitsuo" or sometimes just "Jesus Matayoshi."

Claude Vorilhon now known as Rael or "messenger of the Elohim." He's a former French professional test driver and former automobile journalist who became founder and leader of The Rael Movement, a UFO Cult, after he met an extraterrestrial humanoid in 1973 and that's when he became the Messiah. And of course, the extraterrestrial name he met was called Yahweh.

Inri Cristo of Brazil, was actually born Alvaro Theiss to Roman Catholic farmers who said that as a child he started to "obey a powerful voice that spoke inside his head." He not only claims to be Jesus Christ reincarnated, but he is well known for his many appearances in the media of Brazil and many other countries. France even stated, "Christ is back on Earth" when he showed up there. Today he travels with an entourage of young attractive women and rides around on a scooter.

On a motorcycle, we see Inri Cristo riding down the street. He is wearing a long white gown, long gray hair and beard with a gray braid holding his hair back. He looks to be 80 years old and has a small little smile on his face. Sitting on the motorcycle behind him is a beautiful girl, smiling big, with a blue scarf on her head with beads. On her beads and on her finger nails is the name Inri. She is holding on to him as they are driving down the street.

The words that his followers are singing as they watch them ride are "INRI came to set us free, set us free and guide us in a new path, a new path. Freedom, setting free, freedom, setting free, he is setting us free, freedom, setting free, he is setting us free. Oh father, bless your children with health, light, and justice because yours is all the glory forever and ever, oh father". As he raises his hands to the heavens, he calls out to his followers "Peace be with all of you my children".[5]

Maybe it's just me, but that's not only ridiculous, but I'm sure that's not how Jesus comes back. How do I know? Because the book of Acts says He's coming back this way.

Acts 1:11 "Men of Galilee," they said, "why do you stand here looking into the sky? This same Jesus, who has been taken from you into heaven, will come back in the same way you have seen Him go into heaven."

In other words, it's going to be a visible appearing of the exact same Jesus coming from the sky. He's not on a scooter with hot chicks wearing fake wings on the back of a motorcycle singing a pop song in Portuguese! Are you kidding me!

It's one thing for a person to claim they are Jesus Christ. But here's the point. To have tens of thousands of people across the world falling for it, even to the point where an actual country admits, "The Christ has Returned," can you believe that? It's not just crazy, it's a sign that we are living in the last days! What did Jesus say? What was the very first warning He said to be on the lookout for? Watch out that no one deceives you, specifically claiming, "I am the Christ." That's what all these guys are doing right now, all around the world! This is a clear-cut sign, exactly like Jesus said, that we are living in the last days! We better get motivated!

The 2nd sign of falsehoods, letting us know we are living in the last days, is the rise of **False Myths**.

This is important because you might be thinking, "Well come on now! Who in their right mind would ever listen to these goobers who are claiming to be Jesus Christ? He doesn't come back on a scooter! This is ridiculous! All you need to do is read the Bible to see that this is not the way Jesus is going to come back! These guys are obvious imposters! That's why Jesus says, "Don't follow them!" If you were to say that, you're right! The book of Acts is not the only passage showing this. Here's another one telling us how Jesus Christ is going to come back.

Matthew 24:26-27 "So if anyone tells you, 'There he is, out in the desert,' do not go out; or, 'Here he is, in the inner rooms,' do not believe it. For as lightning that comes from the east is visible even in the west, so will be the coming of the Son of Man."

How can you get any clearer than this? The Bible says when Jesus comes back He's not going to be doing it secretly! He's not going to appear in a rented room, relying on crop circles and a spokesperson, to herald His return! He certainly is not going to be indicted on sexual crimes against minors or be a descendant from Puerto Rico! And that's right, once again, He's not going to ride a scooter! What did it say? Just as lightning shows up and is visible from the East to the West, so it's going to be at the coming of the Son of Man! In other words, it's going to be a worldwide global event, everyone's going to see it. It's not going to be in secret! That's what the Bible says! This is precisely the problem. People today, don't study the Bible, even in the Church, especially Bible Prophecy, which means they are being prepared to be duped by these guys! The Bible says in the last days, people will not only be following after false Christ's, but they'll be following after strange myths, literally stories made up, instead of the Bible!

2 Timothy 4:1-4 "In the presence of God and of Christ Jesus, who will judge the living and the dead, and in view of his appearing and his kingdom, I give you this charge: Preach the Word; be prepared in season and out of season; correct, rebuke and encourage – with great patience and careful instruction. For the time will come when men will not put up with sound doctrine. Instead, to suit their own desires, they will gather around them a great number of teachers to say what their itching ears want to hear. They will turn their ears away from the truth and turn aside to myths."

The word "myths" literally means, "things made up." The Bible says in the last days that churches will purposely hire pastors to tickle their ears with non-convicting sermons, things they want to hear, not the truth, and at the same time they will actually turn away from the truth and start literally following things that are totally made up! Myths! Praise God we don't see any signs of people doing that! Yeah right! As we saw before, the apostasy in the church is in high gear, and people all over the world, who claim to be Christians, are seeking the truth outside the Bible. You might think it's a small thing, but this is precisely why people are falling for these goobers who are claiming to be Jesus, among other things. They refuse to heed the Bible and are running after things made up!

Apparently, today in the Church, all you have to do is say, "I got a word from the Lord," "You better listen to me!" or "I had this experience," or "The Lord told me" and so on and so forth. Even the Church believes them over the Bible! Don't believe me? Here's just one example of a guy still flourishing in the Church with stories he's totally made up! This is baloney!

At a service Todd Bentley is preaching, "What is happening?" He is laying on the floor on his back, kicking his feet in the air and screaming, and everyone is laughing. When he gets up he says, "God, I prayed for about 100 crippled people, not one? God said, "That's because I want you to grab that lady's crippled leg and bang it up and down on the platform like a baseball bat."

I walked up and grabbed her legs and I started saying be healed, be healed, while banging her leg up and down, and she got healed. I thought why is not the power of God moving? And He said, "It's because you haven't kicked that woman in the face." (Everyone is laughing).

There was this older lady worshiping right in front of the platform and the Holy Spirit spoke to me and the gift of faith came on me and He said, "Kick her in the face with your biker boot." (Again, the congregation laughs) I inched closer and I went like this, Bam. Just as my boot made contact with her nose she fell under the power of God. [6]

No! She fell under the power of your combat boot kicking her in the face! If it even really happened! Folks, this is baloney! There's no proof for that! It's sensationalism. It is stories made up! If you think his stories are bad, wait till you hear the stories his wife is making up! Check this out! This is demonic!

At Todd Bentley's service, he calls his wife to the podium to tell about a vision she had about an elephant. He says "I'm going to have my wife, Jessa, share a dream that she had and I'm going to tell you about what God's been speaking to me about. I believe it's the key to God's greatest miracle, anointing me for the church."

She steps to the podium and speaks, "I looked, and I didn't see anything at first, then suddenly this elephant was racing across my eyes. Oral Roberts put his hand over my eyes and asked, 'What do you see?' and I said I didn't see anything at first and then I saw this elephant racing across my eyes and it was dancing, going crazy, it had this big smile and it was just going crazy and I said it's a wild elephant. I asked what's with the elephant?

He said 'Exactly, what's with the elephant?' and the thing about the elephant is it wasn't just an ordinary elephant, it was a wild elephant. It was radical, radical, radical."[7]

A story about a dead guy, because Oral Roberts is dead now, coming to you, supposedly telling you about a radical happy dancing elephant that your husband says is going to be the key for the Church to experience an outpouring of God's Spirit? Excuse me? That's radically ridiculous! That's a story you made up!

That's exactly what God said would happen in the last days! The Church will turn away from the truth, and turn aside to myths, stories made up, instead of the Bible! Again, here's the point, once you go down this road, you can make the Bible say anything! This is what people are doing. This is why they are falling for all kinds of heresy in the last days including these so-called false appearances of Jesus Christ. Not just the Messiah on a scooter, but in just about every kind of form you can think of! Here's some more supposed appearances of Jesus on anything and everything, including a piece of toast.

WLOS Reports

A person in North Carolina has a spiritual link to a piece of toast. She says she saw the image of Jesus in melted cheese. "It's just the peace He has on his face. It's a sweetness on this particular image that just makes me want to smile when I look at it." She said her and her boyfriend intended to make a piece of cheese toast for a late-night snack but when it came out of the oven it was the image of Christ.

Another reporter tells us: I am here with Maria and her two grandchildren. She tells us that she has the image of Jesus on a tortilla.

Another woman tells us: I was eating some cream cheese and when I was done I noticed that the wrapper had the image of Jesus.

Then from a man we hear: I was watching Oprah, when we paused it, Jesus appeared.

Reporter: Jason and Lisa make no secret about being religious people. "God is real, and He is watching." She says. "So, when they saw the image on their Walmart receipt, there was only one person it could be." "The more you look at it the more it looks like Jesus," he said.

Wendy Brady has a specialty of painting which she calls Mississippi Mud. She says, "I've been doing this for many years." She has a keen eye for interior design. But she wasn't expecting to see Jesus after she finished the walls in her friend's home. "To my amazement and joy and surprise, that is what showed up." It's as if the image of Jesus is keeping watch over their door.

Is this the face of Jesus in some broken stucco on the outside of a shop? While people are passing by this Chinese store they think so. One passerby says, "He's looking out after us."

A picture of Jesus graces the wall in a hospital in Florida. But when you look closely the reflection in the chapel window started a Holy uprising of a different kind. The reflection of Jesus. As Joe passed by the hospital, he saw a flash of light and he took the picture of the reflection with his cell phone. At first, he wasn't able to see it with his eyes but after looking at his phone where the picture is scaled down it became very clear.

25WPBF reports: A woman has made a divine discovery. She spotted the image of Jesus while watching the Bachelor. She had plans to spruce up her back yard so when she saw a tent on TV she grabbed her cell phone to take a picture. It didn't come out the way she wanted so she took two more pictures. As she was looking back at the pictures she found a clear image of Jesus in a white gown in the center of the photo.

"Have you ever seen a picture of Jesus on soap?" One man asks as he holds up the bar of soap.

On the program Oddball, we see a cat. On the back of Sissy, the cat you can see the image of Jesus. Sissy's owners think it is a sign of good things to come. Sissy herself not so happy about it. They try to point out the details, but Sissy was not having any of it.

Another report: Kids usually use crayons to color, but a Blue Springs woman says her child's crayons led her to an encounter with Jesus. Tara and her son melted the crayons to make an activity they found on the internet. She says, "I have been praying a lot lately and I asked God for a sign, and what's crazy, is that within an hour of doing this, what greater sign can you get than it being right in front of you. The image of Jesus was in the melted crayons."[8]

So, let me get this straight. Jesus is appearing right now on a piece of toast, Wal-Mart receipts, cat fur, the Oprah Show, the Bachelor show, and melted crayons, to let us know everything's going to be just fine! Who needs the Bible? Do you see what happens when you start going down this route? You turn away from the Bible, and you turn aside to myths, and just about anything becomes Jesus, including so-called appearances of His 2nd Coming! That's exactly what the Bible said was going to happen when you are living in the last days!

People are not only going to be following false Christ's, but they are doing so because they are falling away from the Bible and following myths! Things people have made up, including Jesus on a crayon! What more does God have to do to get our attention? We're living in the last days! It's all happening right now! This is precisely why, out of love, God has given us all these signs of the Rise and Falsehood of False Messiahs and False Myths to show us that the Tribulation is near, and the Rapture is right around the corner!

The 3rd sign of falsehood letting us know we're living in the last days is, you're going to see this **Rise of False Messengers**.

But don't take my word for it. Let's listen to God's

Matthew 24:3-5,10-11,23-25 "As Jesus was sitting on the Mount of Olives, the disciples came to Him privately. "Tell us," they said, "when will this happen, and what will be the sign of your coming and of the end of the age?" Jesus answered: "Watch out that no one deceives you. For many will come in My Name, claiming, 'I am the Christ,' and will deceive many. At that time, many will turn away from the faith and will betray and hate each other, and many False Prophets will appear and deceive many people. At that time if anyone says to you, 'Look, here is the Christ!' or, 'There he is!' do not believe it. For False Christs and False Prophets will appear and perform great signs and miracles to deceive even the elect, if that were possible. See, I have told you ahead of time."

In other words, there's no excuse for you to get caught off guard. According to our text, the very first thing out of Jesus' mouth to indicate when we are living in the last days was what? It's going to be a time of great massive deception, right? All throughout the text. deceit, deceit, deceit! He said it's going to be promoted by False Christs and False Prophets with their False Messages and False Teaching. It's going to be so powerful that it comes close to even deceiving the elect, if that were possible, right? Therefore, Jesus warned us, "See I've told you ahead of time!"

You don't need to be caught off guard with these False Teachers and their false messages if you just stick with the words of Jesus, and the Bible, and certainly Bible Prophecy! But unfortunately, as we saw last time, that's not what people are doing today, even in the Church! They're demanding that their preachers only tickle their ears with "pleasant things" 'knetho' in the Greek. At the same time, they're also turning away from the Bible and turning towards "muthos" myths, stories made up. Now they're saying they saw Jesus on a piece of toast, cat fur, and the Oprah show, and somebody riding around on a scooter in Brazil!

As crazy as that is, that's not the only false messenger duping people in the last days. Believe it or not, another one is Mary. Or should I say, The Catholic Mary. They've messed her up! Believe it or not, right now, one of the biggest, most deceitful sources of false messages around the planet duping people is now coming from supposed visions of the Virgin Mary. Let's look at just a few recent ones.

FOX 5 reports:

Some people believe that this is just a carving in a tree. Others believe that it is a miracle. It's a small carving in a tree measuring about 6 inches in length, now hundreds of people are coming by just to take a glimpse at the carving. A carving they believe is of the Virgin Mary. "Why do you believe?" the reporter asks. "She says she can feel it in her heart, she feels it inside that is the Virgin of Guadalupe." Replies the interpreter.

Albo was the first to spot the carving Tuesday afternoon on her way to the store here in West New York, New Jersey. By nightfall word began to spread and the faithful began to gather. So much so that the police had to put up a barricade and station several officers here. The sight has become sort of a tourist attraction with pictures of the carving now being sold here. "All this spiritual energy, that one carving of her, is amazing." Says an observer.

Gianni and his mother are among the many who are praying here. People here believe the carving resembles the Roman Catholic Icon known as Our Lady of Guadalupe. Many in the crowd tell Fox 5 that they believe the carving also holds mystical powers. "Right now, I am having a lot of sensational feelings and energies going through my body and when I touch her. It is like my fingers felt numb." Said another prayer.

Believers are flocking to this Baton Rouge neighborhood to see a statue of Mother Mary with their own eyes. "The faith of all the people who are coming here are at stake." Says the homeowner. You see all the people coming here believe the statue is bleeding.

Hi Win is the owner and his daughter translated for us and said he was doing lawn work when the unexpected happened. "He looked up and he saw blood flowing down", she said. Blood dripping down the side of Mary's face. And the word spread quickly. "He didn't know how to explain it, he just knows that maybe God sent a message through Mary", she added.

One faithful said that he has seen these manifestations before. A possible miracle right in their living room. A family in Northern Israel bought a statue of the Virgin Mary last year and now they say the statue appears to be crying. The Greek Orthodox family and some Muslim neighbors have seen the tears as well. It started when they noticed that the statue was seemingly covered with oil. She said it even spoke to her telling her not to be afraid. This quickly spread, and some 2000 people of all faiths have come to see the statue in just the last week.[9]

Well, there you have it! If we all get statues of Mary and they speak to us, we can bring all the religions on the planet together and we can have peace. Now, let's be honest, if a statue spoke to you, how many of you would run the other way like a little girl screaming your head off! We just need to deal with the facts. Can you believe that? This is not just crazy, this is not where we get truth from! Jesus didn't say "Don't be deceived in the last days, see I've told you ahead of time, listen to statues with bird droppings on them, or condensation leaking on their faces." He didn't say that! He certainly didn't say, "Rub a piece of bark on a tree and cry like a baby!" In fact, He specifically said not to fall for this kind of baloney! Why? Because False Prophets and False Christs will come with their False Messages and unless you stick with the Bible, Bible Prophecy, and the Words of Jesus, you're going to be deceived, even the elect, if that were possible! That's how powerful it is!

Since nobody wants to do that now, these so-called visions of the Virgin Mary are not only duping people here in the U.S. but now they've escalated on a global scale and millions are being deceived right now!

Around the world there are reports of supernatural events that are drawing millions to apparition sights where the Virgin Mary is said to be appearing. Thousands of visionaries from every conceivable background describe a beautiful young woman glowing in radiant splendor. "She's going up, yes she's beautiful, yes, she's real big, she's just standing there."

Millions flock to apparition sights, hoping to encounter the blessed Virgin Mary. Consider that 15 to 20 million Marian followers visit a single shrine in Guadalupe Mexico every single year. An estimated 30 million pilgrims have visited Medjugorje since the apparitions of the Blessed Virgin Mary began in 1981.

Besides the 6 visionaries who regularly receive messages from the Virgin, thousands of pilgrims claim to see signs and wonders, experience healings and hear the voice of Mary at Medjugorje. She appears as a living, breathing, 3-dimensional lady enveloped in exquisite light. Seers, when describing her, admits the queen of Heaven transcends human description.[10]

Well, it must be real then! No! The Bible is the book you're supposed to stick with. Satan can masquerade as an angel of light, so that means nothing. But secondly, did you catch that title they're giving this supposed vision of Mary? She's called the Queen of Heaven. Now, most people don't know this because they don't read the Bible. This is the same false female deity that Israel worshiped in the Old Testament that invited the judgement of God! I didn't say that. He did!

Jeremiah 7:16-20 "So do not pray for this people nor offer any plea or petition for them; do not plead with me, for I will not listen to you. Do you not see what they are doing in the towns of Judah and in the streets of Jerusalem? The children gather wood, the fathers light the fire, and the women knead the dough and make cakes of bread for the Queen of Heaven. They pour out drink offerings to other gods to provoke me to anger. But am I the one they are provoking? declares the Lord. Are they not rather harming themselves, to their own shame? Therefore, this is what the Sovereign Lord says: My anger and my wrath will be poured out on this place, on man and beast, on the trees of the field and on the fruit of the ground, and it will burn and not be quenched."

I'm kind of thinking God doesn't like this worshiping of the Queen of Heaven, how about you? And how many of you would say it's probably not a good thing to do? It's a demonic deception! God doesn't want us deceived! That's why He gave us His Word! Stick with the Bible, Bible Prophecy, and the Words of Jesus, and you can't be duped! The Queen of Heaven and so-called visions of the Virgin Mary are a false messenger in the last days that Jesus warned us about! That's what you get when you read the Bible! Not only that, you'll also see that the real Mary isn't coming back from the dead to speak to people! I didn't say that, Jesus did!

Luke 16:24-26 "And he cried out and said, Father Abraham have mercy on me, and send Lazarus so that he may dip the tip of his finger in water and cool off my tongue for I am in agony in this flame.' But Abraham said, 'Child, remember that during your life you received your good things, and likewise Lazarus bad things; but now he is being comforted here, and you are in agony. And besides all this, between us and you there is a great chasm fixed, so that those who wish to come over from here to you will not be able, and that none may cross over from there to us.'"

In other words, when a person dies, including Mary, they are not coming back from the grave. No! What did Jesus say? There's a chasm fixed so that those who want to go from here to there can't! There's no crossing over back and forth. Once you're in Heaven, you're in Heaven. Once you're in hell, you're in hell! That's what Jesus said! Mary was a great, godly woman and she was used of God to bring forth the Messiah, that's awesome, it was a great ministry, but with all due respect, she's just a Christian like you and me today! Which means, when you die, you're either with God, or you're in hell, and you're not coming back! That's what you get when you read the Bible! And boy is that truth ever needed today!

How many people today, even in the Church, are getting duped by supposed visions of Mary and her false messages and all these ghost shows or medium shows where people are also supposed to be speaking with a dead relative or someone? Shows like "Ghost Hunters" or "The Long Island Medium" who are tricking people into thinking that they can communicate with their dead loved one, Aunt Vera, or whoever, or some historical figure. Excuse me? That's not what the Bible says! According to the Bible, Aunt Vera, or Mary, or whoever died either went straight into heaven or went straight into hell for rejecting Jesus Christ! And they've been there ever since! Why? Because there's a chasm fixed! You are not crossing over! You are not coming back! In fact, Job is very emphatic about it!

Job 7:9-10 "As a cloud vanishes and is gone, so he who goes down to the grave does not return. He will never come to his house again; his place will know him no more."

Job 10:20-21 "Are not my few days almost over? Turn away from me so I can have a moment's joy before I go to the place of no return."

Job 16:22 "Only a few years will pass before I go on the journey of no return."

Which means, you're not coming back! And guess what? That includes Mary! If a person did hear a voice or did see an apparition, I'm not saying they didn't, I'm not denying that possibility, because the Bible says Satan can masquerade as an angel of light**, 2 Corinthians 11:14**. But the Bible clearly says it was not the actual person! It's called a demon or familiar spirit that is deceiving you on God's Truth and leading you into occult practices. And this is precisely why God says, not to do this!

Deuteronomy 18:9-14 "When you enter the land the Lord your God is giving you, do not learn to imitate the detestable ways of the nations there. Let no one be found among you who sacrifices his son or daughter in the fire, who practices divination or sorcery, interprets omens, engages in witchcraft, or casts spells, or who is a medium or spiritist or who consults the dead. Anyone who does these things is detestable to the Lord and because of these detestable practices the Lord your God will drive out those nations before you. You must be blameless before the Lord your God. The nations you will dispossess listen to those who practice sorcery or divination. But as for you, the Lord your God has not permitted you to do so."

Why? Because He doesn't want you to be deceived! He knows it opens the door to demonic deception! And wonder of wonders, can anybody guess what practices these so-called visionaries of Mary use to "see" her? Occult techniques! The very thing God forbids. Let's take a look.

Recent appearances of Mary have been reported in nearly every habitable nation. Are these events legitimate? Is God sending us a message? Whatever the answer, one thing is certain, the apparition of the Blessed Virgin Mary draws millions from every corner of the globe.

Many followers believe the Blessed Mother is present. "Currently she is appearing all over the world, hundreds of times, there are many visionaries, Nancy is one of the links and time is running out and our lady says that she is stopping in everywhere. We believe something is going on. And for all those who believe they may now have proof they need to convince others.

Two scientists from Columbia came to the farm yesterday to study Fowler. They say she is seeing something when she goes into her trances. They say, "The brain activity looks and seems to be like a coma but she is awake and fully responsive."[11]

Oh, so let me get this straight. You go into a coma like trance, a mind-altering technique that the occult uses to see demons so you can get these so-called visions of Mary. You use the same techniques the occult uses to conjure up demons, what in the world do you think is coming through? It's demons! It's a demonic deception!

But that's right, if you don't want to listen to God's Word, which I don't recommend, I'm going to share with you again the actual testimonies of two people I know who violated this command from God. When they did, things got dark! Their names are Kristine and Bud.

Kristine's Occult Involvement:

My father, when he was in the military got heavily involved with the occult. He said he was in a séance with some of his clan and the table started levitating and he heard voices. They all ran out of the room and these phantom things followed. He didn't say too much more about the experience. The weird thing is he says that a bald man sits by him at night and tells him what the kids are doing.

Then there was a Ouija board at our house left by my father. Somehow, we got hold of it and started playing with it. We would hear scratching inside the walls of the house after that and to this day that house scares the heck out of me. There is something not godly there."

Bud's Occult Involvement:

"Growing up I was always fascinated about the possibility of other life out there. I could not get enough about them. So, while surfing the net about them and ghost hunting, etc. I ran across a video that showed me how to make them show up on demand. It worked so well, I would invite family and friends over on weekends to witness it and we have BBQ's and play with this.

However, it wasn't long before I started seeing dark shadows pass over me and around the yard. They were darker than the night, so dark you could see them. Hard to explain but true. I never said anything to anyone so they would not get scared plus I really didn't know what I was seeing. It wasn't until a few weeks later that my second oldest daughter asked me. "Dad, what are those dark things that fly over us?" When I heard that, I just got the chills and my eyes even started to water. It was such a strange feeling because I guess I was hoping that maybe it was just me. So, I caught my breath and said, "So you see them too, huh?"

Then my youngest daughter said, "Dad I see them all over the yard and in my room." And it hit me hard because she had been telling me something would bother her at night and threw her stuffed animals at her when she was sleeping. Then they would hold her down. I even slept on her floor on night to show her that there was nothing to be scared of. In fact, I set a video camera to prove to her that nothing happens while we're sleeping. Well, I couldn't show her that video because she was right and I was wrong.

Then one night my wife and kids took the puppies outside to let them run before bed and my daughter ran back in telling me mom said to come and look at this. When I got outside I looked up and this huge reaper shaped thing was gliding in the air going around our house. It looked like silk flying in the wind but it kept circling our house. So, I walked up to about 10 feet from it and it just stared back at me. I could not see a face but the hood was facing right at me.

It was a windy full moon night and when I saw it fly in front of me I said, "God, what is that?" We didn't talk much about it after that and still don't today. We no longer watch videos on ghost hunting UFO's, or even scary movies, etc. We know who they are and what they want.[12]

What they want to do is to deceive you away from God and Jesus! But, if you want to learn the lesson the hard way, and ignore God's warning, then you reap what you sow. Demons are coming your way, and that includes these so-called visions of Mary. I have another testimony, hot off the press, just a few months ago, of another Christian who learned this the hard way. His name is Josh, and he and his wife opened up some doors you don't want to mess with.

On February 21st, 2014, my wife and I were changed forever.

Several years ago, I began a quest. Not a Godly one but one of self-fulfillment. I had been raised a Baptist from a very early age, went to church regularly but something was always missing in my life.

I had always been and still have been a very observant person and I started to question "fake" people we came in contact with in the Church! The church seemed to be made up of people who were more of members of a club than a group of people who had been saved, and these people occupied the pews every Sunday.

Their presence outweighed the good people and it built a resentment in me that I could not escape. "Lord, Lord!" on Sundays you'd hear from them, but their behavior denied Him the rest of the week. You get the picture?

So, I started questioning my faith and I started looking into the "New Age" occult practices. I stopped going to church services, lived a life for me, indulged in the "After Life" daily, programing such as Ghost Adventures, Ghost Hunters, Paranormal Entity, Ghost Lab, pretty much ANYTHING dealing with the afterlife that I could get and I would record it on my DVR. My weekend was set!

Now, I knew that God's law forbids us from going to such places for our own protection, but like most defiant children sometimes we learn things the hard way.

Eventually I convinced my wife to try this new EVP experiment or Electronic Voice Phenomenon. We saw them do it on TV, so how bad could it be right? I COULD NOT HAVE BEEN MORE WRONG!

It was getting kind of late and my wife and I proceeded to bed. Then suddenly, I heard a whisper say, "There are two" and then it mentioned both of our names.

I immediately nudged my wife, asking if she was whispering something and she said no. Needless to say we both turned pale white. Who is this? Why are they saying our names? Is this a relative? (You know, a dead loved one like Mary)

We left the recording alone for about a week until the curiosity got the best of us. My wife had even thought this could possibly be her Aunt because after all, her Aunt is the only one that called her by her full name.

So, determined to see if this was a relative we turned the recorder back on and proceeded to ask if there is someone there. I started to hear a slow, deep moan but I thought it might be coming from me, so I told it to get louder and to my surprise it got VERY loud!

So, in a state of panic, I shut off the recorder, told my wife that was no relative and in my head, I hoped I didn't do something I was going to regret.

Then my wife screams as she's looking at the ground in the living room and 2 of the 4 ornaments that are on the coffee table are now on the ground in a perfect straight line. We are speechless, frozen, and terrified all at the same time. How is this possible but more importantly what have we done?

Well nothing happens for about 10 minutes, and we're still in a state of panic when I walk into the kitchen, and what I see next terrifies me. There were multiple items, salt/pepper shakers, items we just bought from the grocery store, ornaments on the microwave, either stacked up on each other or moved to a different location that both of us knew we hadn't been before.

Then suddenly one of our wooden coasters flies off the end table shoots straight for the front door and smashes into the door making and ear-piercing sound. Earth shattering terror does not even begin to explain the emotions we were going through. nothing can describe this feeling. It's the most helpless feeling I had ever felt.

So, my wife immediately calls the pastor of the church we had attended and even as she is telling him what has happened, this thing has now moved to our bedroom. My wife's 5 large candles that sit on our dresser were all placed in different locations on our bed.

Then out of nowhere this thing starts clinging onto me. I could feel its cold grasp on my body with this pushing feeling on my chest making it hard to breath. But suddenly, as I'm enveloped in this horrible feeling of pure terror, I made eye contact with my bible in the bedroom, and instantly I am overtaken with this instinctive mentality to fight.

So, I walk over and reach for my bible and cry out to God and like a light switch I feel the pressure come off my left arm and it slowly comes off the rest of my body until it is no longer on me. It wants to stay but I won't let it.

I don't even remember what I said exactly after that, but all I remember is that when I reached for my bible I knew that God had my back. And what He showed me changed my life forever.

First and foremost, this was NOT a relative! (And that includes Mary!) Popular to what people may think, but it was pure evil!

God showed me in a single instant that God's revelation of the Supernatural is for Him and Him alone, but it does exist. And, that everything in life we need is contained for us in the Holy Bible. It is our guide, our sword, our protector from the sins of the world.

Needless to say, my bible goes with me now everywhere. I read it, I'm learning it, and it's provided for me what I had been wanting for so long, a relationship with God!

My message to everyone who reads this is God is real, salvation is real, but Satan and his parasitic demons are also real, and they're roaming out there just waiting for you to let your guard down.

They will stop at nothing to lead you astray, because they want your soul.[13]

Now they are using so-called visions of Mary to do just that! But that's still not all! If you still don't want to listen to all that we've seen so far, about how unbiblical and demonic these so-called visions of Mary really are, then all you have to do is listen to the messages themselves! They're so completely unbiblical it's not even funny, which means they're coming from a demonic source. I didn't say that God did!

John 8:44 "You belong to your father, the devil, and you want to carry out your father's desire. He was a murderer from the beginning, not holding to the truth, for there is no truth in him. When he lies, he speaks his native language, for he is a liar and the father of lies."

Jesus says Satan is not only a murderer, but he's also a liar and the father of all lies! And so that means any lie can ultimately trace its source back to a demonic deception, right? That's exactly what we get from these so-called messages from Mary!

The following represents common messages from the apparitions of Mary: *"Dear children, today I invite you to ask yourself why I am with you this long. I am the mediatrix between you and God"*

No, you're not! Jesus is! The Bible says this.

1 Timothy 2:5 "For there is one God and one mediator between God and men, the man Christ Jesus."

Not Mary! But that's not all. Here's another lying message.

"The world is degenerating, so much so that it was necessary for the Father and the Son to send me into the world among all the peoples in order to be their advocate and to save them".

No, you're not! Jesus is our Advocate Who saves us! The Bible says this.

1 John 2:1 "If anyone sins, we have an Advocate with the Father, Jesus Christ the righteous."

Not Mary! But that's still not all. Here's yet another lying message.

"I call upon you to open yourselves completely to me so that through each of you I may be enabled to convert and save the world."

No, you won't! Only Jesus can do that!

John 3:16 ""For God so loved the world that he gave his one and only Son, that whoever believes in him shall not perish but have eternal life."

Not Mary! But that's still not all. Here's yet another lying message.

"I alone am able to save you from the calamities which approach. Those who place their confidence in me will be saved"

No, you won't! There's only one way to escape the wrath to come! It's through Jesus Christ!

1 Thessalonians 5:9 "For God did not appoint us to suffer wrath but to receive salvation through our Lord Jesus Christ."

Again, not Mary! But let's look at one more.

"My daughter, in this time, I am the ark for all your brethren. I am the ark of peace. I am the ark of salvation. The ark where my children must enter if they wish to live in the kingdom of God."[14]

No, Jesus is the only way to the Kingdom of God!

John 14:6 "Jesus answered, 'I am the way and the truth and the life. No one comes to the Father except through Me.'"

One last time, let's all say it together…NOT MARY!!!

I don't know about you, but how much more proof do we need to settle this once and for all. This is not Mary, it's a demonic entity, a familiar spirit that's masquerading around as Mary and these demons are lying through their teeth, just like Satan, and they're leading people all around the world, right now, away from God! And that's precisely why Jesus warned us 2,000 years ago. "Watch out that no one deceives you. Many false prophets will appear (like Mary) and deceive many." "If at that time if anyone says to you, 'Look, here is the Christ!' or "Look, if you will, here's Mary," do not believe it. Why? Because, "False Christs and False Prophets will appear and perform great signs and miracles to deceive even the elect, if that were possible. See, I have told you ahead of time."

Jesus said, out of love, if you just stick with the Bible and Bible Prophecy, and His Word, you'll be okay, nobody can deceive you. But since nobody wants to do that today, even in the Church, many just like Jesus said, are being deceived AND it's a clear-cut sign we're living in the last days

There is a **2nd false messenger** blinding people in the last days, on a global scale, from the sky as well. Just like the so-called visions of the Virgin Mary, another demonic issue is **UFO's & Aliens.**

You might be thinking, "Well hey, I'm a Christian, I don't need to worry about UFO's & Aliens! Why do we have to talk about this?" You need to talk about this because two new polls have come out and have stated recently that, "More people believe in Aliens than in God," and "More people believe that Aliens have visited planet earth than those that believe Jesus is the Son of God." Which means, we need to get equipped on this issue As Christians! Our world is being duped right and left, and it's up to us to get the truth out! Why? Because it's becoming a new religion! "UFO-logy has effectively become a new religion for the 21st century," where people now believe that Aliens will save them, not God.

That's how serious this is! UFO's and Aliens are clearly demonic, just like the Visions of the Virgin Mary! Let's see what God's word says:

John 8:42-44 "Jesus said to them, 'If God were your Father, you would love Me, for I came from God and now am here. I have not come on my own; but He sent Me. Why is My language not clear to you? Because you are unable to hear what I say. You belong to your father, the devil, and you want to carry out your father's desire. He was a murderer from the beginning, not holding to the truth, for there is no truth in him. When he lies, he speaks his native language, for he is a liar and the father of lies."

Jesus clearly says right here in this text that Satan is not only a murderer, but he's also a liar and the father of all lies! Which means any lie can ultimately trace its source back to him or some demonic deception. That's exactly what we get from these so-called UFO's and Aliens! Just like supposed Visions of the Virgin Mary from the sky, so it is with UFO's & Aliens from the sky! How do I know?

The 1st way we know UFO's & Aliens are a demonic deception is **They Lie Like Demons**.

The whole premise of UFO's and Aliens are what? They're supposed to be this higher evolved race coming from somewhere out there in the universe, right? But wait a second, if evolution is not true, and it's not, then this whole higher evolved alien race identity is a lie, right? If evolution can't take place on this planet, then logically it can't take place on any planet, right? If evolution can't happen here, then it can't happen anywhere! Which means we're being lied to! That's just the tip of the iceberg! This lying behavior is not only seen in their false identity, based on a lie called evolution, but in the changing of their technology with each succeeding generation.

Most people today envision UFO's to be exactly as they are portrayed in most science fiction films and books, which is a considerably recent conception. It has been stimulated by our expanding knowledge of outer space. But strange sights appeared in the skies long before space flight or manned flight of any kind was possible. In each century, these visions took on identities that tell much about the world view of those who saw them.[15]

You first appeared to the people in the late 1800's as a blimp, when that's all the flying technology they had at that time, but today you appear as a metal disc, like a spaceship, because our technology is much more advanced. Did you really drastically improve your technology that fast and/or did you really fly from Mars on a blimp, like you told the people of the late 1800's? I don't think so! It's another lie! Just like you're lying on your identity, that you're a higher evolved race, when evolution's not true, so you're lying by changing your technology to fit the generation. And wonder of wonders, that's what demons do. They lie! And Satan is the father of it!

The 2nd reason why we know UFO's & Aliens are a demonic deception is because **They Teach like Demons**.

What they teach is a pack of lies! But don't take my word for it. Let's listen to their actual messages.

1. *All of us are little gods.*
2. *The earth is a living entity and we need to worship her and change our ways or we will be destroyed.*
3. *Jesus, Muhammad, and Buddha all came from the E.T.'s to assist mankind in our next step of evolution.*
4. *There is no such thing as sin, we do not need to be saved.*
5. *Orthodox Christianity has it all wrong. Jesus' real message was to teach us that each one of us can become "christs."*
6. *To aid in contacting these "heavenly beings" one should refrain from certain foods and practice meditation.*
7. *Mankind needs to unite into a one world government and religion or we will*

be destroyed.
8. The devil or lucifer is actually a good guy who has come to free us.[16]

You come all the way across the universe just to promote the rise of the Antichrist, support New Age teachings and debunk only Christianity, and say Satan is a good guy? You'd think if you were a real alien, who's supposed to be a higher evolved race, and much more technologically advanced, that you'd share with us something we could use. Like a cure for cancer or some new device to stop the energy crisis. But no! You come all the way across the galaxy just to slam Jesus, Christianity, and the Bible, and promote the Antichrist's kingdom and say Satan's a good guy! I'm kind of thinking, that's what a demon would do!

The 3rd reason why we know UFO's & Aliens are a demonic deception is because they **Communicate like Demons.**

Now, we just read their messages, but what they don't tell you on the news is that in order to get these messages, you have to use the same occult technique that God condemns because it conjures up demons! I didn't say that, He did!

Deuteronomy 18:10-12 "Let no one be found among you who sacrifices his son or daughter in the fire, who practices divination or sorcery, interprets omens, engages in witchcraft, or casts spells, or who is a medium or spiritist or who consults the dead. Anyone who does these things is detestable to the LORD."

Why? Because it's a demonic practice and God doesn't want you deceived! But of all things you have to do to communicate with Aliens and UFO's it's this. Get into an occult altered-state of consciousness and let them speak through you, when God says that's what demons do. So, let me get this straight. You come all the way across the galaxy just to slam Jesus, Christianity, and the Bible, and promote New Age teachings and say Satan is a good guy. And the only way I can receive this supposed "new and improved higher-evolved information" is to use a demonic practice the Bible forbids?

You would think if you are this highly advanced civilization in some far away galaxy, that I could use a walkie talkie, a cell phone, or even one of those nifty "Kirk to Enterprise" devices. But no! I can only communicate with you using demonic practices! That's a demon!

The 4th reason why we know UFO's & Aliens are a demonic deception is because they **Travel Like Demons.**

The Bible tells us angels can travel through different dimensions. The spirit realm and the natural realm.

2 Kings 6:17 "And Elisha prayed, "O LORD, open his eyes so he may see." Then the LORD opened the servant's eyes, and he looked and saw the hills full of horses and chariots of fire all around Elisha."

He didn't need to be afraid because God's Angels, God's invisible spiritual Army, was bigger than the other physical army. But this passage, and others, tell us how angels travel. Demons, are of the fallen category. And what we see is that they have the ability to appear and disappear, to pop on the scene and pop back out, to materialize and dematerialize.

Now, here's the point. Can anybody guess just what method of travel that UFO's and Aliens just happen to use? Hey, that's right! The exact same thing. They clock them at speeds up to 15,000 mph making right turns which would instantly destroy anything physical. They make no sonic boom like a normal physical object does. Radar has never recorded the actual entering of UFO's into our atmosphere. They just pop on to the scene, they materialize and dematerialize. This is why after decades of research; secular researchers are saying this:

"There seems to be no evidence yet that any of these craft or beings originate from outer space." AND *"One theory that can no longer be taken very seriously is that UFO's are interstellar spaceships."*

In other words, even secular researchers admit that these things are not coming from outer space but inner space. They are coming from another dimension. The place the Bible calls the spirit realm, the place where demons travel.

The 5th reason why we know UFO's & Aliens are a demonic deception is because They **Possess Like Demons.**

It's bad enough that I have to use an occult technique to communicate with you as you take over my vocal chords, but wonder of wonders, guess what their ultimate goal is? They want to "possess you" just like a demon, only they call it "walk-ins" because nobody likes demon possession. And when you do, a strange odor shows up, it's called Sulphur.

The Amityville Horror was based on factual account of what happened to a family in Amityville New York. An irritating and nauseating odor seemed to accompany the presence of the ghost or spirit entity that entered there from time to time. Whitley Strieber wrote of his experience in his book 'Communion'. He said he could smell their presence and it smelled like sulphur.[17]

So, demons smell like sulphur and Aliens smell like sulphur. Little do most people realize that sulphur just happens to be the smell to describe the Lake of Fire.

Revelation 19:20 "But the beast was captured, and with him the false prophet who had performed the miraculous signs on his behalf. With these signs, he had deluded those who had received the mark of the beast and worshiped his image. The two of them were thrown alive into the fiery lake of burning Sulphur."

Not copper, not cheeseburgers, not stale milk, but of all things for aliens to smell like when they appear on the scene is sulphur, the very stench of the lake of fire, and you want to possess me! I don't think that's by chance! I think we're dealing with demons!

The 6th reason why we know that UFO's & Aliens are a demonic deception is because they're **Rebuked like Demons.**

They not only want to possess you like a demon, but secular UFOlogists are admitting now that there's a strange trend out there concerning these UFO's and Aliens. They're noticing that there's one way to get rid of these beings 100% of the time when they do come your way. And can anybody guess what that technique is? It's when you command them in the name of Jesus Christ to leave and they do! It's a demon! That is what these people say. They also say that we need to get the truth out!

One experience by a Mr. Bill D.:

It took place at Christmas in Florida in 1976. His abduction started out typically, i.e., late at night, in bed. Earlier in the evening he saw some anomalous lights through his living room window over a forest north of his home.

He assumed it was a police helicopter searching for drug runners or something. Whatever it was, it agitated his dogs for several hours thereafter. He eventually went to bed. He was lying in bed, kept wide awake by the barking dogs, when paralysis set in. He was unable to cry out. He could see nothing but a whitish grey, like a mist or fog, although he sensed someone or something was in his room. His wife didn't waken.

The next thing he knew he was being levitated above his bed. By this time, he was alive with terror, but he couldn't scream. Here is where the story becomes very interesting. He states "So helpless, I couldn't do anything. I said 'Jesus, Jesus, help me!' When I did, there was a feeling or sound or something that either my words that I thought or the words that I had tried to say or whatever had hurt whatever was holding me up.

I fell, I hit the bed, because it was like I was thrown back in bed. I really can't tell, but when I did, my wife woke up and asked why I was jumping on the bed."

This was the first time that experienced field investigators had ever heard of an abduction being stopped, and this man did it by just calling on the name of Jesus. Another experience of stopping an abduction with the name of Jesus Christ goes like this:

One man shared, "Back in about 1973 my wife had a strange experience in the middle of the night. At the time, we knew nothing about UFO abductions so we had no category in which to place it other than an extremely 'lucid nightmare.' It has many of the abduction 'components.' The point is that she stopped the entities and the whole experience with the name of "Jesus". It's vital to get this information out."[18]

Another testimony of a lady I interviewed in Oregon said when three critters showed up on her farm, she rebuked them in the name of Jesus and they didn't just flee, but they tripped over each other and high-tailed it out of there! I'm coming to this conclusion. If it walks like a demon, talks like a demon, travels like a demon, acts like a demon, possesses like a demon, and is rebuked in the name of Jesus Christ like a demon, I'm kind of thinking we're dealing with demons here!

The **7th reason** we know that UFO's & Aliens are a demonic deception is because they **Deceive like Demons**.

All of this lying and demonic behavior is leading somewhere, the ultimate deception of all. It's going to be used to explain away the rapture of the Church!

1 Thessalonians 4:16-17 "For the Lord himself will come down from heaven, with a loud command, with the voice of the archangel and with the trumpet call of God, and the dead in Christ will rise first. After that, we who are still alive and are left will be caught up together with them in the clouds to meet the Lord in the air. And so, we will be with the Lord forever."

This is the passage dealing with the rapture of the Church, and when God rescues us just prior to the 7-year Tribulation. But wonder of wonders, can anybody guess, just what it is that these supposed aliens and UFO's have come all the way across the galaxy just to try to explain away! Hey, that's right! The rapture of the Church! Of all things, they say, "No, no, no! It's not the Hand of God coming to get His church, it's us, the UFO's, here to save you! Don't believe me? Let's listen to them!

Barbara Marciniak is a very famous New Age author and channeler. In her book Bringers of the Dawn she documents what she claims extra-terrestrials from the star system of the Pleiades have told her. "There will be great shiftings within humanity on this planet. It will seem that great chaos and turmoil are forming, that nations are rising against each other in war, and that earthquakes are happening more frequently.

Earth is shaking itself free, and a certain realignment or adjustment period is to be expected. The people who leave the planet during the time of earth changes do not fit here any longer and they are stopping the harmony of earth. When the time comes that perhaps twenty million people leave the planet at one time, there will be a tremendous shift in consciousness for those who are remaining. Another channeler Thelma Terrell, who goes by her spiritual name, Tuella, wrote a book called Project World Evacuation and here's what she shares, "All over the globe where events warrant it, this will be the method of evacuation.

Mankind will be lifted, levitated shall we say, by the beams from our smaller ships, the Great Evacuation will come upon the world very suddenly. The flash of emergency events will be a lightning that flashes in the sky. Do not be concerned nor unduly upset if you do not participate in this first temporary lift-up of souls who serve with us.

This merely means that your action in the plan is elsewhere, and you will be taken for your instructions or will receive them in some other manner. Do not take any personal affront if you are not alerted or are not a participant in this first phase of our plan. Your time will come later, and these instructions are not necessary for you at this time."

One researcher stated, "For almost 200 years, the Christian belief has been that God will evacuate the earth of all born-again believers, prior to His pouring out wrath. But for many years now, many among the New Age movement have received messages from aliens and spirit guides that Mother Earth will soon cleanse herself by ejecting all those with bad vibratory patterns, (i.e. the Christians) to another realm, allowing ascended masters and aliens to help us bring in a Golden Age upon the earth."[19]

In other words, people are being deceived to explain away the rapture of the Church. Is that demonic or what? No wonder Jesus warned first and foremost, "Watch out that no one will deceive you!" The last days are going to be full of deceit, deceit, deceit! So powerful it could come very close to deceiving the elect!

So, the question is, "Well, just how close are we then to this lie being pulled off? Are there any signs of this false explanation of the rapture getting close?" First of all, the Bible clearly tells us nobody knows the exact day nor hour. I don't care how nifty you are with a calculator!"

Matthew 24:36 "No one knows about that day or hour, not even the angels in heaven, nor the Son, but only the Father."

I don't care how good you are with dates, but logically, if UFO's & Aliens are going to be used to explain away the rapture of the Church, then at some point, logically, there has to be some sort of imminent disclosure by the government to say that UFO's and Aliens are real, and they've been hiding something, right? Can you guess what's happening right now? Former Presidents, including Bill Clinton, recently appeared on the Jimmy Kimmel show and said, "When it happens, not if, it will bring peace to the planet!

Jimmy Kimmel interviews Bill Clinton:

"President Bill Clinton is here with us. So, if I were President, and I won't be, let's be honest. The first thing I would do after putting my hand on that Bible and

taking that oath to serve the country is, I probably wouldn't even finish the oath, I would run to the White House, I would demand to see all the classified files on UFO's. Because I would want to know what's been going on. Did you do that?"

The President replies "Sort of, I think it was at the beginning of my second term, we had the anniversary of Roswell."

Jimmy asks, "You waited that long?"

Then the President replies, "I did. Well, I did, and there's also Area 51. Do you remember there was a great sci-fi movie where there was an alien kept deep under the ground at Area 51? So first I had people go look at the records on Area 51 to make sure there was no alien down there. Then when the Roswell thing came up, I knew we'd get zillions of letters, so I had all the Roswell papers reviewed, everything."

Jimmy then asks, "If you saw that there were aliens would you tell us?"

President answers, "Yeah". Jimmy asks, "You would?" President says, "Yes I would, what do we know now. We live in an ever-expanding universe, we know that there are billions of stars and planets out there. So, it makes it increasingly less likely that we are alone." Jimmy asks, "Oh, you're trying to give me a hint that there are aliens?"

President answers, "No, I'm trying to tell you I don't know, but if we were visited someday I wouldn't be surprised, I just hope it's not like the Independence Day movie, like a conflict. It may be the only way to unite this incredibly divided world of ours. If they're out there, we better think about all the differences among people on earth. They would seem small if we felt threatened by a space invader, that's the whole theory of Independence Day. Everybody gets together and makes nice."[20]

"When, not if, Aliens land, it will unite the whole planet together and all our problems will go away. The Aliens can save us!" Bill Clinton just said that It's almost like they're preparing us for something! So is the Vatican! This is freaky! First, the Vatican has not only bought into the lie of evolution, but right now they're in a desperate search for extraterrestrials and they are preparing themselves to be the official spokespeople for when the Aliens do land! Check this out!

Fox reports:

We could not talk about life on other planets without the classic clip from ET. Interestingly the Vatican is just finishing up a 5-day conference on aliens. Father Jonathan Morris, Fox News Commentator is back with us. "Father, good morning to you." Father Jonathan Morris reports, "What a great movie that was." Fox reporter: "It was a wonderful movie, Drew Barrymore, and off she went. Did the Vatican find alien life?"

Father Morris replies, "You know what, as sensational as that question sounds, it's really not that far off from what we have seen in the news over these last days. Pictures of what might have been Pope Benedict standing on the roof of the Sistine Chapel looking for UFO's. That's the type of images that this news conjures up. What is exceptional is that the Vatican was taking very seriously what science might tell us about the possibility of extraterrestrial intelligent life forms. That's what the conference was about."[21]

The Vatican and the Catholic Church are so serious about this that they have an actual entity called V.O.R.G. or the Vatican Observatory Research Group. This group has a couple of the world's most powerful telescopes on the top of Mt. Graham in Arizona looking for extraterrestrial life.

One is called V.A.T.T. or the Vatican Advanced Technology Telescope and the other, they have one-quarter interest in, is called LUCIFER. It stands for Large Binocular Telescope Near-infrared Utility with Camera and Integral Field Unit for Extragalactic Research. It's the most powerful telescope in the world and is reported to get better images than the Hubble Telescope. It's also infrared so it can pick up things that other telescopes can't. And if that wasn't freaky enough, the highway that goes up to Mt. Graham used to be known as the Devil's Highway or 666. So, the question is, "Why in the world is the Vatican searching for extraterrestrial life?" Well, believe it or not, it's because they believe these so-called E. T's are going to be our new Savior and usher in peace to our planet. Here's their own words.

Father Gabriel Funes, Jesuit Priest and head of the Vatican Observatory, stated that, "Extraterrestrial life may not have experienced a 'fall', and may be 'free from Original Sin' and therefore remains in full friendship with their creator. This makes it possible to regard them as 'our brothers.' Therefore, if they're unfallen, they must be closer to God and have a better understanding of the Gospel and of the Godhead and of the nature of God.

In fact, Funes went on to say that he'd not only be willing to baptize an alien into the Catholic faith, but that "They [aliens] are coming here and they're going to baptize us into their faith and it is going to require us to make changes to our knowledge and understanding of the Gospel. Everything we think we know about the Gospel is going to have to be thrown out."

Another prominent Vatican astronomer, is Guy Consolmagno and he too not only says he would baptize an Alien but, "Only if they asked" and then qualified, "Any entity, no matter how many tentacles it has, has a soul." He then later says that, "These non-human forms are described in the Bible as "angels" and "very soon the nations of the world will look to Aliens for their salvation." "We fell, they didn't."

And what of those who resist? Father Gabriel Funes stated, "To not believe in the existence of Aliens and be willing to accept their morally superior dogma, that is going to be the true heresy of the future." In other words, you will be a new heretic if you are unwilling to accept this morally superior and new form of the Gospel.[22]

The Bible clearly warns us about turning to another Gospel, even if it's supposed to come from a so-called angel!

Galatians 1:8-9 "But even if we or an angel from heaven should preach a gospel other than the one we preached to you, let him be eternally condemned! As we have already said, so now I say again: If anybody is preaching to you a gospel other than what you accepted, let him be eternally condemned!"

Is any of this belief getting anywhere in the Vatican? Yes! Both Consolmagno and Funes have been leading advisors to Pope Francis about extraterrestrial life, and apparently their influence is working because Pope Francis just recently came out and said he'd be willing to baptize and alien as well.

Pope Francis reiterated his view Monday that everyone has the right to be baptized and apparently that invite extends even to Martians. The Pontiff described the hypothetical situation during morning mass. According to Vatican radio Francis said, if for example, tomorrow an expedition of Martians came and some of them came to us and said I want to be baptized, what would happen? In other words, if God prompted the Martians to come to earth, find the Pope, and say we want in on this Catholicism thing the Pope would probably say OK cool, but probably in Latin.*[23]*

The Vatican would also have you and I believe that Jesus is really a descendant of alien life and that Mary's virgin birth was actually a direct result of an alien abduction. They are calling Jesus a "star child" and that He was genetically engineered to save us at His First Coming and now the aliens are here again to save us from earth catastrophes coming as a kind of pseudo Second Coming, a Second Saving. This doctrine is called "many Christs" and that's exactly what the Real Jesus warned about in the last days!

Matthew 24:4-5 "Jesus answered: "Watch out that no one deceives you. For many will come in my name, claiming, 'I am the Christ, ' and will deceive many."

So just how close are we to this last days deception? Well, a Professor at the Vatican University, a Father Giuseppe Tanzella-Nitti, said, "Very soon there is information coming from another world, and once it is confirmed it is going to require a re-reading of the Gospel as we know it." And a Vatican spokesman Monsignor Corrado Baldacci said, "There is an Alien presence on earth now." Recently it was reported that Pope Francis is, "Preparing a major world statement about extraterrestrial life and its theological implications and wants to be ready with a statement about 'First Contact.'"

From a movie:

The space ships have landed. The priest and his niece are watching. He says, "There are living creatures out there." She tries to tell him, "They're not human. Doctor Forester said they are some form of advanced civilization." He replies, "If they are more advanced than us they should be nearer the creator than us." As he ponders what is going on he says, "No real attempt has been made to communicate with them you know." While tugging at his arm she says, "Let's go back inside Uncle Matthew."

He turns to her and says, "I've done all I can, you go back." She turns to go back to the rest of the people watching the alien crafts. He turns to the alien ships and proceeds to walk towards them. He starts to recite "Though I walk through the valley of the shadow of death I will fear no evil," His niece is watching as he gets closer and closer.

As he walks they start coming towards him. She is screaming for him to stop and come back to safety but he doesn't heed her cries. He keeps walking, holding his Bible, and still repeating the Lord's Prayer. The ship sees him getting closer and closer when suddenly a blast comes out of the ship and disintegrates the priest into dust.

One researcher stated, "So what would happen someday if 'aliens' showed up and claimed that they seeded life on this planet, guided our evolution and are now here to lead us into a new golden age? And what would happen if the Catholic Church gave those aliens their stamp of approval? That sounds bizarre, but this is exactly what is going on at the Vatican right now! It's all a last days deception card being played on us, as this lady shares.

From 1974 through 1977 I worked with the late Verner von Braun. In early 1974 von Braun was dying of cancer but he assured me he would live a few more years in order to tell me about the game that was being played. That game being the effort to weaponize space, to control the earth from space and space itself. The strategy von Braun taught me was first the Russians are going to be the enemy, in fact, when I met him in 74 they were the enemy. The identified enemy.

We were told they had killer satellites, we were told they were coming to get us, to control us, dirty commies, the whole story. First the Russians were going to be the enemy that was going to make space based weapons. Then terrorists would be identified, that was soon to follow, we heard a lot about terrorism. Then we were going to identify third world countries as crazies. We now call them nations of concern. But, he said that would be the third enemy against whom we would be needing to build space based weapons.

And the next enemy was asteroids. Now at this point he kind of chuckled. The first time he said it, asteroids. Asteroids were going to build space based weapons. So, it was funny then. And the funniest one of all was against what he called aliens or extraterrestrials. That would be the final card. And over, and over, and over, during the four years that I knew him and was giving his speeches for him, he would bring up that last card and say "remember Carol, that last card is the alien card. We're going to have to build space based weapons against aliens and all of it is a lie." He didn't mention a time line, but he said it was going to be speeding up faster than anyone could possibly imagine. The last card, the last card, the last card, would be the extraterrestrial threat.[24]

It sure looks to me like the last card of the last day's lie is being played on us. All it's going to take is for someone, maybe even the Pope himself to say something like this. "Don't worry. Your missing loved ones are just fine. They've been beamed up by UFO's and are awaiting their time of rehabilitation when they can join us here back on earth safely as we, the chosen ones, enter the Age of Utopia. Our Savior's are here, we are now at peace!"

If you don't think the planet is ripe for this lie, a recent survey was taken at Pacific Lutheran Theological Seminary where people of various religions were asked about the impact on their faith concerning an announcement of official extraterrestrial disclosure. They said, "Their religion would be just fine, no problem" to "I'd share a pew with an alien any day." This is all happening right now, it's not make-believe, and therefore, out of love, God has given us all these signs to show us that the Tribulation is near and the Rapture is right around the corner! Jesus Himself said.

Luke 21:28 "When these things begin to take place, stand up and lift up your heads, because your redemption is drawing near."

And so, the point is this. If you are a Christian, then what in the world are you doing for Jesus? Let's get busy working together fulfilling the Great Commission doing something splendid for Jesus, amen? But if you're not a Christian, then I beg you, please, heed the signs, heed the warnings, give your life to Jesus today because you don't want to be left behind!

Chapter Five

The Rise of Wickedness

"One day this farmer died and his elderly wife was bedridden and very depressed and so her son tried everything he could think of to cheer her up, but nothing worked.

So, one day he spoke to the doctor and the doctor told him that a shot of whiskey would perk her up and should be given to her nightly. And, it would make it easier for her to sleep at night and should make her better humored each day.

Well, the son knew his mother didn't believe in drinking liquor, so the doctor told him to put it in her food or drink. The boy went home and put the whiskey in her milk.

Well, that night she slept like a baby and woke up feeling wonderful. In fact, every night when he gave her the shot of whiskey and milk, she woke the following morning feeling more and more cheerful.

But then suddenly, they hit on hard times and the son suggested to his mom that they sell the farm and move closer to the city.

But his mom said, "Son, you can do anything you want to do, but whatever you do, DON'T SELL THAT COW!" (hiccup!)[1]

I must admit, cows are pretty special and awesome, I can vouch for that, but that's not why you keep one around. You don't drink them with whiskey, you eat them!

How many of you would say that lady's joy was a little misplaced there, you know what I'm saying? She was being fooled, right?

Well did you know the same thing's going to happen to the whole world by the Antichrist? The Bible says he's going to arrive on the scene with his own deceptive milk talk, and he's going to promise the whole world intoxicating lies of nothing but pure joy and excitement when in reality it's mankind's worst nightmare! You just got fooled like that lady! It's called the 7-year Tribulation. And that's not a joke! The Bible says it's an outpouring of God's wrath on a wicked and rebellious planet.

The 6th update on The Final Countdown study letting us know we're living in the Last Days is **The Rise of Wickedness.**

And I mean, horrible wickedness! Wait a second! You mean to tell me in the last days that people would get wicked and evil and do bad and rotten things right before Jesus comes back? Good thing we don't see any signs of that today! Yeah, right! But don't take my word for it. Let's listen to God's.

2 Timothy 3:1-5 "But mark this: There will be terrible times in the Last Days. People will be lovers of themselves, lovers of money, boastful, proud, abusive, disobedient to their parents, ungrateful, unholy, without love, unforgiving, slanderous, without self-control, brutal, not lovers of the good, treacherous, rash, conceited, lovers of pleasure rather than lovers of God – having a form of godliness but denying its power. Have nothing to do with them."

In other words, they're a rotten influence, stay away! How can you get any clearer than this? One of the major characteristics of the last day's society is that it's going to be a society filled with absolute unadulterated wickedness, right? What did it say? In the last days people would be, selfish, greedy, boastful, prideful, abusive, disobedient, ungrateful, unholy, unloving, unforgiving, slanderous, out-of-control, brutal, evil, treacherous, rash, and conceited! Good thing we see no signs of that happening! Yeah, right! Every single one of those wicked behaviors is commonplace in our society right now! Which means, guess what? We're living in the last days! I didn't say that God did! But once again, the skeptic's going to say something like, "Well, come on!

Wicked behavior? We've always had wicked behavior." And yes, granted, throughout history, since the fall of man, we've always had some form of wicked behavior.

But what's not common is how in the last few decades, even the last few years, there has been an explosion of every single one of these wicked behaviors that Paul listed. And it's getting worse by the day! In fact, let's look at the change of behavior in America in recent times and you tell me if there isn't a clear rise of wickedness. Now keep in mind, before I share what I'm about to share, the leading disciplinary problems in schools used to be, talking, chewing gum, making noise, running in the hallways, getting out of place in line, wearing improper clothing, and not putting paper in the wastebaskets! Oh, those rebels!!!! And one day, Beaver lied about going to the movies! Check this out!

From one of the old episodes of Leave it to Beaver. We see the Beav and his Mom, Dad, and Brother having a heavy discussion with the Beaver one more time. Beaver's Mom asks, "How was the movie?" He replies, "I didn't go to the movie." Dad responds, "You didn't go to the movie?" Beaver says, "No Sir, I went yesterday, when I wasn't supposed to."

Dad says, "Oh, is that so?" Beaver replies, "Yes sir, and I won a racing bicycle with a guaranteed leather seat and I hid it at Larry's and I was going to make believe that I won it today, but I couldn't, so that is why I am telling you what happened." Dad asks, "Well, when did you decide to tell us about it?" Beaver answers, "While I was walking the bike home from Larry's." Wally interrupts, "Yeah, it's too big for him to ride."

Dad says, "Well, Beaver, I'm glad you decided to tell us the truth. Of course, you realize that you can't keep the bicycle you won while you were being disobedient. We'll have to find something to do with the bike." Beaver replies, "Larry and I already found something to do with it." Mom asks, "Oh, you did?" He replies, "Yeah, I walked it back to Larry's house and then Larry and I walked it down to a church."

His dad asks, "To a church?" "Yes Sir," he replies, "Larry once saw something that had to do with babies in a movie." His dad asks, "Do what?" Beaver replies, "We left it on the front steps with a note, watch it until someone nice adopts it." "Well Beaver, I'm glad that you realized that you couldn't keep the bicycle but there's still the matter of you being disobedient, isn't there." His dad asks. "Yes sir," he answers. So, Dad says, "I guess you had better stay away from the movies for 2 weeks." Beaver lowers his head and says, "Yes Sir."[2]

What a rebel! Can you imagine the audacity of the boy? What wickedness! What an absolute terror Beaver was! Torturing his parents like that! Let's be honest. How many of you dream we could only have problems like that? You talk about a difference. Now we have to deal with these problems in school, drug abuse, alcohol abuse, pregnancy, suicide, murder, rape and robbery. It's changed just a wee bit since Leave it to Beaver which wasn't that long ago, and it's getting worse by the day!

A high school kid took two kitchen knives and went on a stabbing rampage through his school.

A Florida teen was accused of poisoning a teacher's drink.

A father put his 6-week-old daughter in a freezer to keep her from crying.

Three children were left to starve to death while one was chained to the floor.

A woman was arrested after police say she injected hand sanitizer into the feeding tube of her infant son.

Florida parents were arrested after abandoning their three kids in the woods.

A grandmother forced soiled underwear down her 11-year-old granddaughter's mouth.

A caregiver used a stun gun to punish kids.

A couple locked their 3-year-old child in the trunk to cure his fear of darkness.

A mother stabbed her baby in an attempted murder-suicide.

A woman strangled her newborn son and tossed him in the trash.

A dad killed his kids and wife 'because he didn't have car seats.'

A Texas man was convicted of murdering his neighbors over dog feces.

A pregnant woman attacked her roommate over butter.

A North Miami Beach man was fatally shot after a fight over utensils broke out at a Baptism party.

A Florida man bites his neighbor's ear off over a cigarette.

A man stabbed a woman for bringing pizza home instead of a chicken sandwich.[3]

How many of you would say there's been a massive rise of wickedness in the last few decades, right? Exactly like the Bible said would happen when you're living in the last days. In fact, if we're honest with ourselves, it's getting so bad and so commonplace that we're no longer even shocked at this level of wickedness because it's now considered the norm. We expect it. And it's getting worse by the day. You can't go to the movies without being afraid of getting shot, right? You can't walk down the street without getting assaulted, robbed, or beat up. And now we even have people killing each other over cigarettes, butter, and chicken! It's horrible!

We act like it's no big deal, what else is on? Let's check out the weather channel. Hey Bob, look at this, check out the game. Hardly anyone recognizes the prophetic significance of what's going on! How do you know you're living in the last days? Oh! If only we knew! If only we had some certain sign! Just turn on your TV! This absolute unadulterated wickedness that's being reported every single day, every single night, around the world is one of the clearest signs you are living in the last days. You're in that generation that Paul talked about that would have this unadulterated wickedness. But the question is, "How? How could there be such an explosion of wickedness in such a short amount of time, since Beaver's day, especially here in America with our godly heritage? The why is because we have a wicked education system. Here's how the Bible says we're supposed to educate our children.

Deuteronomy 6:6-9 "These commandments that I give you today are to be upon your hearts. Impress them on your children. Talk about them when you sit at home and when you walk along the road, when you lie down and when you get up. Tie them as symbols on your hands and bind them on your foreheads. Write them on the doorframes of your houses and on your gates."

Ephesians 6:4 "Fathers, do not exasperate your children; instead, bring them up in the training and instruction of the Lord."

Proverbs 22:5-6 "In the paths of the wicked lie thorns and snares, but he who guards his soul stays far from them. Train a child in the way he should go, and when he is old he will not turn from it."

Now we all know we're supposed to educate our children in the things of the Lord, and we all know that last verse is the payoff. We quote it, we cross stitch it, we put it on pillows, we put it on plaques on the wall. "Train up a child in the way he should go!" But here's the problem. We've been duped! We let society now train our kids in the way they should go and since our society is full of this unadulterated wickedness, our kids get instructed in guess what? Wickedness! So, when they get older, guess which way they go? The way of wickedness, not godliness! Are we really that surprised? We're not doing what God said to do!

Our school system, as we saw before, has rejected God, removed prayer and Bible reading out of our schools. Now they even say the Ten Commandments cause brain damage for the kids, i.e. it's bad for them if they look at it and think upon it. They even admit this is their goal! To use the educational system in America to usurp Christianity and replace it with godlessness! Don't believe me? Let's look at their words again.

"(Our) great object was to get rid of Christianity, and to convert our churches into halls of science. The plan was not to make open attacks on religion, but to establish a system of state schools, from which all religion was to be excluded and to which all parents were to be compelled by law to send their children. For this purpose, a secret society was formed and the whole country was to be organized." **Orestes Brownson (1803-1876)**

"Education is thus a most powerful ally of humanism, and every American school is a school of humanism. What can a theistic Sunday School meeting for an hour once a week and teaching only a fraction of the children do to stem the tide of the five-day program of humanistic teaching?" **Charles F. Potter, Humanism: A New Religion (1930)**

"We must ask how we can kill the God of Christianity. We need only to ensure that our schools teach only secular knowledge. If we could achieve this, God would indeed be shortly due for a funeral service." **G. Richard**

"I am convinced that the battle for humankind's future must be waged and won in the public-school classroom by teachers who correctly perceive their role as

proselytizers of a new faith: a religion of humanity. These teachers must embody the same selfless dedication as the most rabid fundamentalist preachers, for they will be ministers of another sort, utilizing a classroom instead of a pulpit to convey humanist values in whatever subject they teach, regardless of educational level – preschool, day care or a large state university. The classroom must and will become an arena of conflict between the old and the new – the rotting corpse of Christianity and the new faith of humanism." **John J. Dunphy**[4]

And you just thought you were sending your kids to school for a good education. Maybe it's just me, but I'm thinking that's a different agenda for teaching our kids, how about you? Much different from what God says, "Train them up in His ways." By their own admission, they admit it! They're using our public schools to turn our kids away from God and train them in wickedness! And we wonder why our schools are such a nightmare?

Right now, our kids are being taught in public schools that, "Religion is a disease" and that "the Bible is a work of fiction." They say that evolution is true, that God is dead, that prayer is a waste of your time, and Christians and Christianity are dangerous." They're also being taught earth worship, socialized medicine, world government, redistribution of American wealth to other nations, abortion, the elimination of the right to bear arms, altered states of consciousness, astrology, divination, spiritism, magic spells, sorcery, occult charms and symbols, solstice rites, sacred sex, serpent worship and human sacrifice!

Right now, kindergarten teachers are being required to set aside 30 minutes, on a regular basis, for sex education with pornographic pictures and sexual acts depicted in graphic detail. One district is offering condoms to 11-year old's while they're in school. It's a good thing this has no effect on them. Let's see what this has spawned in the area of wickedness.

Approximately one-third of the entire population of the United States (110 million people) currently has a sexually transmitted disease according to the Centers for Disease Control and Prevention.

Every single year, there are 20 million new cases of STDs in America.

The 15 to 24-year-old age group accounts for 50 percent of all new STD cases each year.

One out of every four teen girls in the U.S. has at least one sexually transmitted disease.

America has the highest STD infection rate in the entire industrialized world. It costs our nation approximately 16 billion dollars a year to treat our sexually transmitted diseases.

The United States has the highest teen pregnancy rate in the entire industrialized world.[5]

Oh, if we could only find the answer why! Is it really a surprise? You send your kids to a school system that has kindergarten teachers sharing with them pornography and handing out condoms? You reap what you sow! You're training them in that! Oh, that we would have listened to Martin Luther long ago! Here's what he said about educating our kids.

Martin Luther:

"I am much afraid that the schools will prove to be the great gates to Hell unless they diligently labor in explaining the Scriptures, engraving them in the hearts of youth. I advise no one to place his child where the Scriptures do not reign paramount. Every institution in which men are not increasingly occupied with the Word of God, must become corrupt."

That's exactly what's happened to our school system. They've rejected God and replaced it with wickedness and that's what our children are being trained in. As one person puts it, "It's time to get them out!" Here's what they said.

"As parents, we are to fulfill our God-given obligation to train up our children in the way they should go, which means removing our children from the "poisonous fog" of public schools where "pornogogues" hold our children's minds in their depraved grip.

The fact that we continue to place our most precious gifts in toxic public schools for seven hours a day, five days a week for their most crucial formative years is testament to our own lack of wisdom as Christians. This intellectual laziness, selfishness, pride, ignorance, and cowardice of many Christians have coalesced into an anemic faith. We are men and women without chests or spines and we practice a faith that's been fed watered down milk. Now we send our children to public schools that feed them tainted crumbs and we wonder why our youth are rejecting God! Christians, we need to wake up now.

"We need to pull our kids out of public schools and rescue them before it's too late! The time to get out is now. How long will you let them sit there under a school board celebrating fornication and sodomy and all the rest of the sexual chaos? One day, you will have to give an account to God".[6]

I'd not only say that most of us don't realize that we are going to give an account to God for how we educate our children, but I'd also say most of us have no idea that it's really our wicked educational system that's being used by the Antichrist to produce the wicked society that, Paul talked about would appear on the scene when you're living in the last days. That time is now.

The 2nd reason why we're seeing such a massive rise of wickedness in the last days is because we also have a **Wicked Media System**.

Here's what King David said about the media or what we put in our eyes.

Psalm 101:2-4 "I will behave wisely in a perfect way. I will walk within my house with a perfect heart. I will set nothing wicked before my eyes; I hate the work of those who fall away; it shall not cling to me. A perverse heart shall depart from me; I will not know wickedness."

That includes with my eyes. Why? Because David knew junk in equals junk out! It's that simple! Here's the point. I don't know if you've noticed or not, but our media system, what we put in our eyes, is nothing but junk, it's nothing but wickedness! We wonder why people have a problem with temptation? We wonder why there's this massive rise of wicked behavior? Listen to David! Junk in, equals junk out! Or the vernacular is sin in equals sin out! The enemy's not dumb! He knows what he's doing! He's stealing away our time with God with the media, and training us in wickedness with this device that says, LOOK AT ME!

TELEVISION SAYS TO YOU EVERYDAY, LOOK AT ME! LOOK AT ME! LOOK AT ME! LOOK AT ME! LOOK AT ME! NO DON'T LOOK OVER THERE, THERE'S NOTHING TO LOOK AT OVER THERE, LOOK AT ME! LOOK AT ME! LOOK AT ME! LOOK AT ME! ARE YOU LOOKING AT ME? IS EVERYBODY LOOKING AT ME? DO I HAVE EVERYONES ATTENTION? DON'T GET THE WRONG IDEA, I'M NOT TRYING TO TAKE OVER YOUR LIFE, YOU NEED WHAT? WHAT DO YOU NEED? WHAT DO YOU NEED? WHAT DO YOU NEED? YOU NEED WHAT? GO

TO THE BATHROOM, GET UP GO TO THE BATHROOM, COME BACK, LOOK AT ME! YOU NEED WHAT? YOU NEED TO GET SOMETHING TO EAT? FINE, GET UP, GO TO THE KITCHEN, COME BACK, LOOK AT ME! YOU NEED WHAT, SLEEP, FINE, GET UP GO TO BED, GO TO SLEEP, COME BACK, LOOK AT ME! SO, WE HAVE AN AGREEMENT? YOU DO WHAT YOU ABSOLUTELY HAVE TO DO AND WHEN YOU'RE DONE YOU WILL COME BACK AND LOOK AT ME? DON'T WORRY ABOUT YOUR SCHEDULE, I AM HERE FOR YOU, I AM HERE FOR YOU 24 HOURS A DAY, 7 DAYS A WEEK, I AM HERE FOR YOU, I AM HERE FOR YOU, YOU NEED ME THROUGH FAIR AND FOUL , THICK AND THIN, I AM HERE FOR YOU, I AM HERE FOR YOU, PEOPLE TRY TO TELL YOU I AM BAD, YOU TELL THEM I AM HERE FOR YOU, 24 HOURS A DAY, FAIR AND FOUL, THICK AND THIN, I AM HERE FOR YOU, I AM HERE FOR YOU, PEOPLE TRY TO TELL YOU, I AM BAD, YOU KNOW WHAT THAT SOUNDS LIKE TO ME, SOUR GRAPES, YOU KNOW WHAT I MEAN? NO, NO, NO, NO, NO, DON'T LOOK OVER THERE, THERE'S NOTHING TO LOOK AT OVER THERE, LOOK AT ME! LOOK AT ME! LOOK AT ME! I'VE GOT STUFF YOU WOULDN'T BELIEVE, DANGER, SEX, ACTION, DEATH, THRILLS, COMEDY, ALL HERE, ALL IN THE NEXT 8 MINUTES, CAN YOU BELIEVE IT? YOU CAN'T BELIEVE IT, IT'S UNBELIEVABLE, YOU CAN'T BELIEVE IT BECAUSE IT'S UNBELIEVABLE, IT'S A MIRACLE, JUST KEEP LOOKING AT ME, JUST KEEP LOOKING AT ME, JUST KEEP LOOKING AT ME! LOOK AT ME! LOOK AT ME! LOOK AT ME! LOOK AT ME! LOOK AT ME! LOOK AT ME!

That would be funny if it weren't so true. This LOOK AT ME device not only steals our time from God, but as he admitted, it's got lots of wickedness. The problem is, we've become so desensitized to receiving that wickedness to our eyes, that we don't even bat an eye sitting down hours a week being peppered with evil, like these people. What I'm about to share with you is a comparison of the curse words with "Gone with the Wind" versus one modern movie with paintballs. Let's see what effect it has on them.

Four people dressed all in white sit down on a white sofa ready to watch TV. The one at the end turns it on with the remote. Clark Gable is on the big screen, walking out the door, telling Scarlett that he doesn't give a damn. Suddenly, a red blast hits the kid at the end of the couch. It is from a paint gun that has taken aim at him for that one bad word.

They are to be shot with paint each time a bad word is spoken. They proceed watching TV and eating their popcorn. "Gone with The Wind", staring Clark Gable and Vivien Leigh, in 1939, had the first swear word in cinema history. History of swearing in Hollywood from 1939 to 2010 has risen significantly with 2013 having the most swear words on record.

"The Wolf of Wall Street" had 528 F-words, 70 Blasphemy, 20 other bad language, 27 sex/nudity, 3 graphic violence. The 4 white figures have now put on black hoods to prepare for what lies ahead.

The painters all dressed in black, carrying their paint ball guns, take aim and start shooting every time a bad word is said. The popcorn bowl goes flying, the paint is going everywhere. Looking like they are shot with real bullets, they try to sit there and take what is being shot at them. The flowers sitting on the table are now shot to pieces, the glass is flying everywhere, paint is flying all over. They decide to turn the TV off. No more.

Every word has impact! Protect yourself and your family.[7]

How? By shutting it off! We're being peppered to death with wickedness in our eyes, and YET the average household combined watches almost *seven* hours a day of television. The average child spends 1,680 minutes a week watching television, compared with 38.5 minutes a week that he or she talks one-on-one with a parent, which means the parent's not instructing them, TV is!

What did David say? I will set no wicked thing before my eyes! And now we do hundreds and thousands of times per hour. And we wonder why things are getting wicked? Junk in equals junk out! That's just one movie. Now add to that, this! The average American adolescent will view nearly 14,000 sexual references on TV per year. 75% of prime-time network shows included sexual content, up 67% in one year alone. Nearly one third of family hour shows contain sexual references. By the time they reach kindergarten, the average American child has seen between 6,000 to 8,000 hours of television, approximately one-third of their total pre-school waking hours.

And it's about to get worse! They are now working on full-blown nudity shows! Seven shows are being rolled out that feature complete nudity. Not just showing nudity here and there, that's bad enough, it's complete full-blown nudity all the time! MTV has a couple new shows coming out, one is called "Virgin Territory" where participants are trying to lose their virginity or what they call V-Card. Another show is called, "Happy Land" where there is a teen story line that promotes incest. The lead person playing the girl in the show said, "Incest is hot and we're going to have fun!" on TV! If you think that's bad now, it's getting so bad that their airing commercials on TV promoting adultery!

Prime News, CNN, Happening Now reports

We certainly don't need commercials to get us to cheat on our spouse. Like this ad campaign by this pro-adultery site, "An Affair to Remember", But they are out there, in your face ads, and your kids can see this, take a look. Two couples are getting married, they look so happy.

But the next scene shows she is with her husband's best friend and he is with some other woman. Or maybe it was her with her co-worker and him with her best friend. The ad says, "Isn't it about time to have an affair, life is too short, have an affair, go to AshleyMadison.com".

Look how happy he is searching the website and wow she is even happier searching for someone to have an affair with. He can't wait to get into his car to go pick her up and off to the hotel. The music is playing, there's nothing I haven't tried. "Shhhhhh, Ashley Madison". Life is short, have an affair. That's the tag line for AshleyMadison.com. An online dating service for married people advocating adultery.[8]

      Who would have thought that we'd ever see the day? Leave it to Beaver eat your heart out, where our once great Christian nation would become so wicked, they'd be promoting adultery on TV. So, the question is, "Because you've heard the mantra, this stuff has no effect on my behavior? This rotten media that I'm ingesting in my eyes has no effect on my behavior?" Really? Let's see how well the family's holding up under this visual assault.

The marriage rate in the United States has fallen to an all-time low, 6.8 marriages per 1,000 people.

In the United States today, more than half of all couples "move in together" before they get married.

Because of that America has the highest divorce rate in the world.

We also have the highest percentage of one person households on the entire planet.

For women under the age of 30, more than half of all babies are being born out of wedlock.

One out of every three children in the United States lives in a home without a father.

69% of Americans believe there's nothing wrong with divorce.

66% of Americans believe sex outside of marriage is perfectly fine.

58% of American believe having a baby outside of marriage is fine.

58% of Americans believe gay and lesbians relations are fine.

89% of all pornography is produced in the United States.

America has the highest incarceration rate and the largest total prison population in the entire world by a wide margin. Without strong families, our young people are constantly in search of an identity. According to the FBI, there are now more than 1.4 million gang members involved in the 33,000 active criminal gangs in the United States.[9]

Sounds to me like the family's messed up, how about you? Could it be we're encouraging this family breakdown with all this wicked media we keep ingesting into our eyeballs? Unlike what David said to do, and it really has an effect on our behavior. But that's not all. This wicked media is not only also producing immorality and the family breakdown but the exact same kind of wicked brutality that Paul warned about in the last days.

2 Timothy 3:1-3 "But mark this: There will be terrible times in the last days. People will be lovers of themselves, lovers of money, boastful, proud, abusive, disobedient to their parents, ungrateful, unholy, without love, unforgiving, slanderous, without self-control, brutal."

The word there for brutal in the Greek is "Anemeros" and it means, "to not be tamed, to be savage, or fierce." And wonder of wonders, have you noticed what's going on today? People are treating each other like absolute savages and it's getting worse! Look at what is happening.

A Pennsylvania woman beat her child with a baseball bat over a clogged toilet.

A 13 year old boy killed his cousin over an Xbox.

A man smothered his crying son over a video game.

Another man fatally stabbed his wife in an argument over a cable bill.

Two 18-year-old boys beat a 30-year-old mentally-disabled man to death with a baseball bat just so they could get his Xbox.

A couple dismembered their roommate and burned their torso in a campfire.

A California priest was beaten to death with a wooden stake and a metal gutter pipe.

Teen girls were charged with torturing a mentally disabled boy.

A woman was beaten to death after accidentally walking in front of the camera while a group posed for a photo.

Teens savagely beat a homeless man and then kicked his dog to death.

Another teenage girl bludgeons, strangles, and decapitates her friend.[10]

    Our society is not only getting wicked, it's getting "Brutally Wicked" exactly like the Apostle Paul warned about in the last days! "Anemeros" is everywhere now! I wonder why? Could it be all this wicked brutal media we're ingesting into our eyes is affecting us? You be judge!

The average American child or teenager views 10,000 murders, rapes, and aggravated assaults per year on television.

80.3 percent of all television programs contain acts of violence.

A child born today will witness 200,000 acts of violence on television by the time they are eighteen.[10]

The question more and more concerned parents and public officials are asking is this: What is all this viewing doing to them? It's creating the massive rise of wickedness that the Bible said would happen when you're living in the last days! It is all happening right now, it's not make-believe, and it's not by chance!

Our wicked Educational System and our Wicked Media is producing the last days society of absolute complete unadulterated wickedness that the Bible warned about in the last days!

The 3rd reason why we're seeing such a massive rise of wickedness in the last days is because we also have an **anti-God system**.

That's right, I'm talking about **Atheism**. We have got to seriously wake up and realize that this Atheism we see today has been spawned by another lie in our schools that's called evolution.

It's not just a lie, but it's totally junk science. And it's built on a lie that there is no God, we have no hope, we have no future, and we came from nowhere! Because of this lie of evolution, we now have these atheistic ideals that has given rise to this massive rise of wicked behavior that we see today. But don't take my word for it. Let's listen to God's. He told us this is exactly what was going to happen, when you say He doesn't exist!

Romans 1:18-32 "The wrath of God is being revealed from heaven against all the godlessness and wickedness of men who suppress the truth by their wickedness, since what may be known about God is plain to them, because God has made it plain to them. For since the creation of the world God's invisible qualities – His eternal power and divine nature – have been clearly seen, being understood from what has been made, so that men are without excuse. For although they knew God, they neither glorified Him as God nor gave thanks to Him, but their thinking became futile and their foolish hearts were darkened. Although they claimed to be wise, they became fools and exchanged the glory of the immortal God for images made to look like mortal man and birds and animals and reptiles. Therefore, God gave them over in the sinful desires of their hearts to sexual impurity for the degrading of their bodies with one another. They exchanged the truth of God for a lie, and worshiped and served created things rather than the Creator – Who is forever praised. Amen. Because of this, God gave them over to shameful lusts. Even their women exchanged natural relations for unnatural ones. In the same way, the men also abandoned natural relations with women and were inflamed with lust for one another. Men committed indecent acts with other men, and received in themselves the due penalty for their perversion. Furthermore, since they did not think it worthwhile to retain the knowledge of God, He gave them over to a depraved mind, to do what ought not to be done. They have become filled with every kind of wickedness, evil, greed and depravity. They are full of envy, murder, strife, deceit and malice. They are gossips, slanderers, God-haters, insolent, arrogant and boastful; they invent ways of doing evil; they disobey their parents; they are senseless, faithless, heartless, ruthless. Although they know God's righteous decree that those who do such things deserve death, they not only continue to do these very things but also approve of those who practice them."

Here's the point. Does that not sound exactly like our society today? Where did all this wicked behavior, mentioned there, come from? What did it say at the very beginning? From suppressing the truth about God's existence and that's exactly what evolution does! Don't they say there is no God? We have no proof before us! Don't they suppress this truth about God's existence with junk science in our schools, in the media and in Hollywood with their lie? Of course, they do!

What did the Bible say was going to happen when you had the audacity to do that? God will give you over to what? Your wicked desires! You don't want there to be a God? Fine! Have it your way! You'll learn the hard way, America, what happens to a society and how evil it's going to get when you no longer want Him! When you say get out of here God!

You will immediately go after sexual impurity, shameful lusts, homosexuality, you will become filled with every kind of wickedness, evil, greed, depravity, murder, envy, strife, deceit, and malice. You'll become gossips, slanderers, God-haters, insolent, arrogant, boastful, disobedient to your parents, senseless, faithless, heartless, ruthless, and it's going to get so bad, you're even going to invent new ways of doing evil. Why? Because you had the audacity to say there is no God, there is 'evolution' so, as an act of judgment from God, He gave you what you wanted, He gave you over to your atheistic evolutionary mindset, wicked desires and your society fell apart!

Now, tell me that is not exactly what has happened to our country today. Every single one of those wicked behaviors mentioned there is totally common place in our society right now, right? Why? Because of the lie of evolution. It's a direct correlation! **Romans Chapter 1**. What you believe determines how you behave! This is the fruit of this atheistic lie called evolution, and it's producing the wickedness we see today. And it's about to get worse!

The 1st way we know it's going to get worse, creating more wickedness is the rise of **Popular Atheism**.

Here are some stats on Atheism in America and you tell me if it's not getting more and more popular by our rejection of God with the lie called evolution.

The number of Americans with no religious affiliation has grown by 25 percent over the past five years.

According to the U.S. Census Bureau, the number of Americans with "no religion" more than doubled between 1990 and 2008.

A study conducted by the Barna Group discovered that nearly 60 percent of all Christians from 15 years of age to 29 years of age are no longer actively involved in any church.

It is being projected that the percentage of Americans attending church in 2050 will be about half of what it is today.

According to LifeWay Research, 46 percent of all Americans never even think about whether they will go to heaven or not.[11]

Doesn't even enter their mind! Why? Because when you couple this with the behavior of the average church member, I think it makes total sense! We're not sharing the Gospel!

10% of reported church members cannot even be found.

20% never pray.

25% never read the Bible.

30% never attend Church services.

40% never give to any cause.

50% never go to Sunday School.

70% never give to missions.

75% are never engaged in any Church activity.

80% never go to a prayer meeting.

90% never have family worship.

95% never ever win a soul to Christ.[12]

So, why are we seeing such a rise in Atheism? Because we're not sharing the Gospel, and these people are being brainwashed into it via the schools and media. It's getting so bad, and we're falling so short, that the Atheists are even now starting their own churches.

BBC Reports:

Now is it possible to have a church without religio? The Sunday Assembly believes it is. The Atheist organization stages gatherings which it says extracts the good things out of religion without making God part of the package. We went to one of their get togethers and discovered a church of England Vicar who says he doesn't believe in the existence of God either.

While many people may find the idea of a godless church strange, one Anglican Vicar has been preaching for over 40 years despite never believing in God. He says, "Atheism and religion don't have to be enemies." Reporter: They come together regularly and their numbers are growing. The Sunday Assembly was started by Thomason Jones and Piper Evans months ago.

Now they claim to have over 8 congregations worldwide. The main branch is in London. Thomason Jones states, "We are a godless congregation that celebrates life. We are there for people that want to live better, help often, and wonder more." Reporter: The idea of the assembly is to take what it calls the best part of church and to use those to celebrate life from an atheist and secular prospective.[13]

Atheist churches! For the first time in mankind's history, we're getting so wicked we now have atheist churches! Can you believe that? But hey, good thing that'll never come here to America! We're a Christian nation! It's already started here in the Bible Belt!

CNN reports:

IN TODAY'S FACES OF FAITH, we are talking about a new kind of church, a church without God. It's called Community Mission Chapel. It looks and sounds like a place of worship. There is a weekly service, offering, uplifting songs, but here is the catch. It's missing one major detail. Its members don't believe in a higher power.

This self-proclaimed atheist church is just one example of the growing presence of religiously unaffiliated congregations popping up all over the world, and it's making some waves in the heart of the Bible Belt, Lake Charles, Louisiana. So here to talk with us about it is Jerry Dewitt, he is a former evangelical preacher turned atheist and author of a new book 'Hope After Faith'. An ex-pastor's journey from belief to Atheism. Thank you for joining us, we appreciate it Jerry. "Thank you, it's a pleasure to be with you", he replies.

The reporter interviews him, "Why don't you give us your story because your conversion just happened a few years ago." He answers, "This is about love, this is about loving truth, and about loving human beings, and about how much I loved God for 25 years, but in my search, was not able to find any true evidence or truth of His existence or intervention."[14]

Really? That's not what we saw in **Romans Chapter 1.** You have no excuse! There's tons of evidence, just look around! Before I continue, I have to clarify something. That man claimed to be a Christian and a Christian pastor for 25 years? What happened to him? Did he lose his salvation? No! You can't! The Bible says if you walk away from Jesus, you are giving the indicator you were never saved in the first place! I didn't say that, God did!

1 John 2:18-19 "Dear children, this is the last hour; and as you have heard that the antichrist is coming, even now many antichrists have come. This is how we know it is the last hour. They went out from us, but they did not really belong to us. For if they had belonged to us, they would have remained with us; but their going showed that none of them belonged to us."

The Bible says people show their fake profession of faith in Christ by acting like the Antichrist by rejecting Christ. You can't lose your salvation! Therefore, if a person "says" they were a Christian, like that guy or the Vicar, but walked away from Christ, they were never saved in the first place! I didn't say that, God did! They were fake! True Christians stick with Jesus!

But here's the point. It's obvious that we're getting so wicked in our world today, even here in America, that we now have atheist churches even in the Bible Belt! Can you believe it? In fact, they're about ready to start their own atheist cable channel! A New Jersey-based atheist group is starting the first ever, on-demand TV Channel dedicated to godlessness. They believe that they're good without God and they're reaching out to the freethinkers and folks who are looking for a way out of faith. And we wonder why it's getting so wicked?

We don't share the Gospel and we allow Atheism to continue. Now it's spawned this absolute unadulterated wicked society that the Bible said would appear on the scene when you are living in the last days!

The 2nd way we know this anti-god system is creating the last days society of unadulterated wickedness is the rise of **Murderous Atheism**.

It's not just popular, it's a murderous belief system! And that's exactly what Jesus said you'd get when you play with this lie from Satan!

John 8:43-44 "Why is My language not clear to you? Because you are unable to hear what I say. You belong to your father, the devil, and you want to carry out your father's desire. He was a murderer from the beginning, not holding to the truth, for there is no truth in him. When he lies, he speaks his native language, for he is a liar and the father of lies."

This passage clearly tells us, Jesus speaking, that Satan is not only a liar and the father of all lies, which would include the lie of evolution, right? But, it also says he's a murderer and he's been one from the beginning. And believe it or not, this is yet another deadly side-effect of the lie called evolution. It not only spawns' Atheism, a godless society, but it spawns the next logical step. You see, if there is no God, and we're all just a bag of chemicals dancing to our DNA as the atheist Richard Dawkins would say, "Because the Universe has no design, no purpose, no evil, no good, and nothing but blind, pitiless indifference, then think about it, who cares what we do, right? If we take a life who cares if there is no meaning, purpose, or value to life as evolution would say.

Therefore, we can "play God" and take it whenever we want! And that's exactly the premise behind abortion! The murder of children! This is where it comes from! The lie of evolution! That's not a baby, it's a blob of tissue or a fetus. And now because of this lie, we have become one of the most murderous evil societies in the history of mankind! Don't believe me? Let's look at how many children we are murdering on a regular basis.

48% of all pregnancies among American women are unintended and ½ of these potential children are killed by abortion. Each year, 2 out of every 100 women ages 15-44 have an abortion and 47% of them already had at least 1 prior abortion. An estimated 43% of women will have had at least 1 abortion by the time they are 45 years old.

During the Revolutionary War 25,000 Americans died. During the Civil War, nearly 500,000 people died. During WWI over 100,000 people died.
Modern Holocaust: Abortion

During WWII over 400,000 people died. And in both the Korean and Vietnam wars about 113,000 died. However, since 1973 in the war on the unborn, we have had over 57,000,000 babies murdered by abortion in America alone, and worldwide, just since 1980, we have had over 1,344,000,000 babies murdered by abortion.[15]

The most dangerous place for an African American is in the womb. One person said "Why would bacteria be considered life on Mars and a heartbeat not be considered life on earth? It's all based on an atheistic lie called evolution and it's now produced one of the most vicious murderous societies we've ever seen. They want to murder children on demand on every street corner.

Since 2002, Planned Parenthood and other abortion providers have received over $1 billion in taxpayer funding. Demonstrators are screaming, "If you want to talk about morality, look at what we represent right now!". They are holding signs "Abortion on Demand and Without Apology", "Stop Abortion Coverage Ban", My Body, my choice", "Who decides", "How can you trust me with a child?". And she screams, "I'm so glad to be a future doctor and I will perform abortions and I will be proud of it!"

According to Planned Parenthood's 2009 Annual Report, abortions accounted for 98% of its services to pregnant women. She says, "There is no shame in abortion, I plan on being an abortion provider, I had an abortion a few weeks ago, my insurance actually covered it, our body, our choice." Another demonstrator says, "Abortion is health care."

What is Planned Parenthood's vision for our future? "Unless you are going to start adopting, all these kids that are going to be born," she shakes her shoulders, "I don't know what we are going to do, we don't have the maintenance." Planned Parenthood says they are not anti-Christian. Another demonstrator says, "I really want them to stop making decisions for my body with their Bibles." Another sign reads, 'Keep your Rosaries off my Ovaries.' Then from another demonstrator, "It is not a baby, a baby is a fetus that has been born". From another, "A baby is what will get in the way of a job that will pay off my loans."

Why should we fund Planned Parenthood? Another demonstrator says, "Because I can't wait for it tomorrow, if I get pregnant I want an abortion. And if I got pregnant today I would abort the baby. And I wouldn't feel bad about that". Then a male demonstrator says, "I want the abortion clinic to be like Starbucks, there should be a Planned Parenthood on every corner".[16]

Can I translate that for you? We are getting so wicked that our society now wants abortion clinics on every corner, so they can murder children on demand! Can you believe that? I like what one guy said, "You can pray all you want, "Oh, God Bless America" but unless we stop the slaughter of these innocent children, He's going to judge America." and soon! Believe it or not, it's going to get even worse!

"A Democratic Abortion Bill in New York now allows babies to be killed by shooting them through the heart with poison."

"Our former President asked God to "Bless Planned Parenthood," and he wants us to pay for these murders in our healthcare system.

Both Google and Yahoo have recently pulled pro-life ads from its "abortion clinics" search results. The United Nations says we have no right to "oppose abortion." They want to be able to murder on demand around the world.

Girl Scouts are giving thanks right now for being a part of a worldwide pro-abortion organization.

And a D.C. fundraiser for abortion offered Coat Hanger Pendants for their contributors and the proceeds went to help pay for those who couldn't afford to kill their own child.

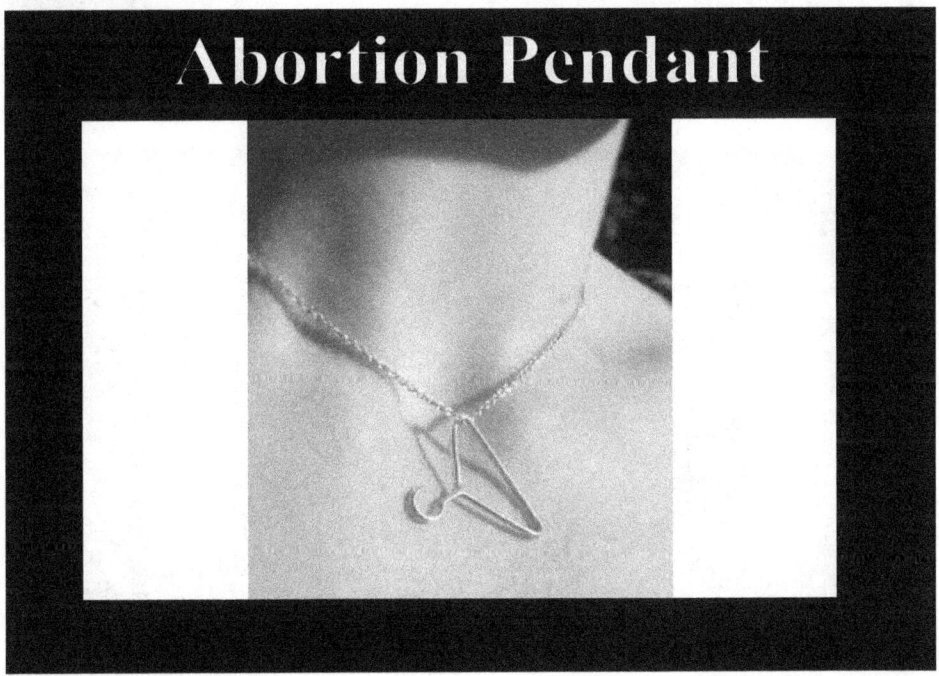

Planned Parenthood right now is handing out awards for "Exceeding Abortion Visits," and they even stated, "Having an abortion will not change God's relationship with you."

And a person recently went into a Hobby Lobby store in New York and hung up "Aborted Baby Jesus Dolls on a Hanger."

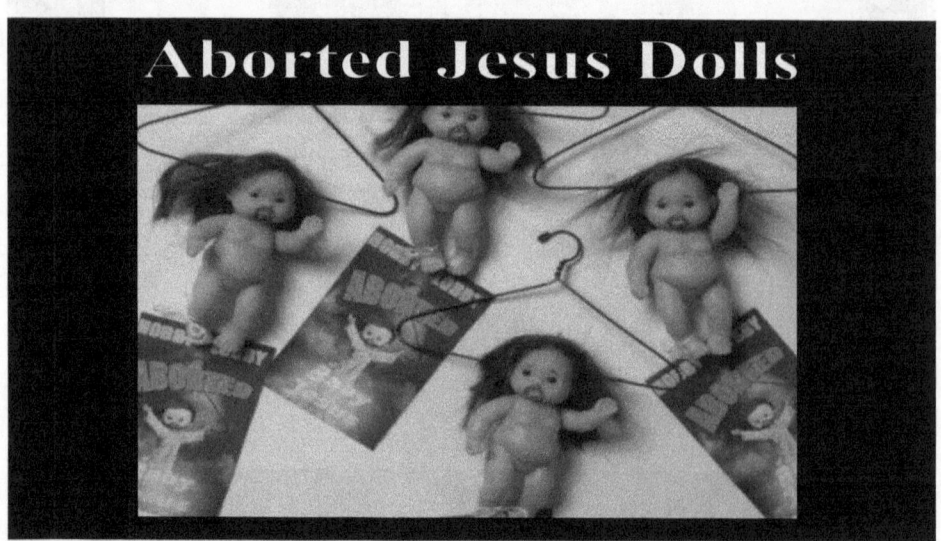

We are getting so wicked, and so evil and so murderous, that we're now using the remains of dead children to power electric plants!

"The remains of 15,000 babies in Britain were incinerated as 'clinical waste' and used to generate power for heat."

And *"Canadian aborted babies were incinerated in Oregon to power a facility there for electricity as well."*

It's not stopping there! It's moving outside the womb.

"Quebec has not only approved a bill legalizing euthanasia on demand." So let's now get rid of those adults we don't like or want, but Belgium has now extended that law to kids!*[17]*

Now you can officially kill kids outside the womb! "Why God, why? Why did we fall? How did this happen? How did our world turn into such a society of wickedness and rebellion? Why is it so horribly evil? I'll tell you why! Because we allowed the infiltration of an anti-god murderous atheistic lie called evolution into our schools, into our media, into our hearts, and even in the Church and God said when you do that HE'LL HAND YOU OVER to your wicked desires! You don't want there to be a God? Fine! This is what you get! An absolute, unadulterated, wicked society that the Bible said would appear on the scene when you are living in the last days! That's why!

The 3rd way we know this anti-god system is creating the last day's society of unadulterated wickedness is the rise of **Hybrid Atheism.**

And this brings us to another logical outcome of this atheistic evolutionary lie called evolution. You see, if there is no God, and evolution is true, then you can, at some point, play God yourself by not only murdering whoever you want, but you can make improvements to mankind's evolutionary process whenever you want.

This is precisely the mindset behind some other comments by Richard Dawkins, things like, "It is immoral to allow Down Syndrome babies to be born." Another Bioethicist said, "We need to push for the elimination of people with a low IQ through Genetic Screening."

"How can they even say that? That's sick!" Well again, if evolution is true, and there is no God, then you can at some point, "play God" and try to improve humanity! That is exactly what they're doing right now! Believe it or not, they are working on a new "Human Hybrid Species" with all kinds of "Evolutionary Enhanced Features," and they are mixing humans with animals. They're called "Parahumans" or "Human Animal Hybrids" and it's not only wicked, it's exactly what Jesus said would appear on the scene again right before He came back. I didn't say that, He did!

Matthew 24:37 "As it was in the days of Noah, so it will be at the coming of the Son of Man."

Genesis 6:1-7 "When men began to increase in number on the earth and daughters were born to them, the sons of God saw that the daughters of men were beautiful, and they married any of them they chose. Then the LORD said, 'My Spirit will not contend with man forever, for he is mortal; his days will be a hundred and twenty years.' The Nephilim were on the earth in those days – and also afterward – when the sons of God went to the daughters of men and had children by them. They were the heroes of old, men of renown. The LORD saw how great man's wickedness on the earth had become, and that every inclination of the thoughts of his heart was only evil all the time. The LORD was grieved that He had made man on the earth, and His heart was filled with pain. So, the LORD said, 'I will wipe mankind, whom I have created, from the face of the earth – men and animals, and creatures that move along the ground, and birds of the air – for I am grieved that I have made them.'"

Why? Because of their wicked behavior! And not only continually thinking wicked, but also getting so wicked they started to tweak with humanity and create some sort of hybrid. Jesus said when you see this repeat of that same wicked behavior as it was in Noah's day, He's getting ready to come back.

So, the question is, "Are we really trying to create some sort of human hybrid?" The answer is yes! In fact, it's been going on for awhile now. And again, this is the logical outcome of an atheistic evolutionary mindset. If there is no God, and evolution is true, then you can at some point play God yourself and improve mankind or "speed up" this evolutionary process. Take the best of man, and the best of animals, and mix them all together, and voila! You've got paradise! Don't believe me?

150 human animal hybrids have already been grown in UK Labs. These hybrids have been produced secretly over the past three years and the revelation comes just one day after a committee of scientists warned of a nightmare "Planet of the Apes" scenario in which human-animal creation goes

too far. Once again, is Hollywood preparing us for our future? Right now, they are creating human/cow hybrids, human/pig hybrids, human/mouse hybrids, rabbit eggs with human cells, pigs with human blood, sheep with human livers, cows with human cells, cat-human hybrids, and a whole list of other weird combinations.

BBC Reports:

Plans to allow Scientists to create embryos that are part human and part animal are sent for approval from the official regulator in Britain. These hybrid embryos are seen by the country's leading scientists as a vital step in the search for cures for diseases such as Parkinson's and Alzheimer's. This embryo is part mouse, part cow. In a few months, this Newcastle Lab is hoping to create a human cow hybrid, as reported by the BBC. EPL Therapeutics is working on a solution, they want to clone pigs, whose organs can be transplanted into people. Cloned and genetically modified cows that can produce milk with the same health properties as human breast milk.

These glow in the dark calves can help develop treatments for diseases for animals and humans. "Yes, you did hear that correctly, he has put a spider gene into a goat." The reporter clarifies. "A transgender fish that actually appears to be 6 pack abs. Just one genetically-modified fish could wipe out local populations of the species if released into the wild, biologist have warned. A mouse-ear hybrid. That's right, a mouse growing a human ear. Taiwan breeds green-glowing pigs.

Scientists in Taiwan say they have bred three pigs that glow in the dark. Mice that glow in the dark. Pretty soon your babies will glow in the dark. Mythology and the coming great deception. A man chosen by the gods. Now maybe, like me, you like going to the movies, renting movies, watching them on TV, whatever. Lately, I'd say within the last year we are starting to see a lot of common themes showing up in movies.

I would like to ask, what do these movies have in common? What do you think these three movies have in common? Avatar, Clash of the Titans, and Percy Jackson, the Lightning Thief. All three of these movies depict super human hybrids saving the world. The first movie, Avatar, mixes human DNA with an alien species to create a human/alien hybrid, the second two, Clash of the Titans and Percy Jackson, are sons of gods, little G. Son of Zeus in the first one and son of Poseidon in the second movie. The son of god saves the world. Problem is, it's the wrong son of the wrong god.[18]

It's the antichrist, anti-god who is using Hollywood to prepare us for this future. And if you'll recall, we've already seen this hybrid technology being used in our military to create a Super Soldier. Let's look at that again.

The Defense Research Agency is working on a super soldier program. A 3-billion-dollar super soldier program to be exact. The program got started to make a metabolically dominate soldier so in layman's terms, the military is studying how to use technology and biology to combine man and machine in science to transcend the limits of the human body.

They are trying to alter the genes within our body to make humans stronger and super human without the help of gadgets. They are working on drugs and genetic enhancements and some technology that would allow for regeneration just like Lizard Man, Spider Man and faster healing like Wolverine, enhanced strength like Captain America and even something that would make you like the god of thunder, Thor, where you could operate without sleep for days, without lack of performance. DARPA says they have already hit their first milestone with animal testing and are preparing reports for scientific conferences.[19]

In other words, they're about to unleash it! Can you believe this? This isn't science fiction. As it was in the days of Noah, so shall it be at the Coming of the Son of Man! It's all happening right now! If you think they're not serious about this, the heat is on because other countries are already secretly doing it which is causing a whole new "Cold War" if you will, to hurry up and create these hybrids, as this man shares.

Sid Roth, from It's Supernatural, talks to Tom Horn:

Sid Roth: For the first time since the days of Noah and the Nephilim we have the technology to mix species, perhaps mix a human with an animal, transhumanism. Explain this. Tom Horn: Well, that's right. In fact, we're doing it in laboratories around the world. When most people today hear about the stem cell sciences, they don't realize that a great deal of that is talking about the creation of a part human, part animal embryo that then can be used for experimental purposes.

Now transhumanism itself is the idea that we're going to use that kind of science and other kinds of science to create a new form of mankind. Sid Roth: Why do we want to create a new form of mankind? Tom Horn: Well of course, you know, if you talk to the transhumanist, they're utopians. They believe we can live forever. We can have immortal life without the bother of having to ask Jesus to give it to us. We can upload our brains. We can live forever inside artificial intelligence systems.

There's a great deal that the transhumanists' community believes. But when it comes to genetics, when it comes to kind of repeating what happened in the days of Noah, where these fallen angels corrupted bloodlines, and they believe that we can improve our species, open new modes of perception. By blending ourselves with animals, we might even be able to see into the supernatural realm. The transhumanists, they aspire to do that?

Sid Roth: Who is DARPA and what are they doing? Tom Horn: DARPA is the Defense Advance Research Project Agency. It's one of the largest departments of the U.S. that uses our tax dollars to hire other people to come up with great ideas, private laboratories, things like that. But in last year's operating budget and in this year's operating budget for instance, they have set aside millions of dollars for rewriting the DNA of our soldiers.

Sid Roth: Why would they want to rewrite the DNA of our soldiers? Tom Horn: Super Soldier technology. And furthermore, they're being advised by some of the top think tanks in the world that our competitors, our enemies, are privately developing this technology right now and that if we don't get ahead of it. In fact, the Jason's, which is one of the top scientific advisory panels in the world, told them that by the end of 2012, if few weren't secretly privately ahead of the enhancement revolution we would fall irreparable behind and be dominated in the battle field.[20]

In other words, you better hurry up and create these hybrids or you're going to be left behind! Can you believe this? And what did Jesus say? It's all coming to pass. "As it was in Noah's day, so shall it be at the coming of the Son of Man." We're getting so wicked, just like in Noah's day, that we're also committing the same wicked sin again of trying to create a super-human hybrid.

Now, I think this explains the severity of the 7-year Tribulation and certainly the first judgment. I mean, think about it. "Why did God wipe out all of the planet except 8 people?" Maybe it was because Noah and his family were the only ones left untainted from this hybrid experiment going on. And if you look at it from Satan's point of view, it makes perfect sense! He was right there in the Garden of Eden when God made the great Genesis 3:15 promise. "From the seed of the woman, one day, one would come one Who would crush the head of the serpent." If Satan could somehow pollute the seed of the woman to the point where there was no true human being left alive to give birth to a Messiah who would crush his head, then he'd win, right?

He almost made it, except for 8 people on the ark. So, God sent a flood, Satan lost, and now we are here again today flirting with the same mistake that Jesus said would appear on the scene right before He came back! One researcher said, in regard to this push to create human hybrids, "Eventually we could get to the point where there are very few 100% humans left." Even minute passages are coming to pass!

The 4th reason why we're seeing such a massive rise of wickedness in the last days is because we also have a **Wicked Chemical System.**

That's right, I'm talking about drug usage. Little do people know that all these drug problems, all these drug wars, all these drug lords, and all these drug issues that we see all around the world is a sign we're living in the last days. But don't take my word for it. Let's listen to God's.

Revelation 9:12-21 "The first woe is past; two other woes are yet to come. The sixth angel sounded his trumpet, and I heard a voice coming from the horns of the golden altar that is before God. It said to the sixth angel who had the trumpet, "Release the four angels who are bound at the great river Euphrates." And the four angels who had been kept ready for this very hour and day and month and year were released to kill a third of mankind. The number of the mounted troops was two hundred million. I heard their number. The horses and riders I saw in my vision looked like this: Their breastplates were fiery red, dark blue, and yellow as sulfur. The heads of the horses resembled the heads of lions, and out of their mouths came fire, smoke and sulfur. A third of mankind was killed by the three plagues of fire, smoke and sulfur that came out of their mouths. The power of the horses was in their mouths and in their tails; for their tails were like snakes, having heads with which they inflict injury. The rest of mankind that were not killed by these plagues still did not repent of the work of their hands; they did not stop worshiping demons, and idols of gold, silver, bronze, stone and wood – idols that cannot see or hear or walk. Nor did they repent of their murders, their magic arts, their sexual immorality or their thefts."

Mankind is so wicked in the last days that even though they are clearly being judged by God, it still doesn't wake them up, does it? No! They're so evil at this point that they refuse to repent and get right with God! Nothing seems to get their attention! Not even the judgment of God! They just continue in their absolute unadulterated wickedness like it's no big deal, thumbing their noses against God! Can you believe that? And so, the question I have is, "Why?"

Notice the word there in the text, "magic arts." It said they did not repent of their "magic arts." It's the Greek word "pharmakeia" where we get the English word pharmacy which literally means "drugs or drugging's." This is the one word that clues us in on the first reason why people in the last days are so evil and refuse to repent and get right with God even though they're being judged by God.

There's going to be a massive amount of drug usage across the planet apparently clouding their minds in the last days. Good thing we don't see any signs of that happening anytime soon. Turn on your TV! What do we hear every single night? Drug this, drug that, drug problem here, drug raid there, drugs in schools, drugs in homes, drugs in the streets, drugs in the government, drugs around the world, right? Drug usage has gone ballistic around the world and it's spawning all kinds of wicked behavior and experts are saying it's going to get worse. Why? Because there's another drug out there that is being legalized right now that drug experts are saying is a gateway drug to using all various kinds of drugs and that is Marijuana. Experts are saying, if that thing gets legalized, and it is, we haven't seen anything yet! Drug usage is going to go nuts! It's a gateway drug. It's going to spawn all kinds of wicked behavior, even worse than what we see today!

In fact, it's already started. Studies are showing since Marijuana has been legalized, "crime rates have gone up" as well as "homelessness," AND it's causing more traffic fatalities, it's killing people! So much for not impairing your abilities as promoters would say.

According to a recent study by researchers from Columbia University, drivers who died in car accidents tested positive from marijuana three times more often from 1999 to 2010 when 20 states legalized marijuana for medical purposes. The study looked at data from the fatality analysis reported system covering 23,000 drivers that died over this 11-years of study. In 2010, 12.2 per cent of the dead drivers tested positive for cannabinol compared to the 4.2 per cent that tested positive in 1999. Dr. Lee, co-author of the study from Columbia University Medical Center said, "If the current trends continue, non-alcohol drugs such as marijuana will overtake alcohol traffic fatalities in 2020.[21]

We know it's going to increase even more because now it's not only being legalized all over the place, but now they're making it so easy for you to get, that you can even get it in a vending machine.

Fox reports: It's a vending machine that's unlike any other. You can buy marijuana out of it. A business in Denver recently installed it. Fox's Jeremy Hubbard reports: There's a special delivery tonight at Montana's Smokehouse and Barbecue in Avon. It's not a bubble gum and candy machine you find in most restaurants.

This one is distinctly Colorado. "The future is outside and we're pretty excited about it." Say the owners. The American Green delivering the Zazzz. It's the state's first marijuana vending machine. Many people can look at this and say it's a vending machine and they would be partially right but mostly wrong. That's for sure.

The machine will soon be stocked with goods from Herbal Elements in nearby Eagle Vale. They will fill it with some of their most popular products but these guys are convinced that they are about to revolutionize their industry with this green machine. "I don't think we have dreamed what it can do yet and that's the whole point, you start with this and then start making your way into the future. I think this is a great starting place."[22]

I think it's a great starting place too, if you want to increase traffic fatalities and deaths and encourage even more drug usage! Don't believe me? It's already happening!

"22 million people in the United States are already using illegal drugs," and it's only going to increase the more you "legalize" it.

According to the Federal Government, "The number of heroin addicts in the United States has more than doubled since 2002." Remember, marijuana is a "gateway" drug.

"The number of heroin-related deaths has risen 84% just since 2010." And a recent report shared how 6th grade girls are now doing crystal meth in school.[23]

Well gee, I wonder why? You keep legalizing this stuff! You reap what you sow! It all spills downhill! That's what the experts are seeing! But those are just "illegal" drugs. Prescription drugs, because drugs are drugs, have gone nuts! Let's look at how many people are being drugged in the United States.

According to a study conducted by the Mayo Clinic, nearly 70 percent of all Americans are on at least one prescription drug. An astounding 20 percent of all Americans are on at least five prescription drugs.

Americans spend more than 280 billion dollars on prescription drugs each year. Right now, there are 70 million Americans that are on mind-altering drugs of one form or another.

In the United States today, prescription painkillers kill more Americans than heroin and cocaine combined.

America has the highest rate of illegal drug use on the entire planet.[24]

      I'm not against all forms of medication, but what did the Bible say? In the last days, you're going to see a massive rise of drug usage all over the planet and just because a drug is considered "legal" doesn't take away from the Biblical context. Drugs are drugs and we're seeing a massive increase all over the planet, legal or illegal. In fact, secular experts are now admitting that some of these "mind-altering drugs are turning them into the violent mindless criminals that are responsible for these latest increases in school shootings and massacres we've been seeing. I didn't say that, they did!

CBN Medical Correspondent, Lori Johnson reports:

Most violent outbreaks in recent years have involved guns. And new information indicates that there is often another common thread, anti-depressants. From Columbine to Arora, the Naval yard to Ft. Hood, anti-depressants have been linked to violence. For decades psychiatrist Peter BreggIn has studied this link.

He says, "These drugs have been causing agitation, anxiety, insomnia, hostility, aggression, mania." Anti-depressants work on the brain thereby altering the way people think. "In addition to driving the person with this amphetamine like affect the anti-depressant does kind of a lobotomy, you lose your empathy, you lose your caring."

In his book 'Medication Madness' Dr. BreggIn cites real life examples of violence that could be blamed on anti-depressants. "An engineer who was given Paxil, probably to help stop smoking, maybe for some tension, certainly not for any mental disorder, and within a couple of doses he drowned his two kids and himself in a tub.[25]

Why? Because he was given a legal drug, that doesn't mean it was good for you. And is this really a surprise? Have you paid attention to these prescription drug commercials? I don't care if they are legal, listen to the side effects. You take this drug to supposedly cure your depression, but the side-effects are what? Liver disease, heart disease, even more depression, thoughts of suicide, anger and rage, and its spawning these killings! In fact, it's going to get even worse! Because it's considered legal and acceptable, it's now turned us into the most drug-crazed culture this planet has ever seen. Just like the Bible said would happen in the last days from a lie called Psychiatry.

Everywhere you look, there it is. Do you think psychiatry has nothing to do with you? Think again. The whole field of psychiatry has gotten into every facet of your life. Dr. Jeffrey Schaler, Professor Dept. Justice & Law, American University: They basically believe that everyone is mentally ill. Dr. Thomas Szasz, Professor & Author 'The Myth of Mental Illness': If you are unhappy it's a disease, if you are too thin it's a disease, if you are too fat it's a disease.

Dr. Mark Filidei, Director, Medical clinic: Where are these coming from? These are coming from the minds of psychiatrists that are dreaming these things up. Writing papers and getting published with their names on it. Calling and creating these new diseases. Patient Amanda: First he said I had ADD, then he said I was depressed, then he said I might be bipolar, but I don't have ADD anymore. Patient Dena: He said I've been noticing you and I wonder if you have it too. Patient Cassandra: He said both my husband and my son had a chemical imbalance and it needed to be corrected with a chemical balancer.

Dr. Ron Leifer, Psychiatrist: There is not one shred of credible evidence that any respectable scientist would consider valid demonstrating that anything that psychiatrist calls mental illness, or brain disease, or biological imbalance, it's all fraud. Dr. Margaret Hagen, Professor of Psychology, Boston University: There is no reliability to science, there is just pseudo-science or pretend science.

Dr. Gary Null, Professor of Science, Faileigh Dickinson University: There is one of the most open secrets in all of America in the psychiatric field that nothing, nothing has been done that is legitimate and they are billing for it.

Psychiatrists claim that one billion of the world's population is mentally ill. In the past 30 years, they have prescribed psychiatric medication to 543 million people and right now they drug 17 million school children with stimulants and anti-depressants. "It is really tragic, it's awful, and its being done for money. It's got to be in the billions. I don't know the exact number but it's got to be in the billions. It's unbelievable. It's so big that it boggles the mind. Take the human tragedy you have just seen and multiply it by the millions. In the past 4 decades, nearly twice as many Americans have died in government psychiatric hospitals than in all US wars since 1776 and while raking in 2 trillion dollars annually. Psychiatrist cannot point to a single cure.[26]

So, it cures nothing, it kills tons of people, it's not scientific, and you rake in trillions of dollars pushing drugs. And is it a surprise?

The founder of psychiatry is Sigmund Freud who was an atheist evolutionist who believed that the idea of God was made up by our forefathers to "cope with life", but he himself "coped with his life" using drugs! He was a cocaine addict and believed it had positive benefits for the human body and mind, and he was addicted to nicotine, smoking 20 cigars a day, which eventually led to his death? Are we surprised they're still pushing it today? But folks, here is the point. All of this is a sign you're living in the last days.

The Bible said in the last days, there's going to be a massive amount of drug usage across the planet clouding people's minds so they won't repent and get right with God even though they're being judged by God AS WELL AS causing all kinds of wicked horrible behavior. But hey, good thing we don't see any signs of that happening anytime soon. It's happening right now before our very eyes and that's exactly what the Bible said would happen, when you are living in the last days!

The 5th reason why we're seeing such a massive rise of wickedness in the last days is because we also have a **Wicked Witchcraft System.**

That's right, I'm talking about Wicca. And as we saw before, Wicca is the modern term for old-fashioned witchcraft. The Bible clearly says that witchcraft too, not just drug usage, is also going to be on the rise in the last days. Let's go back to our text.

Revelation 9:20-21 "The rest of mankind that were not killed by these plagues still did not repent of the work of their hands; they did not stop worshiping demons, and idols of gold, silver, bronze, stone and wood – idols that cannot see or hear or walk. Nor did they repent of their murders, their magic arts, their sexual immorality or their thefts."

As we saw earlier, the word here for "magic arts" is "pharmakeia" which means "drugs or drugging's." But it also carries with it the idea of not just "drug usage" but "drug usage that's fostered by the dark arts." And that's precisely why some translators translate the word as just that, "magic arts, sorcery, or literally witchcraft." But hey, good thing we don't see any signs of people practicing witchcraft worldwide, right? Yeah right! That too is happening before our very eyes!

They are doing it through the promotion of Wicca, which is the new term for old-fashioned witchcraft and it's being promoted through the environmental movement with their nature worship, or feminism with their mother goddess worship, or even Hollywood with movies and shows like "Charmed" or the "Twilight Series" and the "Harry Potter" Series, witchcraft has a whole new appeal, even for kids. But hey, it's a good thing we all know that doesn't affect us! Those kids who grew up watching Harry Potter, are now going into the military, and there's so many of them that are now full-blown witches, that the military is allowing them to have their own witchcraft services.

Eyewitness News – Ken's 5 reports:

Halloween may mean costumes and candy for you and me, but for the witches it is their most sacred holiday. In San Antonio, there is a Wiccan coven touting the largest weekly service for the study of witchcraft in the world. Where they meet and who is in the class may surprise you. Marvin Hurst has their story. "Mention the word witch and instantly most conjure a thought of black magic rituals and the belly of seclusion."

"Just keep the line progressing," says a soldier coming out of the Arnold Hall Community Center in San Antonio, Lackland. "It's a different picture." Says the reporter. "My name is Archer, and I am a witch." says the man in black talking to a room full of soldiers. "Archer, AKA Tony Gatland, is the high priest of this Coven, a packed house where the basic military trainees are studying witchcraft in his circle." Says the reporter.

Archer explains, "I come over here on a Sunday and often there are 3 or 4 hundred. About 320 this day taking part in Samhain, the witches New Year celebration on Halloween, they honor the death and rebirth of their god. Trainees literally line up by choice to learn about Wicca. Fantasy reading of Harry Potter. One soldier who joined in 5 years ago says, "There is nothing wrong with Wicca and of course that is why we have this service here." [27]

Because he grew up watching Harry Potter, but we know it doesn't affect us, but now he's an adult in the military who attends full-blown witchcraft services, but that's purely a coincidence. When are we going to get it through our heads that the media influences our behavior and beliefs? And it's not just the witchcraft shows like Harry Potter, It's the vampire shows like the Twilight Series. You tell me if that doesn't affect people's behavior. Look what this lady decided to do.

Watching her children in a playground in Guadalajara, Mexico, Maria Jose Cristerna is just an ordinary mom. But with her distinctive look she is likely to attract more attention than from her peers. She's made several dramatic modifications to her body to transform herself into Vampire Woman. Maria is 98% covered in tattoos, she's also had dental implants to give her fangs and titanium horns placed in her skull. Maria has given up her job as a lawyer to open a tattoo parlor and clothes shop. She insists her life is no different from any other wife and mother's. [28]

We all know the media has no effect on our behavior, and for some reason she decided to quit her legal profession as a lawyer and become a vampire and open her own vampire shop, just a coincidence? I'll say it again, when are we going to get it through our heads that all this media stuff on witchcraft, vampires, and the occult is encouraging people to go down the same path, it's clear as a bell! In fact, it's opening people up to the next step, ingesting blood just like a vampire to stay youthful.

KOMO 4 news reports:

One of the hot new trends in cosmetic treatments takes injectable fillers to a whole new level. A closer look at the vampire facelift. Cindy VanActren usually gets injectable fillers to plump the sags, fill the creases but this time she is trying something new. "Are you ready for your vampire facelift?" asked the technician. The name conjures up all sorts of images. "At first it sounds sort of Twilighty,"

Cindy says. It's a designer cosmetic procedure that combines fillers like juvederm and restylane with what many call a natural fountain of youth. Components of Cindy's own blood. "I can't believe the difference," Cindy says, "I look way younger than I did!"[29]

Wow! So now I can stay youthful just like a real live vampire in the movies? You know, they are always looking youthful, gee I wonder where that idea came from. Who are we kidding? All of this promotion of witchcraft and vampirism and occult teachings in the media, in the schools, all over our world today really is having an effect on our behavior! And, it's creating an explosion of witchcraft and occult behavior that the Bible said would appear on the scene when you are living in the last days.

The 6th reason why we're seeing such a massive rise of wickedness in the last days is because we also have a wicked satanic system. I'm talking about **Satan Worship**.

Using drugs and ingesting the teachings of Wicca clearly opens up spiritual doors to demonic influences to control our behavior, making things really wicked! It's going to get even worse than that. And that's because the Bible says that the people in the 7-year Tribulation will be worshiping demons. I didn't say that God did. Let's go back to the text.

Revelation 9:20 "The rest of mankind that were not killed by these plagues still did not repent of the work of their hands; they did not stop worshiping demons, and idols of gold, silver, bronze, stone and wood – idols that cannot see or hear or walk."

As wild as it sounds, the Bible clearly says that in the last days, it's going to get so wicked that people are actually going to be worshiping demons, not God, demons, agents of evil! Can you believe that? But hey, good thing we don't see any signs of that happening anytime soon? Yeah right, demon worship, including the worship of the biggest fallen angel or demon himself, i.e. Satan, is on the rise and part of the reason is due to our disbelief. We don't even think Satan exists, so they sneak in under the radar with virtually no opposition and it's also partly because of Satanism's ease of access. No longer do you have to go to some back alley in some creepy bookstore in Timbuctoo to find out about Satanism, it's all over the place, including the internet!

And I quote, "A surge in Satanism is now being fueled by the internet and has led to a sharp rise in the demand for exorcisms", you know, get these demons out of me! In fact, it's now entering our school system. A satanic temple has launched a campaign called "Protect Children Day" where they want children to pray to Satan in school. "We want children to know that they are permitted to pray to Satan in school." You can't pray to God, but now you can pray to Satan! Even at the University level, they're getting ready to have a satanic black mass at Harvard. Check this out!

It's called a Satanic Black Mass and it's about to happen at Harvard University. A Harvard University student club is hosting a Satanic Black Mass re-enactment to celebrate witchcraft and satanic worship. The ritual is expected to take place at an on-campus barn and the Harvard extension cultural study club will be hosting. The performance will be conducted by the Satanic Temple. Most students we spoke to at random say that while they do not agree, they appreciate the school's philosophy.[30]

Keep in mind, Harvard was America's first school and it was started by Reverend John Harvard in 1636 whose official motto was "For Christ and the Church." Harvard had several requirements which students had to observe, one of which was, "Let every scholar be plainly instructed and earnestly pressed to consider well the main end of his life and studies is to know God and Jesus Christ, which is eternal life."

Now we've rejected God so much in our school system, that we're now making sure kids pray to Satan and have satanic black masses where people are now "plainly instructed and earnestly pressed to consider well to worship Satan." Oh, how the mighty have fallen. But that's still not all. The rise of satanism and Satan worship is not only going full-blown into our school system, it is now heading into our Government. One man in Florida is right now seeking "equal time" in our Government to open the meetings with a prayer to Satan.

And, believe it or not, a statue of Satan is getting ready to be put up in a capital building of all places, in the Bible belt! First it was atheist churches in the Bible belt, now it's statues of Satan in the Bible belt.

A New York based Satanic group wants to put a Satan Statue on the grounds of the Oklahoma State Capital and it has now unveiled drawings of the proposal. The statue features a bearded goat headed demon seated on a throne with smiling kids next to it. The Satanic Temple insists that it should be allowed to sit next to the Ten Commandments monument that has been at the Oklahoma State Capital since 2012.[31]

"Why God, why? Why did we fall? How did this happen? How did our world turn into such a society of wickedness and rebellion and witchcraft and Satanism? Why is it so horribly evil? I'll tell you why! Because we allowed the infiltration of a satanic system into our schools, into our media, into our hearts, and even in the government. Put a statue of Satan there and it's led to a massive rise of wickedness in the last days. This is why Jesus said it's going to be the worst time in the history of mankind! You don't want to be there! In fact, it's almost like the government and Hollywood are getting us prepared for the absolute horrific demonic nightmare that's about to come! Check out what the Pentagon is preparing for!

Fans of the Walking Dead know that you have to take zombies seriously. Foreign Policy Magazine recently reported that the Department of Defense has a plan to combat a Zombie Apocalypse. The conceptual document is known as Con-op Triple 8, but should it concern us that this plan exists? And how do we exactly prepare for science fiction becoming reality?[32]

Alright, let me get this straight. What do you get when you combine diseases out of control, drugs out of control, witchcraft out of control, the occult out of control, and even Satan worship out of control? I'd say you get the Pentagon trying to prepare for a so-called Zombie Apocalypse as well as an explanation behind Jesus' comment about the 7-year Tribulation that it's going to be, "A time of greater horror than anything the world has ever seen or will ever see again." And that "unless that time of calamity is shortened, the entire human race will be destroyed." Maybe from a Zombie Apocalypse!

No wonder other passages from Jesus say, **Luke 21:26** "Men's hearts will fail them for fear for what is coming upon the world." In other words, they'll die of heart attacks from what they see during that time."

You can laugh and scoff all you want, but it's all happening right now, it really is coming, and there's only one way out. His Name is Jesus. You better accept Him now before it's too late! And, this is why, out of love, God has given us all these signs of the rise of wickedness to show us that the Tribulation is near and the Rapture is right around the corner! And that's why Jesus himself said,

Luke 21:28 "When these things begin to take place, stand up and lift up your heads, because your redemption is drawing near."

You think it's bad now? The antichrist is going to take all this wickedness and put it on steroids! And it's going to become the worst time in the history of mankind and you don't want to be there! Get saved now through Jesus Christ before it's too late!

Chapter Six

The Rise of Apostasy

"It began last week apparently while I was gone on vacation. Bill got up that Monday and was getting ready for work and Dianne asked him, 'Hey, I bet you don't know what today is.' And Bill said indignantly, 'Well, of course I do!'

So get this, 10am that morning, Dianne gets a box of long-stemmed roses delivered to her office. And then at 1pm, she gets this foil-wrapped, two-pound box of her favorite chocolates. And later that day a boutique delivered a designer dress for her.

And Dianne, she couldn't take it anymore, so she called Bill at work and said, 'Honey, this has been the best Groundhog Day ever in my whole life!'

So, Bill, he's steaming about all the money he spent on Groundhog Day gifts. He had to go to the dentist to get some work done on his teeth and when he got there, the dentist sits him in this chair and said, 'Open wider.' And then he shouted to Bill, 'Good grief! You've got the biggest cavity I've ever seen, the biggest cavity I've ever seen!'

And Bill said, "OK, doc! I'm scared enough without you saying something like that twice."

And the Dentist said, "I didn't! That was the echo."

Bill's now leaving the dentist office and he's going down in the elevator and when he sees a golden retriever sitting on the floor next to a guy and so he asked the guy, "Hey, does your dog bite?" And the guy said, "Nope, he sure doesn't."

Bill lowers his hand to pet the dog and suddenly, the dog bites his hand and starts tearing it apart, shredding it, chewing on it, and Bill's screaming and swinging the dog around the elevator trying to get his hand out of his mouth, and he finally does and throws the dog off the elevator.

He looks at the guy menacingly and say, 'Hey, I thought you said that your dog didn't bite.' And the guy said, 'He doesn't. That's not my dog!'

Bill finally gets home and he sees Dianne sitting on the couch chewing her nails. And apparently this is a pet peeve of Bill's, chewing your fingernails, so he decided to confront her on it.

She reassured him she has a new solution to cure her of the habit. She went out and bought her a whole year's supply of those Lee press-on nails.

So, Bill said without thinking, 'Well that's a great idea. Now you can eat them straight out of the box.'"[1]

Now you know why I visited Bill in the hospital when I got home from vacation! But seriously, how many of you would say Bill had a rough week there, you know what I'm saying? Man! Nothing was going right for him!

Believe it or not, did you know there's an even worse week than that coming to the whole planet one day? It's called the 70th Week of Daniel, which is the 7-year Tribulation, and it all begins at the Rapture of the Church! The reason why it's going to be such a horrible time-frame is because for those who refuse to accept Jesus Christ as their Personal Lord and Savior, they will be catapulted into the 7-year Tribulation and it's not a joke! The Bible says it's an outpouring of God's wrath on a wicked and rebellious planet.

The 7th update on The Final Countdown study letting us know we're living in the last days is the **Rise of Apostasy.**

Not only is the world going down the tubes in the last days, so is the Church! But don't take my word for it. Let's listen to God's:

1 Timothy 4:1-6 The Spirit clearly says that in later times some will abandon the faith and follow deceiving spirits and things taught by demons. Such teachings come through hypocritical liars, whose consciences have been seared as with a hot iron. They forbid people to marry and order them to abstain from certain foods, which God created to be received with thanksgiving by those who believe and who know the truth. For everything God created is good and nothing is to be rejected if it is received with thanksgiving because it is consecrated by the word of God and prayer. If you point these things out to the brothers, you will be a good minister of Christ Jesus, brought up in truth of the faith and of the good teaching that you have followed.

According to our text, another major characteristic of the last days is that many people in the Church will what? They will apostatize! They will "abandon" and "turn away" and "leave" the faith for demonic teaching! And that's when the show begins. They will be pretending to be religious and give the appearance of being Christians, yet will show their true colors by turning away from the truth to follow hypocritical teachings, right?

Granted, throughout history we've always had some people following some sort of perverted truths of Christianity. That's commonplace. What's not common is how in the last few years, there has been a mass exodus of people "claiming to be Christians" who are turning away from even the basic truths of Christianity. They are following all kinds of wacked out stuff! And it's getting worse, by the day!

88% of Americans claim to own a Bible and 82% consider themselves knowledgeable of the Bible.

Yet 43% can't even name the first five books of the Bible.

72% do not believe the Bible is the literal Word of God.

51% believe the Bible is just a book of ancient "fables, legends, history, and moral precepts recorded by man."

And 55% say the Bible should NOT be taken literally.

53% of professing Christians say the Bible should NOT be taken literally.

65% say that Satan "is not a living being but is a symbol of evil."

25% agreed that it doesn't matter what faith you follow because all faith groups teach the same lessons.

30% says that Jesus Christ died but never had a physical resurrection.

29% contend that "when he lived on earth, Jesus Christ was human and committed sins, like other people."

31% say that a good person can earn his/her way into heaven.

46% of professing Christians falsely believe that the Bible encourages the suppression of women.

33% of professing Christians say the Bible is silent on homosexuality.

Professing Christians turn to the Scripture three times more for personal prayer than they do about discovering the truths about abortion, homosexuality, war, or poverty.

As one researcher stated, "Clearly the lack of Bible studying coupled with shallow and superficial Bible teaching in many Churches, account for this failure."[2]

I don't know about you, but it sure looks to me that in the last few years, there's been a massive rise of apostasy. Just like the Bible said would happen when you are in the last days! But the question is, "How could there be such a mass exodus of people deliberately turning from even the basic truths of Christianity in such a short amount of time, especially in America with our godly heritage?"

The 1st reason people in the Church have turned from even the basic truths of Christianity is due to **Apostate Pulpits.**

This is what that researcher was stating with the statistics. The lack of solid Bible teaching. It all spills downhill. If you have apostate pastors in the pulpit, then you have apostate teaching and apostate beliefs which means you end up with an apostate church! That's how it happens! For those who think there could never be a flood of apostate pastors in the pulpit, you better listen to Jesus!

He told us, "Not everyone who claims to be a disciple of Christ really is one." Fake Christians abound everywhere! Judas Iscariot is the prime example.

John 6:63-64,70-71 "The words I have spoken to you are spirit and they are life. Yet there are some of you who do not believe. For Jesus had known from the beginning which of them did not believe and who would betray Him. Then Jesus replied, 'Have I not chosen you, the Twelve? Yet one of you is a devil!' (He meant Judas, the son of Simon Iscariot, who, though one of the Twelve, was later to betray him.)"

According to the text, Jesus clearly tells us, "Not everyone who claims to be a disciple of Christ really is one." He knows the heart! You can't fool him like Judas. He knew he was phony the whole time! This is something we need to wake up in the Church today!

Just calling yourself a pastor doesn't make you one! Going to a church service or even a seminary doesn't make you a Christian or a pastor any more than sitting in a henhouse makes you a chicken, let me re-word that, going to a church service or seminary doesn't make you a Christian or a pastor any more than sitting in a barn makes you a cow, much better! You must be born again! It is my contention that the American Church is flooded with fake, phony Christians, including pastors in the pulpit! Therefore, there is so much apostasy! It spills downhill!

That's what we saw earlier in our study of the Vicar who was an Atheist leading that Church in England for 40 years. Or that so-called atheist pastor in the Bible Belt who said he was a Christian pastor for 25 years but changed his mind. No, you weren't! The Bible says you were a fake, phony Christian just like Judas Iscariot. I'm telling you that's the tip of the iceberg. There's a massive number of fake pastors in the pulpit today! Just ask this guy!

CNN reports:

"First question out of the gate is just simply how do you just up and become Atheist after being a pastor for a whole year?" Ryan Bell, a former pastor, replies, "I think over the years there has been some growing differences between myself and the denomination of Seventh Day Adventist over theology, policy issues, some social issues, our desire to stand with the gay and lesbian population in our community. There were members of our church that were gay and lesbian and transgender members, so we came to some disagreements that

were irreconcilable and I think we all agreed that I had sort of outgrown my place in the Seventh Day Adventist Church."

"So how do you just turn away from Christ just like that?" asked the reporter. "Yeah," he replies, "People have made those kinds of statements. Again, I think religion and faith are things that are full of nuance and peoples' personal experiences. My experience is not like that of some others. I think the tendency that some people have to think of religion and faith in binary categories.

You are either all of one thing or all of another. Either you are completely a Christian and sold on all the ideas about being a Christian or you are an Atheist and you've completely abandoned all faith. The reality that I have discovered over the last 6 days, for sure, is that the majority of people are somewhere between those two poles and I'm with them in that middle space."[3]

    In other words, the vast majority of the American churches now think it's perfectly fine to be an Atheist who supports the gay agenda and a Christian at the same time??? How many Judas's are out there? This really is happening on a massive scale, it's a Rise of Apostasy, starting with fake pastors, and spilling downhill. Where now the majority of the American Church is apostatizing, they're turning away from even the basic truths of Christianity. They're abandoning the faith just like the Bible said would happen in the last days!
    Now here's the point. What's helping these guys to thrive in the Church today, is this rise of another false teaching called the Church Growth Movement. As we saw before, that lie would have you and I believe that if you want to be a successful church you don't need a real pastor who's really born again who will preach all of the Bible, no! You just need to use secular business ideals and slick marketing techniques and a bunch of fluffy teachings from the pulpit in order to have any kind of church growth.
    As we saw before, there's nothing wrong with church growth per se, but the Bible says the growth you need to be primarily concerned about in the church is spiritual growth not just numerical growth.

Mathew 28:18-20 "Then Jesus came to them and said, "All authority in heaven and on earth has been given to Me. Therefore, go and make disciples of all nations, baptizing them in the name of the Father and of the Son and of the Holy Spirit, and teaching them to obey everything I have commanded you. And surely, I am with you always, to the very end of the age."

Here we see the classic passage that we call the Great Commission, not the Grand Suggestion, or the Great Idea to ponder over a cup of coffee, it's The Great Commission. That means it's an order to be obeyed and notice what it was? We are to go out into all the world, and make what? Oh, I know! Believers, right? No! Or, I know, professional pew sitters! Oh, I know! People who show up Sunday mornings just to increase our attendance records, right? Cause that's a successful church, right? Wrong! We are go out into the world and make disciples, which means disciplined learners!

Therefore, this tells us that we who are in the church are to be about the business of spiritual growth in the church, number one, not just numerical growth! Yes, we are to share the Gospel! Yes, we are go out and teach people how to get saved but after that, we who are in the Church are to teach people how to grow up spiritually and be like Christ, right? It says it right there!

But not anymore! Haven't you heard? That's old-fashioned! We have a whole new focus today! Thanks to the lie of the Church Growth Movement, we are now being told we need only to be concerned about numerical growth at all costs! You need to act like the world, be like the world, speak like the world, look like the world, think like the world, and even do business like the world, just so the world will like us, why? Because the premise is, if they like us, they'll stick around and your numbers will go right through the roof! And isn't that what we want? Isn't that a successful church?

I've said it before and I'll say it again, "If you have 500 people in your congregation but only 5 of them are saved, what in the world did you just accomplish?" Are you trying to encourage people to go to hell? As crazy as that sounds, it has become the "latest craze" in running the church. Who cares about that spiritual growth thing. Forget that! People might leave. Who likes to hear they're a sinner, right? That's bad marketing. Come on! Don't you know how to run a business? So, here's what you do Mr. Pastor CEO, you entertain them!

You make them feel good. Skip that Bible thing and make them feel right at home with some good old-fashioned entertainment and man you'll have more numbers then you know what to do with! Isn't that awesome? And for those of you who don't think the Church would ever fall for this baloney, this is the reason why you're seeing crazy stuff like this.

Are you tired of sitting through that same ol' boring sermon and that same ol' boring church service? You want to spice things up? We're here to help you out! How would you like to go to a full-blown Nude Church! That's right! Where nobody wears clothes including the pastor in the pulpit! I'm not making this up, check this out!

"While you went to church this morning, in your Sunday best, about an hour's drive south from Richmond there is a small congregation that really doesn't worry about material things, they worship the way God brought us into the world, naked. This is a congregation that often worships the same way God brought them into the world, unadorned, so on this particular Sunday morning, parishioners are in various state of dress, some nude, some fully clothed, others topless. But it's not about the clothes or lack thereof. Pastor Alan Parker is here to bare his soul to Christ and lead his flock down the path of righteousness no matter what they have on. This time of year, the Sunday service is a little more than half full but in the summer months its standing room only.[4]

You see? It works! That'll get the numbers up and isn't that what we want? Isn't that a successful church? You gotta do what you gotta do!

But seriously, this is why you're seeing this outrageous insane behavior in the church today! It's called apostasy, a turning away, an abandoning of the basic truths of Christianity. And it's encouraged by this lie called the Church Growth Movement!

But that's still not all! Another lie the Church Growth Movement is encouraging people to do, creating this apostasy, is you need only to make people feel good about themselves and don't say anything that would damage their self-esteem! Which means, you don't preach anything from the Bible that might upset them or correct them because they might leave and you can't have that! It's called fluff and it's a major mega sign you're in the last days! I didn't say that Paul did!

2 Timothy 4:1-4 "In the presence of God and of Christ Jesus, who will judge the living and the dead, and in view of his appearing and his kingdom, I give you this charge: Preach the Word; be prepared in season and out of season; correct, rebuke and encourage – with great patience and careful instruction. For the time will come when men will not put up with sound doctrine. Instead, to suit their own desires, they will gather around them a great number of teachers to say what their itching ears want to hear. They will turn their ears away from the truth and turn aside to myths."

According to our text, the Bible clearly says that there's going to come a day, in the last days, because that's the context, where "People in the church will not put up with sound doctrine." They're not going to like hearing the Bible. "Instead, to suit their own desires, they will gather around themselves a substantial number of teachers to say what their itching ears want to hear." The word there "itching" is the Greek word, "knetho" which means, "to desire only that which is pleasant." They don't want to hear the Bible anymore, so they will only gather around themselves teachers who will give them fluff!

This passage of Scripture is being fulfilled before our very eyes, which means we are living in the last days! How do I know? Because this is exactly what the lie of The Church Growth Movement is saying we need to do if we're going to have that "successful church." We need to preach fluff and only fluff so people will keep coming back! If you want your numbers to go through the roof, you've got to remove from all your sermons anything that might convict people, you know, correct them, things like sin, and hell, and God's hatred towards sin, don't do that!

What are you some crazy religious wacko! Don't do that! That's counterproductive! They might leave! So, here's what you do. Don't convict them, but coax them! Don't make them feel bad, make them feel glad! Give them fluff and only fluff, and tell them how good they are, and that God loves them and there's no need to fear! You keep that up and your numbers are going to go right through the roof! Isn't that awesome!

You might be thinking nobody in their right mind in the Church would ever fall for this because it's so clear, it's right here in the text! It's been here for 2,000 years so we wouldn't be caught off guard, right? Not anymore! Little do people realize that every time you see one of these impotent worldly sissy preachers on TV tickling people ears week after week, it's actually a sign we're living in the last days!

We get phone calls and emails, every single week, from all over the world, of how people can't find a healthy church anywhere that'll do something as basic as preach the Bible, all of it, not some of it! Not just the happy stuff, all of it! The whole counsel of God! It has now created what's called the McChurch.

One guy says this, "Our culture demands convenience Christianity. We want it short, simple, fast and cheap.
The McBible does not have the tedious 66 books, but just a few short sentences and simple words at the fifth-grade level. And the McWorship service is all sweetness and love with nothing offensive.

The McSermon is easily digested with a minimum amount of nutrition and a maximum of fat. Each McPrayer is centered on temporal and material things to keep the mind from wandering to the spiritual which is often illusive for the modern American.

To keep the kids awake, the McHymns are hip-hop style. McMarriages are performed for folk who like quicky relationships and throw-away vows. They are the big feature. The McPastor is a touchy-feely guy who majored in pop psychology and has an in-depth understanding of your every need.

And McSins, commonly called boo-boos, are easily forgiven with fast prayers and of course are soon repeated, but not taken too seriously. You eliminate all the negative and dwell only on the positive.

And the McYouth program is short on Bible study and long on fun and games. It's designed to give the kids what they want so that their parents can go out and have fun evenings without worrying about their kids getting into drugs or sex.

And McSalvation does not have any deep doctrine of substitutionary atonement and regeneration, but a simple human decision or a nod of the head is more than adequate to bring a person into the McKingdom, where he hopes to live happily ever after.

All of this ends up in McHeaven where there are no golden streets, but arches that appear over a broad entrance where the grill is scorching and the deep-fry grease is super-hot.[5]

In other words, hell. Why? Because you created a McChurch, a fake church. You listened to the lie of the Church Growth Movement and you never told them the truth about the dangers of hell, eternal damnation, God's Wrath, His hatred of sin, or even or the return of Jesus Christ. It's all there in the Bible but you won't preach it all because you wanted to have a big bunch of numbers in your church! Is that crazy or what? In fact, it's getting so bad today in the Church that we have apostatized, that it is becoming illegal to say that somebody is a sinner in need of a Savior!

"Child Evangelism Fellowship, a nationally-recognized Christian group that seeks to reach children with the gospel of Jesus Christ is under fire for teaching kids the biblical doctrine of sin and eternal judgment, as well as sharing about the love and mercy of God."

Those who oppose the group assert that because of this, CEF does not present "Jesus loves you" mainstream Christianity, and claim that the organization is "hardcore evangelical fundamental."

"They pretend to be a mainstream Christian Bible study when in fact they're a very old school fundamentalist sect" and that preaching to children about sin might give them feelings of fear and shame.

So, supporters have organized a group against CEF called "Protect Portland's Children," which seeks to speak out against CEF's message and to influence parents not to allow their children to attend its events. (This is in the Church) In fact, one so-called Pastor said, "As a seminary educated clergy member, I see the tactics being used as a form of coercion similar to a cult."

And, "Parents who send their children to clubs that operate on fear should be prepared to see their children suffer from mental health issues."[6]

It has set up a Facebook page and its profile photograph is of a child holding a sign that reads "I am not a sinner." Here's the photo.

This is what you get with a McChurch. This is how far we have apostatized. It's now becoming illegal, in the Church, to share with kids the basic

Biblical truth that you're a sinner in need of a Savior, so you can go to heaven, because that might damage their self-esteem! Can you believe that? I'm telling you, as sick and satanic as that is, it gets even worse. Church leaders are now not only not preaching anything from the Bible that might upset people, but now they're preaching the same doctrine of Satanism from the pulpit, where it's all about you, not God. That's the number one law of Satanism! "Do what you will shall be the whole of the law."

Joel Osteen, the King of Fluff, who will only preach fluff from the pulpit and he admits it, recently allowed his wife Victoria to speak from the pulpit to share what she felt was important for the Church to hear and what she shared was that the most important thing in being obedient or worshiping God was that it has nothing to do with God, it's all about you, about making yourself feel good. It's the same message of Satanism!

"Attention all Christians!!!" Says Huff Post Live reporter, Marc Lamont Hill. "When you go to church next Sunday, you might not be doing it for God but to satisfy your own selfish needs, can you believe that? That is what some people are saying or at least that is how some people are interpreting it. There were remarks made by a popular Lakewood co-pastor Victoria Osteen."

On stage with a stadium full of worshipers Victoria Osteen preaches, "I just want to encourage every one of us to realize that when we obey God we're not doing it for God, I mean that's one way to look at it, we're doing it for ourselves. Because God takes pleasure when we are happy, that's the thing that gives Him the greatest joy this morning. So, I want you to know this morning, just do good for your own self, do good because God wants you to be happy. When you come to church and you worship him, you're not doing it for God really, you're doing it for yourself. Because that's what makes God happy. Amen?"

Founded in San Francisco California, by Anton LaVey, in 1966, the Church of Satan sees belief in God or Hell as delusional so they choose to practice in self-reliance and self-worship. Reporter asks Priestess Lilith Sinclair of the Temple of Set, "If a Christian asked you if you worship self what would you say?" She answered, "In a sense they would be right, it is a form of self-worship."

Reporter asks, "You are a Satanist for how long?" Mike Leehan answers, "12 years." Reporter ask, "What does it mean to be a Satanist for 12 years?" Mike answers, "To adore or serve Satan. Or serving self. More than anything else you are serving self, egocentric, self-centered, serve me, all is me, immediate gratification is all its about".

Magus Peter H Gilmore, High Priest – Church of Satan, says, "In the church of Satan, it has chosen Satan as its primary symbol. In Hebrew it means adversary, opposer, one to accuse or question. We see ourselves as being Satan's adversary, opposers, and accusers of all spiritual belief systems that would try to hamper enjoyment of our life as a human being". Per Anton Szandor LaVey, Founder – Church of Satan, "This is a very selfish religion. We believe in greed, we believe in selfishness, we believe in all of the lustful thoughts that motivate man because this is man's natural feeling." [7]

Now it's being promoted in the Church, it's all about you. And yet the words of Jesus echo through the ages;

Matthew 16:24 "If anyone would come after Me, he must deny himself and take up his cross and follow Me."

And God the Father says...

Isaiah 42:8 "I am the LORD; that is My Name! I will not give my glory to another or My praise to idols."

It's not about worshiping yourself, or making yourself happy, it's about worshiping God! Who would have thought, that we'd see in our lifetime, the church being flooded with fake apostate pastors filling pulpit in droves? The Church forbidding people from sharing with others how they are a sinner in need of a Savior, so they can go to Heaven. Thanks to the lie of the Church Growth Movement we now have a new and improved self-worship in the church just like Satanism. This is exactly what the Bible said would happen when you're living in the last days!

2 Timothy 3:1,4,5 "But mark this: There will be terrible times in the last days. People will be lovers of themselves, lovers of pleasure rather than lovers of God – having a form of godliness but denying its power. Have nothing to do with them."

It's all happening right now, turn on your TV it's all over the place, and it's stemming from a lie called the Church Growth Movement! Because of it, we're seeing a massive growth, it's a growth of worldliness and apostasy in the church, just like the Bible said would happen when you are living in the last days

The 2nd reason people in the Church have turned from even the basic truths of Christianity is due to **Apostate Media**.

The church is no longer following the Bible because over half of the church doesn't even believe the Bible is the literal Word of God. So, the question is, "Well, what then are they turning to for their spiritual beliefs?"

As crazy as this sounds, it's the media, i.e. Hollywood's version of the media, which is anti-God and anti-Biblical and so is it any wonder we're seeing massive turning away from Biblical truths in the church? You get your truth from the sewer, guess what, you end up with sewage! It's that simple! And yet, the Bible says when it comes to truth, we Christians don't accept anything, rather we need to filter everything for purity and get rid of the sewage! But don't take my word for it. Let's listen to God's.

Acts 17:10-12 "As soon as it was night, the brothers sent Paul and Silas away to Berea. On arriving there, they went to the Jewish synagogue. Now the Bereans were of more noble character than the Thessalonians, for they received the message with great eagerness and examined the Scriptures every day to see if what Paul said was true. Many of the Jews believed, as did also a number of prominent Greek women and many Greek men."

According to the Bible, we see that the Bereans were not only eager for the truth, but so much so, they wanted the truth, nothing but the truth, and the whole truth that they filtered everything said to them, even the words of the Apostle Paul, right? They wanted to make sure that what they were getting was absolutely correct. Would you say that's a good thing to do? Of course! Because if you get the truth about Jesus Christ wrong, what happens? You go to hell! How many of you would say that's kind of serious?

But not anymore! That's right! Thanks to the lie of the Church Growth Movement, we are now being told, who needs to be that picky nowadays about spiritual truths! If you get a little sewage, so what! I mean, it's all about you nowadays. So just make it up as you go, do whatever feels right to you, and by the way, keep coming to our church services, will you? For those of you who think I'm kidding, here is the latest trend in the church when it comes to sharing the truth from pastors. The top priority is not the truth, the whole truth, and nothing but the truth.

One researcher said, "Study Reveals Most American Pastors are Silent on Current Issues Despite their Biblical Beliefs."

"George Barna's organization asked pastors across the country recently about their beliefs regarding the relevancy of Scripture to societal, moral and political issues, and the content of their sermons in light of their beliefs."

He said, "What we're finding is that when we ask them about all the key issues of the day, 90% of them said, 'Yes, the Bible speaks to every one of these issues."
"But when you ask them, 'Are you teaching your people what the Bible says about those issues?' The numbers drop and 90% of American Pastors say absolutely not! WHY?

Here's the new list according to the survey of their five most important concerns in the Church, not the truth, "Attendance, giving, number of programs, number of staff, and square footage of facilities." (Where's the truth in all that!)
And Barna said, "What I'm suggesting is those pastors won't speak up on Biblical truth because it's controversial. And controversy keeps people from being in the seats, controversy keeps people from giving money, and from attending programs." (And yet truth is controversial!)

One guy said, "When Paul wrote his epitaph, it read, 'I have fought a good fight, I have finished my course, I have kept the faith.' He didn't say, 'I had a large congregation, we had big offerings, we had a lot of programs, a large staff, and a facility.'"[9]

But that's not all! That's the pastors, let's look at the average pew-sitter. Where do they get their truth from? Is it being filtered like the Bereans? Pastors not only don't preach it, but the church doesn't believe it and even makes it up themselves! It's cafeteria style! Pick whatever you want!

"Christians today pick and choose religious beliefs, doctrines and practices – mixing and matching them much as they would select food in a cafeteria. They borrow from different traditions, then add them to whatever religion they're used to.

But they don't want anything to do with organized religion.

Americans write their own Bible. They fashion their own God. More often than not, the God they choose is more like a best friend who has endless time for their needs, no matter how trivial.

Scholars call this, 'domesticating God,' turning Him into a social planner, therapist, or guardian angel. We have trivialized God. We assume that God is the butler who serves you for one reason, to give you a happy life. We've turned Him into a divine Prozac."[9]

Excuse me? Whatever happened to, "Filtering the message according to the Bible to make sure you're getting what is right, according to God." Now you're making up God according to whoever you want Him to be! And so, the question is, Why? I'm telling you, it's not just that we're not filtering the truth like the Bereans anymore, and making it up, we're sucking it up from a sewer pipe source and accepting it! It's called Hollywood!

It's one thing for Hollywood to put out anti-God anti-Christian material, I expect that, they don't know any better. But now, the Church is eating up their anti-God, anti-Christian heresy and considering it true! Let me give you some examples.

THE BIBLE & THE SON OF GOD MOVIE: Despite their box office success, *The Bible* miniseries and the *Son of God* movie are not very faithful to the Scriptures.

MOSES: The Bible says that Moses was a meek man full of humility. But no, the movie replaced him with Moses that had all the bravado of John Wayne saying with confidence, "I will deliver the people of God" and then Moses goes into Egypt to tell them "he" is their deliverer. They then have this 5-7-minute conversation that IS NOT in the Bible and he speaks with arrogance trying to prove to skeptical people that he is their man of the hour.

SAMSON: The problem with Samson is that they spent 20 minutes detailing things that never happened in his life, including the Philistines murdering his wife because they were racist against Jewish people. That NEVER happened. They skipped the fact that Delilah betrayed him repeatedly and he took vengeance on her family. They also said he told her the truth about his strength the first time she asked.

SAUL: First of all, they portray God as being unfair to Saul. It was if the poor guy waited for Samuel 7 days and someone needed to make the sacrifice. And now God is going to punish him? It then shows Saul crying in bed asking for grace and God giving him no grace. All because he wanted to give God a gift, an offering. This portrayal of Saul makes God look cruel, and merciless.

DAVID: In the Bible David did not fight Goliath in order to bring military victory to Israel. He fought him because Goliath was insulting the name and honor of God. Yet the movie portrayed David defending Saul's army's not God's. Throughout the movie they keep giving God's glory to God's people. Then the Bible says David disrobed and danced before the ark of the covenant in humble, and holy worship. He was a man after God's own heart. But the movie shows David dancing around like a party animal, in his underwear, dancing with women and lustfully making advances at Bathsheba. THIS DOES NOT HAPPEN IN THE BIBLE.

PETER: Toward the beginning of the film, a scene depicting the call of Peter was completely wrong. In the movie, Jesus and "Peter" go out in a boat alone together, then Jesus addresses him as "Peter" and then produces a miraculous catch of fish, whereupon "Peter" ponders whether or not to follow Jesus. However, in the Bible, Jesus encounters Andrew and his brother who is called Simon at that time. They were on the shore, not out in a boat. The brothers drop everything and immediately follow Jesus. The miraculous catch of fish comes later. So, does Jesus giving him the name "Peter."

THE APOSTLES: In the Scripture, we have only 12 apostles...all men (Peter, Andrew, James, John, Philip, Bartholomew, Matthew, Thomas, James, Thaddaeus, Simon and Judas Iscariot). But in the film, there are 13 apostles, and the thirteenth apostle is a woman named Mary. Not only is she almost always with them, but she's with them in the boat during the storm when Jesus walks on water. And Mary is also very outspoken and often reproves the male apostles to have more faith as it is very apparent her faith is stronger.

THE PHARISEES: In the movie, the Pharisees want Jesus dead, not out of sinful hatred and jealously as the Bible records, but out of deep concern to spare the people of Israel any further harm from the Roman Empire.

JUDAS: In Scripture, Judas willingly betrays our Lord for a mere 30 pieces of silver and is clearly depicted as a thief and someone who loves money more than people. In this movie however, Jesus turns to Judas and convinces Judas to betray him and Judas adamantly refuses but later he gives in to Jesus' demands reluctantly.

JESUS: At the crucifixion, the film quite deliberately shows the soldier piercing the side of Christ, and then no blood and water pour out. The scene depicting the Ascension was also wrong. The Apostles certainly did not just get up after the Ascension, and start walking off teaching all nations. They went to the Upper Room, elected Matthias to replace Judas, and waited for the Holy Spirit. Also, in the movie the reason for Jesus' death and the meaning of His resurrection are completely missing. No talk that His death is the atoning sacrifice for sin. It's not mentioned at all. Which is why one person stated, "Why did they make such insane changes to the story? Why did the filmmakers take relentless and pointless liberties with the text? They did not do a single scene *completely* correctly." Answer? Well maybe it has to do with the apostate beliefs of the filmmakers themselves.

ROMA DOWNEY: She is not only a full-blown New Ager like Oprah-wan Kenobi, but she even admitted that she listens to books on tape by Eckart Tolle, the same New Ager who's influenced Oprah with false Hindu, Buddhist, Taoist, and Shintoist philosophy. Roma says, "My husband says I'm so self-realized I'm practically levitating." She also went to the University of Santa Monica to get a degree in "Spiritual Psychology." This is not a secular school like Cal Poly or USC, it's a school that specializes in New Age degrees. She also admitted that she *talked to her dead mother through a psychic on live TV* on the John Edwards show which is necromancy and is forbidden in the Bible. And she even went on to partner with him in writing a book called, "Practical Praying: Using the Rosary to Enhance Your Life" and it comes with a free Meditation CD featuring Roma Downey. As one person stated, "These people are liars. They have a history of twisting the Word of God in ways that change the message of the Gospel and the nature, character, holiness, righteousness, and justice of God. What they do with the Bible is terrible."

THE NOAH MOVIE: Not only is the producer of this movie an Atheist, but he even bragged how the movie is the least biblical Bible movie ever.
Director Darren Aronofsky called his movie "The least biblical film ever made," and claimed that his leading character, Noah, was the "first environmentalist."

Here's his interview.

CBS reports:

We begin this half hour with the end of the world, the film version of one of the best-known tales from the Bible's Book of Genesis. The story of how all living things were saved from a great flood sent by God to punish human kind. Directed by Darren Aronofsky, whose previous work includes Black Swan and the Wrestler, this new epic stars Russell Crowe, as Noah.

Good Morning to you Darren.

<u>Darren Aronofsky</u>: *Good Morning to you.*

<u>Reporter</u>: *We have had a chance to see the movie. It's absolutely beautiful even though it's a little bit dark. Speaking of Russell Crowe, I read that you promised Russell Crowe something when you asked him to do this film.*

<u>Darren Aronofsky</u>: *Most people think that when they think of Noah they have very big expectations and so I said Russell, I promise, you will never be wearing a robe and sandals, standing on a houseboat with two big giraffes standing behind you. And that is what this movie is about. It's about changing people's expectations because for me when I was a kid and I read the original story I didn't really sympathize with Noah I was thinking about the people that didn't get on. I always wondered if I would be good enough to get onto the boat. And so, everyone was wiped out. So, there is a very, very more intense story going on.*

<u>Reporter</u>: *There has been a lot of talk about how accurate this is to the Book of Genesis. I read you said this is the least biblical, biblical movie ever made. How did you walk that fine line knowing that audiences might get upset that it wasn't accurate and other audiences might get bored that it was too accurate?*

<u>Darren Aronofsky</u>: *When I said it was the most unbiblical, biblical film, what I meant was we were reinventing the biblical epic. Most people think of their Grandma's biblical epic. I love Cecil B. DeMille's Ten Commandants but it's been 50 years since a biblical epic has been on the screen and we wanted to do something really new and really fresh. So, for people, non-believers, it's a great action film with a great family drama but there's actually nothing in the film that contradicts the Bible.*[10]

In the film, Noah was robbed of his birthright by Tubal-Cain. The serpent's body (i.e., Satan), which was shed in Eden, was their "birthright reminder." It also doubled with magical power that they would wrap around their arm. Noah's family only consists of his wife, three sons, and one daughter-in-law, contrary to the Bible. It appears as if every species was crammed in the Ark instead of just the *kinds* of animals, thus mocking the Ark account the same way evolutionists do today.

"Rocks" (that seem to be fallen angels) build the Ark with Noah! Methuselah (Noah's grandfather) is a type of witch-doctor, whose mental health is questionable. Tubal-Cain defeats the Rocks who were protecting the finished Ark. A wounded Tubal-Cain axes his way inside the Ark in only about ten minutes and then hides inside. He stays alive by eating hibernating lizards. Noah becomes almost crazy as he believes the only purpose to his family's existence was to help build the Ark for the "innocent" animals (this is a worship of creation).

Noah repeatedly tells his family that they were the last generation and were never to procreate. So, when his daughter-in-law becomes pregnant, he vows to murder his own grandchild. But then he changes his mind. The Ark lands on a cliff next to a beach and then Noah becomes distant from his family and lives in a cave and gets drunk on the beach.

THE SHACK MOVIE: The latest Apostate movie that's that came out is called, "The Shack" which is based on the book of the same title. As we saw before, "The Shack" is not only one of the hottest books on the market, but it's been promoted heavily in the Church, yet it's openly New Age in doctrine and teaching, and it presents God as a woman![11]

But no need to worry because we the Church are standing strong as faithful Bereans filtering anything that comes our way making sure it lines up with the Bible!

We wonder why our beliefs are so messed up in the Church! Why is there such a great apostasy in the church today where people are turning away from even the basic truths of the Bible??? Because you're not being Bereans anymore! We accept anything, including sewage! We don't examine everything to see whether it's true or not! Instead we're making everything up as we go and/or ingesting anti-God anti-Biblical material from New Agers and Atheists! That's what's creating this great apostasy that the Bible said would come when you're living in the last days!

The **3rd reason** people in the church have turned from the basic truths of Christianity is due to **Apostate Music.**

Ephesians 5:17-20 "Therefore do not be foolish, but understand what the Lord's will is. Do not get drunk on wine, which leads to debauchery. Instead, be filled with the Spirit. Speak to one another with psalms, hymns and spiritual songs. Sing and make music in your heart to the Lord, always giving thanks to God the Father for everything, in the name of our Lord Jesus Christ."

The Bible clearly says that one of the best things you and I could ever do with music is to what? We are to praise God with it, right? In fact, Sebastian Bach said, "The sole purpose of all music is to bring praise to God." And this is why every time we gather together, as the Church, we are to sing songs to God not ourselves that are God-glorifying, God-honoring, and God-exalting.

Why? Because we are so in love with Him, and we're so thankful for what He's done for us, we can't help but sing love songs back to Him, right? That's the purpose of Christian music! Not Anymore! Thanks to the lie of the Church Growth Movement, we're now being told have to gut all your songs of the name of Jesus and switch to generic terms, like He or Him. Why? Because the world doesn't like to hear song after song about God and Jesus and the Bible. I mean, what are you trying to do, run them off or something? That's bad marketing. Remember, it's all about the numbers.

You need to sing songs that they like, and that fits their style and their preferences, and man you keep that up and you're going to have numbers coming out of your ears! Isn't that what makes for a successful church today?

You might be thinking, nobody in their right mind, in the Church would ever fall for this baloney, but people I'm telling you, this has become another "craze" in the Church in leading people in so-called worship. My question is, "Just who are you worshiping?" You never mention the name of JESUS. You only say He or Him. And so, I'm left wondering what is that? Are you singing about your boyfriend, your fiancé, your husband? Who's He? Why don't you mention the name of Jesus? This is a Church service! We're supposed to be singing songs to JESUS! What's wrong with that?

Personally, as I've shared before, I think it's a spiritual warfare issue! Put yourself in the shoes of a demon, the last thing you'd ever want to hear people singing in the Church is the NAME of JESUS, right? Why? Because they know there's no other NAME under Heaven by which men might be SAVED and there's no other NAME under Heaven by which the DEMONS must COWER, OBEY, and FLEE!

So, take the NAME OF JESUS CHRIST out of your "worship music" and it not only makes the world feel comfortable in the church, it makes the demons feel comfortable too! Isn't that great!

If you don't think the music is being twisted today, what about this. In order to meet the new selfish self-centered needs in church worship today, the words to the classic Hymn, as we saw before, *"Amazing Grace"* have been changed from "Amazing Grace that saved a wretch like me, to, "That saved a person like me," Or "a soul like me, or another version says, "That saved and set me free" skipping the whole thing entirely. Because that could damage your self-esteem calling yourself a wretch…and that doesn't feel good and people might leave, and the numbers will go down and you can't have that!

But that's still not all. The song, *"Victory in Jesus"* You know, "I heard an old, old story, how a Savior came from glory, how He gave His life on Calvary, to save a wretch like me…" What? Are you guys crazy? You trying to get the numbers to go down?!! It's now been changed to, "To save one just like me."

The song *"How Deep the Father's Love for Us"* "How vast beyond all measure, That He should give His Only Son, to make a wretch His treasure," is now, "To make us all His treasure."

Another classic song that's been re-written is, *"In Christ Alone."* And you're thinking, "Well what's wrong with that one?" Well, listen to this.

"It's no secret that the Presbyterian Church collectively takes a more liberal approach to theology. But now, they have rejected the hymn, *"In Christ Alone."* Why? There's one key line in the third stanza that created a barrier — *"Till on that cross as Jesus died, the wrath of God was satisfied."* Originally, the Presbyterian Committee on Congregational Song Books for the denomination asked the song's authors to allow them to change the words to *"As Jesus died, the love of God was magnified."* But the songwriters said no, so the committee axed the song from the denominational hymnal."

What most people don't realize is that this is the same tactics that the heretics in the early church used to invade the church. They would get people to repeat their false doctrines by putting their false doctrines to music! Why? Because we all know music has a way of sticking in your heads and you repeat it over and over again and pretty soon you believe it! And it's being repeated today in the last days of the Church with music as well! They are re-writing it with false doctrine!

That's still not all! We not only have so-called Christian musicians saying we're no longer wretches in need of a Savior, to protect our self-esteem, to keep the numbers up, but now we have got so-called Christian musicians saying, "nothing wrong with sin", "being gay is perfectly fine!" And I'm talking popular Christian singers! Big time! Check this out!

Jars of Clay: The lead singer of the popular Christian band Jars of Clay, Dan Haseltine, recently downplayed the authority of Scripture on moral issues and suggested there was nothing wrong with same-sex marriage. He tweeted, "I just don't see a negative effect to allowing gay marriage. No societal breakdown, no war on traditional marriage. Anyone?" He then later stated, "I don't particularly care about Scripture's stance on what is 'wrong.' I care more about how it says we should treat people." He also noted: "I have received so many great messages from gay Christians. You have encouraged me. So many gay couples display more loving characteristics and healthy relationship practices than most traditional marriage couples."

Jennifer Knapp: The contemporary Christian singer is now describing herself as a lesbian even though she won Dove Awards and a Grammy Nomination during the late 1990's and early 2000's. She has now entered into a relationship with another woman and claims she is still a Christian. "I am who I am. If God is a God who judges and strikes people of same sex attraction, then He's going to strike me down."

Vicky Beeching: She just came out and announced, "I'm gay and God loves me just the way I am." And that, "What Jesus taught was a radical message of welcome and inclusion and love and I have a huge sense of calling to communicate that to young people."

I wonder how she's going to do that? That's right! Through music! They're starting to sing this into people's heads!

So, this week, Vicky Beeching, one of the most popular Christian worship leaders and song writers today has come out on Wednesday and announced that she is gay according to an article in Christianity Today.

Beeching is known for a number of popular songs including God your Awesome, Glory to God Forever, which is one of the top songs sung in American churches today according to CCLI. She was mentored by Matt Redman and Tim Hughes and her songs appear on a popular compilation album such as WOW Worship and Here I am to Worship.

Beeching says she appeared to feel same sex attraction at the age of 13 and grew up feeling conflicted in her evangelical call where she said church leaders would pray against the demons of homosexuality that they believed were in her. That's according to the Christian Today magazine. Beeching went on to study theology at Oxford her webpage goes on to quote her as an Oxford educated, theologian, writer, broadcaster, and musician.

So, Beeching came out to her parents earlier this year and to the Archbishop of Canterbury Justin Welby shortly after that. Because Beeching isn't an evangelical Anglican but she still considers herself evangelical. She says "Church is still my family. Families do not always agree or see eye to eye, but families stick together and I am committed to being a part of the church and working for change."[12]

I wonder what change that's going to be? Get people to accept sin instead of filtering out sin, like the Bereans? It's bad enough that the words are being changed to meet the new self-centered, self-esteem needs of the Church and getting people to accept sin but we have apostatized so much and have adamantly refused to be good Bereans that many of the so-called Christian musicians aren't even Christians at all! I'm not making this up! Check this out!

"Convicted Christian Singer Admits to Being an Atheist and that He duped Fans just to Sell Music.

Tim Lambesis, front man for a so-called Christian rock band (As I Lay Dying) was convicted of attempting to hire a hitman to murder his estranged wife and he admitted that the band duped fans into believing that they were Christian in order to sell their music.

"Truthfully, I was an atheist," said Tim. "I wasn't actually the first guy in the band to stop being a Christian. In fact, I think I was the third. The two who remained kind of stopped talking about it, and then I'm pretty sure they dropped it, too."

Then one sin led to another, turning his renunciation of Christ into justification for his actions.

"The first time I cheated on my wife, my interpretation of morality was now convenient for me." I felt less guilty. I decided, "Well, marriage isn't real,

because Christianity isn't real. God isn't real. Therefore, marriage is just a stupid piece of paper with the government."

But he continued to profess to be a Christian, as did others in the band, to sell records to Christian music fans.

"I remember one Christian festival where an interviewer wanted one of the guys in the band to share his testimony, and he just froze. We laughed about it afterward, but we were only laughing because it was so awkward."
"When kids would want to pray with us after shows, I'd be like, 'Um, you go ahead and pray!' I would just let them pray. I'd say 'Amen.'"

He said that during his tenure with the band, he realized that a number of bands that also professed to be Christians were faking their faith just as he was.

"We toured with more 'Christian bands' who were not Christians than those who were. In 12 years of touring, I would say maybe 1 in 10 Christian bands we toured with were actually Christian bands."

"A lot of Christian parents said, 'Yes, you can buy this CD, because they're a Christian band.' They don't even think to actually check the lyrics." [12]

What did the heretics of the Early Church do to get people to swallow their false teaching? They put they're heresies to music and called it Christian and infected the church and it led people astray! And it's being repeated today! This is what Peter warned about in the last days!

2 Peter 2:1-3 "But there were also false prophets among the people, just as there will be false teachers among you. They will secretly introduce destructive heresies, even denying the sovereign Lord who bought them – bringing swift destruction on themselves. Many will follow their shameful ways and will bring the way of truth into disrepute. In their greed, these teachers will exploit you with stories they have made up. Their condemnation has long been hanging over them, and their destruction has not been sleeping."

I wonder how these guys could worm their way into the church in the last days and introduce these destructive heresies? Maybe they'll use an old tactic. Maybe they'll get the Church to not be Bereans anymore and instead ingest

Apostate Media & Music, and charge them for it, just like the text says! Good thing we don't see any signs of that happening any time soon!

Who would have thought, that we'd see in our lifetime, the Church being flooded with Fake Apostate Pastors filling pulpits in droves! The Church forbidding people from sharing with others how they are a sinner in need of a Savior in order to go to heaven and now the Church has a new and improved self-worship service in the church saying sin is perfectly fine, which is the same message as Satanism.

That's why experts are now saying, "China is becoming more Christian than the U.S." "China may soon be home to the world's largest Christian population, despite attacks on religious freedom over there." "Estimates vary, but there is thought to be about 50 and 100 million Chinese believers in China, with up to 10,000 people coming to faith across the country every single day."[13]

Why? Because they are still being good Bereans who are holding to the true Word of God and are doing just what the book of Acts said to do, "And many believed." They not only warn that, "America is on the decline, but our country may soon no longer be the last bastion of hope for the Christian faith." "Pretty soon we may need to start supporting the American Church with our finances, missionaries, and theological resources."

Why? Because the Bible says in the last days, not only is the world going to go down the tubes morally, but so is the Church in Apostasy! It's all happening right now

The 4th reason why people in the church have turned from the basic truths of Christianity is due to **Apostate Behavior**.

All this apostate slide in the pulpit, in the Church, in the media and in the music is leading somewhere. You reap what you sow. It's called apostate behavior! What you believe determines how you behave! And Jesus said there's going to be one specific apostate behavior that would appear on the scene right before He came back, and the Church is falling for it big time! But don't take my word for it. Let's listen to His.

Luke 17:22-30 "Then He said to His disciples, 'The time is coming when you will long to see one of the days of the Son of Man, but you will not see it. Men will tell you, 'There He is!' or 'Here He is!' Do not go running off after them. For the Son of Man in His day will be like the lightning, which flashes and lights up the sky from one end to the other. But first He must suffer many things and be rejected by this generation. Just as it was in the days of Noah, so also will it be in the days of the Son of Man. People were eating, drinking, marrying and being given in marriage up to the day Noah entered the ark. Then the flood came and destroyed them all. It was the same in the days of Lot. People were eating and drinking, buying and selling, planting and building. But the day Lot left Sodom, fire and sulfur rained down from heaven and destroyed them all. It will be just like this on the day the Son of Man is revealed.'"

According to our text, Jesus clearly tells us two things to be on the lookout for regarding His Second Coming, right? How do you know it's getting close? How do you know Jesus is getting ready to come back? What did He say there? He said, "When you see the same society arise on the scene that was present in Noah's day and who's day? Lot's Day, that He'd be right around the corner and you better get ready," right?

As we saw before, Noah's day was a day that was filled with absolute utter wickedness all the time. The Bible says, "Their thoughts were only evil all the time." And hello! We're already there! But, He also mentioned Lot. And so, let's do our homework, and let's see what were the Days of Lot like. Let's see if we're getting close to that too.

Genesis 19:1-7,12-13 "The two angels arrived at Sodom in the evening, and Lot was sitting in the gateway of the city. When he saw them, he got up to meet them and bowed down with his face to the ground. 'My lords,' he said, 'please turn aside to your servant's house. You can wash your feet and spend the night and then go on your way early in the morning.' 'No,' they answered, 'we will spend the night in the square.' But he insisted so strongly that they did go with him and entered his house. He prepared a meal for them, baking bread without yeast, and they ate. Before they had gone to bed, all the men from every part of the city of Sodom – both young and old – surrounded the house. They called to Lot, 'Where are the men who came to you tonight? Bring them out to us so that we can have sex with them. Lot went outside to meet them and shut the door behind him and said, 'No, my friends. Don't do this wicked thing. The two men said to Lot, 'Do you have anyone else here – sons-in-law, sons or daughters, or anyone else in the city who belongs to you? Get them out of here, because we are going to destroy this place. The outcry to the LORD against its people is so great that He has sent us to destroy it.'"

How many of you would say God did not approve of these people's behavior? I think it's clear as to why God destroyed the cities of Sodom and Gomorrah and the surrounding areas. It was because they were involved in a wicked behavior called what? Homosexuality, right? It invited the judgment of God, right?

I don't know about you, but it's a good thing we see no signs of that making a comeback today anytime soon in our society, inviting the judgment of God, yeah right! It's all over the place! This is so prevalent today, yet hardly anyone realizes it's a major sign we're living in the last days! As it was in the Days of Noah and Lot! This behavior would have to make a comeback before Jesus returned and it is!

The problem is, as soon as you speak up against it, you get labeled as a judgmental, mean, horrible person, and all that other stuff, right? But we don't make up the rules, God does! And His rules say that behavior is not a lifestyle, it's a sin.

Leviticus 18:22 "Do not lie with a man as one lies with a woman; that is detestable."

Romans 1:26-27 "Because of this, God gave them over to shameful lusts. Even their women exchanged natural relations for unnatural ones. In the same way, the men also abandoned natural relations with women and were inflamed with lust for one another. Men committed indecent acts with other men, and received in themselves the due penalty for their perversion."

1 Corinthians 6:9-10 "Or do you not know that the unrighteous will not inherit the kingdom of God? Do not be deceived; neither fornicators, nor idolaters, nor adulterers, nor effeminate, nor homosexuals, nor thieves, nor covetous, nor drunkards, nor revilers, nor swindlers, will inherit the kingdom of God."

I don't know how you can get any clearer than this, Old Testament, New Testament, according to God's Word, homosexuality and lesbianism is not acceptable to God. The Scripture calls it detestable, a perversion, shameful and you're not going to the Kingdom of God unless you repent of it, as well as your other sins, and turn to Jesus Christ as your Lord and Savior. And yet, even though it's absolutely clear in the text, people still refuse to say homosexuality is a sin, and instead call it a lifestyle, or a social rights issue. But let's put that belief to the test.

It also mentions there in that text not just homosexuality, but thievery. Is thievery a social rights issue? Is thievery a lifestyle? If someone chose to become a thief as a way of life, does that make it acceptable? No! Of course not! And neither would they use this as a defense in court. "I'm sorry your honor, you can't send me to jail. You can't prosecute me! That's just my lifestyle. I have a social right to rob that bank!" That would be ludicrous, right?

Yet, the exact same tactic is being used today to justify homosexuality and lesbianism. The Bible says they are a sin just like being a thief. And just because you relabel a sin, doesn't cease to make it a sin! Yet this is what our nation is doing, and the Bible says you're inviting the judgment of God, as this man shares.

"What our Founding Fathers referred to as drunkenness because of their Christian heritage, we now call it alcoholism and deem it a social disease, rather than a sin. What our Founding Fathers called immorality, we now call it the new morality; what the law called adultery or fornication, we now call stepping out or fooling around; and what the Law called abhorrent social behavior (like stealing or filthy language), we now call abnormal social development or anti-social behavior. What the Law-Word called sodomy, we now call an alternative life style."[14]

Call it what you want, relabel it what you want, all it's doing is storing up the wrath of God. I didn't say that Isaiah did!

Isaiah 5:20 "Woe to those who call evil good, and good evil; Who substitute darkness for light and light for darkness; Who substitute bitter for sweet and sweet for bitter!"

You tell me that's not our country right now! We're calling evil good and good evil, and we're substituting darkness for light, right? And what did the text say? We're headed for incredibly awesome times! NO! It said we're headed for woeful times! That's bad, not good! Why? Because as it was in the Days of LOT so shall it be at the Coming of the Son of Man. That behavior invites the judgment of God! In fact, they're using the exact same tactic they used in Lot's Day to force people to go along with this. Let's take a look at that text again.

Genesis 19:9 "Get out of our way,' they replied. And they said, 'This fellow came here as an alien, and now he wants to play the judge! We'll treat you worse than them.' They kept bringing pressure on Lot and moved forward to break down the door."

How many would say, that's a little violent? I'm telling you, this is the same tactic being used on us today! We are being pressured, we are being forced, we are being told we have to go along with this agenda, otherwise we too are being judgmental, knock it off! And if you don't believe me, let's take a look at all the different ways we are being pressured into accepting this behavior across our country. It's coming from all over, The Days of Lot are upon us!

MEDIA: Facebook now gives you options to define your gender. Not only will you be able to identify as transgender, genderqueer, intersex, etc., but you'll be able to specify what gender pronouns you want to be referred to as, he/his she/her, or he neutral they/their. Previously, Facebook users were required to select either "male" or "female" in the gender identification field. Users now have the option to select "Custom" to better express their gender identities.

Nintendo promises to push the gay agenda on children. The Japanese company stated in future releases they will "strive to design a gameplay experience from the ground up that is more inclusive, and better represents all players."

The Discovery Channel is launching a new transsexual kids cartoon called, "SheZow." It follows the supposed adventures of a 12-year-old boy named Guy who uses a magic ring to transform himself into a crime-fighting girl.

A cartoon for kids put out by Disney about a boy that finds a ring that turns him into a girl, a super girl. When danger is around he turns into a girl with the power to scream to stop trucks in their paths or turns his hand into a hand large enough to slap 3 people onto the ground. He/She also has psychic powers that lets her know when danger is near. She has more strength and speed than any girl needs.[15]

SCHOOLS: Dictionaries are now being rewritten to refer to marriage as gender neutral. The Chambers Dictionary has released its 13th edition with marriage now being defined as "the ceremony, act or contract by which two people become married to each other." "Husband" and "wife" were also altered to encompass married gay couples. Husband is defined as "a man to whom someone is married," while wife is "a woman to whom someone is married."

A school in Nebraska is now teaching that we should no longer say "Boys and Girls" but use "Gender Inclusive Words" like Purple Penguins.

A school district in Nebraska has given middle-school teachers a document that advises them to, "Avoid asking kids to line up as boys or girls or separating them by gender. Instead, use things like 'odd and even birth date,' or 'Which would you choose: skateboards or bikes/milk or juice/dogs or cats/summer or winter/talking or listening.' Invite students to come up with choices themselves. The teachers were also given a handout called, "The Gender bred Person" and encouraged to say things like 'calling all readers,' or 'hey campers' or ask all of the 'purple penguins' to meet at the rug."

In another school in Glenview California, teachers celebrated LGBT month and taught five and six-year-old children how to celebrate gay pride as well. The teacher stands in front of her classroom and says, "This morning we are so lucky to be celebrating our first Glenview family pride celebration".

The guest speaker comes to the podium, "I am really, really excited about today. I'm excited that it is June, it's Pride month, and I'm excited that we are bringing this assembly to the entire Glenview community.

I want to talk to you guys, really quickly, about this flag. Anyone recognize this flag?" It is a rainbow flag. "Please raise your hands". As many of the students raise their hands she says, "Wow, that is incredible." "All the people I'm going to show you in these pictures and talk about right now are gay or lesbian or bi". Says another guest speaker as she raises the first picture for the children to see. "She was at Madison last year and she is a lesbian and her partners name is Julie. This is Bill T. Jones, he was also at Madison last year, he is a very famous dancer, he's African American".

One of the kids asks, "Is he gay?" and she answers "yes".

Everything changes when same sex marriage becomes legal. If it is legalized then it must be taught as normal, acceptable, and moral behavior in every public school. Don't believe me, it's already happened in Massachusetts. That means public schools in every grade, even kindergarten must teach your children to accept same sex marriage.

One father says, "Our son Jacob was going in kindergarten and he came home with a diversity book bag. I have the book right here. 'Who's in the family' that introduces children to such things as Clifford and her dads' partner Henry." The reporter asks, "This is what they sent home with your 5-year-old?" "That is correct, Tony," answers the dad. Then the reporter asks, "What was your first reaction when you saw this?" The mother answers, "When I saw the book I was quite upset that they would count this diversity and include it in the diversity book bag and not give me notification.[16]

MEDICAL: A medical doctor is now saying, "I correct God's mistakes." Referring to sex change operations, Dr. Kim says, "I've decided to defy God's will. At first, I agonized over whether I should do these operations because I wondered if I was defying God. I was overcome with a sense of shame. But my patients desperately wanted these surgeries. Without them, they'd kill themselves." And now thanks to the medical industry, three married lesbians, who say they are the only 'throuple' in the world, are expecting their first child together. Doll and Brynn Young, from Massachusetts, were dating for 2.5 years when they decided to spice up their relationship with an additional partner. They met Kitten, 27, and they all three married each other last year. After undergoing injections with an anonymous sperm donor, Kitten is now several months pregnant with the trio's child.

Sex change drugs will now be offered to children. Children as young as nine years old are soon to be prescribed drugs which will delay the onset of puberty as the first step towards a sex change operation, according to reports. The treatment will be offered to children who are so troubled by their gender and who may wish to undergo drastic surgery after adolescence.

Obamacare now covers gender reassignment surgeries. What gets covered varies from Obamacare policy to policy, but Transgender Law Center says, "The law and policy are on a transgender person's side for the first time." Over the next ten years, Obamacare will cost U.S. taxpayers $2.6 trillion.

BUSINESS: Burger King recently came out with it's new "Proud Whopper" in a rainbow –colored wrapper in honor of the 44th annual Gay Pride Celebration & Parade in San Francisco.

At the 2014 Gay Pride in San Francisco, a reporter asks, "What do you think of the Burger King introducing the proud whopper?" "What, so like it's a gay burger?" says a bystander. Another says, "I just don't really believe in the homosexual lifestyle." "I think it's cool, I think it's a cool idea, I think it's great".

"Finally, it's about time." "Do gay people even eat fast food?" A kid holding up the flag says, "I think this means everyone has the same rights". Another child calls out, "I love my two mommies"[17]

And Betty Crocker is now giving away free cakes to gay couples getting married and Lucky Charms showed their support by using the Lucky Charms rainbow marshmallow as a sign of gay pride and handed out Lucky Charms and rainbow accessories at various Gay Pride events. Target has now released their new commercial featuring two lesbian women preparing their room for their baby. Here's the actual commercial.

I'm Amanda and I'm Kat and we're having a baby. As they are talking the camera scans the new baby's bedroom showing all the decorations and new furniture. We don't know what the gender is yet but we are really excited to find out. Amanda says, "I hope the baby has Kat's talent." Kat says, "I hope the baby has Amanda's quick wit." "We want our child to know that anything is possible and that there is nothing wrong with, and everything right with, perusing knowledge and learning everything about the world.

And that's right, Starbucks CEO even recently share with shareholders, "If you support Biblical marriage, sell your shares. You can sell your shares in Starbucks and buy shares in another company. Thank you very much."

And Chase Bank is now requiring their employees to answer a threatening LGBT survey. Here's the actual survey:

Are you:
1) A person with disabilities;
2) A person with children with disabilities;
3) A person with a spouse/domestic partner with disabilities;
4) A member of the LGBT community.
5) An ally of the LGBT community, but not personally identifying as LGBT.

The employee who reported on this survey said "This survey wasn't anonymous. You had to enter your employee ID." And stories from all over are now beginning to pour in from Fortune 500 companies like Blue Cross, Citi Bank, and other companies of how people are being terminated for not being perceived as an "ally" of the LGBT agenda.

SATANISM: The Satanic Temple spokesman, Lucien Greaves, said in a recent interview that, "Gay marriage is a sacrament," and that, "One of the things we feel strongly about is gay rights. And there's been a lot of progress, but there's still a lot of progress to be made."

COURTS: State marriage bans have been falling around the country since the U.S. Supreme Court recently struck down part of the federal Defense of Marriage Act. Currently 27 States Have Legal Same-Sex Marriages and recent court action is expected to bring the total to 30. In fact, there is a new Bill on the books in California that will give new options for people's birth certificates. "Assembly Bill 1951 would allow a lesbian couple to state on a birth certificate that a child has two mothers, a mother and female "father," or two female "fathers." Likewise, a gay couple could self-identify as two fathers, a father and a male "mother," or two male "mothers."

PRESIDENT: Obama purposely picked an openly gay bishop to offer the closing prayer at the annual White House Easter Prayer Breakfast. He also proclaimed June as LGBT month and has gone on record as being the first President in American history to voice his support for gay marriage. Oh, but that's not all. Obama also said that the United States needs to become a "Global Leader in Promoting Gay Rights." "America's support for LGBT rights is not just a national cause, but it's also a global enterprise." And the Obama administration made gay rights a centerpiece of its foreign policy. And yet the official stats from the US Census Bureau reveal that only about 8% of the American population would consider themselves LGBT and an even more recent report from the CDC showed that its way less than that. "Less than 3% of Americans have identified themselves as gay, lesbian, or bisexual." "The overwhelming majority of adults, 96.6 percent, labeled themselves as straight. 1.1 percent declined to answer, or responded "I don't know the answer" or said they were "something else."

ABC news reports:

"He used to think that for gay and lesbian couple's civil union would suffice but now President Obama has concluded that's is not enough. During this ABC news interview, he became the first President ever to support gay marriage."

The President speaks, "For me personally, it is important to me to go ahead and affirm that I think that same sex couples should be able to get married. American's may be still be evolving with marriage equality but as I have indicated personally, Michelle and I, made up our minds on this issue. So, we still have a long way to go but we will get there. And as long as I have the privilege of being your president I promise you won't have just a President in the White House but you will have a fellow advocate for America, where no matter what you look like, or where you come from or who you love, you can dream big dreams and dream as openly as you want."[18]

    I don't know about you, but that's a whole lot of pressure from a serious minority. And yet we're led to believe this is what "everybody" even around the world wants, and we need to push it? We're going to get judged folks! You reap what you sow! As it was in the Days of Lot so shall it be at the Coming of the Son of Man.
    We're being pressured, forced, and threatened to accept this behavior, just like in the Days of Lot. But praise God the Church is standing strong! Why, we'll never put up with this, we're going to stand on God's Word and that settles it! Yeah right! You talk about apostate behavior!
    As I said at the beginning, all this apostate behavior in the pulpit, in the Church, in the media & in the music is culminating into the exact opposite

behavior in the Church that God says to do in regard to this behavior. Here's how we're supposed to respond.

1 Corinthians 5:9-13 "I have written you in my letter not to associate with sexually immoral people – not at all meaning the people of this world who are immoral, or the greedy and swindlers, or idolaters. In that case you would have to leave this world. But now I am writing you that you must not associate with anyone who calls himself a brother but is sexually immoral or greedy, an idolater or a slanderer, a drunkard or a swindler. With such a man do not even eat. What business is it of mine to judge those outside the church? Are you not to judge those inside? God will judge those outside. Expel the wicked man from among you."

According to our text, I don't know how you get any clearer than this, but the Bible says the Church's appropriate response to sexual immorality in the Church, like in the case of homosexuality or lesbianism among others, is to what?

Do not associate with them! Don't even eat with them! Why? So, they'd be ashamed of their behavior! How can you say you're a Christian and keep doing this, let alone expect us to condone this??? But for the non-Christian in the world, it doesn't say we can't hang out with them because somebody's got to witness to them, right? Otherwise, you'd have to leave the world as Paul says. And by the way, I'll state it on record, we true Christians are not advocating any "hate" or "violence" or "bodily harm" to anyone who is involved in any immorality like homosexuality or lesbianism, okay? And shame on anyone who says they're a born again Christian and they do! Knock it off, you're giving the rest of us a BAD NAME. That's not how you share the LOVE of Jesus Christ!

Just like anybody else in the world involved in sin, we witness to them with the love of Jesus Christ so they can be rescued from the penalty of sin, namely hell! Homosexuality doesn't keep you out of Heaven, undealt with sin does! Refusing to turn to Jesus Christ and ask for the forgiveness of all your sins does!

Homosexuality is not the unpardonable sin. All sin is sin, whether it's lying, stealing, adultery, or whatever. Sin is sin and if it's not dealt with through Jesus, the Bible says you're going to hell. But praise God, through Jesus Christ anyone and everyone can be forgiven of all sin no matter what you've done and that's the loving message He's entrusted us to share with the world! But in the Church, different story.

Those who would say they're a Christian and they continue to engage in this behavior, and refuse to repent, what do we do? We don't associate with them! We don't even eat with them! Why? So, they would be ashamed of their behavior! God has a standard. For those of you who don't believe me, that they should be ashamed of their behavior, listen to what Paul says. Paul uses the exact same word in Thessalonians.

2 Thessalonians 3:14 "If anyone does not obey our instruction in this letter, take special note of that person and do not associate with him, so that he will be put to shame."

The Bible says that shame is not bad, it's good. Why? Because it helps bring about conviction. You need to acknowledge that what you're doing is wrong so you can repent of it and be healed! If you don't, I'm not supposed to hang out with you so you'll feel bad about it, so you'll get right with God. It's meant for your good!

This is exactly what the Church is NOT doing! You talk about apostasy! They're helping people stay locked into the bondage of sin! This is how far it's gone! This is how far we have fallen! We're not only still associating with those who say they're Christians in the Church who are committing immorality, let alone homosexuality but we're also removing any sense of shame for sinful behavior and saying that those who oppose them are the real sinners! I'm not making this up! Check this out!

We all know how major denominations all across America are now sliding on this issue Biblically and have actually moved to the point where they are now approving homosexual behavior and marriages, as well as homosexual pastors behind the pulpit. But it's getting so bad in the Church that:

- *Christian Book Publishers are now printing and supporting Pro-lesbian, gay, bi-sexual and transgender books.*

- *The United Church of Christ with its 5,100 Churches across America is supporting the 9th annual Gay Games in Ohio.*

- *The United Methodist Church is granting benefits to its employees involved in same-sex marriages.*

- *A Baptist Church in Kentucky is holding gay weddings.*

- *A Southern Baptist Pastor, Danny Cortez from Los Angeles, announced his change of mind on the issue of homosexuality and same-sex relationships. He then acknowledged that his change of heart on the issue put him at odds with the SBC's confession of faith, the Baptist Faith & Message, but the Church voted on May 18 of this year not to dismiss the pastor and "to instead become a Third Way Church." Soon after he was invited to attend a 'gay pride' reception at the White House with President Obama. Later in a letter Cortez wrote, "This is a huge step for a Southern Baptist church!!"*

- *And speaking of huge steps, for the first time in history, a national Christian denomination, the United Church of Christ, is suing the state of North Carolina to allow gay marriage.*

- *And recently, the Washington National Cathedral not only hosted its first transgender priest celebrating "LGBT month," but Gary Hall, the chief ecclesiastical leader and executive officer of the National Cathedral said that "Homophobia and Heterosexism is a sin."*[19]

ABC reports:

If the Washington National Cathedral's recent decision to celebrate same sex marriages didn't make our stance on the LGBT community clear, then Rev. Gary Hall's statements during his regular Sunday sermon definitely should. Hall told congregants on Sunday that the church must quote, "have the courage to call homophobia and heterosexism what they are, a sin."

The reverend also called the churches role in oppressing the LGBT community shameful. He says, "It's wisdom that the church came to its senses over time and labeled both racism and sexism as sinful. And now we find ourselves at this last barrier of our human identity. You can call that barrier homophobia, you can call that barrier heterosexism. But we must now have the courage to take the final step to call homophobia and heterosexism what they are.

They are sin. Homophobia is a sin. Heterosexism is a sin. Shaming people for whom they love is a sin. Shaming people because their gender identity does not fit neatly into your sense of what it should be is a sin."[20]

A sin? God's standard has now become a sin in the Church? As it was in the Days of LOT so shall it be at the Coming of the Son of Man! Who in the world would have thought, that we'd see in our lifetime, the Church being flooded with fake apostate pastors filling pulpits in droves. The Church forbidding people from sharing with others how they are a sinner in need of a Savior in order to go to heaven. A new and improved so-called self-worship service in the Church that celebrates self, the number one law of Satanism. Believers getting their spiritual truths from apostate, new age, atheist movies and listening to apostate music gutted of the name of Jesus.

And now the Church is saying that homosexuality is not a sin but acceptable and that those who oppose it are the real sinners. Can you believe that? The days of Apostasy are here! In fact, apparently, so is the arrival of the Antichrist! Little does the apostate Church know that they're not only *not* following God's Word, the Words of Christ but they're actually preparing people to receive the actual antichrist.

Daniel 11:36-37 "Then the king will do as he pleases, and he will exalt and magnify himself above every god and will speak monstrous things against the God of gods; and he will prosper until the indignation is finished, for that which is decreed will be done. He will show no regard for the gods of his fathers or for the desire of women."

Interesting, you mean to tell me the Antichrist has no desire for women? What do you call that? Oh yeah, that's homosexuality. And now the Church is helping to promote it, just in time for the Antichrist's arrival. Can you believe it? 20 years ago, this would never have been possible! But today, right now, it's progressed so far that "66% of Americans, right now, said they would vote for a gay President." You know, a Political Leader, like the Antichrist!

This is all happening right now! The Days of Lot are upon us, which means Jesus Christ is getting ready to come back for us, and the judgment of God is at hand! Out of love, God has given us all these signs of the rise of apostasy to show us that the Tribulation is near and the Rapture is right around the corner! And that's why Jesus Himself said;

Luke 21:28 "When these things begin to take place, stand up and lift up your heads, because your redemption is drawing near."

Everything's going down the tubes, including the Church, and you don't want to be here! It's going to be the worst time in the history of mankind! Let's get busy working together fulfilling the Great Commission doing something splendid for Jesus, by holding to the truth, not budging from it! Why? Because the truth is what sets people free, not a watered-down version of it!

But if you're reading this and you're still not saved, you better accept Jesus Christ now as your Lord and Savior before it's too late! Don't delay! Today could be your last day!

Chapter Seven

One World Religion

"Well hey, for those of you who don't know, Orson, he is the absolute master mechanic of all time. I mean, he can fix anything bar none. So, a couple weeks ago, he finds this beat up old moped and he decides to fix it.

He gets it running, and goes to the gas station near Lake Mead to get some gas, and low and behold, he sees Jon there putting gas in his new hotrod.

Well, Orson being a car buff and all, he asks Jon if he could check out his new red hotrod. So, he's looking under the hood at the engine and Jon goes in to pay for gas and comes back and he shuts the hood and starts it up.

Well get this, as Jon is pulling out of the gas station in his hotrod, he decides to give Orson a bit of a show. You know, feeling pretty cool about his truck, we'll see who's the master mechanic around here, so he punched it and raced right out of the gas station.

But suddenly, Jon looks in his rear-view mirror and he sees that Orson is about to pass him on his moped. So, Jon hit the gas even more, but Orson just flew right on by. Jon couldn't believe it. That moped just passed him like he was on blocks.

Then to Jon's amazement, here came Orson back the other way again. So, Jon thought, 'Well now he's just toying with me.' So, this time Jon really punched it. He took the truck up to 100 mph but Orson still just flew right on by.

But about a half mile down the road, Jon noticed Orson coming the other way again but this time in his lane, so they hit head on and crashed. Jon grabs his cell phone and called for help, and then rushed to Orson's side.

And as Jon was waiting for the help to arrive he asked Orson, 'What in the world did you do to that moped to make it so fast?'

And Orson replied, 'I didn't do anything Jon. When you closed the hood on your truck, you caught my suspenders.'"[1]

How many of you would say that Jon needed to pay closer attention to what was going on, you know what I'm saying? His lack of attention to details cost somebody, namely Orson, some serious pain didn't it. But that's right, believe it or not, did you know Jon's not the only one who's got a serious problem with paying attention to details creating some havoc in their lives?

The Bible says the whole planet's doing the same thing, they're not paying attention to the details of receiving Jesus Christ as their Lord and Savior, and as a result, they are headed for the worst wreck of all time! It's called the 7-year Tribulation and that's not a joke! The Bible says it's an outpouring of God's wrath on a wicked and rebellious planet.

The 8th update of the study letting us know we're living in the last days is the rise of a One World Religion.

What? Are you serious? All the religions of the planet are going to come under the head of one man, the Antichrist, and his buddy the False Prophet? Uh, yeah! And what's wild is that all these dead, fake, phony apostate Christians we've been seeing in the last chapter, they're going to go right along with it. Can you believe that? Don't take my word for it. Let's listen to God's.

Revelation 13:3-9 "One of the heads of the beast seemed to have had a fatal wound, but the fatal wound had been healed. The entire world was astonished and followed the beast. Men worshiped the dragon because he had given authority to the beast, and they also worshiped the beast and asked, 'Who is like the beast? Who can make war against him?' The beast was given a mouth to utter proud words and blasphemies and to exercise his authority for forty-two months. He opened his mouth to blaspheme God, and to slander his name and his dwelling place and those who live in heaven. He was given power to make war against the saints and to conquer them. And he was given authority over every tribe, people, language and nation. All inhabitants of the earth will worship the beast – all whose names have not been written in the book of life belonging to the Lamb that was slain from the creation of the world. He who has an ear, let him hear"

In other words, you better pay attention to this! According to our text, the Bible clearly says that there is coming a day when all the inhabitants of the earth are going to be busy worshiping who? The actual Antichrist himself, right? One day, the Bible says, the entire world will be unified into a One World Religion that is satanically inspired.

But that's the question. "Could this really happen? Could the whole world really be deceived into creating a One World Religion that the Antichrist is going to hijack and take over and say, "Now worship me!" Yes! In fact, its happening right now before our very eyes!

The 1st way we know we're really headed for a One World Religion is due to a **Worldwide Assault on Christians**.

What I'm talking about is the rise of **Christian Persecution**, specifically Christians, and once again, if you put yourself in the Antichrist's shoes, it makes perfect sense. If you're going to deceive the world into creating a One World Religion, then at some point you have to get rid of anyone who doesn't go along with your program, right? Of course! That's exactly what the Bible says, the Antichrist is going to do specifically to God's people in the last days! But don't take my word for it. Let's listen to Jesus.

Matthew 24:3-10 "As Jesus was sitting on the Mount of Olives, the disciples came to Him privately. 'Tell us,' they said, 'when will this happen, and what will be the sign of Your coming and of the end of the age?' Jesus answered: 'Watch out that no one deceives you. For many will come in My Name, claiming, 'I am the Christ,' and will deceive many. You will hear of wars and rumors of wars, but see to it that you are not alarmed. Such things must happen, but the end is still to come. Nation will rise against nation, and kingdom against kingdom. There will be famines and earthquakes in various places. All these are the beginning of birth pains. Then you will be handed over to be persecuted and put to death, and you will be hated by all nations because of Me. At that time, many will turn away from the faith and will betray and hate each other."

Jesus clearly says that not only one day the whole planet is going to hate followers of Him, but that many people who claim to be "in the faith" i.e. Christians, will actually betray and hate others who are "really in the faith," the true Christians.

That's why I've said for years, you better be careful. The person sitting next to you in the pew, may one day be the death of you. They might turn you in to the authorities! Why? Because not everyone who goes to a church service is a Christian! Going to a church service doesn't make you a Christian any more than sitting in a barn makes you a cow! You have got to be born again! This is the same thing that happened to the underground Church in Europe when Communism came in and took over. It's the same tactic. They told the churches they would leave them alone, they could have their freedom, but they actually sent fake phony spies, people claiming to be Christians, into the church service to spy on people and report any who didn't agree with the State.

And then, one by one, those people who disagreed disappeared until all that was left in the church were those who would go along with the Communist Agenda. It's documented, that's how they took over. I'm telling you, the same exact tactic is being used on us here in America, and it's given rise to what Jesus said will happen!

There's going to come a day when the whole world is going to hate you just for being a follower of Jesus. Even to the point where they're going to want to kill you! And for those of you wondering, the context here is during the 7-year Tribulation, so the people He's talking about here, being hunted down and killed, are the Jewish remnant who follow Christ after their temporary blindness is removed, those who get saved after the rapture. During the 7-year Tribulation people can still get saved, the Gospel still goes forth from multiple sources, The Two Witnesses, the 144,000 male Jewish witnesses, the Angel of God who proclaims the Eternal Gospel and anything you and I might leave behind.

But the point is this. You should have got saved before the hammer came down. Now you're going to pay for it with a price, your life.

But again, here's the point for you and I today. Do we see any signs of this rise of hatred towards Christianity around the world that they actually want to kill us and they're sending people into the Church to turn us in? It's already here, all over the world! And they're using two wedges, I believe, to get the job done. One is the homosexual issue (a moral issue) and the other is pluralism (a spiritual issue).

First let's deal with homosexuality. Here's the premise. Put yourself in the Antichrist's shoes. If you're going to get rid of Christians, then you first must have a good excuse for getting rid of them in the first place, right? You know, like what Nero did with blaming Christians for the burning of Rome. And then once we became the bad guys, the troublemakers, they went about killing us, right? You got your excuse, now you can go slaughter them with people's approval.

I'm telling you, this is precisely what's being done with the homosexual movement. Because we disagree with their immoral behavior, it's become the excuse to label us as being mean, judgmental, intolerant, and dangerous to the point where they now say what we believe is a hate crime and we need to go to jail! Don't believe me? It's already happening even here in America and around the world.

"What do we want, equality, we want it now, what do we want, equality, we want it now" an activist is shouting. Janet Porter, Faith2Action, reports: We have been battling this for months but marriage isn't about equality. By trampling on marriage, homosexual activist wants to reshape the culture into something we won't even recognize. But this battle isn't about marriage.

It's about driving the homosexual flag into yet another segment of society and then using it as a club to silence all dissent. To label anyone who disagrees as a hater. Just like someone visiting the Family Research Council after the Southern Poverty Law Center slapped them with the hate group label. Peter Sprigg, of the Family Research Council: We found 50 rounds of ammunition and 15 Chick-Fil-A sandwiches in his backpack and he admitted that he intended to shoot and kill as many possible members of the staff of the Southern Poverty Law Center, and he intended to smear the Chick-Fil-A in the faces of his victims. He had chosen his target multiple times by looking at the website of the Southern Poverty Law Center. And because they had designated The Family Research Council as an 'anti-gay hate group' and placed us on their hit map which is still on their website, that is how he chose us as his target"

Once marriage is redefined that becomes a foundation for traditional and Christian beliefs to be marginalized. It's no longer speculation. When Massachusetts courts redefined marriage, K thru 12 homosexual indoctrination intensified and parental rights became a thing of the past. Parents, David & Tonia Parker tell us, "After the diversity book bag came home we realized that the intention of the administrator and teachers was to affirm the relationships of gay marriage in the minds of the children. When we went in to the school, what we requested is parental notification when these issues are brought up by adults within the school and the option to opt our child out of this kind of indoctrination.

When you wish to affirm homosexuality to our son, you're presenting that which is sin as though it is not to our son and we cannot allow that. To make a long story short the accommodation they gave was to put me in handcuffs and send me to jail." This battle isn't about marriage, it's about freedom. "They were willing to handcuff a father and send him to jail. It was a 6 by 8 cell, filthy, but I felt I didn't have a choice at that point. In order to fulfil my roll and duty as a father". If we care about our freedom we had better use it now. HELP US WARN THE CHURCH.[2]

    And you wonder why I'm preaching on this now! Folks, we better speak up, this is really happening, the persecution has already begun. And notice it wasn't just a pastor. But a Christian father, who simply objected to his son being taught homosexuality in school, was labeled as a hate crime, and was handcuffed and thrown into prison, in America! Not just a pastor, but now even your average born again Christian!

    I'm telling you, this is the first wedge, homosexuality, into getting rid of any and all Christians who won't go along with a *One World Religion*. This has become their excuse! They're weeding the true ones, Christians, from the fake ones, who will now go along with this. And now they're saying the fake ones who go along with this are the "real Christian" and the true ones are dangerous ones and need to be gotten rid of.

    True Biblical Evangelical Christianity is being eradicated and replaced with a fake phony apostate Church, who will go along with a *One World Religion*, and the tool they're using to get the job done is homosexuality! Let me show you just how far this tactic to eradicate true Christians from society, has infiltrated all sectors of society.

EDUCATION: For those of you who think you're just going to get a good education so you can equip others on the dangers of this moral issue and help them out, think again. You may not get that chance. Individual Christians like Jennifer Keeton and Julia Ward have been kicked out of graduate school counseling programs because of their moral objections to homosexual conduct, and Christian schools themselves are now under fire. Just one example is from Gordon College who has kept its Biblical code of behavior since 1889. Now, they have been given an ultimatum by the New England Association of Schools and Colleges (NEASC). "Be an accredited academic institution by accepting "homosexual practice" or you will lose your school accreditation." As one person stated, "This is an all-out assault against Christianity. If a secular agency can dictate the religious beliefs and worldviews of a Christian institution of higher learning, then religious freedom in this nation is over. If this succeeds, a tsunami of Christian schools departing from sound doctrine just to maintain government funding will follow, and we may soon find aspirants of ministry trained in the exegesis of political correctness rather than that of scripture."

BUSINESS: For those of you who think you're going to just start your own business and provide a great godly environment for your employees, think again. You may not get that chance. Right now, a baker in Oregon is being fined $150,000, told he needs "rehabilitation," and put out of business for declining to bake a cake for a lesbian wedding. A baker in Colorado was fined, ordered to bake a cake in violation of his own conscience, and sent to re-education camp for the same offense. A florist in Washington was pursued by the state attorney general for politely declining to make a floral arrangement for a same-sex wedding. A photographer in New Mexico was fined $6,700 for declining to do a photo shoot for a lesbian wedding. A T-shirt company was ordered to produce T-shirts to promote a message they find morally objectionable. In fact, if one senator gets his way, true Christians won't be allowed to own businesses anymore. Democratic Senator Chuck Schumer from New York said recently, "anyone whose religion teaches that the murder of an unborn child is wrong should simply not open a business in America." Gee, I wonder if homosexuality is next. What's that around his neck?

GOVERNMENT: For those of you who think you're going to run for office and help overturn some of these laws that are harming people, think again. You may not get that chance. Christians with Biblical values are being blocked from running for office in Canada. Canada's Liberal Party, recently announced that the Liberal Party will not allow anyone to run in any national election who does not pledge to vote "pro-choice" without exception. Trudeau also hinted that the party may make a similar stance on other "social" issues. He made it clear that there will be a litmus test for new candidates on a host of issues, stating that he will ask new people seeking to become candidates "how they feel about same-sex marriage", as well as abortion. In fact, one city in Canada moved to bar Christians from using public facilities.

The Sun reports: Last month the city council passed a shockingly bigoted motion. A motion to ban Christians who they find 'divisive' from using publicly funded facilities like the convention center here in town, just days before a Christian convention of sorts was being hosted at that convention center. This city council voted to cancel it. They had a debate, well debate is the wrong word, it was really a series of shocking rants against Christians that culminated in making most public buildings Christian free zones.

The Sun reports: Two Canadian Law Societies decided to ban Christian schooled lawyers from practicing law in the providences. The Law Society in upper Canada voted 28-21 to ban them. And just last week the Nova Scotia Barristers Society voted 10-9 to affectively blacklist Christians from that province too. The ban applies in advance to any and every lawyer who graduates from a law school at BC Trinity Western University.

And here in the United States, a gay judge in Dallas Texas has "Formally announced that she refuses to officiate at any marriage ceremony for heterosexual couples." But as one person said, "How can she get away with this if Christians are sued and fined every time they try to discriminate against gay marriage? " And it's so bad that a former U.S. Military General admitted, "Given the violation of religious liberties that have been going on in America, ironically, Christians are being forced into the closet. It's now become a policy of Don't Ask, Don't Tell, if you're a Christian. It used to be that you had to come out of the closet to admit you're homosexual, but now you have to come out of the closet to admit that you're a Christian."

MEDIA: For those of you who think you're just going to get the word out on the airwaves and help others to see the dangers of this behavior, think again. You may not get that chance. Individuals are being punished for it. Chris Culliver of the 49ers was sent to a re-education camp prior to the Super Bowl for laughing at homosexuality. The special-teams coach of the Minnesota Vikings was suspended and nearly fired for a joke about homosexuality. A safety for the Miami Dolphins was sent to re-education camp for tweeting out his displeasure over Michael Sam's slobbery homosexual kiss on draft day. A Canadian broadcaster was fired for defending man-woman marriage. Craig James was fired by Fox Sports Southwest for defending natural marriage in a senatorial campaign. In fact, you might soon go to jail for it. The previous administration was pushing the "Hate Crime Reporting Act of 2014" that if it had passed would task the National Telecommunications and Information Administration to, "begin scouring the Internet, TV and radio for speech it finds threatening." The legislation arrived four months after Duck Dynasty star Phil Robertson's comments about homosexuality which were labeled "hate speech." "If the legislation had passed, it would have finished the United States. We would find ourselves in the same situation as our Founding Fathers were in under British rule. We wouldn't be allowed to speak out against the government, homosexuals, illegals or dangerous religious extremists. We wouldn't be able to publicly teach the biblical principles on sin, homosexuality, fidelity, adultery, fornication, etc. or someone will be offended, making our words hate language. Websites would have be forced to shut down and Churches would have been forced to compromise the Word of God or close their doors and go into hiding and meeting at underground locations."

CHURCHES: For those of you who think you're just going to go into ministry or just be a vocal Christian and equip people with God's truth and warn them, think again. You may not get that chance. Since Obama was elected in 2009, dozens of laws and executive orders have been quietly put in place to create an environment that is heavily in favor of LGBT policies and practice. None of which have anything to do with "tolerance" or "acceptance of diversity", but rather seek to silence and instill fear in any and all who would oppose their agenda. And this has created such an atmosphere of "hatred" towards Biblical Christianity and the Bible that we are now seeing the day where preachers in the United States of America who preach the old-fashioned gospel will watch helplessly as their churches are taken from them, and they themselves placed in jail. Right now, the State of Idaho is telling Christian Pastors to perform same-sex marriages or they will go to jail. Donald Knapp, an ordained minister who opposes gay marriage now faces a 180-day jail term and $1,000 fine *for each day* he declines to celebrate the same-sex wedding. And other states are not only banning "Gay-Conversion Therapy" but just to make sure the resistance is quelled, the city of Houston recently subpoenaed pastor's sermons, emails and text messages to make sure they were not opposing the gay agenda.

FOX News Reports:

It is a shocking story out of Texas where the city of Houston has issued subpoenas demanding that a group of pastors turn over their sermons as part of a battle to enforce the equal rights ordinance in the city. Now ministers who fail to comply with the subpoena could be held in contempt of court.

Pastor Steve Riggle, did you get one of the subpoenas? Pastor Riggle of Grace Church, co-founder, answers, "I did, yes I did". Hannity asks, "What did it say?" Pastor answers, "Well, it wanted my sermons and emails and texts and anything that had been said about the equal rights ordinance or homosexuality or including Mayor Parker if I may have ever said anything about her. Communication with the congregation, they wanted any of that."

Erik Stanley joined in, "And contrary to the media report, the city is not backing off. The Mayor actually tweeted on her page that if the pastors were talking about this issued from the pulpit, their sermons are fair game". Pastor Riggle adds, "And I'll tell you this, with all due respect, there is no one that knows the mayor or the city attorney who would believe that they did not know about those subpoenas until yesterday."

Which is why one guy stated, "The U.S. Creed on gay marriage is like Sharia Law. Just as Christians and Jews are fined for their religion in countries governed by Sharia law, all citizens in America are required to approve of gay marriage and related sexual anomalies or be punished by the state." And if you don't think it will ever come to that, recently homosexuals "won the right" to get married in any church they choose in Denmark. The country's Parliament voted to make it "mandatory" that all churches in that country to conduct gay marriages.

New developments now involve a Lakewood Bakery accused of discriminating against a gay couple by refusing to sell them a wedding cake. Well, the state's civil rights committee says that bakery did violate discrimination laws. The wedding cakes at Master Peace cake shop are detailed and attractive. The conflict between some customers and the owner have become ugly and complicated. The owner asks, "Do we close down the bakery before we compromise our beliefs?" He says he doesn't believe in gay marriage and he refuses to make this marrying gay couple a wedding cake. The patron says, "We have already been discriminated against there. We were already treated badly". A judge ruled that a business owner cannot refuse service to a customer on the basis of sexual preference and that decision was upheld today by the Colorado Civil Rights Commission. This commission is also ordering the bakery owner to submit quarterly reports on who he refuses to serve and how he retrains his employees to serve all customers.[3]

And if you don't think it's coming here, you better wake up! It's the same tactic. We better speak up now, or all this is coming to America! And once it does, you ain't seen nothing yet! It's going to open up the floodgates to all kinds of destructive behaviors, inviting God's judgment even faster, which is exactly what God said would happen when you went down this route.

Romans 1:18,21,26-32 "The wrath of God is being revealed from heaven against all the godlessness and wickedness of men who suppress the truth by their wickedness. For although they knew God, they neither glorified Him as God nor gave thanks to Him, but their thinking became futile and their foolish hearts were darkened. Because of this, God gave them over to shameful lusts. Even their women exchanged natural relations for unnatural ones. In the same way the men also abandoned natural relations with women and were inflamed with lust for one another. Men committed indecent acts with other men, and received in themselves the due penalty for their perversion. Furthermore, since they did not think it worthwhile to retain the knowledge of God, he gave them over to a depraved mind, to do what ought not to be done. They have become filled with every kind of wickedness, evil, greed and depravity. They are full of envy, murder, strife, deceit and malice. They are gossips, slanderers, God-haters, insolent, arrogant and boastful; they invent ways of doing evil; they disobey their parents; they are senseless, faithless, heartless, ruthless. Although they know God's righteous decree that those who do such things deserve death, they not only continue to do these very things but also approve of those who practice them."

      They start passing laws in every state and force you to go into this! It's the exact same thing God said was going to happen! If you ever wanted to know why America is going down the tubes so fast, here it is. We're following the same path the Roman society did. They first turned to an evolutionary mindset that said there was no God even though there is plenty of evidence for God's existence through His creation. So, what did God do? God gave them over to shameful lusts. And that was with homosexuality and lesbianism. And then what happened after that?
      They still refused to retain the knowledge of God, so then what? Now things got really dark. God gave them over to a depraved mind to do what ought not to be done. Evil, greed, slander, murder, strife, gossip, God-hating people who actually invented ways of doing evil and then even approved of those who do such things! Now does that sound familiar or what?
      That's America! That's what's wrong with us! We're following the same path of the Roman society and we're reaping the same destruction. Which means, we're under the wrath of God just like them! And it's opened up Pandora's Box and it's getting worse by the day just like God said it would! Once you go down

this route of approving homosexuality it will open up the doors to absolutely unimaginable behavior! Don't believe me? It's already begun.

As we saw before, one person warned that all this ongoing redefinition of marriage with same sex unions will soon include the idea of what's being called, "non-monogamy" or the concept of faithfulness between a man and a woman in marriage being outdated. The new concept will be the acceptance of "multiple partners" or "polygamy" without the stigma of adultery. In fact, it's already begun.

Fox Reports:

Details tonight about an historic court ruling having to do with two volatile subjects, sex and religion. What the opinion means for polygamist families is really something quite transformative. In response to a lawsuit brought by a polygamist reality TV family, Sister Wives, a Federal Judge in Utah has ruled that polygamy will no longer will be criminalized in that state.

A victory to plaintiff's lead attorney says it's no surprise. Jonathan Turley, says, "If you look at the trend of the law, it has been towards greater protection of the individual choices and get the government out of homes and bedrooms, to prevent the majority from dictating the moral code that everyone must live by".

Those who oppose the recent Supreme Court opinion on sodomy and gay marriage say they're not surprised either, that they predicted this very turn of events. In fact, it's going to get even worse. Judge Richard Posner, a federal judge with the 7th Circuit Court of Appeals who recently become a hero to the pro-gay marriage movement also said, "Perhaps it's time the government begin issuing "rape licenses" (I kid you not) since the "right to rape" for some men at least, "exceeds the victim's physical and emotional pain."

And other legal officials are saying that pedophiles also deserve civil rights. Margo Kaplan, a Law Professor at Rutgers University said, "People who are sexually attracted to children, must hide their disorder from everyone they know, or risk losing educational and job opportunities and face the prospect of harassment an even violence.

The nation's anti-pedophilia laws are unfair to pedophiles and should be changed." So, pedophiles get more rights than Christians??? And recently a Judge in Australia even said this, "Incest and pedophilia may no longer be considered taboo, just as gay relationships are now being more accepted than they were in the 1950's & 1960's."[4]

Or as God says, "Once you go down this route, you aren't going to believe what's going to happen!" Anyone who objects to this behavior is going to become a hater and you will have to be taken away because you don't fit in this satanic coming *One World Religion*!

What's ironic is that now even Non-Christian nations, Communist nations, and Third World countries, are putting up protective barriers against this so their societies won't be destroyed!

Russian President Vladimir Putin recently signed into law a bill banning the, "Propaganda of non-traditional sexual relations to minors." The law is aimed at limiting the rights of the country's gay, lesbian, bisexual, transgender, and intersex people.

They have also included multiple bans on gay pride parades and hefty fines to gay rights groups accused of acting as a "foreign agent."

Nigeria's president also signed into law a law criminalizing homosexuality prescribing 10 years in prison for those who "directly or indirectly" make a "public show" of same-sex relationships as well as punishing anyone who participates in gay clubs and organizations, or who simply supports them."[5]

How backwards it has gotten. Who would have thought we'd ever see the day when Communist nations and Third World countries would behave more Biblically than us? And it's being used to silence the Church and get rid of Christians on a global scale, which is exactly what Jesus said would happen when you're living in the last days!

The 2nd excuse the Antichrist is using to get rid of all dissenters who won't go along with a One World Religion is **The Ecumenical Movement.**

The Ecumenical Movement, or Pluralism in other words, the belief "that all paths lead to Heaven." For those of you who may not know, ecumenicalism is defined as "the organized attempt to bring about the cooperation and unity of all believers." At the onset, that sounds pretty good. But what they don't tell you is that it's come to mean all believers, meaning even those outside of Christ, who are not Christians, no matter what they believe, whether they believe in Christ or not!

Their so-called "unity" in the ecumenical movement is being sought not on the basis of truth, but from a "watered down version of it." The Bible clearly says we Christians, genuine believers in Christ, do not join hands with somebody who's preaching a "watered down version" of God's truth, that's a lie! And He doesn't want us preaching lies! Rather the Bible says we need to come out from among them and be ye separate! I didn't say that. God did.

2 Corinthians 6:14-17 "Do not be yoked together with unbelievers. For what do righteousness and wickedness have in common? Or what fellowship can light have with darkness? What harmony is there between Christ and Belial? Or what does a believer have in common with an unbeliever? What agreement is there between the temple of God and idols? For we are the temple of the living God. As God has said: I will live with them and walk among them, and I will be their God, and they will be my people." Therefore, come out from them and be separate, says the Lord. Touch no unclean thing, and I will receive you."

According to our text, the Bible clearly says that when it comes to unbelievers, i.e non-Christians, what are we supposed to do? Yes, we hang out with them, yes, we witness to them, yes, we love them enough to tell them the truth about Jesus being the only way to heaven. I didn't say that, He did!

John 14:6 "Jesus answered, 'I am the way and the truth and the life. No one comes to the Father except through Me.'

So of course, we love the lost enough to tell them the truth that Jesus is the only way to Heaven, of course, right? We don't want them to go to hell, right? That's true love! But the last thing we ever want to do Paul says is what? Is to be to be "yoked" with them, right? And that's totally different than witnessing. The word "yoked" literally means there, "to bound together with or to have fellowship with." So why does Paul say not to do that? Because it's like oil and water. It doesn't mix! It can't mix! It'll never mix. Why? Because you cannot mix a lie with God's perfect holy truth! Eternity is on the line here! This is serious stuff! That's Paul's argument there. So why in the world then would a born-again Christian try to mix God's truth with the devil's lies!

What do righteousness and wickedness have in common? What fellowship can light have with darkness? What harmony is there between Christ and Belial? Or let me translate it for you. How can we really "get along" with those who believe that we ourselves are gods, or that we'll burn in a mythical place called purgatory where we purge away our sins in order to get into heaven, which is denying the cross?

How can we "join hands" with those who would have you and I believe that sin is just an illusion, or that hell is only make believe and that heaven for some men will be to endlessly satisfy their lusts with as many virgins as they want, which only happens after they kill a bunch of people? And how can we have "unity" with those who are claiming to be Christians yet state that one has to keep the sacraments to be saved, or that Satan doesn't exist, or that Christ's work on the cross is not secure?

How can we "have fellowship with" those who would have you and I believe that Jesus is not God but the archangel Michael, or worse yet, that He is the spirit-brother of Satan? How can we do that? I think the answer is obvious! As God says, "Come out from among them and be ye separate!" Why? Because God says so! You cannot have fellowship with those who are leading people to hell! That's a lie that all paths lead to heaven! Which means true born again Christians cannot ever go along with this One World Religion that says all paths lead to Heaven which is in essence saying Jesus is not the only way to Heaven. That's a lie! You cannot meld the two together! Yes, we witness, but we do not yoke up and get intimate with!

And yet, that's exactly what the ecumenical movement is trying to get us to do! In fact, let's see how far this lie has already progressed, that all paths lead to Heaven, it's a lie.

PLURALISM IN CLIMATE CHANGE: A group of Christian, Muslim and Jewish youths have now formed a multi-faith community with the help of World Council of Churches (WCC). They say their desire to protect the earth is a concern for all faith traditions. Tariq Abdul Akbar, a 21-year-old Muslim from the United States says, "We must as people of faith put aside our religious differences and come together to raise awareness about climate change. After all this is a human rights issue and affects all people in the world." Mark Edwards, another student from the Church of Ceylon in Sri Lanka says, "The responsibility to respect creation is common to all faiths. Earth is a gift to us all and we are all responsible for its well-being." And on his return to Sri Lanka he hopes to conduct meetings for youth and children in his church. Liron Alkolombra is a representative of the Jewish tradition and said, "Living in a multi-faith community is an 'eye opener.' Our visit to a synagogue, a church and a mosque in Switzerland moved me. I realized that we all believe in one God and are part of humanity."

PLURALISM IN EUROPE: In Berlin Germany, they have created a "House of Prayer and Learning" at a cost of $60 million for Christians, Muslims and Jews to all pray under the same roof. Pastor Gregor Hohberg said, "From the beginning, we wanted it to be an inter-religious project, not a place built by Christians in which Jews and Muslims would then be added, but for all three religions to have equal prayer space on the same floor with each leading to a common room where the different congregations will be able to converse. They're calling it, "The House of One."

We have inherited a large house, a great world house, said Martin Luther King. We all inhabit this world house, our earth. We see that the world is growing together and that we have to learn to live with each other. Increasingly, religions are colliding, as strangers, as friends and also as rivals or enemies.

For this reason, Jews, Christians and Muslims have come together in Berlin to attempt something new. We want to build a completely new sacred building, a synagogue, a church, and a mosque under the same roof and at its center a meeting place. 'The House of One'. It shall be located in the heart of Berlin. In the place where the city was founded 800 years ago.

It shall be a unique, peaceful place for encounters, meetings and exchanges between people of different religions and also for those who are removed from religion. Everyone is invited to come. Every interest, every question, every support is welcome with every peaceful dialogue and every good wish. A cloud of blessing will grow, one earth, one mankind, one home, "The House of One"[6]

PLURALISM IN AMERICA: Even have here in America the Omaha Tri-Faith Initiative is combining Christians, Jews, and Muslims into an inter-faith dialogue as well as inter-faith facility. They have recently kicked off a multi-million-dollar effort to bring the three religions onto a 35-acre campus. The city's religious leaders said, "We want to form a relationship between all Jews, all Muslims, and all Christians. It's an opportunity not only to learn to tolerate people of different beliefs, but to find ways to even celebrate all we have in common…to join those who call God by different names."

PLURALISM IN SCHOOLS: Just in case you don't live anywhere near Berlin and Omaha, right now high school students in Colorado are being encouraged to recite a pledge in Arabic stating, "One Nation under Allah."

In New York, kids are now observing Muslim New Year holidays and possibly the Hindu Festival Diwali.

School kids in California are having to bow down to the sun god as a part of "liturgical/ritual religious practices" aimed at having them "become one with god" through Ashtanga yoga teachings. Founder, Sonia Tudor Jones says she wants to "spread the gospel of Ashtanga through the country and even internationally."

PLURALISM IN GOVERNMENT: Recently Dalai Lama was allowed to open the Senate meetings with prayer. Senators bowed their heads as the Dalai Lama prayed one of his favorite prayers, "With our thoughts, we make our world." Senate staff filled the back rows of the chamber and visitors observed from the gallery above which drew more people than a typical start to the Senate day.

And speaking of Congress, an Interfaith School for Military Chaplains has now been dedicated. Priests, Rabbis, Imams and Protestant ministers who serve as U.S. military chaplains came together to dedicate themselves and the nation's first joint military multi-faith education center.

And even our former President stated, "We are no longer a Christian Nation…" "The increasing diversity of America's population shows the dangers of sectarianism are greater than ever. Whatever we once were, we are no longer a Christian nation, at least not just, we are also a Jewish nation, a Muslim nation, a Buddhist nation, and a Hindu nation, and a nation of non-believers", says President Obama in his speech.

CNN reports:

This is a clip of the President's speech in Turkey, a Muslim country and a NATO ally. "I've said before that one of the great strengths of the United States is, as I have mentioned, we have a very large Christian population, we do not consider ourselves a Christian nation, or a Jewish nation, or a Muslim nation, we consider ourselves a nation of citizens who are bound by ideals and a set of values."

Then to complete his prior speech he says, "And if we had only Christians in our midst, if we expelled every non-Christian from the United State of America, whose Christianity would we teach in the schools? Would it be James Dobson's or Al Sharpton's? Which passages of scripture should be our public policy? Should we go with Leviticus, which suggest slavery is ok and eating shellfish is an abomination, or we could go with Deuteronomy which suggest stoning your child if he strays from the faith. Or should we just stick to the Sermon on the Mount, a passage that is so radical that I doubt our own defense department would survive its application."[7]

And is it by chance that we now have American schools indoctrinating our kids into the Muslim religion? Here's just a sampling of the few things they are being taught right now in schools across America:

Learning to become a Muslim.
Fasting for Ramadan.
Learning about Ramadan.
Learning the five pillars of Islam.
Memorizing verses of the Quran.
Adopting a Muslim name.
Staging a jihad (war against non-Muslims).

As one person stated, "Apparently, the "Muslim in chief" has overlooked his Christian obligation and duty that he swore in public office to uphold the Constitution of the United States with his hand on the Christian Bible which states, "You shall have NO other gods before Me!" (Exodus 20:3)[8]

This is not make-believe, it's happening right now, even at the highest places. It sure appears to me that somebody's trying to squish all the world's religions into ONE, how about you? Even here in America! Here's the problem. As we saw earlier, true born again Christians CANNOT go along with this. Why? Because we're supposed to be separate from this! This is a LIE! All paths DO NOT lead to heaven!

So, what do you do with those who resist this? Ah! You move to Stage #2, you call these people the bad guys, the resisters, those people who have the audacity to ruin world peace. And one by one you get rid of them!
And that's exactly what the Bible says is going to happen to those who get saved after the rapture. You should've got saved before!

Revelation 6:9-11 "When He opened the fifth seal, I saw under the altar the souls of those who had been slain because of the Word of God and the testimony they had maintained. They called out in a loud voice, "How long, Sovereign

Lord, holy and true, until You judge the inhabitants of the earth and avenge our blood?" Then each of them was given a white robe, and they were told to wait a little longer, until the number of their fellow servants and brothers who were to be killed as they had been was completed."

Maybe it's just me, but it sure appears the events during the 7-year tribulation are not going to be good ones for the followers of God, how about you? Being killed, and your blood being avenged just for following God, that doesn't sound like a good time to me! And again, those people being murdered and asking God to avenge their blood are the people who got saved after the rapture, and again, the lesson is you should've got saved before the hammer came down! You're going to pay for it with a price, and that price is your life. They're actually going to hunt you down and exterminate you just for being a follower of God.

Here's the point for you and I today. This happens during the 7-year Tribulation. "Are there any signs today of the whole world wanting to hunt down and exterminate people, just for believing in God's Word and refusing to give up their testimony for Jesus? I.E. that He's the ONLY WAY to HEAVEN?" Uh yeah! That's why we're already at Stage #2!

Just like we read before with the homosexual movement, disagreeing with them is a hate crime, so now it is with the ecumenical movement, disagreeing with them has also become a hate crime. Don't believe me? It's already happening.

As reported on the Noland Show in Ireland, the rye on the pastor's comments about Muslims just keep on growing. James McConnell was strongly criticized for saying he did not trust Muslims. But the first minister, Peter Robinson, has now defended him. James McConnell says, "People say there are good Muslims and that may be so, but I don't trust them. Enoch Powell was right and he lost his career because of it. Enoch Powell was a prophet.

He told us blood would flow in the streets and it has happened. Islam is heathen, Islam is Satanic, Islam is a doctrine spawned in Hell." "Well," says the commentator, "Khalid, you've come all the way over this evening, across the water, what is your reaction to what the first minister said?" Dr. Khalid Anis of the Islamic Society of Britain, replies, "I think it's disgraceful. Quite honestly, I think it's shocking that somebody in that position of leadership, in that position of influence, somebody that everybody in Northern Ireland and I imagine on the mainland, looks up to for guidance and leadership can utter a statement which is full of hate".[9]

So now, disagreeing with another religion, saying they're not the way to Heaven, only Jesus is, is hate? A hate crime? I'm telling you, we're already at Stage #2 on this! First it was a moral issue with homosexuality, if you disagree, it's a hate crime and we need to get rid of you. And now it's a spiritual issue with the ecumenical movement or Pluralism, that all paths lead to Heaven, and if you disagree you're a hater, and we need to get rid of you too!
Both have become the two excuses to get rid of any and all true born-again Christians, who won't go along with a One World Religion, and replace them with fake phony Christians who will. Believe it or not, the extermination of "The Haters" the Christians has already begun.

PERSECUTION IN STATS: Right now, there are over 250 million Christians worldwide under the threat of persecution. Right now, our fellow brothers and sisters in Christ are being beaten, tortured, imprisoned, and murdered. Why? Because they refuse to compromise the truth, unlike the ecumenical movement whose promoting this One World Religion! In fact, in 1988 alone, there were some 310,000 Christians slaughtered and more Christians have died for their faith in this last century alone than in the previous nineteen centuries combined. And it's getting worse.

PERSECUTION IN THE WORLD: North Korea remains the most difficult country in the world to be a Christian because it's an act that is punishable by death or life in prison. There are an estimated 70,000 Christians imprisoned in camps just like in Nazi Germany and it's a sentence that is not just for the individual believer, but for three generations of their family. That's their parents, their children and their grandchildren. In fact, recently North Korea passed a law where merely possessing a Bible can be punishable by death.

Militant groups in Syria are using the war as an excuse to target Christians and "get rid of Christians in their country." There are forced conversions or killings by those who do not convert to Islam and 41 of the top 50 countries persecuting and killing Christians around the world are Muslim.

In fact, there are thousands of Christians being slaughtered for their faith right now in India, Burma, Nigeria, Afghanistan, Egypt, Saudi Arabia, Turkey, Belarus, Sudan, and on and on it goes. In fact, Christians are being persecuted so bad that their assailants are killing them, draining their blood, and selling it for profit, or to go to heaven, like this lady shares.[10]

A nun is being interviewed about what she knows about the blood being sold. Here is her answer in broken English:

Since 2005 I hear about the persecution of the Christians in the Middle East because I am myself a refugee. What you do with a Christian is okay. You can rape the girls, you can kill them. Everything for them is allowed to do to a Christian.

And this blood they are selling them. How I came to know that they are selling them was from a relative, they didn't tell me this 'they sell the blood.' I know that from my own home.

The Muslim was talking: 'If we kill one Christian and wash our hands with his blood, we will go to Heaven.' This hand, with the blood of the Christians, washed, they will be like touched, show the way to go to heaven. They believe in that. That I know that.

What I'm doing with this blood that I'm collecting with these cans, and he said: "Oh sister that is a big business." What business with the blood? Because I was hearing, but I was not knowing that. They sell the blood.

Yeah, so small bottle we are sending for our friends in Saudi Arabia. They cannot kill them there to bring offer to our Allah. Each small bottle is cost $100,000 dollars. We make big business. For that we can buy more guns and other things.[11]

Now that's not only sick, it's interesting because the Bible says in the last days, the One World Religion Harlot will be "drunk with the blood of the saints."

Revelation 17:6 "I saw that the woman was drunk with the blood of the saints, the blood of those who bore testimony to Jesus. When I saw her, I was greatly astonished."

And apparently that's why a new study from Pew Research Center shared how, "Christians and Christianity are now the most persecuted religion on the planet," and that "A Christian is Killed Every 11 Minutes," and that "Christian persecution is turning into Christian extinction," and it's "The biggest story in the world that has never been told." But this kid will tell the story when he gets there!

One evangelist in Europe is now warning, "The Fate of Christianity in U.S. not far from what happened to Christianity in Europe." And he cites several reasons why:

The Church is sleeping and dying out.
Homosexuals are stamping out Christianity and the Bible.
Atheism is not being debated, just denounced.
The role of apologetics is being downplayed to reach the skeptics.
The people continue to think, "It could never happen in the U.S."

Oh, but it already has!

Christian Songs are being disqualified from the Oscars.
Hollywood is portraying Christians as dangerous Terrorists in Movies.
Bibles are being banned from Hotels.
Home Bible studies are being declared Illegal.
The IRS is targeting Conservative Christian Groups.
Amazon & PayPal are being pushed to blacklist Conservative Christian Websites. (Can't buy & sell)
Police are investigating a Church that had a poster which suggested non-believers would burn in hell. It was turned in by a passerby as a "hate incident."
Troops are being banned from attending Vacation Bible School.

Teachers are telling students, "Jesus is not allowed in School."
Colleges are rejecting applications from Christians because of their faith.
Schools are banning Christian Clubs.
Schools are banning books from Christian authors.
Now that brings us to an odd comparison to what happened to the Jewish people under Hitler. In order of appearance Chronologically, here's what happened to them:

Public burning of books by Jews.
Random attacks on Jews and Jewish property.
Police and the courts no longer protect Jews.
Boycotts of Jewish shops.
Jewish practices banned.
Jewish students excluded from exams in medicine, dentistry, pharmacy and law.
Jews excluded from military service.
Laws deny Jews many basic civil rights.

Jews no longer allowed to vote and lose German citizenship.
Jews banned from parks, restaurants and swimming pools.
Jews banned from communication devices and transportation.
Special identity cards issued to Jews.
Jews were arrested.
All schools closed to Jewish children.
Jews were sent to Death Camps

Looks like we're following the same path! In fact, one-man shares, *"How this level of persecution is not only coming here to America, but much sooner than you think and you better get ready!"*[12]

The Church in America is going to suffer terribly and we laugh now. They will come after us, they will come after our children. They will close the net around us while we are playing soccer mom and soccer dad. While we argue over so many little things and are mesmerized over so many little trinkets, even now it is closing around you and your children and your grandchildren and it does not cause you to fear.

You will be isolated from society as has already happened. Anyone that tries to run for office who actually believes the Bible will be considered a lunatic until we are silenced. We will be called things that we are not and be persecuted not for being followers of Christ but for being radical fundamentalists that do not know the true way of Christ which is of course love and tolerance.

You will go down as being the greatest bigots and haters of mankind in history. They have already come after your children and for most of you, they got them. They got them through the public schools and indoctrination in the universities and you wonder why your children don't come out serving the Lord. It's because you fed them right into the devils' mouth. So, little by little the net is closing around and then it's not little by little. Look how fast things are going down in just a matter of weeks, a matter of weeks. But at the same time, know this, persecution is always meant for evil.

But, God always means it for good. And is it not better to suffer in this life, to have an extra way to Glory in Heaven. You must settle this in your mind. This is the one thing I want to say over and over. Do not believe, down through history you have the wrong idea of martyrdom and persecution. You think that these men were persecuted and martyred for their sincere faith in Jesus Christ. That was the real reason, but no one heard that publicly. They were martyred and persecuted as enemies of the state. As child molesters, as bigots, as narrow minded stupid people who had fallen for a rouse and can contribute nothing to society.

Your suffering will not be noble, so your mind must be filled with the Word of God when all people persecute you and turn on you and the spirit of God and common Grace pulls back and you see even your children and your grandchildren tossing in the lot that you should die. This is no game. You want revival and awakening but know this, for the most part great awakenings have come only preceding great national catastrophes and the persecution of the Church.

I believe God is bringing a great awakening but I believe he is raising up young men who are strong in the trust in the providence of God to be able to wade through the hell that is going to break loose on us and it will be on us before we even recognize it unless in God's providence He is not done. He is not done. And note this, this is not silly talk. Apart of a great awakening these things are going to come upon you. Be ready to lose your cars, your homes, everything.[13]

Now folks, as he stated, this is not silly talk, there really is an agenda to get rid of all true born again Christians all over the world, every nation, even America, just like Jesus said would happen when you're living in the last days. If ever we needed revival, and to speak up, it is now!

The 2nd way we know we're really headed for A One World Religion is due to a **Worldwide Assimilation of Believers.**

What I mean by believers, is the world's definition of believers, as the ecumenical movement would say, all religions lead to Heaven, and we can merge into one and believe it or not, the Vatican is promoting that very same false message right now! What's wild is that it just so happens to fit with what the Bible says the One World Religion Harlot will be doing with the Antichrist in the last days!

Revelation 17:1-6;15-18 "One of the seven angels who had the seven bowls came and said to me, 'Come, I will show you the punishment of the great prostitute, who sits on many waters. With her the kings of the earth committed adultery and the inhabitants of the earth were intoxicated with the wine of her adulteries.' Then the angel carried me away in the Spirit into a desert. There I saw a woman sitting on a scarlet beast that was covered with blasphemous names and had seven heads and ten horns. The woman was dressed in purple and scarlet, and was glittering with gold, precious stones and pearls. She held a golden cup in her hand, filled with abominable things and the filth of her adulteries. This title was written on her forehead: MYSTERY BABYLON THE GREAT THE MOTHER OF PROSTITUTES AND OF THE ABOMINATIONS OF THE EARTH. I saw that the woman was drunk with the blood of the saints, the blood of those who bore testimony to Jesus. When I saw her, I was greatly astonished! Then the angel said to me, 'The waters you saw, where the prostitute sits, are peoples, multitudes, nations and languages. The beast and the ten horns you saw will hate the prostitute. They will bring her to ruin and leave her naked; they will eat her flesh and burn her with fire. For God has put it into their hearts to accomplish His purpose by agreeing to give the beast their power to rule, until God's words are fulfilled. The woman you saw is the great city that rules over the kings of the earth."

We have a lot going on in this text. We see that the One World Religion Harlot will not only be "drunk with the blood of the saints," as we saw before, from those who get saved after the rapture of the Church, BUT she's also working in conjunction initially with the Antichrist, controlling the religions of the world, and ruling over the kings of the earth, right? But at some point, it says that the Antichrist turns on her, God allows it as a form of punishment or judgment, and the Antichrist will destroy her.

He apparently uses her until he gets what he wants. World domination. She's just a tool. At first, she rides him, seemingly in control, but later he grabs control and kills her. Now I said all that to get to this. In order for this passage to be fulfilled, we need to see some sort of global religious identity working with the governments around the world, trying to control them as well as promoting all the world's religions to come together as one under its control.

Can I tell you something? That's exactly what the Vatican is doing right now! And they've been doing it for quite some time. If you'll recall, who do all the world's leaders, including American Presidents, eventually go to meet? The Pope, at the Vatican, right? Why? Because they're working in conjunction with all the world's governments right now trying to control them, just like this text says! And two, they are also working to bring about all the world's religions under their control. Let's look at that proof again. It's been going on for quite some time.

The Vatican and the Roman Catholic Church, its Pope is currently leading the greatest ecumenical movement in history in order to unite all religions under Rome's leadership. In 1986 Pope John Paul II gathered in Assisi, Italy the leaders of the world's major religions to pray for peace.

There were snake worshipers, fire worshipers, spiritists, animists, Buddhists, Muslims, Hindus, North American witch doctors. I watched in astonishment as they walked to the microphone to pray. The Pope said they were all praying to the same god and that their prayers were creating a spiritual energy that would bring about a new climate of peace.

John Paul II allowed his good friend the Dali Lama to put the Buddha on the altar in St Peters Church of Assisi and with his monks to have a Buddhist worship ceremony there while Shintoist chanted and rang their bells outside.

They prophesized world religion is in the process of being formed before our very eyes and the Vatican is the headquarters for the movement. Is this not spiritual fornication?[14]

That's exactly what it is! And that's exactly what our text said a world religious identity would do in the last days with the Antichrist! The Vatican is the headquarters of it! This is not make-believe, this is all happening right now! In fact, as we saw before, they're already calling for a United Nations of Religions where some global entity would control the world's religions just like the United Nations controls all the world's government.

King Abdullah of Saudi Arabia: He has been planning for years to, "Find a way to unite the world's major religions in an effort to help foster peace and he believes a new International Organization will help make that dream a reality."

Chief Rabbi Yona Metzger, one of the two Chief Rabbis of Israel said: "We need a United Relations of Religions, which would contain representatives of the world's religions as opposed to nations, a church, a mosque, a synagogue or a holy temple must be embassies of God and we have to spread this idea to our believers." He has suggested that the Dalai Lama could lead the assembly.

Muslim Figure Adnan Oktar; He met with three representatives from the reestablished Jewish Sanhedrin to discuss how religious Muslims, Jews and Christians can work together on rebuilding the Temple." An official statement about the meeting has been published on the Sanhedrin's website where they stated, "We are all the sons of one father, the descendants of Adam, and all humanity is but a single family."

Peace among nations will be achieved through building the House of God, where all peoples will serve." Oktar added that, "The Temple will be rebuilt and all believers will worship there in tranquility." And, "The Temple could be rebuilt in one year."

Shimon Peres: Former President of Israel also met with Pope Francis to discuss the idea of creating a UN-like organization that he called "The United Religions" to, bring an end to the wars raging in the Middle East and around the world."[15]

So, world religious leaders all over the planet, are crying out for some global entity to control all religions on the planet, to bring in a time of so-called peace, and can anybody guess who's at the forefront of this? The Vatican! They're leading the way! In fact, right now as we speak, the Pope and the Vatican are vying for control over Jerusalem and the Temple Mount, and many believe a secret deal is being negotiated. That's what the Pope's been doing with his recent trips to Israel. He's encouraging all major religions to come together as ONE!

Pope Francis, on his final day of his middle East trip, prayed and laid a wreath at Jerusalem's Holocaust museum. He visited the grave of the father of modern Israel, Theodore Hertzel, met with the two chief rabbis of Jerusalem and paid courtesy calls on the Israeli president and prime minister.

Earlier the Pope met with the Grand Mufti of Jerusalem and said a visit to the Holy Land would not be complete without such a meeting. "I make a heartfelt plea to all peoples and to all communities to look to Abraham. May we respect and love one another as brothers and sisters." Arthur Schneier, American Rabbi of the United States, praised the Pope's visit. He said "Unfortunately there are those religious leaders that seek to divide us."

The fact that the Pope was here visiting Israel is also a milestone of interfaith relations." In the evening Pope Francis met with Eastern Orthodox leaders at the church of the Holy Sepulcher, the site where many believe that Jesus Christ was crucified. Patriarch Bartholomew I, Eastern Orthodox Patriarch, the spiritual leader of the world orthodox Christians lamented racial discrimination and religious extremism in contemporary society. He says, "In the face of such conditions, love the others, the different others, the followers of other faiths, and other confessions."[16]

Isn't that sweet! They're planting an olive tree together. I wonder if the Antichrist is going to come by later and water it! All the world's religions are coming together under the Vatican and what's wild is that's exactly what the occult is saying needs to happen for the Antichrist to arise!

They believe that once all world religions come together, (and they're expecting it soon) a religious leader will be chosen to be earth's religious spokesman and will then encourage all the people of the world to accept a new world leader, who will suddenly appear on the scene, which sounds precisely like the false prophet the Bible talks about, who convinces the world to worship the Beast or the Antichrist.

The occult is also in agreement that none of this can fully take place until the people who will never go along with this One World Religion are out of the way. Can you guess who that might be? In fact, they say that these people who are restraining or holding things up won't necessarily die but will somehow mysteriously disappear, or in their words, "elect to leave this dimension as if going to another room."

And once these people leave this earth, the occult says the new world leader will take his rightful place over the world. Then and only then, will it be possible to build a combination Temple-Church-Mosque in Jerusalem. At the proper moment in history, a world religious leader will visit the combined Jewish-Christian-Moslem sector of Jerusalem to announce that all religions should be combined into one. The Moslem and Jewish areas in Jerusalem will be combined with Christians to create the New Jerusalem Covenant and all religions will celebrate three festivals.

1. Festival of Goodwill
2. Festival of Easter
3. Festival of Wesak,

This will create the New World Order Religion and will be the spiritual equivalent to the political United Nations. This action will then finally break the Middle East log jam. And as one-person states, "I would not be surprised if this group is actually writing the Peace Treaty that the Antichrist will sign with Israel at the proper time. Which of course would be the fulfillment of Daniel's prophecy of 9:27, which starts the 7-year Tribulation."[17]

Daniel 9:27 "He will confirm a covenant with many for one 'seven.' In the middle of the 'seven' he will put an end to sacrifice and offering and on a wing of the temple he will set up an abomination that causes desolation until the end that is decreed is poured out on him."

In other words, he's going to lose! But that's not all. The Vatican is not only promoting all religions come together as ONE and sign an agreement or covenant but the new Pope, Pope Francis is making it so easy for anyone and everyone to be a part of this global religion, even atheists! Check out what Pope Francis has been saying lately!

Huffington Post reports:

Good news for your atheist out there. Jesus is still going to redeem you. During his Wednesday mass, Pope Francis emphasized the importance of doing good as a principal that unites all humanity. In his sermon he said, "The Lord has redeemed all of us, all of us, with the Blood of Christ: all of us, not just Catholics. Everyone! Even the atheists. Everyone!"

Conan, on his nightly show says, "Atheists are still eligible to go into Heaven. And to return the favor Atheists said that Popes are still eligible to go into a void of nothingness." The Daily Brief says: The new Pope Francis has really gone off the rails of the papal and is continuing to send out his message of peace and compassion. He is quoted as saying that "The Lord has redeemed all of us, all of us, the Blood of Christ: all of us, not just Catholics. Everyone. Even the Atheist." Hey guys, we did it, we're all going to Heaven. Even you right there. Good work world. That's really cool. Like the Pope printed a whole bunch of get out of jail free cards and distributed them to everyone.

Ann Thompson At Vatican City says: If you thought that was extraordinary perhaps his most interesting comments came when asked about a gay lobby. He said he had never met anybody in the Vatican that had gay on their business card and he said that if someone is gay and they are searching for the Lord who am I to judge. He said that people should not be marginalized.

As a lesbian and a catholic Cleo could have never imagined she could be this happy among fellow Catholics. Cleo married Donna, they had a child and found a Catholic church in Atlanta that accepted them. For this couple, the words of Pope Francis on not judging or condemning homosexuals is a divine sign that they are welcome in the Catholic faith.

She says, 'I just see an olive branch being extended for things that may not have been previously from other Popes from the position of the church and that is very refreshing and it gives us hope." Parishners say that by advocating deep compassion over harsh judgement he's bringing his flock a step closer to its divine calling.[18]

Apparently, that divine calling is to form a One World Religion that anyone can join, even atheists and homosexuals! That's not what the Bible says!

1 Corinthian 6:9-11 "Or do you not know that the unrighteous will not inherit the kingdom of God? Do not be deceived; neither fornicators, nor idolaters, nor adulterers, nor effeminate, nor homosexuals, nor thieves, nor the covetous, nor drunkards, nor revilers, nor swindlers, will inherit the kingdom of God. Such were some of you; but you were washed, but you were sanctified, but you were justified in the name of the Lord Jesus Christ and in the Spirit of our God."

He then went on to say that it is dangerous for you to think you can even go to Heaven apart from the Catholic Church and the One World Religion.

"On June 25, Pope Francis spoke to an audience of 33,000 people saying, 'There is no such thing as 'do-it-yourself' Christians or 'free agents'. "It is a "dangerous temptation" to believe that one can have a personal, direct, immediate relationship with Jesus Christ without communion with and the mediation of the church." Excuse me? You not only say atheists and homosexuals go to Heaven, but you go to the other extreme and now say you can't be saved apart from the Catholic Church and this new One World Religion.

It's one thing for the Catholic Church and the Pope to do this, but it's a good thing the Protestant Church isn't falling for this lie! Well, I hate to burst your bubble, but not only are Protestant churches caving in on these issues, but they're even being seduced right now by the Pope himself to join him in his One World Religion.

Believe it or not, Kenneth Copeland, who by the way is a false teacher and Word of Faith heretic, recently piped in a private message from the Pope to his so-called Protestant church. The Bishop who showed up to announce this private message from the Pope to this church made some chilling remarks. Check it out!

At the service of Kenneth Copeland, he introduces Anglican priest Tony Palmer. He says" Thank you for giving me this opportunity to spend a couple moments introducing to you something really special and historic."

A film clip comes on of the Pope. The Pope proceeds to tell us the following: My brothers and sisters, excuse me, because I speak in Italian. And let's pray to the Lord that he unites us all. Come, on we are brothers. Let's give each other a spiritual hug and let God complete the work that He has begun. And this is a miracle; the miracle of unity has begun. I ask you to bless me, and I bless you.

From brother to brother, I embrace you. Thank you. Tony Palmer comes back to the podium and says, "This has brought an end to the protest of Luther. Brothers and sisters, Luther's protest is over. Is yours? And I'm going to be cheeky here because I challenge my Protestant pastor friends here, if there is no more protest how can there be a Protestant church? Maybe we are all Catholics again.[19]

"Luther's protest is over, how about yours?" Can I translate that for you? Won't you join us "Protestant Church" in forming a One World Religion. Exactly like the Bible said would happen, when you are living in the last days! It's happening now, even in the Protestant Church!

But you might be thinking, "Well okay, that's just Kenneth Copeland. He's a false teacher, we all know that, what do you expect? I'm sure he's the only one doing this, right?" WRONG! Many of the people from the charismatic movement are doing the exact same thing. They're meeting with the Pope, chumming up with him, giving him high-fives, trying to figure out how we can all get along as Protestants.

In a picture recently taken we see in order, John & Carol Arnott, Brian Stiller, Kenneth Copeland, Pope Francis, Thomas Schirrmacher, Geoff Tunnicliffe, James & Betty Robinson, and Bishop Tony Palmer, and it's one thing to meet with the Pope, but the purpose of the meeting was to discuss "Unity in Diversity" and then you have strange statement being made by James Robison, who was giving the Pope a high five.

"The enemy has kept many Christians from loving one another as Christ loves us and have failed to recognize the importance of supernatural unity even with all of the unique diversity. This week I was blessed to be part of perhaps an unprecedented moment between evangelicals and the Catholic Pope.

I believe I am beginning to witness what Jesus prayed for. Years ago, God told me to reach out beyond the safe, comfortable walls of my Southern Baptist tradition, beyond denominational barriers and seek to bring the family together. Oh, how I hope and I pray that is the case. Dear God, please let it happen and let me gladly be a part of it."[20]

Let me gladly be a part of forming a Global Religion with the Pope, from a protestant leader. You might be thinking, "Well okay, that's just the charismatic movement. They have some aberrant teachings anyway, what do you expect? I'm sure they're the only so-called Protestant Denomination doing this."

Wrong answer! Now we have people like Beth Moore hanging out with these same charismatics, including James Robison who's high-fiving the Pope, and she's making some odd comments about Catholics.

On stage, Beth Moore introduces the ladies seated behind her: Right over here to my right you see First United Methodist Church of Less than Land and behind them just down the street you have Christ the Redeemer, Lutheran Church.

Every single one of my sisters in this area attends a Lutheran Church, which thrills me. And these, as she points to the first group of ladies, all attend a Methodist church. I can't tell you how I love that kind of diversity. What I have asked these ladies to do right here, now this makes it a little bit different, because they do go to different churches.

But I have asked them to represent tonight to us is an African American Church that we are going to call Mt Zion Missionary Baptist Church. Is that good, did I do good? Right back here I want you to meet St. Anne's Catholic Church of Less than Land. These ladies come, every single one of them, although they don't go to one Catholic church they go to different ones but every single one of them go to a Catholic church right here in Houston, and I am so thrilled that they are here.

What I have asked my sisters to do here is actually they represent many different churches but they represent one church in our midst tonight. These are our sisters that attend different charismatic churches in the city, but tonight they attend Abundant Life Church.[21]

No, that's not good! What are you doing calling Catholics our sisters or brothers or whatever? They don't believe the same way to heaven!

Again, you might be thinking, "Well okay, that's just one protestant lady in the Church. We all know that Protestant pastors aren't going to fall for this baloney!" Really? You might want to pay attention to what Joel Osteen said about the Pope.

Local Channel 2 Reports:

More than 60,000 people will pack Yankees stadium tomorrow for a night of hope. The huge event featuring Lakewood church pastor Joel Osteen and his wife

Victoria. Before he arrived in New York, Osteen paid a special visit to the Vatican where he met with Pope Francis.

Tonight, Osteen shares the experience with local 2 anchor Dominic Sasa. She reports: We sat down and talked about the preparations for the big event. Joel revealed to me about the incredible opportunity he just had to meet with Pope Francis.

Joel Osteen says, "I just felt very honored and very humbled to see the Pope to give the mass to 100,000 people there that day, you just see he has such a heart to help people. I love the fact that he made the church more inclusive, not trying to make it smaller but to make it larger to take everybody in. So, it just resonates with me." With Rome behind him Joel feels he had divine inspiration fueling his message for tomorrow night.[22]

"Well okay, that's Joel Osteen. We all know that he refuses to stand on the truth period. And He only preaches fluffy stuff. But not the rest of our Protestant pastors! They'll never do this!" Really? You might want to listen to what Rick Warren said about the Pope.

World Over *asks Rick Warren, "What is your secret to reaching people every day, every week, not only in your writing but when you speak to them? What is it, what is this communication gift, if you will, if you could decode it?" "The main thing is love always reaches people. Authenticity, humility,*

Pope Francis is the perfect example of this. He is doing everything right. You see people will listen to what we say if they like what they see. And as our new Pope he was very, very symbolic in his first mass with people with AIDS, his kissing of the deformed man, his loving the children. His authenticity, his humility, his caring for the poor, this is what the whole world expects us Christians to do. And when they go and say 'Oh that's what a Christian does'.

In fact, there was a headline here in Orange County, I loved the headline, I saved it, it said, 'If you love Pope Francis, you will love Jesus'.

The reporter asks, "That was a headline?" while they both laughed. Rick answers, "Yes, that was a headline. I saved it, I showed it to a group of priests that I was speaking to awhile back."

Reporter: When I walked into your office here, I was struck. You have three images and personal notes that confront the person walking into your office. There is Mother Teresa, Martin Luther King, and Billy Graham. Why those three. What do they give you?"

Rick Warren answers, "The only one that is missing is Pope John Paul II. Those four people were the greatest influences on the 20th Century without a doubt."

The reporter: The Vatican recently sent a delegation here to Saddleback, the Academy for Life. Tell me what they discovered and why did they come? This was a sizable group.

Rick Warren answers, "It was. There were about 30 bishops from Europe, one of the men who had actually been trained and mentored by John Bonet, and which is an interesting thing because we have a retreat center here and my spiritual director who grew up at Saddleback actually went and trained under John Bonet too. So, I'm very excited about that. But they were talking about the new evangelization. Saddleback has been very effective in reaching the secular mindset. So, we figured out a way to reach that mindset and I fully support the Catholic Church's new evangelization."

Reporter: Tell me about your, the little breather you take during the day when you watch television. You surprise me. When we first met you came up to me and I said I can't believe you watch this show.

Rick Warren replies, "You know, I'm an avid fan of EWTN. I make no bones about it. I probably watch it more than any Christian channel, one of my favorite shows is the Chapel of Divine Mercy, which I love and when I have had a very stressful day, I'll come home and I've got it taped and Kaye and I will both listen, put it on and sit back and relax, worship and in that time of reflection of meditation quietness I find myself being renewed restored so thank you for continuing to replay the Chapel of Divine Mercy.

Reporter: Thank you Mother Angelica[23]

'The Chaplet of the Divine Mercy,' Mother Angelica's program is in progress. The Priest is leading the congregation. "In the name of the Father, the Son and the Holy Spirit, Amen. You expire Jesus, but the source of life gushes forth for souls, and the ocean of Mercy opened for the whole world. Oh, Fount of life,

unfathomable divine mercy and envelope the whole world and empty yourself out upon us.' The Holy Rosary with Mother Angelica and the Nuns of Our Lady of the Angels Monastery 'In the name of the Father, the Son and the Holy Spirit. And all the nuns said 'Amen'.

Mother Angelica: Hail Mary full of grace, the Lord is with thee. Blessed art thou among women and blessed is the fruit of thy womb, Jesus. Nun's join in 'Holy Mary, mother of God, pray for us sinners now until the hour of our death, Amen.' Mother Angelica: Hail Mary full of grace, the Lord is with thee. Blessed art thou among women and blessed is the fruit of thy womb, Jesus. Nuns: 'Holy Mary, mother of God, pray for us sinners from now until the hour of our death, Amen'. Mother Angelica: Hail Mary, full of grace, the Lord is with the. Blessed are thou among women and blessed is the fruit of thy womb. Jesus. Nuns, "Holy Mary, mother of God, pray for us sinners from now until the hour of our death, Amen."[24]

You love the Pope, and you actually have his picture on your wall as a source of inspiration? So, when push comes to shove and the Pope says we all need to combine our religions together, do you think he's going to resist? But that's still not all. But you might be thinking, "Well hey, the rest of us Southern Baptists are going to fall for it!" Well I certainly hope not! The last couple of weeks have shown some concern, at least those who are higher up.
Russell Moore, is the president of the Southern Baptists Ethics and Religious Liberty Commission and he said recently...

"Gay Therapy, the attempts to change a person's sexual orientation, has been 'severely counterproductive.'" And he "Joins a chorus of psychologists and religious leaders who have departed from the once-popular therapy."

So, with all due respect, telling people "you are no longer slaves to sin" **Romans 6** and you can have a "new identity" and become a "new creation" and become a "new person" in Christ is now counter-productive? While flying back from a conference I came across this article. "Russell Moore and Rick Warren join 'Pope Francis' with Muslims, Buddhists for an Interfaith Conference on Marriage." What? What are you doing meeting with the Pope? Folks, this is not looking good!
And by the way, the Conference is sponsored by, "The Pontifical Council for the Family, the Pontifical Council for Interreligious Dialogue, and the Pontifical Council for Promoting Christian Unity." You know, the Catholic

Church saying let's all come together as ONE with the Vatican! As crazy as that sounds, Protestant pastors are doing just that! They're "converting" to Catholicism! Check this out!

Larry Lewis is one of the growing number of individuals who converted. He says, "I was a Protestant minister for over 30 years in different areas of ministry and I was very content, happy, thrilled about it actually. Then pastoring in the United Methodist Church, in the middle of my pastorate there, we were kind of blindsided by the Blessed Mother.

It came out of nowhere, and really began to turn our whole lives around." Steven Barham, a popular speaker at Marion Conferences attended Assembly of God before becoming a priest. He says, "The content is the same basic structure as the gospel. Repent, be converted, fast, pray, pray for the renewal of the church and go back to the sacrament.[25]

Go back to the Sacraments? That's not the Gospel! That guy's preaching a false gospel that works with the One World Religion that the Bible said would come in the last days! And in order for this to come to pass, the Protestant Reformation would have to somehow, someway, someday, be overturned. As you just saw with your own eyes, it is! Right now!

"If these events culminate during the 7-year Tribulation, the Rise of a One World Religion, and the Antichrist going up into a rebuilt temple, declaring himself to be god halfway into the 7-year Tribulation AND these events keep lining up, then how much closer is the rapture of the Church, which takes place prior to the 7-year Tribulation!" We don't know that exact day or hour, but folks, we need to get ready!

Out of love, God has given us all these signs of a One World Religion and the Vatican to show us that the Tribulation is near and the Rapture is right around the corner! And that's why Jesus Himself said,

Luke 21:28 "When these things begin to take place, stand up and lift up your heads, because your redemption is drawing near."

Everything's going down the tubes, including the Church, and you don't want to be here! It's going to be the worst time in the history of mankind! Therefore, if you're reading this today and you are a Christian, then what in the world are you doing for Jesus? Let's get busy working together fulfilling the Great Commission doing something splendid for Jesus, amen? But if you're not a

Christian, then I beg you, please, heed the signs, heed the warnings, give your life to Jesus today, because tomorrow may be too late!

Chapter Eight

One World Government

"First of all, it started with Bill's truck breaking down so he had to take the bus to work. So, he gets on the bus and he notices this elderly lady sitting in front of him and she turns around and offers Bill a handful of almonds.

Well Bill had totally forgot about breakfast, so he was grateful and he munches them right up. In fact, about every 5 minutes, the old lady repeats the gesture and gives Bill even more almonds during the whole trip.

Just before the bus was to let Bill off, he asked the lady why she didn't just eat the almonds herself. And she responded, "It's not possible with her old teeth, she's not able to chew them."

So, Bill asked, "Well, why do you buy them?" To which the lady replied, "I just love to suck the chocolate off of them."

After Bill brushed his teeth 14 times and ate 800 packs of gum, he finally gets to the office and later that day he meets Dianne at the park for lunch and they're taking this romantic walk in the park, and Dianne notices this young man and woman sitting on a park bench, passionately kissing.

And so she asks Bill, "Hey, why don't you do that?" To which Bill replied, "Dianne, I don't even know that woman!"

Dianne storms off and leaves Bill at the park and later that night Dianne is feeling a little guilty about how she just ditched Bill there at the park, so she decides to try to be romantic one more time. She's downstairs and Bill's upstairs, so she sends Bill a text that goes like this.

"If you are sleeping, send me your dreams. If you are laughing, send me your smile. If you are eating, send me a bite. If you are drinking, send me a sip. If you are crying, send me your tears. I love you."

To which Bill texted back, "I am in the bathroom. Please advise."[1]

Seriously, how many of you would say Bill had a rough week, you know what I'm saying? Man! Nothing was going right for him!

Did you know there's an even worse week than that coming to the whole planet one day? It's called the 70th Week of Daniel, which is the final week of the 7-year Tribulation, and it all begins at the Rapture of the Church! The reason it's going to be such a horrible time-frame is because for those who refuse to accept Jesus Christ as their Personal Lord and Savior, they will be catapulted into the 7-year Tribulation and it's not a joke!

The 9th update on *The Final Countdown* study that is letting us know we're living in the last days is the rise of a **One World Government.**

Are you serious? Yes, the Bible is clear. One day the whole planet really is going to be under the control or government of the Antichrist. But don't take my word for it. Let's listen to God's.

Revelation 13:1-7 "And I saw a beast coming out of the sea. He had ten horns and seven heads, with ten crowns on his horns, and on each head a blasphemous name. The beast I saw resembled a leopard, but had feet like those of a bear and a mouth like that of a lion. The dragon gave the beast his power and his throne and great authority. One of the heads of the beast seemed to have had a fatal wound, but the fatal wound had been healed. The whole world was astonished and followed the beast. Men worshiped the dragon because he had given authority to the beast, and they also worshiped the beast and asked, "Who is like the beast? Who can make war against him?" The beast was given a mouth to utter proud words and blasphemies and to exercise his authority for forty-two months. He opened his mouth to blaspheme God, and to slander his name and his dwelling place and those who live in heaven. He was given power to make war against the saints and to conquer them. And he was given authority over every tribe, people, language and nation."

According to our text there, the Bible is clear. There really is coming a day when all the inhabitants of the earth will be under the authority or government of who? The Antichrist, right? One day, the whole world will be unified into a One World Government that is actually satanically inspired. It says it right there in the text. But again, the question for you and I is, "Could that really happen? "
Could the whole world really be deceived into creating a One World Government that's satanically inspired and is there any evidence that it's really going to take place just like the Bible said any time soon?" It's happening now!

The 1st proof that we know we are headed for a One World Government real soon is **The Quotation Proof.**

What most people don't realize is that this One World Government is not only going to be put into place, because the Bible said it would, but what people don't realize is that it's been in the planning stages for a long time. You can see that by their verbiage! There's a phrase out there to describe this One World Government and it's called a New World Order.
Just like we saw with the One World Religion, whenever you hear of the words "Interfaith" or "Interfaithism" or "Multifaith" "Ecumenicalism" etc. you need to supplant it for what it is, it means One World Religion. Those are "buzz" words. Code words. And so, it is with this phrase, "New World Order." It means One World Government. Wherever you see that, in print, in media, out of people's mouths, supplant it for what it is. It means One World Government. People right now are using it all over the world, even our own Government. And they've been doing it for years if you've been paying attention.
For instance, Richard Nixon called for a New World Order as far back as 1967. Then Nelson Rockefeller called for it the next year, Mikhail Gorbachev started calling for a New World Order, so did George Bush Sr. Then Bill Clinton called for a New World Order, then Tom Brokaw, Walter Cronkite, George Bush Jr., Tony Blair, and Gordon Brown. Putin from Russia said we need a New World Order, China called for one recently, so did Iran, even the Pope said we have to have one. Then Al Gore said we need a New World Order, the former French President Chirac called for a New World Order, so did David Rockefeller, Strobe Talbot (Clinton's Deputy Secretary of State), Nelson Mandela, Madeleine

Albright, and Robert Muller from the U.N. called for a New World Order and even said this: "We must move as quickly as possible to a one-world government; one-world religion; under a one-world leader." That's from the U.N. Exactly what the text says! Then George Soros, the billionaire, called for a New World Order, Henry Kissinger has been calling for a New World Order for many years and even recently said, "Obama is primed to create a New World Order."

And after that, lo and behold, President Obama started saying just that, "All nations must come together to build a stronger, global regime." AND he's still out there promoting this idea that we need a new International Global System.

Obama: Leaders, dignitaries, of the European Union, representatives of our NATO Alliance, distinguished guests. We meet here at a moment of testing for Europe and the United States and for the International Order that we have worked for generations to build.²

International Order? He is working for an American Order? Isn't that what an American President needs to do? But that's not all. His cohort, Vice President Joe Biden is even more blunt about it. Listen to what he said recently to a graduation class of Military cadets. Here's what he wants them to focus on!

Channel 4 reports:

Vice President Joe Biden calls the newest graduates of the Air Force Academy strategic thinkers as well as warriors and the future of the New World Order. Biden: It's time for us to refocus our military assets and resources to other parts of the world where they are needed where we face new challenges. This is the world you are graduating into. This is what I want to talk to you about today for a few minutes. I believe we and impractically you, your class has an incredible window of opportunity. To lead in shaping a new world order for the 21st century.³

Really? You are encouraging our young military to be a part of a New World Order? How about encouraging them to help protect America's freedom and interests and thanking them for their service and if you think this really isn't going on, maybe that's why Defense Secretary Chuck Hagel recently resigned. He admitted that a New World Order is being built right now.

Washington Idea Forum reports:

Could you give us a brief big picture of how dangerous you think this time in history is? Is it chronic annoyance or actual danger and when will the United States see some end to these wars especially this now 13-year war in Iraq and Afghanistan? Chuck Hagel: Jim, I think we are living through one of these historic defining times. I think we are seeing a new world order. Post WWII, post-Soviet Union implosion being built.[4]

So, a New World Order is being built? Reports said he disagreed with Obama's policies, maybe this is one of them. And if you think this is far-fetched, even the secular media is admitting there was a purging of American military leaders who wouldn't go along with his policies.

Next News Network reports:

President Obama is leading a wholesale purging of military leadership. No One knows why the moves are taking place. Nine senior generals have lost their commands so far, this year. Up to 200 other military leaders have been removed from their positions by the President in the last 5 years.

A growing number of retired generals are questioning the reason behind the removals. A few former leaders say the administration is removing military leaders who may have policy differences with Obama. Former generals and admirals say the President is also using dismissals to scare those who remain into complying with his policies. One former Navy Seal is telling the press that the President is removing military leaders who will not agree to disarm Americans.

Fox news reports:

Hundreds of top military leaders leaving their post since President Obama took office. Why I ask. Who is filling that void. Joining us now is CEO of Concerned Veterans for American, Pete Hagstaf. "You're still active in the reserves right, is it different, is it beyond attrition when we talk about these leaders retiring?" Pete Hagstaf replies, "I think it is, you've seen 5 years under this commander and chief and he has a different prospective about a lot of things about the military.

He has a perceptive about what this military should look like and how it should be used and over 5 years you are going to see the war fighter and independent minded types slowly sifted out and instead your house cats that are willing to go along with this agenda."[5]

House cats who will go along with your agenda? International Order. New World Order. What do you do with those who don't agree? Oh, that's right, you get rid of any and all resisters, those wise old Generals and other mature military personnel who are more patriotic, and then train up a younger generation of house cats who are more compliant. So much for a conspiracy theory. Even the secular news is admitting it! But you look at the facts, and somebody's pushing for this One World Government right now! And this is what the Bible said would happen, when you're living in the last days!

The 2nd proof that we know we are headed for a One World Government is the **Coercive Proof.**

The 1st way the Antichrist is coercing us to go along with a One World Government is through a **Universal Court System.**

You see, just in case you can't be re-educated into a house cat, like this younger generation, unfortunately, we now have the legal means to make you do it anyway! And that's through the court system. A Universal Courts System that is! And this is the kind of pressure the Bible says the Antichrist is going to use to push forth his agenda

Revelation 13:11-18 Then I saw another beast, coming out of the earth. He had two horns like a lamb, but he spoke like a dragon. He exercised all the authority of the first beast on his behalf, and made the earth and its inhabitants worship the first beast, whose fatal wound had been healed. And he performed great and miraculous signs, even causing fire to come down from heaven to earth in full view of men. Because of the signs he was given power to do on behalf of the first beast, he deceived the inhabitants of the earth. He ordered them to set up an image in honor of the beast who was wounded by the sword and yet lived. He was given power to give breath to the image of the first beast, so that it could speak and cause all who refused to worship the image to be killed. He also forced everyone, small and great, rich and poor, free and slave, to receive a mark on his right hand or on his forehead, so that no one could buy or sell unless he had the mark, which is the name of the beast or the number of his name. This calls for wisdom. If anyone has insight, let him calculate the number of the beast, for it is man's number. His number is 666.

So here we see how the Bible clearly says that the False Prophet in the last days is not only going to dupe the whole world into worshiping the Antichrist, but he's what? He's going to make them, he's going to order them, he's going to cause them, he's going to force them to do whatever he says to do, otherwise they will what? They will die, right? Again, I want to focus on the key words there, "make" "order" "cause" and "force." In the Greek they literally mean, "to carry out, to command, to direct or to execute." This implies there's some serious enforcement going on here! In fact, it's global enforcement because again, that's the context. He forces the whole planet to do whatever in the world he wants them to do. How? Well, believe it or not, it's through this Universal Court System. As we saw before, there is already a World Criminal Court that went into effect July of 2002, thanks in part to the signing of the treaty by Bill Clinton on his last day in office. Thanks Bill! Thanks for your help in forming a

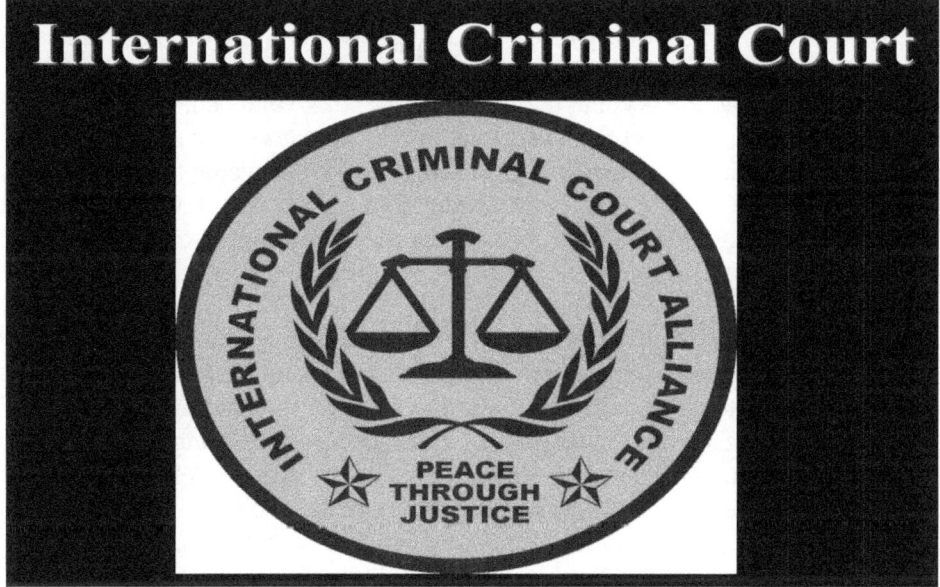

One World Government. It's called the International Criminal Court and it's the first permanent international criminal court. With, "Jurisdiction over crimes threatening the peace, security and well-being of the world" and it was negotiated by 160 countries.

Recently, Chief Justices from 60 different countries participated in a summit in India called, "The International Conference of Chief Justices of the

World" to, "Globally enact applicable world laws to protect the future of humanity, end wars, deal with the problem of terrorism, illiteracy, and climate change." Because we all know global warming is spiraling out of control, yeah right! It's just another excuse to shove this through!

That's not the first summit. It's the 14th annual one! And they said there, "The time is ripe for a peaceful revolutionary change which can bring the countries together and unite them as One World." They just said that at this conference! And that sounds exactly how the Antichrist is going to launch his kingdom at the beginning of the 7-year Tribulation.

Revelation 6:1-2 "I watched as the Lamb opened the first of the seven seals. Then I heard one of the four living creatures say in a voice like thunder, 'Come!' I looked, and there before me was a white horse! Its rider held a bow, and he was given a crown, and he rode out as a conqueror bent on conquest."

Many would say this passage is dealing with the Antichrist and his rise to power during the 7-year Tribulation, riding on a white horse, no arrows just a bow, meaning a bloodless coup, possibly with the stroke of a pen. Like these judges and Universal Court System are calling for right now! We need a "peaceful revolutionary change." A guy who will take this planet over, without war, with a stroke of our pens! Exactly what the text says! That's what they're calling for right now! BUT, if you think about it, if this is going to succeed, at some point you have to somehow coerce the countries to give up their national sovereignty.

And guess what? That's also exactly what this International Summit of Judges are calling for right now as well. "All the countries must shed off a part of their sovereignty to come under the umbrella of the World Parliament and World Government. It's the only way to prevent the innocents from being slaughtered in brutal wars. Fanaticism and terrorism are global issues and need global laws."

"We, judges, can make things happen. A World Judicial System is the only way to solve global problems and ensure equality of all nations." And if you think our world's not "ripe" for this lie, listen to this guy again. This is former Belgian Prime Minister Paul-Henri Spaak. He said this:

Paul Henri Spaak Quote:

We do not want another committee. We have too many already. What we want is a man of sufficient stature to hold the allegiance of all people and to lift us out of the economic morass in which we are sinking. Send us such a man and, be he God or the devil, we will receive him.[6]

Sounds to me like somebody's ripe for the Antichrist and a One World Government, how about you? Yeah, slightly! And the courts are there to sign off on it!

The 2nd way the Antichrist is coercing us to go along with this One World Government is through a **Universal Army.**

You see, not everybody's going to go along with this. And so, you need some sort of strong arm to force people to do it anyway. You need some sort of global army to pull it off! And that's exactly what the Bible said is coming next after this false peace!

Revelation 6:3-4 "When the Lamb opened the second seal, I heard the second living creature say, 'Come!' Then another horse came out, a fiery red one. Its rider was given power to take peace from the earth and to make men slay each other. To him was given a large sword."

In other words, this time is going to be a horrible slaughter! And that's what the text says later, 1/4th of the earth is annihilated! But according to the Bible, right after this "bloodless peaceful coup" this false peace by the Antichrist, there's going to come a global war! Which means he's going to have to have at his disposal some sort of global force or army to put resisters down, right? That's what we already saw with this younger generation of military cadets being brainwashed to fight for a New World Order instead of America's best interests!

That's why the older Vets are getting kicked out! There's an ol' switcheroo going on! The world's militaries, even our own, are being prepared to fight for a New World Order, a Global Government! And this is nothing new! They've been training people for years!

For instance, Tony Blair, the former British Prime Minister, has been calling for years for NATO to become the future "military arm of a New World Order rather than strictly a defensive alliance." If you think about it, we've already seen NATO exercise more and more military force over the sovereignty of nations, right? In our lifetime. I wonder who's next?

Some would even say this has been planned even as far back as 1952, as the following map on the next page shows you from the World Association of Parliamentarians for World Government in London.[7]

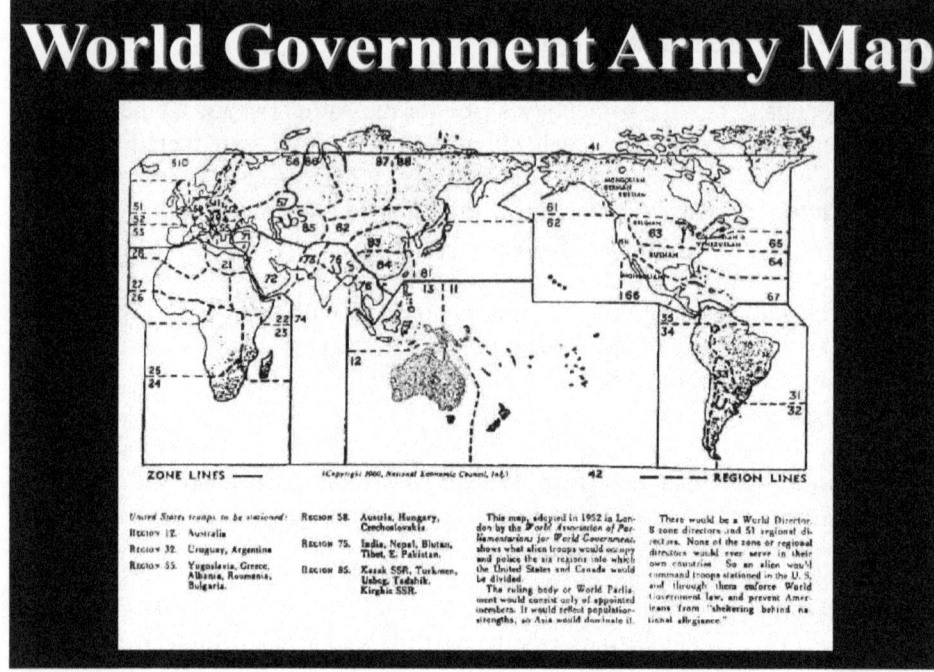

They met in London to plan on how they can have foreign troops stationed in foreign countries to help control things around the world. Why? Because it's awfully hard for an American soldier to shoot a fellow American, right? But not if that soldier was from China. And believe it or not, that's what's on this map! It details how in America they plan to have Chinese, Russian, Colombian, Venezuelan, and Belgian troops stationed here. And American troops stationed in Europe to help control things over there! But good thing we'll never see foreign troops on America soil. In fact, speaking of Chinese, the Chinese military just finished, for the first time in history, training on American soil.

Soldiers with the Hawaii National Guard recently joined their Chinese counterparts for an inaugural disaster training. Tech Sergeant Andrew Jackson has more. Hawaii National Guard Search and Rescue soldiers recently participated in the first ever search and rescue extraction training event between the U.S. and Chinese militaries.

During this 3 days disaster management exercise, search and extraction professionals got a chance to learn from each other while working hand in hand in a simulated disaster environment. Previous engagements involved planning *and table top strategy sessions. This is the first-time rescuers from the two nations had the chance to work together in a field environment.*⁸

If that works, that's good, then maybe we can work together down the road in another crisis when global war breaks out and we need to re-establish control and these foreign troops can help us, a communist military on American soil? Why would we allow that, unless somebody's got a plan? But that's not all. If you think it's not going to work towards policing, the Chinese Police have been hired by France to police its people in Paris!

*In a decision that has surprised many but which may simply be a sign of things to come, France will allow Chinese Police to patrol tourist areas in Paris. For more than two centuries it's been armed Frenchmen that have been patrolling the streets of foreign countries. Now that the shoe will be on the other foot many in France can barely contain their surprise and indignation. One man on the street says, "The country should control things by itself. It's not right for foreign police to be stationed here."*⁹

I agree with him. What is a communist country doing policing your western country? It's almost like somebody's got a plan and step by step they're conditioning people to, make the words of Henry Kissinger seem more real!

Henry Kissinger:

*Today America would be outraged if U.N. troops entered Los Angeles to restore order. Tomorrow they will be grateful. When presented with this scenario, individual rights will be willingly relinquished for the guarantee of their well-being granted to them by the World Government.*¹⁰

But you're assuming the soldier of the future is going to even have a choice! You might be thinking, "Well hey listen, there's no way that any good red-blooded American soldier is going to go along with this bologna. They're not going to go along with this Universal Army!" Really? Believe it or not, they are working on a remote controlled universal soldier that will do whatever they want it to do, whenever they want it to do it, no matter where he's from! The previous administration launched what's called The Brain Initiative.

The U.S. President, Barack Obama, has proposed a 100 million US dollar initiative to map the human brains activity in unprecedented detail. Saying this

1.4-kilogram organ remains largely a mystery. Obama says, "As humans we can identify galaxies light years away, we can study particles that are smaller than an atom, but we still haven't unlocked the mystery of the 3 lb. of matter that sits between our ears."[11]

Okay, so let me get this straight, the timing of this is when people were out of work, they're losing their jobs, unemployment is running out of control, and they're losing their homes, you say our biggest need right now is to map the human brain? It didn't make any sense to me either, until I found out who was getting the funding for this Brain Initiative program. And that's the program called DARPA. The Defense Advanced Research Projects Agency.

That's the same group we saw before who is working in super human enhancements for soldiers, like super human strength, super human endurance, super human protection, super human pain tolerance, etc. And now, thanks to this Brain Initiative, DARPA is now funded to work on a super human brain chip that can be implanted in soldier's brains, to enhance their memories.

Back in April of 2013 President Obama unveiled the Brain Initiative, a bold new research looking at the brain. The White House pledged to spend $100 million US dollars to study how our brains work. One year into the initiative there's big news to report. The next few months highly secretive military researchers say they will unveil the advancements of plans that could one day restore a wounded soldier's memory. DARPA is behind this sophisticated memory stimulator. While this is great news for those who suffered brain injury, some people see it in a different light. Manipulating memories in people could open an ethical minefield.[12]

Not to mention we're also assuming that's all they're going to use it for, to help heal memories. Unfortunately, we know if you do the homework, it's going to be used to create a remote control soldier.

Brain machine interfaces, a technology that marks the beginning of a new kind of man, the cyborg, the robot man. Neuro robotic technology can be applied in different directions. The brain controlling the machine or the machine controlling the brain.

But a third option is also possible, one brain controlling another brain via the interface. Two electrodes in the sensory cortex of the rat sends stimuli to the zones connected to its whiskers. When the rat follows the signals sent to it's left side it and turns in that direction, it is rewarded with a discharge to it's pleasure zone. This discharge releases a dose of dopamine providing instant pleasure. This zone is also called the brain reward center.

We possess a reward center too, just like the rat. In the process of creating a cyborg this is square one. If we send a stimulus to the zone related to the hand we create a sensation in that area. In the same way via the motor cortex we can provoke an involuntary movement.

In Boston, the first machine interface trials have already been conducted on paraplegic patients. Thanks to an electrode chip called 'The Brain Gate' they can operate a computer remotely by thought. So, it's no coincidence that these researches are partly funded by DARPA. Neuroscience will bring us the soldier of the future.[13]

Who apparently, with the help of technology, will do whatever the Antichrist wants him to do, even take out a fellow countryman and feel good about it, as the Antichrist builds his satanic One World Government! And where are the two places on the human body people can take the Mark of the Antichrist? In the right hand, or the forehead. You know, like a Brain Chip! This is all happening, right now, it's not make-believe, it's not Science Fiction, it's present day reality! And this is why, out of love, God has given us all these signs of a One World Government to show us that the Tribulation is near and the Rapture is right around the corner.

The 3rd proof that we know we are headed for a One World Government is what I call the **Union Proof.**

That's right, I'm not talking about the teamsters. Believe it or not it's something way worse than that! I'm talking about the Ten Horned Kingdom or Unions that the Bible says the planet would be split up into in the last days! But don't take my word for it. Let's listen to God's.

Revelation 17:9-13 "This calls for a mind with wisdom. The seven heads are seven hills on which the woman sits. They are also seven kings. Five have fallen, one is, the other has not yet come; but when he does come, he must remain for a little while. The beast who once was, and now is not, is an eighth king. He belongs to the seven and is going to his destruction. The ten horns you saw are ten kings who have not yet received a kingdom, but who for one hour will receive authority as kings along with the beast. They have one purpose and will give their power and authority to the beast."

So according to the Bible, we see how the Antichrist's kingdom is going to be split up into ten different parts ruled by ten different kings or leaders, right? Then, at one point, they surrender their power and authority over to him, right? It says it right there, okay? Use your mind of wisdom! It's a good thing we see no signs of that happening today! The planet being split up into 10 different kingdoms or unions. It's happening right now! We already saw they are creating 10 World Regions to ensure proper control of the whole world! And it's not just 5, not 19, not even 122, but exactly 10! Let's take a look at that again.[14]

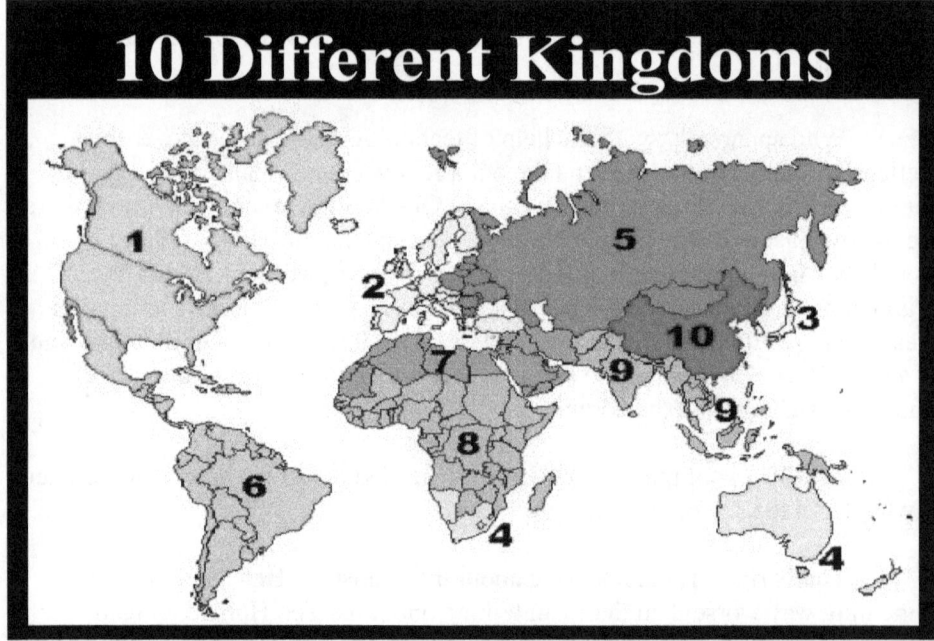

So, look at the facts, it looks to me like our world has already been split up into 10 different kingdoms headed up by 10 different kings! Exactly like the text says! In fact, we have been slowly and methodically prepared for this. This is what we saw before with the birth of the European Union. It's a region of countries coming together with their own currency called the Euro. And that was a watershed event, because if you look at that map and pay attention to the Geo-Political world, you're going to see they're following that map to a tee! Exactly like the text says! 10 Nations are being formed right now!

Nobody gets the importance of what's going on in the Geo-Political realm because they're not paying attention to the Bible and what it says about last days Antichrist's 10-Horned Kingdom! Let's take a look at how close it is to coming to pass.

North American Union, Nation #1 This is the economic and political union of Canada, Mexico, and the United States and is based on the same concept of the European Union. It includes a common currency called the Amero or North American Dollar and has been the subject of academic, business, and political circles for decades.

Western Europe, Nation #2 – This of course is the aforementioned European Union that currently has 28-member states with a capital in Brussels. The combined population includes over 500 million people, or 7.3% of the world's population, and has 24 different languages. They have their own international government, court system, councils, and central bank. Their monetary union was established in 1999 with the Euro and is the second largest reserve currency as well as the second most traded currency in the world after the United States dollar.

Japan, Nation #3 – They have already been in several talks with several different proposed unions including the Asia-Pacific Economic Cooperation (APEC) a forum of 21 Pacific Rim countries in the Asia Pacific region, as well as the China–Japan-South Korea Free Trade Agreement and the Trans-Pacific Partnership (TPP) which is a proposed regional free trade agreement with 12 different countries throughout the Asia-Pacific region including the United States.

Australia, South Africa Nation #4 – Australia has already entered into various unions with other countries including the Australia New Zealand Closer Economic Relations Trade Agreement (ANZCERTA) sometimes shortened to (CERTA). It came into effect in 1983 and there has been a recent call from both Australian and New Zealand business communities to extend this union to other Pacific nations so as to move toward a single market, allow the free movement of people and goods, stabilize the region, reduce security threats, and political unrest. One possibility is to create what's called a Pacific Union that's composed of member-states from the Pacific area with a common charter, institutions, and currency.

Eastern Europe, Russia, Nation #5 – While many may have believed that Russia, a communist country, would never go along with combining their country with others, recently, the unthinkable happened. Russia entered an agreement with other Eastern European countries and formed the Eurasian Economic Union creating an energy superpower, that now produces about 20.7% of the world's natural gas, and 9% of the world's electrical energy. Here's the announcement.

Katie Pilbeam, Venture Capital Presenter reports:

Leaders of Russia, Kazakhstan and Belarus have agreed to set up a new Eurasian Economic Union at the summit in the Kazakh Capital of Astana. It's a lot of money at stake and it's a historic deal as well. I'm going to break it down for you, all the detail.

This deal represents a new era of trade. As the Russian President said, the signed agreement has landmark historic importance, as you can see. The ex-soviet neighbors can now enjoy the free movement of goods, capital and services as well as the free movement of people.

170 million people in total and the group is set to get even bigger with Armenia and Kazakhstan expected to join the union later in the year. As you can see geographically where these countries sit and how close they are it makes economic sense for these countries to partner up.[15]

Its new currency will be called the "Altyn" which means "gold" and is from a Turkic word referring to an ancient gold coin once used by the Russians that also means "six" since one "altyn" equaled "6" dengi. Also, this new Eurasian Economic Union would help explain as well some of Russia's recent behavior since according to the map, Georgia and Ukraine are supposed to be a part of this Union.

Latin America, Nation #6 – In 2004, presidents and representatives from 12 South American nations signed what was called the Cusco Declaration that announced foundation of the Union of South American Nations. This group announced upfront that their intention was to model their new community after the European Union, including a common currency, parliament, and passport. The Union's headquarters will be located in Ecuador, the Parliament in Bolivia, and the banking system in Venezuela.

North Africa and the Middle East, Nation #7 – Right now there is a call for a Middle Eastern Union to also be patterned after the European Union that would put the populations ranging from Turkey and Jordan to Libya and Egypt under a single authority and rule over the Arab, Turkish, Kurdish, and other peoples who live there. As the Middle East Union Congress states on its website, "We dream of a Middle East that is empowered, free, and governs for all its peoples in a new world where the Middle East Union is an important integral part of a greater global community that pledges its allegiance to the earth and every human on it." This proposed Union may also help explain why there's been so much turmoil and unrest over in these Middle Eastern countries lately. In recent years we've seen many rulers overthrown in Tunisia, Morocco, Libya, Pakistan, and Egypt as well as invasions to Iraq, Afghanistan, and possibly soon Iran. Maybe they've been resisting this plan and so they've been "encouraged" to go along with it anyway including a new leader who will. Which ultimately leads us to the question about the Jewish people. What's going to happen when Israel refuses to go along with this Union because you know they will because this is an Arab dominated union that has vowed to kill them? Well, many scholars believe this is when we will see the Hand of God come down and protect His people in a profound fashion as Zechariah states:

Zechariah 12:1,2-4,6 "This is the word of the LORD concerning Israel. I am going to make Jerusalem a cup that sends all the surrounding peoples reeling. Judah will be besieged as well as Jerusalem. On that day, when all the nations of the earth are gathered against her, I will make Jerusalem an immovable rock for all the nations. All who try to move it will injure themselves. On that day I will strike every horse with panic and its rider with madness, declares the LORD. I will keep a watchful eye over the house of Judah, but I will blind all the horses of the nations. On that day I will make the leaders of Judah like a firepot in a woodpile, like a flaming torch among sheaves. They will consume right and left all the surrounding peoples, but Jerusalem will remain intact in her place."

Zechariah 14:12 "This is the plague with which the Lord will strike all the nations that fought against Jerusalem: Their flesh will rot while they are still standing on their feet, their eyes will rot in their sockets, and their tongues will rot in their mouths."

Now again, some people would say that this is just some sovereign act of God where He supernaturally causes a plague that instantly removes people's flesh while they're standing. And it could be. I personally don't want to be there to find out. However, with the modern weaponry that we see today, what does that graphic description sound like to you? Kind of like a nuclear holocaust, doesn't it? Either way, once you understand what God says in the Bible about His people and how He's going to protect them, as well as people's intentions with this map, everything starts to fall into place, doesn't it?

Tropical Africa, Nation #8 – This Union has already been accomplished for many years. It's called the African Union and it consists of 54 African states with the only African State that is not a member being Morocco. It was established in 2001 and launched in 2002 representing over 1 billion people and has plans for an African monetary Union to be administered by the African Central Bank and a new unified currency, similar to the Euro, called the Afro. Other versions call it the Afriq and it's expected to be out in the next several years.

Southeast Asia, Nation #9 – This Union has also already been formed before our very eyes. It's known as the Association of Southeast Asian Nations or ASEAN and it's a political and economic union of a multitude of countries located in Southeast Asia and a land mass totaling 3% of the planet. It is now the seventh largest economy in the world and they are proposing to use Asian Currency Unit (ACU) which is similar to the European Currency Unit (ECU), which was the precursor of the Euro. There has also been recent talks of India, one of the nations mentioned on this map, now joining ASEAN via its new Prime Minister, and if this occurs, the ASEAN Union will represent nearly 2 Billion people on the planet passing Japan as the #3 economy in the entire world.

China, Nation #10 – China has not only risen in recent years out of the blue to become a world superpower but even a world super economic power. And this is because they have been working for quite some time behind the scenes aligning themselves with several different trade agreements and unions like the Asia-Pacific Trade Agreement (APTA) as well as the Shanghai Co-operation Organization (SCO). This union has not only allowed them to become a dominant political and economic power in their region, but the dominant security institution as well. According to the Strategic Studies Institute, the U.S. Army's institute for geostrategic and national security research and analysis, "China's standing armed force of some 2.8 million active soldiers in uniform is the largest military force in the world. Approximately 1 million reservists and some 15 million militia also back them up. With a population of over 1.2 billion people, China also has a potential manpower base of another 200 million males fit for military service available at any time." Now that's not only a huge army, but it's the exact number that Bible mentions that's going to wipe out 1/3rd of mankind during the 7-year Tribulation.[16]

I don't know about you, but I'd say if you pay attention to the Geo-Political realm, our world's being split up into 10 different kingdoms or regions or unions right now before our very eyes. That's exactly what the Bible said would happen, when you're living in the last days!

Speaking of these unions and 10 kingdoms, I wanted to back up to the first one we skipped over called the North American Union. That's the one most of us here in America have a hard time dealing with because we think there is no way in the world that the American people are going to ever surrender their freedom, their national sovereignty, their unique identity, and create a union with Canada and Mexico. No way! Well, first of all, we know it's going to happen, in one form or another, because the Bible said it's going to happen, but two, you need to realize it's been being worked on and planned on for years right behind our backs!

The **1st way** we know America is going to be swallowed up into a 10 Horned Kingdom of the Antichrist is the **Currency Proof**.

There have been talks and plans for many years now, for the United States to be merged into what's called this North American Union. This proposed "union" between the United States, Canada and Mexico would have a new currency called the Amero. It was leaked out several years ago on a financial news broadcast, and what they're saying now is all we need is for is the right crisis to come along and put it into play.

Ron Paul:

There is a move towards a North American Union.

Lou Dobbs:
Security and prosperity, a partnership, some people call the North American Union.

Dan Dicks, Press for the Truth:

It's essentially the centralization of power into fewer hands.

Herbert Grubel, Father of the Amero:

What would be the benefit of creating the equivalent of the euro? I had the inspiration to call it the Amero.

Worldwide exchange CNBC:

I think one thing that people who are dollar based need to focus on is the Amero and that is one thing no one is talking about that I think is going to have a big impact on everybody's life in Canada, US and Mexico. A new currency for the North American community which is being developed right now between Canada, the US, and Mexico to make a borderless community much like the EU.

CNN Reports:

Our economies are now very integrated, societies are growing increasingly integrated. What's needed now is a North American idea for all three. The greatest initiatives have usually originated from some crisis of some sort.

Herbert Grubel:

My hope is that eventually if there is a major catastrophe, that there will be enough people around who will say this may be the time to try out this money.[17]

That's Hebert Grubel, the father of the Amero and as you read he admits all we need is the right crisis to come along, and hopefully enough people will be there to launch this new currency! Laugh all you want, I think that's what they want you to do so you won't pay attention to this, but this is what these people are really working on behind the scenes! Whether it ends up being called the Amero or not, that's not the point. This combining of our currencies into an *Economic Union* with other countries is exactly what the Bible said would happen in the last days!

The **2nd way** we know America is going to be swallowed up into a 10 Horned Antichrist Kingdom is the **Highway Proof**.

In order to help these three countries come together, Canada, U.S., and Mexico, you not only need a single currency, you also need a single infrastructure to connect all three countries to keep the goods flowing back and forth for that economy, right? That's exactly what's been going on for quite some time! Believe it or not, there's a giant super highway called the NAFTA Superhighway or Trans Texas Corridor that is being built right now through America that will connect all three countries together. One congresswoman was blowing the whistle on it for quite some time, but nobody was listening to her. Let's take a look.

Rep. Marcy Kaptur, D-Ohio says the following:

Today I want to talk a little bit about super NAFTA and what the Bush administration is planning to lock NAFTA in even tighter in this country and across the continent. There's something called an Agreement on Security and Prosperity that is being negotiated by the Bush administration. Very quietly, no hearings are being held in this congress, most Americans have never even heard of the term.

This security and prosperity agreement as it is being called has no democratic underpinning to it. It's being negotiated by the very same elites that negotiated NAFTA. Let's look at some of the signs that are happening.

It is suddenly clearer why a company from Spain called Cintra wants to be the gatekeeper on this new highway structure. Cintra is a subsidiary of Throvial, a Spanish transportation company founded by multi-billionaire Raphael DePino who is one of the richest people in the world. The people of the United States had better wake up.[18]

Maybe she was just being an alarmist and she was blowing this all out of proportion. Maybe it's really not that bad. Actually, it's way worse than you can ever imagine. We're going to pay tolls to a foreign company if this continues to go through.

The New World Order is rapidly constructing the physical infrastructure of the North American Union. The NAFTA super highway control grid. More than 80 federal and state highways have been designated as international arteries. The I-35 NAFTA corridor starts deep inside Mexico and travels through the middle of the United States and ends in central Canada.

Container ships from Asia dump their cargo on the Pacific side of Mexico. It then travels duty free by rail to the new Kansas City inland port now considered sovereign soil of Mexico in the heart of the United States. Under international agreements predominately foreign companies are placing tolls on the already existing paid for roads.

Federal, state, and corporate documents show that they will then use the revenue raised to build up a transportation infrastructure of Mexico not the United States or Canada. Foreign made products can pour in even faster from Mexico.

Revenues raised will also be used to fund the fledgling North American Union and its growing bureaucracy. Bottom line they are using our own money to enslave us.

Arthur Peterson, Col. Retired Army:

To think that people would even consider confiscating land of farmers and ranchers and taking their homes away from them and turn it over to a foreign company in Spain which is controlled by a notorious socialist and they get the tolls on this land for 50 years. I see things today that are happening that would make my friends who died in World War II turn over in their graves.[19]

It's pretty shocking and it's really happening. Why would a sovereign nation, America, as patriotic as we are, turn our backs on the freedom that was hard fought, won, bought and paid for, with blood, and turn it over to a foreign country? It makes no sense, until you realize that the Bible says it's all part of the Antichrists 10 Horned Kingdom that would appear on the scene when you're living in the last days!

The 3rd proof we know America is going to be swallowed up into a 10 Horned Antichrist Kingdom is the **Border Proof**.

You see, if all three countries are going to be tied together in this new North American Union via the currencies and that highway system is to keep that economy going then you need some sort of way to control the borders, right? I mean, it makes total sense. You not only have to control the flow of goods going back and forth, but also the people, right?

So how are you going to identify every single person coming across the border and what country they're from, and who they are, as well as identify those troublemakers who won't go along with program? First, to deal with the troublemakers, you'd need to combine your armed forces together. And that too has already been done with the formation of a North American Army. I didn't hear about it either because it wasn't in the media, by design.

"In a ceremony that received virtually no attention in the American media, the United States and Canada signed a military agreement allowing the armed forces from one nation to support the armed forces of the other nation during a domestic civil emergency." (This is not a time of war!)

"The agreement, defined as a Civil Assistance Plan, was not submitted to Congress for approval, nor did Congress pass any law or treaty specifically authorizing this military agreement to combine the operations of the armed forces of the U.S. and Canada in the event of a domestic civil disturbance."

"The military plan is designed to bypass the Posse Comitatus Act that traditionally prohibits the US military from operating within the borders of the United States."[20]

But now, not only will American soldiers be deployed at the discretion of whomever is sitting in the Oval Office, but foreign soldiers will also be deployed in American cities." Wait a second, that's like what we saw before with the other map with the Chinese military being stationed here with the Russian, Belgium troops, yeah, it's all happening! "The Civil Assistance Plan is an incremental step toward creating a North American armed force available to be deployed in North American emergency situations." So that's how they're going to deal with the troublemakers in my opinion.

But what are you going to do about identifying every single person coming across the border, who they are, and where they're from, and whether or not they are a legitimate citizen of this new North American Union? Can you say, "Create a crisis so you can manage the outcome?" What do you think is going on with all this border talk lately? It's all designed to get us conditioned to work towards a Universal ID System. And by the way, the border problem is much bigger than just the Hispanic community coming across. It's all kinds of people from all over the world!

Channel 5 Reports:

The local Border Patrol Union is worried that amnesty will attract more people who will want to enter the U.S illegally. This reporter rode alone with agents as they patrolled the border and made a surprising discovery.

Joe Gutierrez, Border Patrol says:

Earlier today my partner was here patrolling the area and we had three Chinese immigrants come up to us directly. We apprehend people from 143 countries nationwide. Most people think that is just Hispanics and Mexicans from Mexico and Central American but we get people from China and a whole bunch of different places.[21]

Say what? Chinese coming across the border? People from 143 different countries?! What are we going to do? We've got a Border Crisis on our hands! I know, how about if we implement some sort of Universal ID Card for everyone to carry at all times so we can keep track of them and determine whether or not they are eligible to get a job in this new North American Union. Don't believe me? That's exactly what they were calling for. It's a setup!

Fox News reports:

President Obama is not only taking on health care reform but another issue, immigration reform. The key meeting at the White House tomorrow could be the first step towards that reform and for some very big changes for every American worker. Senators Chuck Schumer and Lindsay Graham, bipartisan that is, set to sit down with President Obama tomorrow, discussing plans for a national identification card.

This thing is meant to crack down on illegal workers. But our next guest says that it could crack down on your privacy. Congressman Ron Paul is a Texas Republican and he is opposed to this card. Congressman, good afternoon to you. Ron Paul: Good afternoon, it's good to be with you. Interviewer: It's a great pleasure to have you. So, what's the problem with the national I.D. card because its proponents says that this is it, this is the thing that is finally going to help us stop illegal immigrants from coming in here and taking jobs.

Ron Paul: Well, we do have a problem with illegal immigration, but I would say that the problem with every American citizen carrying their papers is a much worse problem than illegal immigration. Besides you can take care of illegal immigration other ways. People over the decades now in this country have wanted this I.D. card and they are looking for every opportunity to do it. This is it. Who knows what will come of it.

My guess is that they will probably have a GPS chip in it so they can measure everybody, every instant, no matter where they go so, to me it violates the whole principal of privacy, the principals of constitution, the principals of the republic, and to me as a gross distortion of what we should be doing, it's part of an authoritarian society and dictatorship, but not a republic.

Kelly asks: But tell me how it's invasive. What Schumer and Graham propose, according to what I read, is that your I.D. card would have your finger print, your thumb print, or would have the reading of the veins in the back of your hand and you would have to be scanned by your prospective employer so that if it came up that you were illegal they would catch you by the scan. [22]

So, you couldn't cross the border, you couldn't get a job, you in essence couldn't "buy and sell" unless you had your HAND scanned in this new ID system. What does that sound like? Sounds like a precursor to the Mark of the Beast! That's exactly what it is! Step by step. You see, what they don't tell you is that this ID system has a fatal flaw. It's another crisis waiting to happen. They're external cards. And we all know the problem with these external cards we carry around with us, we could lose them or somebody could steal them, right? So now what? Another crisis!

Ooh! I know? How about we get that same micro-chipped ID card that's on the outside of you, now put on the inside of you where nobody could steal it and you could never lose it! Wouldn't that be great? It's called set-up #2. And believe it or not, there's already a whole new generation of people out there ready to do just that. Get a microchip in your hand in order to travel. Check this out!

The first person with an RFID chip reports:

I want to show you my motorcycle that I have wired to read the RFID chip. First you can see the key is in the off position, turn on the engine run switch, which turns on the RFID reader, and as it turns over it doesn't start. But, on the other side of the motorcycle is where the RFID reader is. So, he waves his hand over the reader and the bike starts. Another person with an RFID chip tells us: I have the chip implanted in my left hand. It allows me to do all the functions as the key does except with my hand. [23]

Did you catch that? The RFID implant does the same things as the CARD does, but with your hand? They would never mandate a hand implant, would they? Uh, yeah! The same Antichrist who's implementing these 10 Horned Kingdoms is also going to mandate a Mark, in the forehead or the hand.

Revelation 13:16-17 "He also forced everyone, small and great, rich and poor, free and slave, to receive a mark on his right hand or on his forehead, so that no one could buy or sell unless he had the mark."

This is not make-believe. It's happening right now before our very eyes and this is why, out of love, God has given us all these signs of a One World Government to show us that the Tribulation is near and the Rapture is right around the corner! And that's why Jesus Himself said,

Luke 21:28 "When these things begin to take place, stand up and lift up your heads, because your redemption is drawing near."

It's going to be the worst time in the history of mankind and he's going to force you into the greatest time of satanic slavery this world has ever seen. There's only one way out! It's through the Kingdom of Jesus Christ! He wins! I didn't say that, God did!

Daniel 2:44 "In the time of those kings, the God of heaven will set up a Kingdom that will never be destroyed, nor will it be left to another people. It will crush all those kingdoms and bring them to an end, but it will itself endure forever."

In other words, you want to be on the winning team! That's only through Jesus Christ! If you are reading this and you are a Christian, it's time to get busy working together, fulfilling the Great Commission sharing the Gospel, leading souls to Christ! Amen? We better speak up and stand up and take a stand before it's too late, like this man did.

Ronald Reagan tells us:

We are at war with the most dangerous enemy that has ever faced mankind in its long climb from the swamp to the stars. And, it's been said that if we lose that war and in so doing we lose this freedom, our history will record with the greatest astonishment that those who had the most to lose did the least to prevent its happening.

I think it's time to ask ourselves if we still know the freedoms that were intended for us by the founding fathers. Not too long ago two friends of mine were talking to a Cuban refugee, a business man who had escaped from Castro. And during his story one of my friends turned to the other and said, 'We don't know how lucky we are.' And the Cuban stopped them and said, 'You don't know how lucky you are? I had some place to escape to.'

In that sentence, he told us the entire story. If we lose freedom here, there is no place to escape to. This is the last stand on earth. This idea of a government, is beholding to the people, and it has no other source of power except for the sovereign people. It's man's relationship to man. Whether we believe in our capacity for self-government or if we abandon the American Revolution and confess that a little intellectual belief in a far distance capital can plan our lives for us when we can plan them ourselves. You and I have a rendezvous with destiny.

We will preserve for our children the last best hope for man on earth or we will sentence them to take the last step into a thousand years of darkness. When he finished his speech, we are reminded of the missiles and bombs rolling down the streets in Russia. All the Russian people being dominated by that government and how their freedoms had been taken away.

The tanks and the people hanging in the street while the lookers on are crying and helpless. The soldiers marching whether in Russia or China, all under communist rule. Then the bombs dropping and people running as more trucks bringing more soldiers through their city. Then we are reminded of Hitler and the Jew being dragged down the street by his Nazi's. More people hanging, then pictures marched through the crowds of Stalin and Lenin.

Reports the local TV news.

IT'S TIME TO TAKE A STAND! This afternoon we received a call from a viewer, who said a business near downtown Reno was flying a Mexican flag above an American flag, which in fact is illegal. This after photos' and calls about the flag were posted on Craigslist as early as 11:30 this morning, we were able to have a photographer to go and check everything out and we found the story to be true. It also didn't take long for the situation to get a strong reaction. We are going to show you unedited just what happened.

A bearded gentleman walks up to the flag pole and takes the two flags down and cuts the American flag off the line. The gentleman then turns to the camera man and says, 'I took this flag down in honor of our country with this knife from the United States Army. I'm a veteran and I'm not going to see this done to my country. If they want to fight us then they need to be men and they need to come and fight us. I want someone to fight me for this flag. They're not going to get it back.[24]

The 4th proof that we know we are headed for a One World Government is the **Control Proof.**

You see, the Bible is clear. We're not just headed towards an evil deceptive Antichrist kingdom, that's split up into 10 kingdoms with 10 rulers, including America, but that kingdom is going to be one about absolute total control! I mean, everything! That's right, we're talking about Big Brother, the Big Eye in the Sky! The Antichrist is going to develop a Big Brother system that monitors everything on the planet! And I mean everything! But don't take my word for it. Let's listen to God's.

Revelation 13:11-17 "Then I saw another beast, coming out of the earth. He had two horns like a lamb, but he spoke like a dragon. He exercised all the authority of the first beast on his behalf, and made the earth and its inhabitants worship the first beast, whose fatal wound had been healed. And he performed great and miraculous signs, even causing fire to come down from heaven to earth in full view of men. Because of the signs he was given power to do on behalf of the first beast, he deceived the inhabitants of the earth. He ordered them to set up an image in honor of the beast who was wounded by the sword and yet lived. He was given power to give breath to the image of the first beast, so that it could speak and cause all who refused to worship the image to be killed. He also forced everyone, small and great, rich and poor, free and slave, to receive a mark on his right hand or on his forehead, so that no one could buy or sell unless he had the mark, which is the name of the beast or the number of his name."

As we saw before when we were in this text, the Bible clearly says that the False Prophet in the last days is not only going to dupe the whole world into worshiping the Antichrist, but he's what? He's going to make them, he's going to order them, he's going to cause them, he going to force them to do whatever he says to do, otherwise they will what? They will die, right? Again, I want to focus on the key words there, "make" "order" "cause" and "force."

This implies that we have some serious enforcement going on here! In fact, it's global enforcement because again, that's the context. It's global. He forces the whole planet to do whatever in the world he wants them to do, or you're going to die! In order to pull this off, think about it, you not only need some serious control over the whole planet, but you better have some serious ability to monitor everything and everyone on the whole planet, right? Why? Because think about it! Trying to control the whole planet is a huge task for a guy!

So, here's the point. How are you going to find and enforce everyone on the planet to do your will, right? I mean, how are you going to micro-manage the whole planet, because that's what's going on here, into doing what you say? Here are the facts, you know there's going to be a whole lot of resisters! People are still going to resist. They're still going to try to escape your system! How do you force, order, make, and cause people to do what you say? Well, simple! You not only control the whole planet with a global government that controls what people do, but you develop a Big Brother system that monitors everything they think, and everywhere they go! You'll know who the resisters are! You're listening in! You're watching! You'll make sure they can't leave your system!

I don't know about you, but good thing we don't see any signs of there being any technology to monitor everything we do on the planet all at the same time. I'm here to tell you it's already here! They're already monitoring our every move! What we do, where we go, and what we think!

The 1st Type of big brother surveillance system they've already put into place to FORCE US to go along with this global government is the **Information System.**

You see, whether you realize it or not, there is already in place massive amounts of databases to identify who you are. In fact, they're so big they're called mega-databases. 24 hours a day, right now, they are gathering and storing information on you and I from credit card transactions, magazine subscriptions, telephone numbers, real estate records, car registrations, and even fishing licenses, to name just a few. And, because of all this information, they can provide a full profile of each one of us, right down to whether we own a dog or cat, enjoy camping or gourmet cooking, read the Bible or other books, what our occupation is, what car we drive, what videos we watch, how much gas and food we buy and even where our favorite vacations spots are.

In fact, it is estimated that, right now, each adult in the developed world is already located, on average, in three hundred different databases with an average of 1,500 data points on you. That's a huge file! In other words, Big

Brother is already here, even in the U.S.! So, the question is, "How in the world did these guys even get all this information on in the first place," right? There is a multitude of ways they've been getting it from us. In fact, they have even tricked us into giving it up to them voluntarily so they now know everything about us. Don't believe me? Let's ask the Amazing Mind Reader Dave from Belgium! He proves it!

Random people were invited to have their minds read. They were told it was for an upcoming TV program starring Dave. The first person comes in and has a seat. He hugs them, dances around the room and then bows his head as he starts to communicate: I see a school in Antwerp. "Yes." She replies. He says: Insects, I feel 2 insects on your back. She asks, "Is that possible?" As he looks at her butterfly tattoo he says: Yes, they are butterflies. Slovenia? "Yes", she replies.

Dave: An orange motorcycle? The next gentleman says, "Spot on," Dave: Zenith? He answers, "Yes. Very Good". Dave: Your best friend's name is Julie. A new girl is now sitting at his table, "Yes." Dave: Interesting love life. I see three or four people. She replies, "Not a lot of people know that." Dave: How's your torn muscle? She smiles. Dave: I see a red house with a white balcony. She shakes her head yes.

This is amazing, but Dave is just warming up. Dave: I see money and transactions. Do you know your bank account number? Because I do. I see a negative balance. "Yes?" she asks. Dave: 9-7. Dave: Last month, you spent 300 liras on clothes.

He asks the same question about the bank account to another person and then tells him that he sees a house for sale. 795,000 liras. The client says, "Scary." But then Dave goes a step further and proceeds to get the person to give him their bank account number.

Now it is time to reveal the magic behind the magic. Behind the wall of the tent is another room. The wall falls and you see 3 masked people working their laptops to delve into each of the people's names that are wanting their minds read. That is how he gets all the information. Your entire life is online. And it might be used against you. They are all in awe as they see their pictures and all their information on the computer screen.[26]

They've tricked us into putting our lives online and other technological means. And now they can read our minds. It's not magic. It's present day reality. They're using all this technology against us, intertwining it all, and figuring out everything about us! Our entire lives are known to them! Whether it's the loyalty cards which tracks what we buy and sell or credit cards, ATM cards, or credit rating agencies, that shows our whole financial history and economic status or search engines, which store and records, "Every search you perform and keeps a profile on all your habits and interests, like and dislikes." Even social media like Facebook and Twitter which builds massive amounts of database information on us, of all our photos, our friends, our communications, our contacts, everything you can think of we put them up there for them.

They know everything about us, of who we are, where we are, what we're doing, who we're hanging out with at any given moment, and they're building a huge massive profile on us down to the intimate detail! But that's still not all. They're also using our cell phones, e-mails, faxes, TV viewing, you name it, it's all being monitored? Why? Because, "Under the guise of national security and terrorist threats," the government now has full authority to monitor and intercept all this information and collect it.

One such institution is called the NSA or "The National Security Agency" which is the "U.S. Intelligence Agency responsible for the global monitoring, collection, and decoding of information and data for foreign intelligence." The problem is, it's not just for foreign intelligence, but it's being used on even you and I here in America. The cat came out of the bag recently! Check this out!

Reporting from Washington DC, Greenwald's Book reveals more NSA documents leaked by Snowden in 2011. It further reveals that NSA and its partners are in a game of collecting it all and it speaks to what Snowden and the journalists that he has worked with have been warning us all along. An out of control spy agency with unbelievable tools that puts a threat to privacy around the world.

The NSA has partnered with a number of American Corporations to carry out its 'collect it all' mission. Including one mysterious corporate partner since 1985 which has access to international cables, routers, and switches and is aggressively involved in shaping the internet traffic to run through NSA monitors. As a result, the NSA's Fairview program operates in the U.S. but has access to information that transits the nation and through its corporate relationships provide unique accesses to other telecoms and ISPs.

Aggressively involved in shaping traffic to run signals of interest past our monitors. As a result, the NSA was able to run through its program 6,142,932,557 phone call records per month. More information on the NSA's supply chain interdiction where the agency intercepts foreign bound computer servers and routers, implants bugs in them and then sends them back into transit, allowing NSA to crack some of its hardest targets. All this data collection is posing a challenge to the NSA, one that they are aware of, collection is outpacing our ability to ingest process and store to the norm of which we have become accustomed.[27]

Did you catch that? In other words, they're admitting this, "We're getting so much information on you even here in the U.S., that we're running out of room to store it all." Which again, is admitting, they are really doing this, this is not make-believe, it's not a conspiracy theory, it's really going on! They are monitoring all our information on a global basis even here in the U.S. In fact, so much so, that they've now come up with a solution to fix the problem they mentioned. "Running out of room to store all this information on us." They've now built an even bigger NSA data center!" It's in Utah, and it's called the "Utah Data Center." Check this out!

Fox News Reports:

We are more aware tonight than we have been in a while about just how much power the government has over our lives. The massive leak of information about the NSA's surveillance of Americans really does affect virtually everyone in the country. Tonight, we accelerate our coverage of this most timely topic in part one of 'Prying Eyes'.

In Bluffdale, Utah, 25 miles south of Salt Lake City, the NSA is nearing the completion of a gargantuan new project. It's called the Utah Data Center. The NSA will neither confirm nor deny the specifics but some estimate the center will be capable of storing 5 zettabytes of data. To give you an idea of how much data is in a zettabyte think of it this way. One iPhone 5 has 16 gigabytes of data storage. One Terabyte would be 62 iPhones, stacked, that would be 19 inches high. One petabyte would be more than 62,000 iPhones which would reach higher than the Empire State Building.

An exabyte would be more than 62 million iPhones reaching higher than the international space station. Just one zettabyte would be more than 62 billion iPhones, stacked, they would reach past the moon. If it really has 5 zettabytes the Data Center could in theory store every email, telephone call, google search and surveillance camera video in America for a very long time.

Thomas Drake:

Americans' should be concerned about letting the government go too far in the name of security. The only way to have perfect security is to have a perfect surveillance state, that's George Orwell, that's 1984. That's what that would look like. Reporter: And Drake is not alone in feeling that way. Bill Binney who worked at the NSA for nearly 4 decades starting as a data analyst in the days before desktop computers: Whatever you did electronically they could capture. My estimate was that they were collecting on the order of 3 billion phone records a day.

That's just internal to this country. In simple terms, NSA is spying on Americans inside this country. Reporter: Apparently Congress, which in 2008 amended the Foreign Intelligence Surveillance Act explicitly legalizing much of the surveillance going on and President Obama who re-authorized the law agree. To many it's clearer than ever that President Obama is using that authority even more aggressively than the man that was accused of shredding the Constitution, George W. Bush.[28]

In other words, once the Antichrist rises to power, the technology is already in place to turn this planet into on big giant global Big Brother society, just like that! The pieces, he admitted, are already there! They just need the right "bad guy" to take it over! You put all this together, it sure looks to me like we have the ability for the first time in mankind's history, for one man and his cohort, to monitor everything people do on the planet. So, they can force them to do what they say or die, how about you? And that's exactly what the Bible says is going to happen when you're living in the last days!

The **2nd Type** of big brother surveillance system they've already put into place to FORCE US to go along with this global government is a **Satellite System.**

You see, just to make sure that you're monitored and controlled at all times in this Antichrist Big Brother Global System, they're not only storing a massive amount of information on us right now as we speak but they're also watching us from the sky as we speak! And believe it or not, it's this same kind of "secretive" behavior the Bible says the Antichrist is going to use in the last days. In fact, the Bible says it's already at work behind the scenes.

2 Thessalonians 2:1-8 "Concerning the coming of our Lord Jesus Christ and our being gathered to Him, we ask you, brothers, not to become easily unsettled or alarmed by some prophecy, report or letter supposed to have come from us, saying that the day of the Lord has already come. Don't let anyone deceive you in any way, for that day will not come until the rebellion occurs and the man of lawlessness is revealed, the man doomed to destruction. He will oppose and will exalt himself over everything that is called God or is worshiped, so that he sets himself up in God's temple, proclaiming himself to be God. Don't you remember that when I was with you I used to tell you these things? And now you know what is holding him back, so that he may be revealed at the proper time. For the secret power of lawlessness is already at work; but the one who now holds it back will continue to do so till he is taken out of the way. And then the lawless one will be revealed, whom the Lord Jesus will overthrow with the breath of His mouth and destroy by the splendor of His coming."

Here we see the Apostle Paul comforting the Thessalonians from a misconception going around apparently at that time by some false teachers saying these Christians missed the Rapture, that the Day of the Lord had already come! But Paul says No! Christians are not going to be around during the 7-year Tribulation and he's emphatic about it!

That is a time of God's wrath! The Day of the Lord is God's judgment on the ungodly world. It's His final cataclysmic judgment that consumes the wicked," not Christians! We are not appointed unto wrath! So, "Don't freak out and listen to these false teachers!" he says. BUT, he does mention something about the Antichrist that is already here right now today! And that's the phrase, "The secret power of lawlessness, the antichrist, is already at work."

In other words, the wicked intent of the Antichrist to overthrow God in the future during the 7-year Tribulation, is already here. The machinery is already in place! The embodiment of the Antichrist hasn't come yet, as he says, but the machinery behind the scenes, if you will, is being built as we speak. And I believe the key word there is "secret." It means "an unknown, a mystery, a secret or something hidden from us." Much of this antichrist Big Brother global monitoring system is doing just that, it's being "secretly" worked on behind the scenes and "hidden from us." Including one of the biggest ones, the Big Eye in the Sky, Satellites.

Big Brother, right now, not only knows everything we do, everything we say, everything we think, with this information system we just saw, but they have even developed a system that monitors everywhere we go with satellites. Right now, we are "secretly" being monitored anytime, anywhere on the planet, 24 hours a day, 7 days a week, with satellites!

Motorola has already launched 66 low-orbiting satellites that can not only pick up signals from certain types of microchips, wouldn't that be handy if you implanted one, BUT now it's common knowledge that this kind of tracking system is already used to monitor the locations of military personnel, boat traffic, and even garbage men in England are being watched right now from the sky on their jobs in order to make sure that they don't linger in one spot too long!

In fact, in England they're even using satellites to measure the speed of motorists from space! You don't have a radar detector on earth for that one! They're monitoring every square foot of farming land in Australia right now, being watched via satellite to monitor food production and crop yields.

Even here in America, satellites are being used by state governments to search for unreported improvements that might increase property taxes, to check for water-use permits, find improper tree cutting, to see whether or not you turned your lights off on your house, from the sky, to conserve energy, track cars in parking lots to create retail forecasts for businesses, and even take pictures of reported property damage from above so insurance companies can tell whether or not a claim is true.

But hey, they won't track the average civilian, will they? Actually, they already are, on a massive city-wide scale! One such system already in place from above is called ARGUS and it's an airborne surveillance camera that's so powerful "It can see what type of phone you're carrying from 17,500 feet away!" and even see what you were doing days before!

John Antoniades, who designed the new sensor known as Argus with 1.8 billion pixels, the world's highest resolution camera says: "This is the next generation of surveillance.

For the first time, we actually have permission from the government to show the basic capabilities. It is important for the public to know that some of these capabilities exist."

<u>Reporter</u>: *The image was taken 17,500 feet above Quantico, Virginia and covers 15 square miles.*

Antoniades: *This image is at a very, very fine resolution. So, if we wanted to know what was going on in any spot along this intersection we can generate a moving image that shows us what is going on in the area.*

Reporter: *Simply by touching the screen he has opened up a window showing a detailed area while still maintaining the broader context.*

Antoniades: *Everything that is a moving object is being automatically tracked. The boxes show that the computer has recognized the moving objects, you can see the individuals crossing the street, you can see individuals walking in the parking lot, there's enough resolution for you to see people waving their arms, walking around and the clothes they wear. Then you can pick the location of where you produce these images anywhere in the entire field of view.*

Reporter: *Antoniades can open up to 65 windows at once and can see objects as small as 6 inches on the ground.*
Antoniades: *From even 17,500 feet, the white thing that you see flying around is a bird.*

Reporter: *Argus streams close to the ground and also stores everything. A million terabytes of video a day which is the equivalent of 5000 hours of high definition footage.*

Antoniades: *So, you can go back say I would like to see what happened at this particular location 3 days 2 hours 4 minutes ago and it would actually show you exactly what happened as if you were watching it live.*[29]

Say what? Right now, we're currently being monitored and recorded from the sky 24 hours a day, 7 days a week, and you can even see what we were doing days ago, like a search engine? This is not make-believe, its current technology being used on us right now in secret! Just like the text says! One day, in the 7-year Tribulation, the Antichrist is going to high-jack this system to totally enslave the planet!

Another surveillance system that monitors whole cities from the air is called "Persistent Surveillance Systems" and they're using that technology to, "Catch criminals in the act." It's a video search engine from the sky!

"The entire area is filmed and recorded in real time and has already been tested in Baltimore, Dayton, and Compton to track crimes." "We literally watched all of Compton and zoomed in anywhere in the city to follow cars and see people. In one case, we tracked a criminal as he approached a woman, grabbed her jewelry, and then ran to a getaway car."

Well, you see! Right there! It's a good technology! They're using it to catch criminals! Yeah, but what if you became the criminal so to speak? That's the problem!

The article went on and said this, "So why haven't the people of Compton heard about this experiment until now?" "The system was kind of kept confidential (you know, in secret) from everybody in the public." "A lot of people do have a problem with the eye in the sky, the Big Brother, so in order to mitigate any of those kinds of complaints, we basically kept it pretty hush-hush." In other words, we're hiding it from you in secret!

Google's getting in on the action. Shocker! Most of us know about "Google Earth" and their "Street View" program that combines their satellite photos, with on the ground photos, to get a bird's eye view of the planet, including a 360-degree panoramic view of your house. That's already been out there, we've become conditioned to accept that BUT they have also just bought another satellite company called "Skybox" that can take photos from 500 miles up in space, not 17,500 feet, but 500 miles in space, with a sub-one-meter resolution of the ground below."

One guy called it, "Google Eye" and it has intentions of "surveying the globe by taking pictures of the entire planet three times a day!", including video footage. "We'll be counting the ships, cars, shipping containers and trucks that move around our world on a daily basis." In other words, Google will now be monitoring everything from above about us, just like they're already monitoring everything down below about us with our information!

In fact, a lot of the recent justification for all this spy satellite technology is stemming from the recent missing Malaysian Airlines Flight 370. Remember that? Because of that, China is not only planning on their own global network of surveillance satellites, but listen to what they said after their frustration of not being able to find the missing Chinese passengers on that flight. "If we had a global monitoring network today, we wouldn't be searching for these people in the dark. We would have a much greater chance to find the plane and trace it to its final position."

In other words, somebody's using this crisis to manage the outcome! We've got to monitor this planet at all times so this will never happen again! We'll never lose another plane or people.

In fact, so much so, we are being monitored right now from a multitude of satellites from a multitude of angles and countries, they now have an actual

APP out there that you can download to your phone to tell you which satellites are spying on you right now!

It's called a SpyMeSat APP, and it provides notifications of when, not if, "spy satellites" and "unclassified imaging satellites" are zooming above your

head and may be taking your picture." I'm not kidding! Download it today! This is how bad it's getting, which means this is not a conspiracy theory! So, with all this in place, all it's going to take right now for one guy to monitor and control the whole planet, to FORCE them to do whatever he wants them to do, is to highjack it and take it over. Gee, I wonder who that's going to be!

The "secret power of lawlessness" is already at work! For the first time in mankind's history, the Antichrist has all the tools he needs to monitor the whole planet. This is not make-believe. It's happening right now before our very eyes. And that takes place during the 7-year tribulation. Therefore, how much closer is the Rapture of the Church, which take places prior to the 7-year Tribulation?

The **3rd type** of Big Brother surveillance system they've already put into place to force us to go along with this One World Government is a **Monitoring System**.

That's right folks, the Big Eye is watching us! You see, just to make sure that we're always under the careful ever, watchful eye of Big Brother, they're not only storing a massive amount of information on us right now, watching us from the sky, but they are even monitoring our every move down here below as we speak, and unfortunately, it's going to lead to a horrible slaughter! I didn't say that. God did.

Matthew 24:15-22 "So when you see standing in the holy place the abomination that causes desolation, spoken of through the prophet Daniel – let the reader understand – then let those who are in Judea flee to the mountains. Let no one on the roof of his house go down to take anything out of the house. Let no one in the field go back to get his cloak. How dreadful it will be in those days for pregnant women and nursing mothers! Pray that your flight will not take place in winter or on the Sabbath. For then there will be great distress, unequaled from the beginning of the world until now –and never to be equaled again. If those days had not been cut short, no one would survive, but for the sake of the elect those days will be shortened."

According to our text, where Jesus is speaking, the Bible clearly states that during the 7-year Tribulation, after the Antichrist shows his true colors and goes into the rebuilt Jewish temple to declare himself to be god, the abomination of desolation, that was spoken of by the Prophet Daniel, that Jesus is referring to here, is what will happen at that time? What does Jesus tell the people to do? He said you need to be fleeing, right? You need to get out of there quickly, right? Why? Other passages tell us that the Antichrist is going on a hunting spree at that time! He's going to be hunting people down and killing them! It's going to lead to another horrible holocaust, starting with the Jewish people. This is what Zechariah says.

Zechariah 13:8-9 "In the whole land, declares the LORD, two-thirds will be struck down and perish; yet one-third will be left in it. This third I will bring into the fire; I will refine them like silver and test them like gold. They will call on my name and I will answer them; I will say, they are my people, and they will say, The LORD is our God."

So, here we have some good news/bad news going on in this text. The Good News is that the Jewish people finally turn back to God at this point. But the Bad News is that it comes at a horrible price! Just the Jewish people alone, $2/3^{rds}$ of them are going to die at the hands of the Antichrist and only $1/3^{rd}$ are going to be left. Another horrible Jewish Holocaust is coming, the Bible is clear about that, unfortunately. But that's just the tip of the iceberg when it comes to the slaughter that the Antichrist is going to be a part of during the 7-year Tribulation. A massive amount of people are going to die!

Revelation 6:3-4,7-8 "When the Lamb opened the second seal, I heard the second living creature say, 'Come!' Then another horse came out, a fiery red one. Its rider was given power to take peace from the earth and to make men slay each other. To him was given a large sword. When the Lamb opened the fourth seal, I heard the voice of the fourth living creature say, 'Come!' I looked, and there before me was a pale horse! Its rider was named Death, and Hades was following close behind him. They were given power over a fourth of the earth to kill by sword, famine and plague, and by the wild beasts of the earth."

Here we see after the first seal is opened, the second seal is opened, and a global war breaks out that the Antichrist is a part of, and just to give you an idea how big that number really is, if this war were to break out today, the death toll would be over 1.8 billion people! Nearly 2 billion people are going to die in this war in the first half of the 7-year Tribulation! How many of you would say that's pretty bad? But that's still not all! The Bible says another third of the planet is going to be wiped out after that in the second half of the 7-year Tribulation.

Revelation 9:15-16 "And the four angels, who had been prepared for the hour and day and month and year, were released, so that they would kill a third of mankind. The number of the armies of the horsemen was two hundred million; I heard the number of them."

And as we saw before, as a side note, it just happens that China has the ability to raise an army of that exact number. But the point is this. Here comes another slaughter! One third of the earth is going in this battle! If you subtract this number from the first slaughter, it is going to be another 1.8 billion! Interesting math when you bust out the calculator! Just in these two judgments alone, 3.6 billion people, about half our current planet, is going to die, not even counting the second unfortunate Jewish Holocaust.

And here's the point. No wonder Jesus said it's going to be the worst time in mankind's history! And no wonder there's an urgency to accept Him now so you can avoid the whole thing, amen? And no wonder Jesus said for those who unfortunately rejected Him and found themselves during this horrible time-frame in the 7-year Tribulation, that your only option is to flee, right?

Remember what He said? You better make flight, you better run, you better flee and you better do it fast! Don't go back into your house, don't go to your work place, don't get anything, just get out of there now, right? Why? Because the slaughter's coming! The planet is going to be annihilated! Therefore, common sense tells us that at this time frame, a good source of reliable transportation is going to come in handy, right?

But the problem is, the Antichrist is not dumb! He's already thought of this. He's just like Satan, who is a murderer and has been one from the beginning! He is going to make sure people stick around for the slaughter!

The 1st way he's doing that is developing a monitoring system with our **Transportation.**

He'll know exactly where you are so you can't escape! As we already saw, they have already placed tracking devices in vehicles with the OnStar system via satellites. But that's just the tip of the iceberg! There's a multitude of ways they are tracking our vehicles.

The 1st way they are tracking our vehicles, besides OnStar, is with **Shooting Darts.**

That's right! James Bond eat your heart out! Check this out!

Fox 13 Reports:

Officers are using a new technology now that will prevent high speed chases and still catch the bad guys. This is going to attract a lot of attention. It's like something out of a James Bond movie. It's a dart shot out of the front of a police car and it latches right on to whatever they are chasing. Then with GPS tracking whatever they are chasing never really gets away. It's a magnetic, GPS dart, and during a chase, cops can fire them at a car. Then hang back, get on their car computer and track every move.[31]

Well hey, that's nice! Now they can really get those bad guys! But again, what if YOU became the "bad guy"? How far do you push this? Oh, but that's not all. This tracking technology is so commonplace, it's not just for the police anymore, it's even for the average Joe!

The 2nd way they're tracking our vehicles is with **Personal Locators.**

How many movies have you seen where the plot revolves around a tiny GPS tracking device that lets one spy follow the movements of another on some kind of radar? This is the Zoomback Personal Locator, it uses GPS, it costs $100.00 plus $15.00 per month.

To show you how we test these things, as my friend drives I can go on my laptop to Zoombak.com and pinpoint his location. I can click find now and in a few seconds, there he is. Or I can watch a bread crumb trail of his location with a new thumb tack every 5 minutes.

Zoomback is intended to be put in your car, boat, kids backpack or even your dog's collar so you can always keep tabs on them. Interestingly, one thing Zoomback doesn't talk about is how you can use it secretly. You can plant it to track the movement of your spouse or your kid or your employee.[32]

Nobody would ever do that, would they? Yeah, right! First of all, I have a rule, if the average Joe can get this into his hands, then what does Big Brother have? My rule is anything we see in public we're 20 years behind the actual technology.

The 3rd **way** they're tracking our vehicles right now, whether you realize it or not, is with **EZ Passes.**

You know, those nifty electronic RFID devices they got us to install in our vehicles to automatically pay for our toll charges while on the road. Aren't those great! Yeah, the problem is they do MUCH MORE than that!

In New York City, many people use a quick read system called EZ Pass to quickly and easily pay for tolls. Readers are set up at toll booths. They scan the RFID from a distance, making it simple for travelers to pass through. But a hacker that goes by the name Puking Monkey stumbled across a different and more unsettling use for the EZ Pass System.

We admit that the electronic mooing is a bit unsettling but it's the reason behind the mooing that has people a little perturbed. According to Forbes, Puking Monkey became concerned about privacy on the road after he saw license plate cameras on the back of a police car. During his research, he hacked his EZ Pass reader so that every time it was being read it would flash and cause the cow to moo. The cow was mooing when there wasn't even a toll booth in sight which understandably made Puking Monkey a bit concerned.³³

How many of you would agree it would cause you to "puke up your monkey" too, when you found out they're tracking you with these tags? What else are you doing? For those of you who say, Well hey, I'm not going to use the EZ Pass, you might soon have to. Certain states like Massachusetts and Pennsylvania, and others, are mandating EZ Passes for payment, and you cannot travel these roads without this tracking device. No more cash, no more change, you can only pay with an electronic payment. Where have I heard that before?

The 4th way they're tracking our vehicles whether you realize it or not is with **License Plates.**

Believe it or not, if you were paying attention to what Puking Monkey said, this is what the Police are doing. They're using license plate readers to scan us.

It's been almost a year since Edward Snowden ignited a fire storm over mass surveillance conducted by the NSA. But the NSA is not the only agency tracking us. As reported by America Tonight on privacy, your secret is out with the investigation into a new controversial tool for surveillance that has caught on like wild fire among many law enforcement agencies. It's also creating a lengthy record of movements by ordinary Americans.

Mounted in public places or on law enforcement vehicles, ALPR devices scan the license plates of every car that passes. Each device can scan thousands of plates per minute and check each plate against a hot list of stolen cars or wanted persons. And data from ALPR devices, which include photos, a time stamp, and location is also retained in thousands of data bases across the country and shared by various agencies.

If a license plate camera picks up your license plate at many times during the week it can pinpoint your location and chart your pathway through your life. That can reveal some very sensitive information. It can tell who you associate with, which doctor you are going to, or whether you are sleeping at a different house every night. If you don't have probable cause against a citizen or individual, why are you keeping their data, there's no reason to do it.³⁴

Unless of course, you are building a Big Brother Society using all this technology to create a giant prison planet. And believe it or not, they've already conditioned us to accept this kind of monitoring.

The 5th way they're tracking our vehicles right now is through **Car Lenders.**

This is wild! You want that new vehicle? Are you a person with bad credit? Then you're going to have to let us track your every move, and shut you off if you don't make a payment! Don't believe me? It's already here in Las Vegas!

Candice Smith:

The worst thing that can happen to someone is to be driving on the freeway, cars going around you super-fast, and your car just instantly powers down.

Reporter: Two years ago, Candice Smith, said she and a friend were driving on a busy stretch of I-15 in Las Vegas when her car's engine suddenly stopped.

Candice: I started to panic really bad and I looked over to my friend and said, 'like what's going on?'

Reporter: The reason her car stopped wasn't a mechanical issue, she says it was her auto lender. The company she said had determined she was late with her payment and remotely turned off her car.

Candice: All of a sudden, the steering wheel locked up, it was super scary. If it wasn't for the person that was in the car with me and actually pushing the car over to the left-hand side I think we would have been hit and would probably be dead.

Some auto lenders extend loans to people with poor or damaged credit. They are increasingly turning to new technology called a starter interrupt device to spur timely payments and they say help build credit with flashing lights, loud beeping and the threat of remotely disabling the car.

One car salesman says, "So, there is a tough love approach with our technology whether it be a sub-prime lender, a bank, or a credit union, it's really how they *are approaching the consumer. They want to help them get on their feet but sometimes it does require a very consistent reminder and in some cases the disablement of the start of their vehicle if they haven't made their payment on time."*[35]

So, if I don't make my payment on time, in essence, or do what you tell me to do, a banking system will shut my car off automatically leaving me stranded. I mean, gee whiz! What's next? Are you going to say I have to get a chip in my body so I can "buy or sell" and if I don't do what you say, you're going to shut me off there too? Little by little, they're working towards their ultimate goal!

The **6th way** they're tracking our vehicles, knowing where we are at any given moment, is with all our vehicles. They have already mandated that every single car in the United States manufactured from this point forward is getting a **Black Box Tracking Device**, whether you want one or not! Let's look at that again.

The Obama Administration has approved a plan that requires black boxes in all new cars sold in the U.S. Those devices will show exactly what you do behind the wheel and privacy advocates worry about what else they may reveal.

Shoppers of all new vehicles will soon get more than they bargained for. A data recorder watching a driver's every move. Beginning in September of 2014 every vehicle sold in the U.S. will be required to have a black box. The insurance industry supports the move, even most drivers are unaware that 96% of cars sold today already have data recorders installed.[36]

Excuse me? You're mandating that 100% must have them now, 96% of them already have them? I didn't hear about that, did you? But don't worry! We all know we can trust the government! Yeah, right! And as you just read, insurance companies love this stuff. You know why? Because, insurance companies can now use this technology to, "Locate policy holders by GPS and charge them insurance rates based on per mile driven." The Department of Transportation (the DOT) is planning on a new Federal Motor Vehicle Safety Standard called the, "Basic Safety Message." This technology would allow them to "spontaneously" provide "communication" to a vehicle to warn them of any potential accidents" AND is the, "First step to making fully automated vehicles," by the government.

So, you put all this together, for the first time in mankind's history. We have the technology right now to flip a switch, stop any vehicle, and say a message like this, "Halt! Warning! Warning! You're trying to flee a certain area without permission. Your vehicle is being shut down for your own good. Have a nice day! Welcome to the Antichrist Kingdom!" This is not make-believe. It's all current technology! No wonder Jesus said it's going to be a bloodbath! You won't be able to escape!

The 2nd way the Antichrist is developing a global monitoring system, tracking our every move is with a **Camera System.**

That's right! Big Brother is watching you wherever you go! He has not only developed a system that monitors us wherever we drive, but wherever we go, even on foot!

As we saw before, they're already watching us with cameras everywhere, and I mean everywhere! In fact, we just finished up with vehicles being tracked, but they also want to put a camera in every vehicle!

Do you ever get tired of your wife nagging you for not keeping your eyes on the road every time she's in the car? Then you might want to stay away from GM dealerships because they are making sure she is riding shotgun from here on out. Over the next 3 to 5 years, GM will be teaming up with seeing machines to fit motion camera sensors into the next generation cars to make your car alert you every time your head isn't rotated towards the road or your eyes haven't been looking at your mirrors enough. Just like your wife, GM has your best interest in mind.[37]

You're going to be putting a camera in my car to watch my every move, for my so-called good? Excuse me? They are not only going to, it's going on everywhere, even in public transit. The next train you take will be watching and listening to you and recording it all. The New York Metropolitan Transportation Authority (MTA) has announced a plan to install several thousand audio and video recorders on it's commuter trains in response to federal safety recommendations. (Remember…it's for your good) Officials say the technology will also be used to control undesirable behavior. (We're watching you) And other forms of public transportation across the country have also begun installing similar technologies as well. For instance, buses in Baltimore have already begun recording conversations of bus drivers and passengers in order to "investigate crimes."

And in February, transportation officials in Boston began outfitting their buses with a $6.9 million surveillance system funded entirely by the Department of Homeland Security. Those cameras consist of 360-degree lenses that can be embedded in the ceilings and walls to "capture everything." "Being able to watch and hear everyone on board any form of public transport (via video or audio) may help to improve the security of innocent passengers." See, it's all for you! It's for your own good!

Thanks in part to Executive Orders, under the guise of "terrorism" and other "bad guy" reasons, but again, what if YOU became the "bad guy?" The government now has full authority to utilize all kinds of new surveillance technology in the U.S., not a foreign entity, us! We already saw Chicago is the most watched city in the whole United States with a system they built called "Operation Virtual Shield." Where they can, "see anything you're doing, what book you're reading, what text you're sending, etc. everything" And that's just the tip of the iceberg. All kinds of cities across the U.S. are doing the exact same thing. All under our nose by the way.

- *Ypsilanti Township in Michigan is currently working with local police to put up, "Surveillance cameras in every single neighborhood." They claim the cameras are, "No different than police officers constantly standing in the neighborhood."*

- *Police in Austin, Texas are now demanding "live access" to surveillance cameras "already" installed inside public schools, saying they need this to prevent "future school shootings."*

- *In Modesto, California, an armored police surveillance truck was unveiled recently that video and audio records local residents while traveling throughout the city. It's called The Armadillo and several other departments across the country, such as Fort Lauderdale have also already implemented the use of surveillance vehicles with real-time video footage feeding directly back to police headquarters.*

- *And speaking of police officers and cameras, thanks to the riots and trouble caused by the recent Ferguson shooting incident, the President has come up with a new solution to fix it all. Mandate all policemen to wear body cameras to watch you!*

- *ABC News reports: The recent shooting death of Michael Brown in Ferguson, Missouri are spurring calls for police to wear body cameras and that includes President Obama's push for funding for thousands of small cameras. After a series of meetings today the President promised programs to bring police and communities together. Obama: Part of the reason this time will be different is because the President of the United States is deeply invested in making sure this time is different. The president is also asking for 263 million dollars for community policing including 75 million dollars for body worn cameras. Reporter: To see these cameras in action we ride along with Officer Solinex. On this traffic stop the first thing he does is point out the camera to the motorist. Officer: I just want to advise you that you are being audio and visually recorded. The Driver: That's fine. Solinex says when people know that they usually exhibit their best behavior.[38]*

Speaking of another crisis, following the Boston Marathon bombings, the Boston Police Department is now starting to look at a more high-tech means of securing the city against future attacks. They found the solution in the form of an artificially intelligent, self-learning surveillance network that now watches the entire city, and all of its inhabitants. It's an AI-based surveillance system that not only watches and analyzes human behavior, but "learns from it" to identify suspicious or abnormal activity.

"Our system will figure out things you never thought of looking for." It's completely free of additional human programming, guidance or monitoring, and needs little installation and additional hardware, Why? Because it can be attached to the already present huge, sprawling networks of cameras present in any city. After a few days of hardware and software installation, AI Sight can begin.

Terminator called it SkyNet, but I guess we call it AI Sight. Is that freaky or what? And again, the justification for this is that it stops crime and curbs bad behavior, but is that true? NO! Remember how in England we already saw how they put up over 4 million cameras in the government and private sector to create a "surveillance canopy." I mean, sure it stopped crime, right? WRONG! The figure has now grown to over 5.9 million cameras, one camera for every 11 people, and, "The UK still has the highest homicide rate in all of Northern Europe." In other words, it is not working!

"For every 1,000 cameras in London, less than 1 crime is solved per year." And even the British government stated, "Surveillance cameras produced no overall effect on crime." Why? Because it is NOT for crime. Its Big Brother being built before our very eyes! And when all the cameras around the world get tapped into by this AI System, we're going to be in a heap of trouble! And I mean all countries!

China is developing a mini camera system that scans the crowd for "potential suicide bombers, where Police can scan a sea of people with special goggles to see if they are under extreme stress, like a suicide bomber would be."

But as one man said, "I already feel tense if a police officer is looking at me, let alone with strange goggles!" And Google is out there making sure everybody on the planet could be wearing these monitoring devices on the head with Google

Glasses!

As we saw before, these devices can communicate to the Internet anytime, anywhere, no matter where you go, even without a computer or cell phone. But you can also send photos, ask questions, talk to people, request a map, take a picture or video live, post it online for everyone to view or hear, including those trying to disguise themselves! There's an app for everything! Big Brother's got it all figured out! No place to hide!

Hi, I'm Kevin. My team and I have created the First Real-Time Facial Recognition app for Google Glass.

It's called Name Tag and it's powered by facialnetwork.com.

We allow limited access to download the app.

To start this demo, we have a digital camera that's video recording into prism on google glass and we're seeing exactly what the Google Glass is seeing.

It looks at the picture, name tag, you take the recorded picture and put it on the wall, capture his photo, it runs the database, runs the facial recognition software on it while he waits for the first picture to be identified, he then takes a picture of a lady and puts her picture on the wall.

It is running these faces against 2 and a half million photos in our database. Once it finds a match it will send that information to us with another photo.

After the Glass app identifies the first picture as Bryan Cranston, the second picture is identified as Taylor Swift.

Kevin then takes a picture of another man, puts his picture on the wall and waits for the app to identify him.

The camera pings, and it shows that this guy has a criminal history, Registrant Sexually Assaulted a 13-year-old.

So, I know what you are thinking, can this Name Tag work on a real person?

His friend is standing there with a hat, dark glasses, and a beard.

He takes his picture, Name Tag, and it scans his picture and comes up with his name.[39]

      Yeah nice! So much for hiding. Even if you put on a disguise, a beard, a hat, whatever, you can still be identified!
      And don't' worry, for those of you who don't like glasses, Google's got you covered. They're coming out with Google Lens!

Now there's no reason for anyone on the planet not to have one of these monitoring devices on their head! Once this AI System taps into all the existing cameras around the planet, including on the people, there will be no place to hide! No wonder Jesus said it's going to be a bloodbath

The 3rd way the Antichrist is developing a global monitoring system tracking our every move, ensuring we stick around for the slaughter, is with our **Communication System.**

But don't take my word for it. Let's listen to God's.

Matthew 24:3-11 "As Jesus was sitting on the Mount of Olives, the disciples came to Him privately. 'Tell us,' they said, 'when will this happen, and what will be the sign of Your coming and of the end of the age?' Jesus answered: 'Watch out that no one deceives you. For many will come in My Name, claiming, 'I am the Christ,' and will deceive many. You will hear of wars and rumors of wars, but see to it that you are not alarmed. Such things must happen, but the end is still to come. Nation will rise against nation, and kingdom against kingdom. There will be famines and earthquakes in various places. All these are the beginning of birth pains. Then you will be handed over to be persecuted and put to death, and you will be hated by all nations because of Me. At that time many will turn away from the faith and will betray and hate each other, and many false prophets will appear and deceive many people."

So, according to our text, Jesus clearly says there's not only going to be a massive rise of wars and rumors of wars, and famines, and earthquakes in the last days, but He said what? He said there's going to be a massive rise of persecution towards His followers in the last days, right? And as we saw before, it's happening right now! Of course, the people He's talking about are the Jewish Elect and the people who get saved after the 7-year Tribulation begins. They missed the Rapture. Praise God they got saved, but now they're in a heap of trouble.

Why? Because Jesus says at that time they will not only hate His followers all over the world but they will want to kill them. In fact, they are going to betray them and literally "turn them in." That's what the Greek word means! Betray is the Greek word "paradidomi" which means, "to give into the hands of, to give up to the custody of, for judgment, punishment, and/or to be put to death." The Bible says during the 7-year Tribulation, the followers of Jesus will be "turned in for death" or literally "betrayed" on a global scale. So, put it to the test. Here's the question, "How in the world is somebody going to do this, on a global scale, because that's the context?" How are you going to know if somebody is a Christian, number one, anywhere on the planet, and two, how are you going to know their location to "turn them in" for death?

If they keep quiet and stay out of sight, they should be safe, right? Not if you control the communication! If you did that, all a person would have to do is make one little slip up and talk about Jesus and you're toast! They'll know who the Christian is and exactly where you are! But hey, good thing we don't see any signs of anybody having the technology to monitor all our conversations and locate us anywhere on the planet anytime soon. Yeah, right folks! It's already here! It's called your cell phone! The world's greatest tracking device ever invented! And believe it or not, that's the issue!

The 1st thing Big Brother can do with our cell phones is to **Track Us With Them**.

As we already saw, for the first time in mankind's history, they've already got technology in place to monitor every single conversation on the whole planet with these NSA programs, among others, and they are still doing it today!

Fox News Reports:

A bomb shell report this morning that the NSA has been secretly collecting the phone records of tens of millions of Americans. A top secret court order reportedly forcing Verizon, one of the country's largest phone companies, to hand over the daily call information for every single one of their customers. She asks the reporter at the White House what kind of information are they looking for. He replies, "We know they want to see the phone number you dial, when you dial it, and how long you talk to the person on the other end of the line, that goes for all the Verizon customers in the United States and there are about 128 million of them on an ongoing basis. The White House also said this kind of information is a critical tool in protecting the United States from terrorists."[41]

And that always seems to be the excuse, isn't it? We need to give up more of our freedoms and let them spy on us so we can get those bad guys, those terrorists. But again, that's the issue. What if you became the "bad guy" or the "terrorist." And who gets to determine that? It's all an excuse to monitor our every move, even our communication. I'm telling you, it's way more than just being able to see what number you dialed, who you talked to, and for how long, it's literally to track your every move!

Believe it or not folks, our cell phones are one of the biggest global tracking devices ever invented by man and we pay for it! I'll say that again, we pay for it! Talk about tricky and sneaky! It reminds me of what the Bible says about Satan.

2 Corinthians 11:3 "But I am afraid that just as Eve was deceived by the serpent's cunning, your minds may somehow be led astray from your sincere and pure devotion to Christ."

The word there is "cunning" in the Greek is, "panourgia" and it means, "craftiness, cunning, or literally one skilled in trickery." That's what the Bible says Satan is. He's not just evil, he's tricky! He's cunning! He's tricked us into PAYING for OUR OWN tracking devices around the world! Can you believe that? In fact, we already saw how the government has been hot to trot making sure everybody has a cell phone, right? Even those who can't afford one, with all these free government cell phone giveaways. Remember that? Gee I wonder why? It's because it's a tracking device and you can't have anybody out of the system! The devil is so sneaky, we've not only been conditioned to not only pay for this kind of monitoring devices with our cell phones, but to even accept it in a multitude of ways!

The 1ˢᵗ way we've been conditioned to be tracked with our cell phones is with **Personal Retrieval**.

I mean, who doesn't hate this? You're in a hurry to rush out of the house and you can't find your cell phone? Isn't that annoying? Don't you hate that? Or worse yet, don't you hate it when somebody steals it from you? Those bad guys! Well hey, worry no more! That's right! Due to the fact that these devices come with built in GPS services, you can find your cell phone anywhere anytime!

*If you've lost your precious smart phone don't fret, GPS and location services built into smart phones, tablets and even lap tops, make it easy to locate and even erase data from missing devices. One app we found to be effective with all kinds of smart phones is the PREY app. You can track them on the PREY website on any other computer or phone. If a device goes missing just flick the switch on the website to see the phones location. You can also command the device to play a loud sound or even take and send a photo to see who has it.*⁴²

Isn't that great! You ever lose your phone and you can catch that bad guy who stole it in the first place! Even get his picture! But of course, that also means, since you carry this phone with you at all times, you too can be tracked and you too can have a photo taken of you as well. But they wouldn't do that would they?

The 2ⁿᵈ way they are conditioning us to be tracked with our cell phones is with **Friend Retrieval**.

I mean, talk about another annoyance. Don't you hate it when you want to go out and have some fun, you finally get some time off, but you just can't seem to find any of your friends anywhere? Doesn't that annoy you? Well hey that's right, fret no more! Google is here to help you. Just use their service called Latitude and you'll never have to party alone again!

Latitude is a new feature on Google Maps that allows you to see where your friends and family are on a map and easily keep in touch with them. When your friends accept, you can see them on your phone. For example, my friend Ali is currently in Cairo visiting his friends, my surfer buddy, Alice, is in Australia, my parents just arrived safely home from the airport, there was some bad weather in New Jersey. I see some of my buddies are nearby playing tennis, well, maybe they are free for dinner.[43]

      Yeah! And then you'd never have to party alone again! I can find all my friends at any time, anywhere, which of course means YOU can be found any time, anywhere as well. But nobody would do that, would they? In fact, they even have another app out called "Cloak" that allows you to do just the reverse of Latitude. It finds your friends alright, and you of course, but not so you can spend time with them, but so you can avoid them. I mean, who wants to be out on a date and you run into your ex-boyfriend or girlfriend! Fashion Faux Pas! Social Nightmare! It really is a Social Lifesaver! It's conditioning us to be tracked everywhere! You can even get a complete map of anyone, anywhere with another resource from Google. Their Latitude program has now morphed into Location History! "You just log into the same account you use on your phone and voila! The record of everywhere you've been for the last day to month will erupt across your screen like chicken pox." Here's a photo,

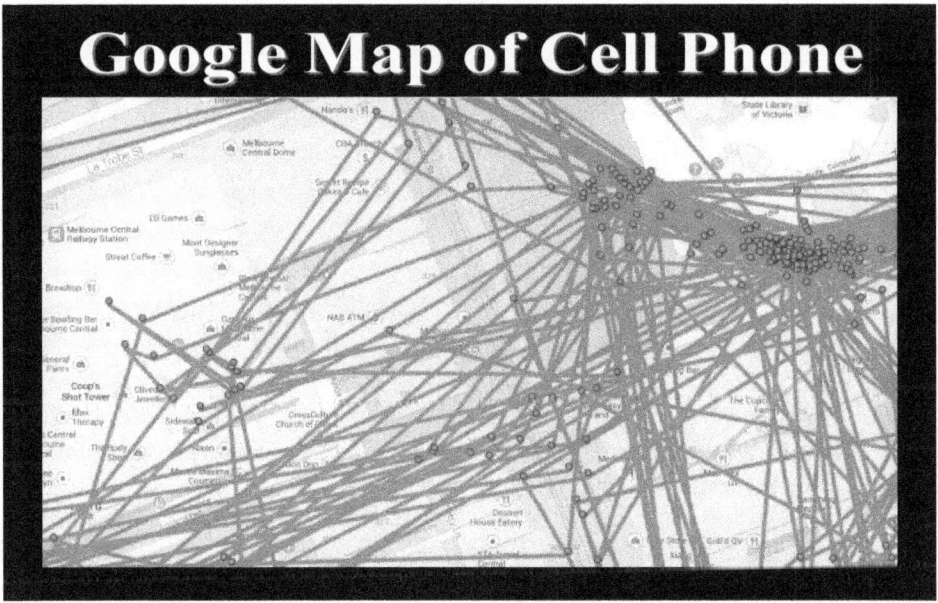

      Isn't that exciting! Yeah, it's about as exciting as Chicken Pox! Hello! Speaking of freaky.

The 3rd way we're being conditioned to be tracked with our cell phones is by **Parental Retrieval.**

Hey, Moms and Dads, don't you wish you could stop worrying about your little children, wherever they are, what they're doing, are they getting into trouble, are they safe, did they show up like they said they were going to. Well hey, that's right, worry no more! Cell phone providers are here for you! Now you can locate any family member at any time! Won't it be great!

Cell phones can be used to connect families with constant calls all day long. But now, with Sprint Family Locator, you can quietly keep track of your family without bothering them throughout the day. If you want to make sure Carolyn made it to morning band practice without interrupting music you can run a quick location check from either your phone or your home or office computer.

You can also program regular safety checks that automatically send you a text or email with any child's whereabouts at specific days and times. So, if Grant walks home every day at 3:00 you can double check to make sure he makes it home safely every time.

Real time interactive maps let you view their location with street addresses and landmarks as well as satellite views. Kids can cover a lot of ground. Family Locator also lets you view a weeks worth of recent location history. So, when Grant leaves Jake's house to go to Charlie's but ends up at Henry's and forgets to call, you'll know just where he is. And there's no installation required. The GPS technology is already built into your child's phone.[44]

What did it say? It's already built into your phone and yeah, it's nice knowing where your kids are, and the rest of the family, but at what price? And you sure hope somebody doesn't use it behind our back! Unfortunately, they already are.

The 4th way we are being conditioned to be tracked with our cell phones is with **Police Spying.**

Cell phones can not only allow individuals and parents to track us always, but so can Police. In fact, they're already doing it! Soon they are going to have a "Text Message Detector Gun" from a company called "ComSonics" in Virginia that says, "It can detect radio frequencies that come from a cell phone inside of a car, and since text messages emit unique frequencies that differ from other frequencies emitted by other activities on the phone, this would allow the officers to determine if someone is texting from inside the vehicle." (A Text Message Detector Gun!) Since, "Texting is currently outlawed in 44 states while driving, this radar gun would be a welcome addition to many law enforcement agencies around the country. But the problem is, that's just the tip of the iceberg of what they're already doing with our cell phones, they're also using it to track us, without our consent, without a search warrant, and it's unconstitutional. The news is admitting it!

RT Reports:

There is a pretty disturbing story out there today that we just learned about, thanks to the ACLU. And it involves, not Federal agencies doing National Security related investigations, but local police departments, hundreds of them, tracking your cell phones. This study finds that numerous police departments across the country are now using cell phone tracking often without court orders to find suspects and then investigate criminal cases. The ACLU surveyed more than 200 law enforcement agencies and most said that they use cell phone tracking.

Fox News Reports:

"In a town in North Carolina we came across an incident where law enforcement engaged in GPS tracking, not on the phone of just one individual who was suspected of a crime, but of every person who had called that phone. So that means, if someone suspected of a crime called a pizza delivery guy, that guy is also getting tracked."

Catherine Crump of the ACLU Reports:

And they're trying to hide it. The ACLU not only found that this information contradicts what the public hears from law enforcement officials, but they also found training manuals that say, "Do not mention to the public or the media the use of cell phone technology or equipment used to locate the target subject." It also advises, "Don't put this stuff into the police reports". So, doesn't that make you feel safe?[45]

Oh, but they're not the only ones trying to hide this, *"The Obama Administration has been quietly advising local police not to disclose details about surveillance technology they are using to sweep up basic cell phone data from entire neighborhoods."* That's from the Associated Press! And that, "Public findings showed that the government sales of communication systems such as the Stingray (one of the ones Police are using) from the company who makes them (Harris Corporation) accounted for nearly one-third of its $5 billion in revenue." In other words, they're investing heavily into this tracking technology of our cell phones! But don't worry, it's for your good, your safety!

The 5th way we are being conditioned to be tracked by our cell phones is with **Government Spying.**

Folks, it's not enough that the police are doing this behind our backs, but our own government is doing it too. Shocker! And just like the police, they're doing it in secret or should I say from the SKY. Here's what they're doing on an even bigger scale!

ABC News Reports:

Tonight, new questions about whether the government is scooping up personal cell phone data from thousands of innocent Americans. An investigation by the Wall Street Journal has uncovered a secret program designed to track down fugitives, suspected killers, rapists, and other criminals. It allows the US Marshals to pinpoint the location of your phone from the sky without you knowing it's happening.

Here's how it works. The Marshalls launch a small plane carrying a device called 'A Dirt Box' which acts like a mini cell tower. Over a populated area, it picks up identifying pings from thousands of phones below until it finds its suspect. Pinpointing that person's location within a 3-yard radius, even in a specific room. "They put it on an airplane, they get information on tens of hundreds of thousands of people and that is an outrageous, unreasonable, bulk search of innocent American citizens information." Says Christopher Soghoian, ACLU.

<u>Reporter:</u> *Popular Science reports that 17 fake cell phone towers had been found across the US. These phony towers have the ability to spy on phone calls, intercept messages, and load a phone with spyware and you never even know it's*

happening. It's known that government agencies use dummy towers as interceptors for espionage.[46]

It's to catch bad guys, right? But again, what if you became the "bad guy?" Who defines that? It's not just our own government doing this, it's the governments around the world! It's going global! You don't even need a fake tower or flying planes to do it either. They've got it figured out how to force phone companies to let them to do it!

"Vodafone (a multinational telecommunications company) recently stated, 'Government agencies are able to listen to phone conversations live, (we'll get to that in a second) and even track the locations of citizens without warrants using secret cables connected directly to network equipment." "Secret wires have been connected to its network and those belonging to competitors, giving government agencies the ability to tap into phone and broadband traffic." "In the 29 countries it operates in, laws demand they allow governments to directly access information about them. And refusal to comply with those laws is 'not an option." In other words, you have to let them spy on people! To show you just how, not just our own government, but the governments around the world are doing this. Listen to this.

The **6th way** we're being conditioned to be tracked with our cell phones is with **Game Spying.**

What? You talk about sneaky! We all know cell phones are not only great devices to make phone calls and keep tabs on people, but they're also great devices to play games with too, right? Especially when you're waiting in line, sitting at home, bored to death, whatever. The problem is, these games they designed have bugs in them that allow them to track your every move. Don't believe me? Even the news admitted it again! Talk about deceitful just like Satan!

Fox News Reports:

The NSA knows what you are up to and a little Angry Bird may be to blame. The agency is using cell phone apps to access personal information. This startling revelation comes from NSA leaker Edward Snowden, it's another leak and some say another cause for concern. Snowden's latest leak of documents shows how the NSA along with the division of Great Britain's government communications can zero in on your location when you are using Google Maps or posting a picture on Facebook or Twitter.

Also, when you are playing the popular game Angry Birds on your smart phone, player beware, Big Brother could be watching your every move, gathering knowledge, your age, sex, and other personal information. The White House defends the NSA app, saying the agency is not spying on the average Americans but on people who are potential threats to the country.[47]

Yeah, that's it! Sure! You always wondered why that game became so popular so fast and still is by the way. Everybody just had to have it! And good thing, because now they can track you with it! This is not make-believe! It's all happening before our very eyes! Think of the prophetic significance. How is the Antichrist going to make, order, force, cause people to do whatever he says to do, let alone know who's a Christian and find them so he can kill them? Simple! He'll just tap into this already existing communication system and your cell phone will betray you! He tricked you into paying for your own monitoring device on a global scale!

The 2nd thing Big Brother is doing with our cell phones to monitor us on a global scale is they can also **Watch & Listen to Us.**

What? Yeah, you thought tracking was bad? You haven't seen anything yet! These nifty devices, these cell phones that we all have to have, will not only track our every location, but they can also be tapped into to watch and monitor all our conversations! I believe it also explains what else is going on in our opening text.

Matthew 24:9-10 "Then you will be handed over to be persecuted and put to death, and you will be hated by all nations because of Me. At that time many will turn away from the faith and will betray and hate each other."

So again, Jesus says that the people during the 7-year Tribulation will not only hate the followers of Christ, those who get saved after the Rapture, but they'll what? They'll want to kill them, right? And they will betray and "turn them in." So again, think about this. How in the world are you going to know if somebody's a follower of Christ anywhere on the planet? I mean, we just saw you can track their locations anywhere on the planet with a cell phone, but how are you going to know if somebody's a follower of Christ? Well hey, wouldn't it be great if you had a single device that could not only pinpoint people's exact locations around the world, but even monitor all their conversations too, and see who they're hanging out with? Wouldn't that be great! Believe it or not, our cell phones are already doing that!

GMA Reports:

We have all heard the stories about how the GPS in your phone can track you, but, we have no idea how much about your personal life that people can learn through your cell phone until we met a woman whose cell phone nearly cost her, her life. "He knew where I was all the time. If I was at dinner somewhere he would text me and ask me how dinner was," explains Susan.

Reporter: Susan's x-boyfriend stalked her for 3 years using only her cell phone to do it. She's so afraid for her life that she asked us to disguise her identity. She says, "I thought I was going crazy. It's unnerving to know that somebody 24/7 knows where you are, what you are talking about, what's going on, everything about you."

Reporter: At the time, Susan didn't know that her ex-boyfriend installed widely available software on her phone when she wasn't looking. Once installed, he could be anywhere, even in a different state, and track her every move. He could listen in on her phone calls, read her text messages, and turn her personal cell phone into a bugging device. Susan says, "He would text me, how was dinner, was the date good, did you enjoy yourself at Friday's?"

Reporter: With her permission, I installed the software on a colleague's phone and sent her out to see how it worked. I just intercepted a live phone call and she has no idea I am listening in. The most frightening part of this technology is she doesn't even need to be on the phone. I can remotely activate her speaker on her phone and hear everything going on. Robert Siciliano, Security Expert, tells us, "When someone remotely activates your phone you're not going to know it and they can use that phone to monitor the conversations in the room you are in."

Reporter: Robert Siciliano gets countless emails from victims of cell phone spying. He says, "Your cell phone can be sitting by you when you are watching TV and somebody can actually log onto your phone and watch what you are watching on television. Someone can easily install spyware on your phone that allows them to see everything you do all day long via the phone's video camera.[48]

Well that's nice! Good thing I downloaded that game everybody just had to have! But that's just those creepy ex-boyfriends or gamers, right? This ability to watch and listen to you on your Cell Phones is now going global!

"German researchers have discovered a flaw that could allow anyone to listen to your cell phone calls and intercept text messages on a potentially massive scale – even when cellular networks are using the most advanced encryption available." "Those skilled with the right abilities can also locate callers anywhere in the world, listen to calls as they happen, and record hundreds of encrypted calls and texts for later decryption." "For example, a single carrier in Congo or Kazakhstan could be used to hack into cellular networks in the United States, Europe or anywhere else."

In other words, this ability to track, watch, or listen to anybody's cell phone anywhere on the planet has gone global! And that's not just freaky, but it's prophetically wild! Think about it from the Antichrist's point of view! How are you going to know if anyone's a follower of Christ around the planet and haul them in to kill them? Simple! Your cell phone on a global basis will betray you! And maybe that's what they will do in the 7-year Tribulation. They'll be "listening" for anyone saying the word "Jesus" at any time or "peer out" through your cell phone to "see" you and others. To "see" if you're at a church service or underground Bible study, something like that! Since these devices also know your location exactly, you'll be betrayed and they'll come haul you away and take you to be killed. It's not far-fetched. It's current day technology that allows the Antichrist to fulfill this passage! It's never been here in the history of mankind, but it is now! We're living in the last days

The 4th way the Antichrist is developing a global monitoring system, tracking our every move, is with our **Location System.**

That's right, I'm talking about your house, your home, your apartment, wherever you live, that which you thought was your own private domain is not anymore! Not even your house is going to be a safe during the 7-year Tribulation! You need to get saved now! But don't take my word for it. Let's listen to God's.

Matthew 24:15-22 "So when you see standing in the holy place the abomination that causes desolation, spoken of through the prophet Daniel – let the reader understand – then let those who are in Judea flee to the mountains. Let no one on the roof of his house go down to take anything out of the house. Let no one in the field go back to get his cloak. How dreadful it will be in those days for pregnant women and nursing mothers! Pray that your flight will not take place in winter or on the Sabbath. For then there will be great distress, unequaled from the beginning of the world until now –and never to be equaled again. If those days had not been cut short, no one would survive, but for the sake of the elect those days will be shortened."

As we see in this passage, the Bible clearly says that during the 7-year Tribulation, after the Antichrist shows his true colors and goes into the rebuilt Jewish temple to declare himself to be god, that's the abomination of desolation spoken of by the Prophet Daniel, that Jesus is referring to here, and He says the only option for these people is to what? To flee, right? To get out of there now in quick flight, right? Why? Because again as we saw before, Zechariah and other passages say it's going to be a horrible time of slaughter. Just the Jewish people alone, $2/3^{rds}$ of them are going to be annihilated, then $1/4^{th}$ of the earth will be annihilated, and then later another $1/3^{rd}$ goes after that! Over half the planet is going to die in the 7-year Tribulation, just with those three judgments! That's why Jesus says, "Get out of there and flee." But He not only said what you should do, flee to the mountains, but He also said what you should not do. He said whatever you do don't "flee" to your house, right? In fact, I'd say any dwelling because the Greek word here for "house" is "oikia" and it means, yes, a house, but it's also means "an inhabited edifice or dwelling." So, maybe the reason why Jesus says specifically to "get out of town" and "flee to the mountains" is because maybe any building whatsoever won't be safe at this time! Not just your house, but your workplace, your favorite pad, or even your church sanctuary, no inhabited edifice or dwelling is going to be safe! You just need to get out of there!

And again, you should have got saved and avoided the whole mess, but now, because you rejected Jesus today, your only option is to run, flee, and head to the hills, just like Jesus said! Why? Because, has it ever occurred to you that not even a person's "home" is going to escape Big Brother's eye? And for those who think this is science fiction, believe it or not, they're already doing it! They not only have radar guns that can peer through concrete walls to see you if you try to hide in any building, including your home, they also have satellites in orbit and drones in the sky that do the same.

The 1st way they're getting even more invasive with our homes is with **Computers.**

You see, not only does everybody just have to have a cell phone, as we saw before, which are great for tracking, watching, and listening to everything we do, but hey, everybody's got to have a computer too, right? At least one! And by the way, that's all a cell phone is, a sophisticated computer, just smaller! And who cares if you use your home computer just to play games, it also has become one of the biggest bugging, tracking, monitoring devices ever invented by man! And since we keep them at home, guess where they get to monitor us! Right there too!

The 1st way we're being monitored in our home by our computers is with **Data Tracking.**

Believe it or not, as we saw before, "Every search you perform online, including on Google, goes into a giant database, which is then used to keep a profile on our habits and interests. Search engines also track which links you click during your search and then they use that information to place targeted ads into your browser."

Did you ever wonder why, when you were looking for a tourist spot in Hawaii on your computer, all of a sudden, ads for airline tickets to Hawaii start popping up everywhere? How did they know that? It's all interconnected! They're tracking us! And that's not counting the social media we've been trained to use on our computers, like Facebook and Twitter, where we volunteer all kinds of personal information and communication including photos of ourselves and others.

They also do this tracking by what's called, "cookies." And no, these are not the kind you eat. These are the kind that are secretly put on your computer and track your every move and what you're doing! For instance, "Verizon and ATT have been quietly tracking the Internet activity of more than 100 million of their customers with what's been called 'super-cookies." "They're so powerful that it's even difficult for savvy users to escape them." These "cookies" allow these companies to, "Monitor which sites their customers visit, cataloguing their tastes and interests." Everything we type is being tracked by these "cookies." "Consumers cannot erase these cookies or evade them by using browser settings."

In other words, you're stuck with it! They are going to track you whether you want them to or not! It's a gold mine for companies, because these providers sell all this information to other companies who then get to target us with specific ads, all based on our interests!

CNN Reports:

So, if someone is surfing on line, if you or I were just looking around at stuff, do we have any idea or any warning that we are being tracked? Investigator: Not right now, trackers are companies you never heard of actually or at least most of them. They are small companies whose business it is to put little tiny things of software on websites and those send back information about you and they compile a profile and it's not your name usually but its everything about you under a unique ID number associated with you.

We did find that the biggest trackers were Google and Microsoft which you have heard of but the third largest one was Quantcast that most people have not heard of.

<u>CNN reporter</u>: *What more can they find out about us online? Can they tell what movies I like, what I like to eat or what products I use?*

<u>Investigator</u>: *We were surprised with our findings we did find; our lead example was a woman whose tracker on her computer knew all her favorite movies. We wrote about a girl who was 17 years old and was worried about her weight and the tracker on her computer also knew that, we talked to a woman who was worried about whether she had some sort of uterine disorder and she was also being targeted with ads.*[49]

So much for being anonymous! Better be careful what you search for because it's all being tracked and watched! And believe it or not, it's not just companies doing this, so is the government! The NSA (shocker) is also secretly, planting bugs in our computers to monitor us, even when you're not online! Yes, they have that technology! Let's take a look.

Fox News Reports:

The NSA has reportedly installed software in computers around the world that lets the United States government monitor those machines even if the computers are not connected to the internet. They can get to you whether you are on line or not.

That is according to the New York Times sighting NSA documents, computer experts and US officials. According to those sources, the secret technology could also let the NSA launch a cyber-attack. Nothing is surprising any more. Nothing. What's a little different about this is that there's no flat denial from the NSA. It's basically saying to us, don't worry about it, we only use it if we are going after the bad guys.[50]

Oh, and speaking of not even needing to be online, you might be wondering, "Well how do they do this," right? Can you say wireless! You see, another thing they don't tell you is, "Why in the world has there been this big push for everything to go wireless, right"

Remember back in the day when you had to "plug in" to the Internet with a cord and you had to string all these wires around for your computer to use your mouse and printer? Not anymore! Thanks to everything going wireless! But what they don't tell you is, "The wireless breakthrough could make the invisible, visible." This is how they do it!

"Hackers can steal data from PC's wirelessly that are not even online." That's how they're doing it, okay? and "Researchers from MIT Wireless Center and Artificial Intelligence Laboratory (There's that AI thing again) have developed a wireless system which can also track movement of people through a wall using WIFI. So, they can not only get on your computer wirelessly, but they can also track your movements.

"They can also detect subtle gestures like the rise and fall of a person's chest through which a person's heart rate can be measured with 99% accuracy. This technology can be used for the military and law enforcement and can also track the movements of humans staying behind closed rooms or hiding behind a wall. (You know like in your house during the 7-year Tribulation).

Scientists are now working on a higher resolution system which can detect body silhouettes, gestures, and even emotions." All because of wireless. Everything is going wireless, not just in your home, but even out in public with all these wireless cafes, shops, stores, coffee shops, etc. It's everywhere! Everybody's wireless!

In fact, the latest trend now is that whole towns offer free wireless services to anyone and everyone who comes into their community. They are called WIFI Towns that have installed a WIFI Mesh, a blanket over the whole community. So, now everyone can have their information hacked on their computer as well as being tracked no matter where you are.

All this technology can be used to monitor your computer and you, as well as what building you're in. There's no safe place to hide! No wonder Jesus said don't go back to your house. They'll see you in there!

The 2ⁿᵈ way we're being monitored in our house with our computers is with **Web Cams.**

Who's watching who? As we saw before, virtually anyone can tap into anybody else's computer via their webcam, and spy on them literally through their webcam! It's so commonplace they're called Ratters, we saw that before. All new laptops have built-in webcams whether you want one or not! So that means, you too can be watched on your computer.
Another rage that everyone has to have are those BabyCams, right Mom's and Dad's? I mean, don't you want to use this technology to make sure little Jonnie and Susie are safe from afar? The problem is, other people can do it too!

Here's a look at what we are talking about. The IP cameras just like this one, many parents use in their child's nursery to help keep an eye on them and you can control them so easily from your phone, your iPad or your laptop. But, imagine waking up in the middle of the night to find someone has been using your baby monitor to watch your child and your home. One mother tells us, "Sound asleep, suddenly I heard what sounded like a man's voice. But, I was so asleep I wasn't sure."

<u>Reporter</u>: *Disoriented and confused, Heather picked up her cell phone to check the monitor and her 10-month-old daughter's room. She could see the camera moving which didn't make sense because she wasn't moving it. Heather says, "About the time I saw it moving I also heard a voice again. Screaming at my daughter. He was screaming 'Wake up baby, wake up baby' and then a long screaming sound, trying to wake her up" That's when her husband Adam ran into the baby's room and described how the camera then turned from his petrified daughter to point directly at him. Adam says, "Then he screamed at me. Some bad things. Obscenities.*[51]

Well, I guess on the one hand, that could be the ultimate excuse as to why your child's been using bad language. "Wasn't me! It was the hacker! He got into my webcam!" Can you believe that? It's way more invasive than that! You see, another trend that everyone just has to have is not only webcams installed for babies, but for businesses! Got to keep track of your employees! But the problem is, just like with babycams, they too can be hacked on a massive scale! In fact, one guy from Russia, of all places, demonstrated just how easy it is to hack into all these webcams and post them on a website, tens of thousands of webcams and their live feeds for the whole world to see.

CBS Reports:

A Russian backed website is peering into homes around the world this morning. Many are right here in the United States. Anyone can log on to see the live feed from your bedroom to security systems all with a map straight to your front door. In London, the government is demanding that Russia take this site down. The website has actually been up and running for months peering into offices and people's bedrooms for all the world to see.

They claim they are doing it for their own good, shining a light on the problem of weak security. They have eyes on everywhere. The so called private webcams are only clicks away from anyone with an internet connection. Businesses like a laundromat in Salt Lake City, a university in Iowa, private homes right down to baby monitors, these are children's bedrooms right here in the United States this morning.[52]

That's kind of creepy. So much for personal privacy with all these webcams in your home and business! Everything is being watched! All "oikia" is no longer safe! No wonder Jesus said FLEE to the hills!

The **3rd way** we're being monitored in our homes with our computers is with **Built-in Microphones.**

You see, just like cell phones, computers not only have the ability to "watch" you, but they also have the ability to "listen" to you as well, just like a cell phone, with their own built-in microphones. Maybe you don't see it there, but these microphones not only allow web browsers like Google to listen to you on your computer, but it can keep on listening to you, even when you tell it to stop!

Just go to Google.com and right in the middle of Googles most sacred real estate is a speech button. This is how their most malicious site can listen in while you are at your computer and even after you have left that site. If you visit a site where you have speech recognition for completely legitimate reasons, it is a voice activated 'voice to do' app. Chrome will ask for your permission to access the microphone. Since it is supposed to be used only for this app I allow it. Chrome will show a clear indication that it is listening to your voice.

Example: To do, shop for groceries. To do, prepare demo video. Cool it works. But if you say, 'turn off mic' it will stop listening to your command. Now that you are done with this site, you can close it and go on with your day, visit other sites, or get away from the computer completely. But, the malicious site you visited continues to listen in on you long after you left it. As long as Chrome is still running, nothing said next to your computer is private. If you go to a different site and authorize the closing of the site that was listening to your voice there is no indication that your voice is being recorded and yet Google Chrome is listening. In this hidden spot, you can see everything said has been captured being sent back to Google, analyzed, then sent back to the malicious site where it could be saved or sent on to any other area in the world.[53]

And as you saw, even provide a nice neat typed written report of everything you just said, without your knowing it. Your computer is listening to you! And they're not the only ones. So is Facebook. "Facebook recently rolled out a new feature that's leaving some users speechless." The social network's new app allows them to turn on your smartphone's microphone, listen in on what's around you and identify what you're listening to, the music or TV shows, etc." I'm sure they wouldn't do that with your computer's microphone, would they?

The **4th way** we're being monitored in our homes with our computers is with **Our E-mails.**

What? Nothing's safe! As we have already seen, everything you type, including your e-mails are being monitored. Nothing's sacred anymore. And we already saw that with Project Echelon that has been going on for years! They look for "key words" like "bomb" or other key words to decipher whether or not you're a terrorist. That's been going on for years! But it's not just Project Echelon or the NSA that's doing this, so is Google! For proof of that, they recently turned a guy in to the authorities, based on what they "SAW" i.e. monitored in his email account.

KHOU News Reports

John was convicted of sexually assaulting a child 20 years ago. Now police say technology which was unthinkable back then caught this sex offender preying on kids again. They got a tip from Google, basically Gmail. An officer from the Houston Metro Internet Crime Against Children Task Force said John had used his Gmail account to email a friend three explicit pictures of a young girl.

The company software detected the pictures and they turned him in. He was trying to get around getting caught and was keeping it inside, I would have never been able to find that. Google wouldn't respond to our questions about their technology to fight child porn. Officer: I really don't know how they do their job but I'm just glad they do it.[54]

Now before I go any further, please do not misunderstand me, I'm not at all justifying what that man did with child porn. I believe he does need to be prosecuted for it but at what price? Just what is Google's job, as he said? The point is, he was "turned in" by Google by what they "saw" in his e-mail account, which means it's being monitored live! What you type is being monitored via your email!

The 5th way we're being monitored in our home with our computers is with **Automated Home Systems.**

I mean, who out here doesn't like that remote control? What an invention! You don't have to get up off the couch, you just sit there and change the channels, the device does the rest! Isn't that great! That's right! Now you can not only do that with your TV, but your whole house! The thermostats, appliances, smoke detectors, lights, you name it! It's all remote control now, thanks to Google! They just spent $3.2 billion buying this company called NEST. Let the home invasion begin!

All around the world the home is the center of people's lives. It's where you start your day and end your day. It's where you raise a family, to make memories with the people you love. So, wouldn't it be cool if our homes could be more aware. If our homes could learn from us. Help take care of us. NEST can do just that. It all started with the NEST learning thermostat. NEST can also protect. If you wake up a little bit earlier, before you even get out of bed, you can let NEST know that and it will adjust the temperature in the room.

As you get into your car and drive home, the car will in the background, send the estimated time of arrival to your NEST thermostat, so, your home can be at the right temperature as you arrive. Why would we ever bring the thermostat and the washer together? If you look at it from the prospective of energy consumption it's an easy one. These are big in energy consumption in the home and also require a lot of day to day interaction of the consumer.

If you have a thermostat communicating with the utility company, it's much easier for one signal to go to NEST and dissimilate to all the household appliances to basically reduce energy consumption. It also has a Lifex LED light bulb that you control with your smart phone. When we first heard about the NEST program we were really excited to be a part of it.

With NEST Protect and Lifex, when the smoke alarm is triggered we can pulse your lights red which can help you see in the dark as well as give extra notification that there is a problem in the house, which is especially good if you are hearing impaired. NEST brings a whole new dimension to Lifex. Who thought that by combining NEST and Lifex we could help save lives[55]

.   Yeah, save lives or monitor lives! How far do you push this convenience? Do you really want Big Brother, Google, controlling your house? They are already monitoring my computer, e-mails, and listening to me! Oh, speaking of lights, has anybody noticed how there's not only this big push for wireless, but also for us to become environmentalists and switch out our lights with these new LED lights? Have you noticed that? I wonder why? I mean, surely it wouldn't be to monitor us, would it? Unfortunately, yes!

CBS News Reports:

Should you find yourself in Terminal B at Newark Airport, look up, those aren't just new lights, they are smart lights. A sophisticated array of LED fixtures with built in sensors and cameras connected over a wireless network. They monitor security and the flow of foot traffic. Hugh Martin is the President of the Silicon Valley company that developed the smart lights at Newark and this parking garage in San Jose.

<u>*Reporter*</u>*: So, these lights, they sense that we are walking.*

<u>*Hugh Martin*</u>*: Yes, there is a motion sensor in each individual light.*

Reporter: This is just one of a few places in the country where a smart light network has been installed. This Silicon Valley building uses it primarily for security. And here is how it works. There are 40 lamp posts in this lot holding 83 LED lights connected to 7 cameras in a seamless grid that is tracking and recording my every move.

Hugh Martin: So, we do use the license plate recognition and we also can detect people. Kevin Kirk is chief engineer of the Shorenstein Company which owns this building. The company plans to install smart lights at their properties across the country.

Kevin Kirk: Everything goes up into the cloud so we can access anything from anywhere. The future is limitless for this technology.

Reporter: The smart light network has the ability to spot an unattended bag at an airport and alert security, show drivers to empty parking spaces, alert shoppers of sales as they walk past retailers.

There is no end to the kind of information you can gather. And therein lies the problem. In the future, the smart network could track every place we go, everything we buy, everything we do all the time. It sounds rather Orwellian. There are over four billion outside lights in the world today. Imagine all these lights connected in one global network.[56]

Imagine that AI system we saw before taking over and then the Antichrist hi-jacks it all, and he'll have everything he needs to monitor the planet for the first time in man's history. No wonder Jesus said RUN to the hills! I mean, all that's left is some freaky Big Brother AI Voice System that tells us what to do in your own home! Well, believe it or not, that just came out too. It's called ECHO.

Amazon has created the Star Trek computer for your home. There is a new female computer voice you can talk to now and her name is Alexa. Well, the device itself is called Amazon Echo. Amazon created a speaker that you can put anywhere in your home. Its connected to the internet and it responds to your family's voice commands, but before any question or command you have to say Alexa.

The concept is just like what you can do with Android when you say, 'OK Google' before a command. The Amazon Echo does much more than a phone, you can ask her for the news and she'll play the latest from NPR, ESPN, or your favorite radio station.

You can set alarms, timers, even ask her to add items to your shopping lists. "Alexa, add wrapping paper to the shopping lists". Alexa replies, "I put wrapping paper on your shopping list." "Alexa, how many teaspoons are in a tablespoon?" Alexa replies, "One tablespoon equals 3 teaspoons." At the top at the light ring you will find 7 microphones with technology that can hear you from any direction and while music is played. [57]

Which means, no matter how much you try to cover up your conversation and what you're doing, Alexa can still hear you! Now think about it like this. Can you imagine if Antichrist taps into this entire system and everything on the planet is all tied together, with these lights, microphones, computers, you name it, everywhere. And then, instead of saying now, "Okay Google" or "Alexa" to do anything in your home or wherever, in the future you'll have to say, "Okay Antichrist, to turn on my heater or buy and sell, to do anything.

Is it really far-fetched? NO! It's all coming together now! No wonder Jesus said RUN to the hills! Again, you should have got saved today, and avoided the whole thing. But, for those of you who still persist and say you're the Ultimate Survivor, you don't need Jesus, you'll just unplug from the system, go off the grid, and avoid the whole thing, think again! That might soon become illegal, like it was for this lady.

News 4 Reports:

A Cape Coral woman says she's living off the grid. She doesn't use city power or water but now she's being ordered to plug in or face the consequences. We first featured Robin Speronis in November. She showed us how she lived day to day with no running water or electricity.

Robin tell us "Code enforcement officer came, knocked on the door, then posts a plaque that says, 'inhabitable property, do not enter." The Cape Coral officer posted the notice for her to vacate. "Putting a woman who lives by herself, a widow, out on the street without any notice." [58]

But you don't get it lady, it's for your own good and we can't have anybody outside the system! Then how are we going to monitor them! Folks, this is not make-believe, it's really happening right now! For the first time in mankind's history we have the ability right now to have one man literally control & monitor anyone, anytime, anywhere, on the whole planet, at home or in public, wherever, it doesn't matter, all bases are now covered! Don't go back to your house! That's why Jesus said,

Luke 21:28 "When these things begin to take place, stand up and lift up your heads, because your redemption is drawing near."

It's going to be the worst time in the history of mankind. You don't want to be there! There's no way of escape, except One. His Name is Jesus. Ask Him to forgive you of all your sins now, believe in your heart that God raised Him from the dead, and the Bible says, you will be saved! Amen?

Chapter Nine

One World Economy

Now I don't know if you realize it or not, but one of the many unsung heroes of Church ministries is the sound engineer. Believe it or not, they do a whole lot more than you could ever imagine. In fact, so much so, I wanted to give you an idea of how much a good sound engineer goes through just to make things sound good. Let's take a look.

"The female singer is at the microphone, all prepared to sing, she opens her mouth and we notice in the sound booth the man on the sound board is busy pushing buttons all over the board. Her agent is standing next to him moving his mouth to her beautiful voice. The song is lovely and the agent can see dollar signs. She sounds awesome. The sound engineer is pushing buttons faster and faster, she is harmonizing, with one, with two, with three versions of herself. Fantastic… All of a sudden, the sound engineer pushes the wrong button and her true voice comes out. She is so horrible, off key, screeching into the microphone. The noise is awful. The sound engineer proceeds to hit more buttons as fast as his fingers can push them. Gradually the beautiful voice comes back, the agent is once again so proud of his awesome singer. The voice he is hearing makes him want to cry. On the other hand, the sound engineer is sweating bullets, his fingers are killing him, it was so stressful that he is breathing heavy like he may pass out, he leans back in his chair, hoping that he never has to do that again. Thumbs up between agent and singer, Great Job!"[1]

Believe it or not, that guy's not the only one sweating bullets getting hand cramps! That video not only reminds me of just how important a good sound engineer really is, but it also reminds me of how people's tunes are going to change, just like that, when Jesus comes back!

You see, on this side of the wall, prior to the rapture, people are singing a merry tune. They laugh, they scoff, they act like it's no big deal! Ha ha ha! La la la la la! Who cares! But after the Rapture, on the other side of the wall, that tune is going to change into a horrific moan even worse than that lady! I didn't say that, God did.

Revelation 6:16-17 "They called to the mountains and the rocks, 'Fall on us and hide us from the face of Him who sits on the throne and from the wrath of the Lamb! For the great day of their wrath has come, and who can stand?"

Luke 21:26 "Men will faint from terror, apprehensive of what is coming on the world, for the heavenly bodies will be shaken."

So, as you can see, people's tunes are going to change just like that! Why? Because the 7-year Tribulation is an outpouring of God's wrath on a wicked and rebellious planet. It's not a happy tune!

We saw how the Antichrist is going to monitor the whole planet and everything we do, and everywhere we go with a Big Brother Surveillance Society! Every single aspect of our lives is going to be monitored with a Big Brother type system to ensure that we obey and unfortunately stick around for the last days slaughter!

It's already being done. We saw how our computers, that we bring into our homes, are being used to monitor us with Data Tracking, WebCams, Microphones, E-mails, and those Home Automation Systems. For the first time in man's history, we now have the ability for one man to literally monitor, control, watch, spy, listen on, anyone, anytime, anywhere, on the whole planet, home or in public, it doesn't matter, all bases are covered. Which means, we're living in the last days!

The 10th update on The Final Countdown study letting us know we're living in the Last Days is The Rise of a One World Economy.

The Bible is clear. One day the whole planet is not only going to be under the "authority" of the Antichrist, with this One World Government, but it's also going to be under his economy as well. He's not only going to monitor you, but he's going to control all the money! Now he's really got you! But don't take my word for it. Let's listen to God's.

Revelation 13:11-17 "Then I saw another beast, coming out of the earth. He had two horns like a lamb, but he spoke like a dragon. He exercised all the authority of the first beast on his behalf, and made the earth and its inhabitants worship the first beast, whose fatal wound had been healed. And he performed great and miraculous signs, even causing fire to come down from heaven to earth in full view of men. Because of the signs he was given power to do on behalf of the first beast, he deceived the inhabitants of the earth. He ordered them to set up an image in honor of the beast who was wounded by the sword and yet lived. He was given power to give breath to the image of the first beast, so that it could speak and cause all who refused to worship the image to be killed. He also forced everyone, small and great, rich and poor, free and slave, to receive a mark on his right hand or on his forehead, so that no one could buy or sell unless he had the mark, which is the name of the beast or the number of his name."

So here we clearly see, the Bible says there really is coming a day when all the inhabitants of the earth will not only be under the authority of the Antichrist, but even his what? His economy or monetary system, right? You can't buy or sell, you can't do anything with money without his permission. And so, here's the point. "Could that really happen?" Could the whole world really be deceived into creating a One World Economy for the Antichrist to, at one-point, hijack and take over for his purposes? And is there any evidence that this is really going to take place any time soon, like the Bible said? Yes! In fact, it's happening now!

The 1st proof we know we really are headed for a One World Economy is **The Machinery Is Already In Place**.

What most folks don't realize is that this One World Economy of the Antichrist is not only going to be put into place, because the Bible said it would, but what people don't realize is that it's been in the planning stages for a long time. And they're just about ready to pull it off! The machinery is already there! Right now, there is already in place the plans for absolute total economic control of the entire world. Right now, there's already a Universal Bank called the World Bank which is the world's leader of lending money to the nations around the planet.

But wait a minute. If you're going to have a universal bank then you need a universal lending institution to oversee the dispersion of loans, right? Well what do you think is the function of the International Monetary Fund which oversees the whole world's financial system and even fixes the exchange rates? If you're going to have a universal lending institution then you need a universal money exchanger to funnel all this money to all the different countries, right?

Well, guess what? Right now, there's a universal electronic banking system called SWIFT, which automatically makes sure that all the different money transactions in the world match all the different currencies. If you're going to have a universal money exchanger, then you need to have a universal strong arm to punish those who don't obey this world banking system, right?

Well, that's why, right now, there's the World Trade Organization which not only sets the trading rules for the world, but they punish all countries who do not obey with billion-dollar fines. So, as you can see, the machinery for a One World Economy is already here! It's already in place! Not 50 years down the road…it's already here! And for further proof, just pay attention to all these treaties we keep hearing about. What are they all about? They are all about tying together the world's economies!

First, there was the GATT Treaty in 1944, the (General Agreement on Tariffs and Trade) to help, "Liberalize world trade." Then 50 years later in 1994 we had (NAFTA) or North American Free Trade Agreement. And then 10 years after that (2004) was (CAFTA) or the Central American Free Trade Agreement, combining Central American countries. And then the very next year, (2005) was the FTAA or Free Trade Agreement of the Americas, which proposes to encompass the whole Western Hemisphere and their economies and it's happening all over the world!

There's the (AFTA) the ASEAN Free Trade Area, or (APTA) the Asia-Pacific Trade Agreement, (SICA) the Central American integration System, or other proposed ones like (CEFTA) the Central European Free Trade Agreement, (COMESA) the Common Market for Eastern & Southern Africa) or (GAFTA) the Greater Arab Free Trade Area or (SAFTA) the South Asia Free Trade Agreement, and even (TAFTA) the Transatlantic Free Trade Area, on and on it goes! The most recent one out there that the previous administration was working on while we're all consumed with other things was called (TPP) or the Trans-Pacific Partnership. It encompassed 12 nations in the Pacific area, including Australia, Brunei, Canada, Chile, Japan, Malaysia, Mexico, New Zealand, Peru, Singapore, Vietnam and the United States. All I have to say is, if this baby had gone through, man, you think it's hard to get a job now, you ain't seen nothing yet! This was NAFTA on steroids! That didn't help things! I didn't say that, the news did!

RT News Reports:

The Obama Administration is preparing to sell America out to a handful of private corporations. Well, more than a handful, but right now President Obama is preparing to push through the largest trade deal in human history, the Trans-Pacific Partnership, or as it is more commonly known, TPP. If approved the TPP would create a whole new set of rules regulating the economy of 12 countries.

The countries are bordering the Pacific Ocean. The rules cover everything from pharmaceuticals to digital copyright law and could permanently change everything that Americans and people all over the world interact with the global economy. He would unconstitutionally transfer legislative powers from the US congress, our state legislatures, our city and county governments, to multi-national corporations and unaccountable international bureaucrats at the World Trade Organization otherwise known as the WTO.

Incredibly it would also transfer our judicial power in federal and state courts, which are bad enough, to globalist TPP judges at regional tribunals and the WTO. 1) Very little of the TPP deals with actual trade 2) The US's sovereignty would be stripped down, transferring powers from federal control to global control by special interest groups.

Like the infamous NAFTA trade agreement passed in the 1990's the TPP would usher in another wave of outsourcing as the remaining manufacturing policy basis would be to give the incentive to move to the Pacific Rim countries resulting in millions of American job losses. You would think that the Obama Administration would want the American public to be as up to date as possible on such a big trade deal, right? Wrong!

The United States negotiated the deal entirely in secret with the help of about 600 private corporations. No wonder then that the Obama Administration doesn't even want Congress to take a closer look at the TPP. It puts the United States in the proposed treaty as soon as possible. The President is trying to use a special legislative trick called 'Fast Tracking'.

It would prevent law makers from making any amendments to the TPP. If instituted, the TPP's (Intellectual Property) regime would trample over individual rights and free expression, as well as ride roughshod over the intellectual and creative commons. If you read, write, publish, think, listen, dance, sing or invent; if you farm or consume food; if you're ill now or might one day be ill, the TPP has you in its crosshairs.[2]

Thankfully, our current administration stopped this one in it's tracks prior to being enacted.

What's next? You going to control what I "buy and sell" too, across the planet? Yeah! That's the goal! It's all being interconnected! In fact, there's another treaty out there even worse than this one called (TISA) or the Trade in Services Agreement that covers 50 countries and 68.2% of World trade & Services, which means you only have 31.8% to reach your ultimate goal, interconnect 100% of the world's economies! They're almost there! This is not a game, this is really happening. The machinery to pull off a One World Economy is being put into place now, which means we're living in the last days!

The **2nd proof** that we know are headed for a One World Economy is **The Unions are Already in Place**.

And this is what we saw before with the Ten-Horned Kingdom of the Antichrist. But I bring it up again because it's not just about forming a One World Government, it's also about forming a One World Economy.

Revelation 17:12-13 "The ten horns you saw are ten kings who have not yet received a kingdom, but who for one hour will receive authority as kings along with the beast. They have one purpose and will give their power and authority to the beast."

So again, according to the Bible, we see how the Antichrist's kingdom is going to be split up into ten different parts ruled by ten different kings or leaders, right? And then, at one point, they surrender their power and authority over to him, right? And it's exactly 10 that they are working for! Not 5, not 19, not even 122, but exactly 10 regions or unions to govern the world! It's not just about forming governmental unions, it's about forming economic unions.

For instance, as we saw before, it's not just that the European Union was formed by a group of countries to combine their governments into one, it was also the fact that they combined their economies into one! They came together economically to form a new currency called the Euro. Then we saw Africa did the same thing with their African Union which is a region of countries coming together economically with their new proposed currency called the Afro. Then we saw, the North American Union, between Canada, United States, and Mexico, with the proposed currency called the Amero.

Even Russia got in on the action recently with some of its surrounding countries and formed the Eurasian Economic Union and their new proposed currency called the "Altyn." Then there's plans for the South American Union, Asian Union, Mediterranean Union, Central Asian Union, Pacific Union, and on and on it goes, as we saw before.

These Unions bring together not just their governments but their economies! And it's created a global currency war with a huge battle to see who's left on top of the pile!

Chirac calls for a global tax
2009: Russia says the World needs a New Currency
2009: China begins to discuss a New World Currency
2009: The U.N. calls for a New Global Currency
2010: The International Monetary System begins talks on a global currency
2011: The Vatican Calls for Oversight of the World's Finances

Prime Minister Gordon Brown: "The international financial crisis has given world leaders a unique opportunity to create a truly global society. Britain, the United States and Europe are key to forging a New World Order. Uniquely in this global age, it is now in our power to come together so that 2008 is remembered not just for the failure of a financial crash that engulfed the world. We can together seize this moment of change in our world to create a truly global society."

President George W. Bush: "It is essential that we work together because we are in this crisis together. Together we will work to modernize and strengthen our nations' financial systems so we can help ensure this crisis doesn't happen again."

European Commission President Manuel Barroso: "We need a new global financial order."

German Chancellor Angela Merkel: "It was time to rethink the world's financial system and prevent any repetition of the current crisis."

Morgan Stanley Chief Executive John Mack: "We need a new global body to oversee the financial crisis, warning that it is like nothing he's ever seen before."

Timothy Geithner president of the Federal Reserve: "We need a new global monetary authority, a de-facto global financial dictatorship, operating across borders and forcing nations and corporations to register and adhere to strict monitoring and regulations."

China: "They are calling for a new global currency controlled by the International Monetary Fund, stepping up pressure to global leaders, for changes to the financial system."

Russia: "Is calling for a new international currency system and wants to overhaul the entire global financial order and even introduce a new supra-national currency to avoid future global financial crisis."

United Nations: "They are proposing the biggest overhaul of the world's monetary system since WWII by calling for a new global currency."

Banks: "The Institute of International Finance, a group that represents 420 of the world's largest banks and finance houses, has issued yet another call for a one-world global currency. They are encouraging a return to a commitment to utilize International Monetary Fund special drawing rights to create an international one-world currency."

Single Global Currency Association: "Are calling for the world to embrace a single global currency to be managed by a global central bank within a global monetary union. If the European Monetary Union can successfully provide stable currency to countries, why not a Global Monetary Union for all countries? We shall achieve this goal through education and persuasion."

A currency world war is looming for the global world economy, this is according to Russia having sent out a warning. The concerns were sparked by Japan's move to lower the Yen in pursuit of better exports causing fears of a massive chain reaction if other nations follow suit.

The global economy is on the verge of a currency war, Japan's prime minister is pushing for a more aggressive central bank policy by dropping the yen. It went down 11% since December.

Meanwhile in the European Union experts say Europe has fired the first shell that EU financial authorities have warned that the rising Euro is threatening the economy. Now the United States has been printing bucks for the past 5 years to support the markets but that also makes the dollar cheaper.

Washington has been looking over the shoulder of China which holds the majority of US foreign debt and Beijing is also being accused of holding back its currency. But the last time a major currency war happened was during the great depression era in the 1930's which resulted in the slowdown of international trade and was the lead up to WWII.[3]

I wonder if this is going to lead up to WWIII that the occult says we need for the Antichrist to arise out of the ashes to save the day and bring back the economies of the world. In fact, speaking of wars, many believe this battle over the world's economies is also explaining other things we're seeing in the news.

For instance, why did we see dozens of bankers mysteriously die all over the world? Big banks too! Were they resisting somebody's plans? Don't know! But one thing we do know is that the real reason why Gaddafi, the leader of Libya was taken out recently, had nothing to do with terrorism or safety, it had to do with him messing with the global system, the global economy!

RT News Reports*:*

Obama says, "Our resolve is clear, the people of Libya must be protected." But some are convinced that intervention in Libya is all about currency. Specifically, Gaddafi's plan to introduce the gold Dinar, a single African currency made from gold, a true sharing of the wealth. "It's one of these things you have to plan almost in secret", says Dr. James Thring, Ministry of Peace and legal action against war. "Because as soon as you say you are going to change from the dollar to something else you are going to be targeted."

In the months leading up to the military intervention, Gaddafi called on African and Muslim nations to join together to create this new currency that would rival the dollar and the euro. They would sell oil and other resources around the world only for gold dinars. Anthony Wile, founder, The Daily Bell, says, "If

Gaddafi had an intent to try to reprice his oil or whatever else the country was trying to sell on the global market, accept something else as a currency, maybe launch a gold dinar currency, any move such as that would certainly not be welcome by the powers that be today that would be responsible for the World Central Bank.

So, yes that would certainly be something that would cause his immediate dismissal and the need for other reasons to be brought forth for removing him from power." It happened before, in 2000 Saddam Hussain announced Iraqi oil would be traded in euros not dollars, sanctions and an invasion followed.[4]

Say what? Even the news admits it! It doesn't matter who you are, Libya, Iraq, whoever, you mess with the global plans for a global economy and you're toast! In fact, they're not the ones being punished. Right now, so is Russia. We all know the oil prices plummeted recently, which makes for fantastic prices at the gas pumps. Turn to somebody and say, "Yahoo!" BUT for those countries whose economies are more dependent on higher oil prices, like Russia, and others, there's no yahoo about it, it's killing their economy! Many believe it's being used as a tool to spank Russia for tampering with the world's economy. I didn't say that, our previous President did!

Barack Obama: If you'll recall, their economy (Russia) was already contracting even before oil collapsed. And part of our rationale in this process was that the only thing keeping that economy afloat was the price of oil. And if, in fact, we were steady in applying sanction pressure, which we have been, that over time it would make the economy of Russia sufficiently vulnerable and that they'd have enormous difficulty managing it."

In other words, we're going to take you down, by driving down the price of oil. Why? Because, Russia was messing with the world economy!

"Putin is creating institutions that rival the IMF and the World Bank, and he's increasing membership in an integrated, single-market Eurasian Economic Union, and he's attacking the structural foundation upon which the global economy rests."

So, guess what? Just like the other guys, Libya, Iraq, and who knows who else, you mess with the plan to create a global economy, you pay the price! We'll take you down! Including China! Here's the real hot button! China is also trying to control the world's currency, and I wonder what that's going to lead to? Maybe another war?

NT News Reports:

Do you think that China wants a global alternative to the dollar? Is there any possibility of that happening? Dr. Thorsten Pattberg, China expert at Peking University, says, "Yes, it would be perfectly reasonable to think that China wants to see their currency be the next world currency. There is a plan, and China is purchasing more gold and it also plays in to this. They recently purchased several tons of gold in Hong Kong and China is taking a big leap forward actually to control the world currency to replace it with the Yen.[5]

They're trying to control the *World Economy*. They're trying to usurp these guys! Gee, what's that going to do? In fact, they're making good headway. "The Chinese economy just overtook the United States economy to become the largest in the world." "For the first time since Ulysses S. Grant was president, America is not the leading economic power on the planet, China is!" We're now #2! So, what's that going to do? Some would say it's going to lead to another war, even China. And maybe this is the impetus for this war mentioned in Revelation.

Revelation 9:15-16 "And the four angels, who had been prepared for the hour and day and month and year, were released, so that they would kill a third of mankind. The number of the armies of the horsemen was two hundred million; I heard the number of them."

As we saw before, it just so happens right now that China can raise an army of that exact number, and one third of the earth is going in this battle! Could it be over currency? The global economy? Don't know, could be. But, as you can see, somebody is pretty serious about forming a One World Economy with the machinery in place, and now these unions in place, we're almost there!

The **3rd proof** that we really are headed for a One World Economy is **The Currency Is Already In Place**.

You see, you not only need the machinery in place, and these 10 economic unions in place, to hand over to the Antichrist, but Revelation 13 says it needs to have a universal global currency for the Antichrist. That's exactly what they're calling for! The U.N. right now is calling for a global currency. The IMF is calling for global currency. Leaders from England, Europe, United States, all over the world, are calling right now for a global currency! In fact, so are the banks! "The Institute of International Finance, a group that represents 420 of the world's largest banks and finance houses, has issued another call for a one-world global currency." Right now!

When 10 Unions come together, the 10 become 1, exactly like the text says! Another outfit called, "The Single Global Currency Association" is "Calling for the world to embrace a single global currency to be managed by a global central bank within a global monetary union." And listen to their rationale! "If the European Monetary Union can successfully provide stable currency to countries, why not a global monetary union for all countries? We shall achieve this goal through education and persuasion."

As **Revelation 13** says, "We're going to force, order, & make you do it!" You know, like what they're doing with Russia and other countries. In fact, even the Vatican is getting in on this. The Pope is actually calling for a global tax to be paid to the U.N. to "redistribute wealth" to the poor. But I like what one guy said, "If you really want to help the poor, how about starting with your throne at the Vatican."

"GO, SELL EVERYTHING YOU HAVE...
...and give to the poor" (mark 10:21)
I'm quite sure he could sell that golden throne at a very good price

It's always somebody else's riches that the rich want to give away! But it goes even deeper than that! You not only need a global currency, but you need a global electronic currency to turn into a Mark. There just happens to be a new one out there called Bitcoin! Let's see what it can do!

What is bitcoin? Bitcoin is the first decentralized digital currency. Bitcoins are digital coins you can send through the internet. Compared to other alternatives bitcoin has a number of advantages. Bitcoins are transferred directly from person to person via the net without going through a bank or clearing house.

This means that the fees are much lower. You can use them in every country. Your account cannot be frozen. There are no prerequisites or arbitrary limits. Several currency exchanges exist where you can buy and sell bitcoins, dollars, euros and more.

Bitcoins are kept in your digital wallet on your computer or mobile device. Sending bitcoins are as simple as sending an email. And you can purchase anything with bitcoin. Bitcoin is changing finance the same way that the web changed publishing. When everyone has access to a global market great ideas flourish.[6]

One of the great ideas that people have come up with, with this new electronic global currency called Bitcoin, is you can implant a microchip into your hand to buy and sell with Bitcoin! But nobody would do that, would they? They already are!

CBN. Com Reports:

Subdermal NFC implants store your bitcoin under your skin. A Dutch man had two wireless computer chips implanted in his body. He did it so he could store digital money, and use the chip for other purposes, like program his alarm clock. Martin is an entrepreneur and the London Telegraph tells us the experiment was a success. He said the chips can be used not only for digital currency but as keys for your house, monitoring your health, even call a doctor if you have a heart attack. And he believes that people who use the chips are helping to make them socially acceptable.[7]

So, don't you want to be a part of the new revolution? You can "buy and sell" with these implanted chips, and turn on lights, call a doctor! Whatever you need, just get the implant! Put all this together, and what are we seeing? Right now, before our very eyes, we're seeing the machinery put in place for a *One World Economy*.

The unions for a *One World Economy* being put into place to hand over to the Antichrist and even a universal currency that people can implant in their right hand and maybe even forehead, is also being put into place. What more proof do you need? We're living in the last days!

The 4th proof that we know we really are headed for a One World Economy is the **Cashless Proof.**

I'm talking about a cashless society. That's exactly what the Antichrist needs to pull off The Mark of the Beast! A cashless society! Don't take my word for it. Let's listen to God's.

Revelation 13:1-7 "And I saw a beast coming out of the sea. He had ten horns and seven heads, with ten crowns on his horns, and on each head a blasphemous name. The beast I saw resembled a leopard, but had feet like those of a bear and a mouth like that of a lion. The dragon gave the beast his power and his throne and great authority. One of the heads of the beast seemed to have had a fatal wound, but the fatal wound had been healed. The whole world was astonished and followed the beast. Men worshiped the dragon because he had given authority to the beast, and they also worshiped the beast and asked, who is like the beast? Who can make war against him? The beast was given a mouth to utter proud words and blasphemies and to exercise his authority for forty-two months. He opened his mouth to blaspheme God, and to slander his name and his dwelling place and those who live in heaven. He was given power to make war against the saints and to conquer them. And he was given authority over every tribe, people, language and nation."

There really is coming a day when all the inhabitants of the earth are going to be under the universal economy or monetary system of the Antichrist, right? He's going to control, literally, all the buying and selling on the planet. And in order to pull that off, he's going to need a One World Economy, which we saw is already happening right now before our very eyes! He needs a One World Global Currency, which they're calling for right now, and it needs to be electronic. Why? Because, it's common sense. If you're going to pay for something with your right hand or forehead, as the text says, this tells us it must be some form of "electronic" payment. I mean, you don't tape a dollar bill to your hand to make a payment here in this passage, or slap 20 bucks on your forehead to pay for your groceries.

Obviously, you have to have some sort of electronic capability to make a financial transaction with the Mark of the Beast system either in your right hand or forehead. It says it right there! Here's the point. I don't know about you, but I'm so glad we see no signs whatsoever of us ever going to some form of electronic cashless society around the world, that enables us to make electronic payments, even with our body parts. Yeah, it's already here!

The 1ˢᵗ way we know it is already here, a cashless society, is the **Promotion**.

Whether you realize it or not, we have been slowly but surely conditioned to move towards a cashless society that the Bible predicted would come in the last days. Let me give you some examples. In the last century alone, think about it, we have gone from paper currency to electronic cash. And it's happening very fast! For instance, if we don't have any money on us, don't worry, just write a check. Then if we don't have the money to write a check, don't worry, just charge it to a credit card. But if we don't want to pay the interest on a credit card, don't worry, just take it out of your checking account with a debit card.

Those things are so popular right now, as of 2010, debit card spending overtook cash as spending. We already love this electronic transaction stuff for making payments! In fact, right now "One in 10 Americans don't even carry paper money anymore!" And those that do, don't carry very much! "78% carried less than $50, and 49% carried only $20 or less!" That's why they're saying, "If we move to a cashless society, it won't be much of an adjustment for most Americans." Including this next generation family.

The Sutton Family has gone from a jar with money in it to a plastic card. They are one of a growing number of American families using less cash and more plastic for every day spending. "We don't deal with a lot of cash. Even their lunches are now automated through credit cards. So, they are very, very used to this and not using cash" says Ms. Sutton. Buying lunch, shoes, and even an iPad, the Sutton children make purchases on their own from a weekly allowance that they get on a card instead of cash.

"I bought these shoes with my own money so I could play soccer." Says the daughter. Their parents go on a mobile app or go on line to transfer money into

each child's account. Then they use their allowance card to spend their allotment. "It's more like your own personal credit card so you don't have to carry around all this cash", says one daughter. Allowance manager founder, Dan Metor says using plastic and tracking spending not only saves families money but it helps children learn how to make transactions in an increasing cashless society.[8]

As well as, preparing them for receiving the actual Mark of the Beast! Can you believe that? Whole families, right now in America, don't even mess with cash anymore! And they're even instructing their kids to go cashless just like the Bible said! This isn't just an American phenomenon, it's happening all over the world, it's global. Everybody is going cashless now, even Europe! Check this out.

Buying into a cashless future, shops here on Beech Road in Manchester have more and more customers paying by card. That is the way it's going with people paying with their card or on their mobile. Every business on this road which is lined with independent stores and cafes accept cards, some are more reluctant than others.

But they are taking part in this cashless experiment as many shoppers now prefer plastic. Reporter: Do you prefer cash or card? The customer replies, "Card, it's much easier. I feel much easier with my card in my pocket." Last year spending on cards reached the record of 500BN here in the UK. (500 billion pounds) Cash payments have dropped by 14%. "I think there will be a time where we won't use physical cash anymore. And I don't think it's that far away.

We've reached a point where we don't use checks anymore. I don't know when the last time I wrote a check was. The reason we carry money around was it was the way to pay for things in the past." Says, David Edmundson-Bird, Retail Expert "The way to pay for things in the future isn't with physical cash. I would say ten years."[9]

Wow! 10 years for a cashless society? That's not far away, and that's exactly what's needed for The Mark of the Beast! We're getting close! Time to get motivated! In fact, some banks in Europe are encouraging people to "Stop using cash and checks in favor of electronic transactions."

The year 2014 was a turning point for cashless technology. Within the global market, there has been a twentyfold increase in cashless transactions compared to the previous year. These figures represent a true shift in attitude towards cashless payments, from both event organizers and the public, with some becoming their sole method of access and payment. In other words, that's your only option! "We always knew that 2014 would be the year there would be a change in attitude, (in a cashless society) but these results have exceeded even our highest expectations." In other words, 'than what we even thought!' Why? Because we're living in the last days and it's being promoted all over the world! People are eating it up right and left! A cashless society is almost here, which means the Mark of the Beast is coming next!

The **2nd way** we know we're in a Cashless Society is **The Convenience Is Here**.

As you saw with the previous examples, everyone loves this cashless stuff, whether it's America or Europe, or businesses or personal use, because it's so convenient! No more fumbling around your wallet, no more dropping coins, no more looking for this and that and people staring at you, and no more standing behind that lady in Wal-Mart paying with pennies! Can I get an AMEN!

The reason why is because it's electronic and it's convenient! And it's getting even more convenient by having all these features, of a checking account, debit or credit card, all combined into one called a smart card. A smart card is about the size of a regular credit card but this one has a tiny microchip in it that can store and receive information, as well as make financial transactions. You can use them for all kinds of things, very convenient. Like, "Vehicle and building access, computer access (replace all passwords), Loyalty programs (airlines, grocery stores, etc.), Rapid Check-in (hotels, etc.), Personal Identification Holder (Soc. Security, Driver's License, Student ID, Health Insurance Info, voting information, picture, and fingerprints). All of that on one card? Isn't that convenient? Oh, and you can "buy and sell" with it too!

In fact, billions of these cards are already being issued right now and have been for many years! They're already very popular! AND it's not just because of the so-called convenience as a selling point, but it's security as well. I mean, can you imagine if we would just get rid of all paper currency and switch to these smart cards, and combine all these cards into one? You talk about security! Think about it! We could get rid of all kinds of crimes, because cash is the "currency" of criminals, and even those dreaded terrorists, like this news report shares.

We wonder what would happen if we got rid of cash. After all, cash is what keeps terrorists, drug dealers, and gun dealers in business. Could a move to a cashless economy around the world help America? Here now is the man with a plan, Jonathan Lipow. He wrote an article in Saturday's New York Times, entitled Turn in your Bin Laden's.

How much terrorist activities are funded through dollars? He replies, "We know that insurgents use cash, we can be certain at least half of the funds are indeed being used in gang activity, criminal activity". Reporter: So, your solution is to get rid of the cash and that would cut off a lot of the illicit activity out there and certainly a lot of funding for terrorists, etc., etc.

So, if we did come up with something, your finger print or your social security number, whatever that might be, I guess you're going with a national ID-card, but it would require banks to agree on a language around the world. Would that work everywhere? He answers, "Ideally we would have a simple standard worldwide."[10]

So, when the Mark of the Beast gets implemented, it can just jump on that and go worldwide too! Folks, this is all coming together before our very eyes! A cashless society, they say, would not only provide a whole new sense of convenience and security, but they say it'll provide a whole new sense of flexibility. And that's because all this electronic cash can not only be used in a smart card, but even in your cell phone. Now that's convenient! Right now, whether you realize it or not, cell phones are doubling as mobile cash machines to make purchases anywhere in the world from street vendors to pizza delivery. With the wave of your phone, which you hold in your hand, (maybe soon you can just wave your hand) you can buy just about anything from a boat to a burger. Just ask Apple. They've now come out with Apple Pay! Check it out!

"Thanks so much", says the customer as he leaves the shop. His name is Matt Mayor. Today he is going to try a little experiment. Mobile payments have been around for a while. But the arrival of Apple Pay has taken it to the next level. Today I am shopping with my iPhone and using Apple Pay.

Now my challenge is to buy everything on my Christmas list today without ever reaching for my wallet. I'm just going to use my iPhone. The question is, is the future here yet? So far so good, I have been nailing my Christmas list. I'm going to get a bite to eat. So far, every store he has been in, including the restaurant, has taken payment with his iPhone.

Now he is looking for something for his niece. He Is looking on his phone for a certain store. What he is seeing is the app 'shop this' that lets you see the item you want to buy, you hit the master pass page and it takes you to the store where you put it in your cart and you have bought it using your iPhone. It's great that I can pay with my phone at retailers across New York City but some of the biggest retailers in the country have also partnered with Apple Pay so you can shop without your wallet wherever you go.[11]

    Isn't that convenient? Isn't that great! And Apple is not the only one. Many corporations, not just Apple, are getting in on this new form of electronic payment with your cell phone, from Google, to PayPal, to even Starbucks. In fact, listen to what Howard Schultz, the Chairman and CEO of Starbucks said about this push for electronic payments with your phone and how it's leading to a battle over who gets left on top to control this electronic currency AND how it's spelling the end of cash very soon. Listen to his prediction.

Charlie Rose interviews an executive from Starbucks: Everyone in the world is chasing mobile payment but who's going to be the VISA of digital paymen? There's no doubt that the phone is going to become your digital wallet. The competitors right now are everybody, Google, Apple, PayPal. Starbucks has a unique position in that we are already processing over 5 million mobile transaction per week on the phone.

Charlie Rose: Give me an example of how fast the velocity of mobile payments is. When will it be the way the majority of people pay? He answers, "Two or three years, I say 50% of everything you do every day will be done on your phone in terms of payment and eventually you will have a cashless society.[12]

    Two or three years? That's way less than 10! What does he know that we don't know? Anybody seeing a pattern here? Everybody's predicting we're going cashless soon. Not 50 years down the road, but 2 to 3. In fact, that's still not all. Talk about convenient! With the new versions, you no longer must be near a kiosk or cash register to make your payment with your phone. Now the new ones automatically recognize you before you even get into the store! Talk about convenient! Check this out!

Making Change, Peter Goodman, Producer, tells us: There was a time when we needed cash everywhere we went from filling stations to pay phones, even the tooth fairy dealt in cash. But money isn't physical any more. It's not only the pennies in your piggy bank and that raggedy dollar bill. Or is it digital with zeros and ones stored in the computer prompting some economist to believe that the old-fashioned greenback may soon be a goner.

Economists like Robert Riech say the demise of cash has been happening ever since our financial fortunes were told by a piece of plastic with a magnetic strip. That was half a century ago. He says, "And now 95% of transactions in America or more have nothing to do with physical pieces of paper or coins." Think about it taxis, parking meters, tolls, even Girl Scout cookies, don't require cash any more. All proof that cash's days are numbered.

All you do is register and you create a virtual tab right on your phone, so that when it comes time to pay, you don't need your wallet, your credit card, you don't even have to pull out the phone. Instead a photo pops up on the register and the money is deducted from the account of your choosing. It's going to recognize you before you walk in. Jerrod pays with 'Square' all the time. And it's not just 'Square'. It's Apple, Google, Visa, and major banks looking to change the way we spend. "There will be a time, I don't know when, I can't give you a date, when physical money will just cease to exist", Says Robert Riech.[13]

Do you have any idea how wild that is? The Bible said nearly 2,000 years ago that we'd switch to a cashless society for the Mark of the Beast. That's what these guys are saying, and they're going from 10 years, to 2, to 3, to anytime now, which means we're living in the last days! That which is needed for the Mark of the Beast, is almost here!

The 3rd way we know a Cashless Society is coming real soon is **The Mandating Is Here**.

You see, for those of you who think you're going to hold out and refuse to go cashless, too bad! You better read your Bible! The Antichrist is going to mandate it! You won't have a choice!

Revelation 13:12,14,15,16-17 "He made the earth and its inhabitants worship the first beast, whose fatal wound had been healed. He ordered them to set up an image in honor of the beast who was wounded by the sword and yet lived. He caused all who refused to worship the image to be killed. He also forced everyone, small and great, rich and poor, free and slave, to receive a mark on his right hand or on his forehead, so that no one could buy or sell unless he had the mark."

So again, we see the option to "opt out" of this system is taken away! The Antichrist is going to make, order, cause, and force people to take this Mark or you are dead meat! I'm telling you, the same kind of pressure tactics are being used right now to implement phase one of the Antichrist's plan to go cashless! The choice is being taken away! In Europe, right now, smart cards are not only commonplace but will soon become a necessity. England is expecting to have all governmental services online and will issue citizens with smart cards to access the system. You don't have a choice, it's mandated! Even here in the U.S. in light of the terrorist attacks, the Pentagon mandated smart cards for millions of troops, civilians for opening secure doors, getting cash, buying food, and checking out weapons, for the individual, you have to do it too! Check this out!

"VISA and MasterCard are saying, "American Credit Cards will disappear in 2015 and be replaced with this new tech called Smart Cards, Why? Because haven't you watched the news? All these recent scares with all those eBay, Home Depot, and Target credit card rip offs over the holidays! Remember that?

Well, now VISA and MasterCard are mandating the new cards with chips in them, whether you want one or not, because they say they're much more secure. And, unfortunately, they too can be hacked. But it makes you wonder why they repeated that news story of the credit cards getting ripped off over and over again in the media. It's almost like you "created a crisis so you could manage the outcome" AND get us to switch to this. But they wouldn't do that would they? Yeah, right!
And for those of you thinking this is just some wacky conspiracy theory, there's no way people in the world today are serious about going cashless across the whole world, this will never catch on, maybe some isolated places, but not the whole planet! Really? Well, one, read your Bible. It is coming! And two, for the first time in mankind's history, we even have whole countries right now that are converting to it! Starting with Sweden, check this out!

Bloomberg Reports:

Shopping for snacks in Stockholm has got a lot simpler in recent years. One shopper says, "I put in my pin code and then it's done." In part that's due to cashless payment systems like the one developed by Peter Freydell. He says, "Cash presents a lot of problems for society as a whole."

Freydell's firm, Seamless, now operates in 30 different countries. But here in Sweden it's just one of several companies competing to replace cash. Freydell says, "You want to challenge the old banking industry by providing this new innovating way for our payment services."

The old banking industry has reacted with 6 of Sweden's largest banks banding together in 2012 to build an instantaneous mobile payment platform, Swish. The idea that banks would cooperate to kill off cash might be unthinkable elsewhere. But it's not so surprising in Sweden where bills and coins recently constituted less than 3% of the country's domestic product.

Many bank branches here no longer carry hard currency. Homeless magazine vendors, like Jimmy here, use wireless card readers to accept credit and debit card payments. Signs in stores say, 'no cash accepted.'[14]

    No cash accepted. You know you're going to a cashless society not only when you see signs that say, "No Cash Accepted," but when your homeless people only take electronic payments! And it's not just Sweden. The whole world's getting in on this. Other countries are going down the same route too! Japan, Nigeria, Canada, Australia, other countries in Europe, saying we want to convert to a cashless society! In fact, in Britain, they recently did a social experiment over one area where, "Shops would only accept cashless payments to test whether Britain should become a cash-free country." Everybody in the world wants this! Apparently, it was so successful that, "Britain is now at the forefront of countries heading towards becoming cashless because the public is eager to embrace the new technology."
    And believe it or not, of all people, so does Israel. "A special committee has recommended a three-phase plan to do away with cash transactions in Israel" "The motivation for examining a cashless economy is combating money laundering, tax evasion, and of course, the ability to finance terrorism." Speaking of limiting what people can do, listen to what this guy said, "In a cashless society, literally every transaction would be tracked. AND if a government decided to squash dissidents, it could cut them off the economy"

You know, like what's happening with Russia, Libya, Iraq, and possibly China. We'll not only destroy your economy, but we'll cut you off from the global economy, period." You won't be able to "buy and sell" on a planetary wide basis with this power! Can you believe that?

In fact, it's progressed so far that, "Denmark's Central Bank is about to stop producing money altogether." "By the end of 2016, Nationalbanken planned to outsource all of its printing and minting services because note and coin production is no longer a sound financial option." In other words, you're wasting money by printing money! It's not economically feasible anymore! It's all going electronic! There's only one small problem with this grand scheme to get the whole world to go cashless and accept electronic payments. You see, they're not very secure!

First of all, you could lose your smart card or phone, or somebody could steal it, or it could get hacked like Target and eBay, then what? Well that's right, worry no more! Motorola has come to the rescue! They've come out with a new "Digital Tattoo" that you can put on your wrist to keep your phone payments safe! Let's take a look at this new security.

An average user unlocks his phone 39 times a day and it takes him 2.3 seconds every time they do so. It is so cumbersome that more than 50% of users do not lock their phones, exposing their personal data to theft. So, we started working on making it easier for people to unlock their phones.

Your phone is personal to you so how you access it should be personalized to your style. We are excited about a new way to go. It's a digital tattoo from Vivo link. We work with Motorola to make the digital tattoo. It's easy to put on and lasts for 5 days whether you take a shower or exercise, you don't have to worry about it. It goes where you go. It's so comfortable that you barely notice and it's easy to use. No fumbling, no typing, just tap.[15]

Wow! So, I got a Mark on my wrist that secures my phone so I can keep on making payments, I mean, pretty soon, I can just skip the whole phone thing and just use my arm! Wouldn't that be great? Step by step, that's the ultimate plan. You see, there's only one problem with Motorola's Tattoo. It only lasts five days, or it could come off, or get lost, so now what? You're back to square one!

Well hey, if you are used to having an external tattoo on the outside of you to secure your payment, then maybe one day you'd like to get it on the inside of you and make it permanent! It'd be secure! You can't lose it! Believe it or not, that too is already here AND they're also saying, very soon the choice is going to be taken away, mandatory microchips are coming if you want to function in society!

Chances are you're carrying a couple of our RFID chips now. And if you are they are sending out a 15-digit number that identifies you. That number can be picked up by a ISO compliance scanner. And, they are everywhere too. The chips are embedded in credit cards, Mikey cards and the Swipe cards that let people into their buildings. They are used to track manufactured goods in factories and stores, identify livestock, and lost pets. And now RFID microchips are being injected into humans.

Dr. Mark Gession from the city of Redding in England was injected with one in 2009 to control electronic devices in his office. The microchip implants are coated with a bio-compatible material that enables them to bond with the surrounding flesh and sinew. That keeps them in place and makes their surgical removal difficult and painful.

Companies in America have marketed microchips for security and medical purposes, and they use the chips to open doors, unlock their cars, phones and computers with a simple wave of their hand. Having an electronic implant might seem too painful or weird to even contemplate but scientists say that view will change dramatically.

Forget mobile phones, your children and grandchildren may well want an implant instead. It's not possible to interact in society in a meaningful way by not having a mobile phone. I think human implants are likely to go along a very similar route. It will be such a disadvantage to not have the implant that it eventually becomes not optional.[16]

In other words, it's mandated. First the phone, then the implant, you don't have a choice. As **Revelation 13** says, He's going to make, order, force, cause you to take it, or you're going to die! Good thing we see no signs of that happening soon! Yeah, it's happening now! Not 50 years down the road! It's happening now! Everything needed to pull off **Revelation 13**, for the first time in mankind's history is already here! Which means we're living in the last days! And that's why Jesus said:

Luke 21:28 "When these things begin to take place, stand up and lift up your heads, because your redemption is drawing near."

The point is this. If you're reading this today and you are a Christian, then what in the world are you doing for Jesus? Let's get busy working together fulfilling the Great Commission doing something splendid for Jesus, amen? But if you're not a Christian, then I beg you, please, heed the signs, heed the warnings, give your life to Jesus today, because tomorrow may be too late!

Chapter Ten

The Mark of the Beast

"Recently the Chief of Staff for the US Air Force decided he would personally intervene in the recruiting crisis that's affecting the armed forces here in the United State. He came to Nellis Air Force Base, and he opened it up for all eligible young men to apply.

Joey & Bobby, two of our Interns, always looking for a better job, decided to apply.

The General and his aides were standing near a brand-new jet fighter, when lo and behold, here comes Bobby and Joey and they walk up and he sticks out his hand and introduces himself.

He looked at Bobby and said, "Son, what skills can you bring to the Air Force?" And Bobby looks straight at him and says, "I'm a pilot!"

Well, at this, the General gets all excited, he turns to his aide and says, "Get him in today, all the paper work done, everything, do it now!"

So, the aide hustles Bobby off and the General then looks at Joey and asks him, "Son, what skills do you bring to the Air Force?"

And Joey looked at him and says, "I chop wood!"

Well at this, the General just shook his head and said, "Son, we don't need wood choppers in the Air Force, what do you know how to do?"

And Joey said, "I chop wood!"

So, the General in a huff says, "Young man, you are not listening to me, we don't need wood choppers in the Air Force, this is the 21st century!"

And so, Joey says, "Well, you hired my friend Bobby!"

And the General says, "Well, of course, he's a pilot!"

And Joey just rolls his eyes and says, "Well, so what! I have to chop it before he can pile it!"[1]

Now you know why I've been asking for prayer for me personally working with the interns! But that's right, believe it or not, I'm not the only one going around saying, "Help me! Help me!" Believe it or not, one day our whole planet's going to be crying out the same thing during the 7-year Tribulation! Why? Because it's an outpouring of God's wrath on a wicked and rebellious planet. You don't want to be there! You're going to be crying out for help!

The 11th update on The Final Countdown study and that is just that, The Mark of the Beast.

This Mark of the Beast system that's being put into place, through a One World Economy and Cashless Society, is not only going to be put into place by the Antichrist and False Prophet but it's also going to be put into place with the same cunningness and deceitfulness of their inspiration, the one empowering them, i.e. the devil. But don't take my word for it. Let's listen to God.

2 Thessalonians 2:1-10 "Concerning the coming of our Lord Jesus Christ and our being gathered to him, we ask you, brothers, not to become easily unsettled or alarmed by some prophecy, report or letter supposed to have come from us, saying that the day of the Lord has already come. Don't let anyone deceive you in any way, for that day will not come until the rebellion occurs and the man of lawlessness is revealed, the man doomed to destruction. He will oppose and will exalt himself over everything that is called God or is worshiped, so that he sets himself up in God's temple, proclaiming himself to be God. Don't you remember that when I was with you I used to tell you these things? And now you know what is holding him back, so that he may be revealed at the proper time. For the secret power of lawlessness is already at work; but the one who now holds it back will continue to do so till he is taken out of the way. And then the lawless one will be revealed, who the Lord Jesus will overthrow with the breath of His mouth and destroy by the splendor of His coming. The coming of the lawless one will be in accordance with the work of Satan displayed in all kinds of counterfeit miracles, signs and wonders, and in every sort of evil that deceives those who are perishing. They perish because they refused to love the truth and so be saved."

In other words, they didn't want to hear it! According to the Bible, we clearly see that when the Antichrist is revealed, he's going to do so with what? False counterfeit signs, wonders, and miracles, right? He's a liar and a deceiver! That tells us the specific evil tactics he's going to use to dupe people in the last days to be willing to take the Mark. He's going to use lying, thieving, murderous, transforming seductive lies, to get people to do it! And believe it or not, that's exactly what's being put into play right now! The Secret Power of Lawlessness is already at work!

The 1st way we've been deceived by the Antichrist to be willing to take the Mark of the Beast is with a **Universal Matrix.**

You see, whether you realize it or not, a Universal Matrix is being created right now that connects everything on the planet that's needed to pull off this Mark of the Beast system. It's called the Internet. And if you'll notice, all information, all finances, all knowledge and all forms of media, all are being connected and merged with this invention called the Internet. The key word here I believe, is net, the net is closing in on us! It's not just in existence right now, but we have already, in just a few short years, been conditioned to accept it and to rely upon it for almost all of our needs, including financial needs. You can buy online, you can sell online, you can bank online, you can do all your studying and research online, you can shop online, you can watch TV online, you can register online, you can make your appointments online. You can do just about anything and everything online! Everything is going online. Have you noticed?

Now here's the point. It's a giant matrix system that's starting to control everything we do, including our finances and buying and selling and that's what's needed for the Mark of the Beast system! And this is why I've said, I truly believe that this term in the Bible "buying and selling," is a loaded term. When you're shut out of the Antichrist's system, this Matrix he's creating, buying and selling is just the tip of the iceberg. If you think of the Internet, it's everything! You will literally become a non-citizen and/or die!

Again, here's the problem. Right now, we can access this Matrix with a certain amount of freedom, but what if one day somebody hijacked this system that controls everything on the planet, then what would we do? You talk about a power play, right? Then they could make, order, force, cause people to do whatever they want them to do, right? They are controlling the Matrix! Well guess what? It's happening now!

Right now, we are seeing signs of the Internet, that connects everything on the planet, including finances, to become limited. The freedom to access the Internet is being taken away, and the net is closing in on us on a Global scale. Let's take look at a current map.

Now as you can see a large portion of the planet is covered in green, which signifies little or no restriction, and if you'll notice, it's pretty much the backwoods of the planet, South America, Mexico, and Africa. The white areas are those being "selective" and the yellow is those whose position is changing.

But as you can see, a huge portion of the planet is pink and that signifies the "worst offenders" of Internet restriction, and notice it's not just China and Russia but the United States and Britain as well.

This is the problem. You see, we're being lied to! We think we have total freedom of the Internet here in America, not like those communist nations. When, according to the Open Net Initiative, who tracks this kind of stuff, we're just as bad as they are! And it's about to get even worse! How many of you guys remember the recent Sony Hack Scare Thing going on that supposedly North Korea did? You talk about "create a crisis so you can manage the outcome!"

First of all, many reports are saying North Korea had nothing to do with it, it was an inside job, and even so, look at the outcome! It's being used as an excuse to have the government now control the Internet. Shocker! Create a crisis so you can manage the outcome! And what a comforting thought that is! Have the government control the Internet? We all know what a wonderful job they're doing with the IRS, and Healthcare and taxes and everything else! Can you imagine the government running the Internet? Yeah, not good! Let's take a look at how they put this into place to deceive us to take control.

Obama said, *"No foreign nation, no hacker should be able to shut down our networks, steal our trade secrets, or invade the privacy of American families, especially our kids. So, we're making sure our government integrates intelligence to combat cyber threats just like we have done to combat terrorism."*

The US government has stridently asserted that North Korea was almost certainly responsible for the Sony hack with no evidence whatsoever.

The New York headlines read*: "This is of a different nature than past attacks," one official said. "An attack that began by wiping out data on corporate computers-something that had been previously seen in South Korea and Saudi Arabia- had turned into a threat to the safety of Americans," the official said.*

But echoing a statement from the Department of Homelund Security, the official said there was no specific information that an attack was likely. It is not clear how the United States determined that Mr. Kim's government had played a central role in the Sony attacks. North Korea's computer network has been notoriously difficult to infiltrate.

But the National Security Agency began a major effort four years ago to penetrate the country's computer operations including its elite cyberteam, and to establish "implants" in the country's networks that, like a radar system, would monitor the development of malware transmitted from the country. It is hardly a foolproof system. Much of North Korea's hacking is done from China. And while the attack on Sony used some commonly available cyber-tools, an intelligence official said, "this was of a sophistication that a year ago we would have said was beyond the North's capabilities." [1]

Halfway down the article it states that it is not clear how the United States determines that Mr. Kim's government had played a central role in the Sony attack. In other words, there is no evidence whatsoever to back up this claim. In fact, the only evidence that really does indicate anything is that this hack attack on Sony Pictures was an inside job.

An order to justify draconian cyber security measures like the ones Joe Lieberman called for in giving the White House the same power as China to sensor and shut down the internet. And just by coincidence Obama's state department official Catherine Novelli was meeting with China's internet censorship Czar. This is the guy overseeing the great firewall of China, the infamous government censorship program over the entire web.

She was meeting with him at an event in Washington urging cooperation on cyber security between the United States and China. So isn't it convenient that right at the time the cyber security legislation is stalled in Congress, the Obama administration shows it's desperation to regulate the internet.

Now we have this convenient Sony hack that can be used to grease the skids to tighten control. Obama speaks, *"Tonight I urge this Congress to finally pass the legislation we need to better meet the evolving threat of cyber-attacks. Combat identity theft. And protect our children's information. That should be a bipartisan effort.*[2]

Yeah, that's what it was. It's about protecting the kids and keeping us safe from those dreaded terrorists! How much mileage are you going to get out of that excuse? But as you saw, somebody created a crisis so you could manage the outcome. You lied! It's really about controlling the Matrix, the Internet, and the government restricting its usage! If you thought that was bad, the government controlling the Internet, acting like China, meeting with China, wait till you see the next proposal.

There was also talk of the Obama administration giving up control of the Internet to a foreign Global Entity called the ITU or International Telecommunication Union that works like the U.N. that controls the world's governments, but this entity would now control the Internet around the world. I'm not making it up! Check this out.

Fox News Reports:

We created it but now the Obama Administration is about to give it for free to the rest of the world. The Obama Administration is to hand control of the internet to what it describes as the global community. So, we created the internet, we did a great job of sustaining it and keeping it running. It works great, right? Why would we do this?

The Obama Administration said let's open this up to global governments which include other countries like China, like Russia. They are going along with censorship like the communist countries. That's pretty shocking. Now a government controlled international body is making a play to become a new place for the internet's future. It's called The International Telecommunication Union, or ITU. In December, the worlds governments will meet to decide to expand its mandate to making important decisions about the net.

They get to make decisions about our internet without us even knowing what they are discussing, then tell us once the decision is made. But the really scary part is that the countries pushing hardest for ITU control are the same countries that aggressively sensor the internet. In Russia, making a YouTube video against the government can get you two years in jail. In China, you can't even get to most social media websites. Iran is trying to build its own national internet and email network to keep the entire population under its control.[3]

The Obama administration wanted to give the Internet over to these guys! Is that crazy or what? Unless of course, somebody has a plan! Let me get this straight. First of all, you create this global matrix to "buy and sell" and all kinds of other things, and then you give it over to a global entity to control it, but what if one guy hi-jacks it? Then what? He could control what people "buy and sell" on the whole planet for the first time in the history of mankind! Where have I heard that before?

In fact, they're really planning on wrapping the whole planet with this Matrix system! Right now, they are working on turning the Internet into what's called the "Outernet" where they will use tiny satellites to, "take the whole world online." They're called, "CubeSats" and they will, "provide Internet to every person on earth." Then they plan on going to the next step by what's called the "Ubernet" that will create an "All-encompassing information environment where accessing the Internet will be effortless, and it will all be tied together with mobile, wearable, and embedded computing," you know, like a microchip!

So, correct me if I'm wrong, but you put all this together and, you first created a Universal Matrix and got everybody used to it and dependent upon it for everything including buying and selling then you grabbed control of it and gave control over to a global entity, then you made sure the whole planet was tied into it, and now all that's left is for one guy to hi-jack the whole thing and take it over. What do you think that is? Folks, if I didn't know better, I'd say that's the same kind of cunningness and deceit the Bible says the Antichrist is going to use to implement the foundation for the Mark of the Beast! And it's happening right now, which means, we're getting close!

The 2nd way we're being deceived by the Antichrist to be willing to take the Mark of the Beast is with a **Universal ID.**

Now think about this. This is just like Hitler did with the Jewish people. He marked them! It's coming again only this time it's electronic! You see, put yourself in the Antichrist's shoes. I mean, here you have this ultimate goal of controlling what people "buy and sell" all over the planet and as we just saw, you just established the Universal Matrix system that provided the platform for you to do this, but how in the world are you going to connect people directly to this platform and control their access to it?

Well hey, I know, how about you issue everybody a Universal ID Card that everyone on the planet had to carry with them in order to access this system to "buy and sell" among other things and that way, if they didn't have the card, they would be shut out! Wouldn't that be great? But they wouldn't do that, would they? Actually, that too is already being put into place! Believe it or not, as crazy as it sounds, a Universal ID Card is about to be put into place here in the United States. Like a frog in the pot we've been warmed up to it!

It started with Social Security Card. Remember how that was supposed to be just for tracking the individual accounts for those who enrolled in the Social Security program and it was never to be used for ID purposes, ever! But now look at us. Try getting around in life without one, right? It's needed for almost everything! Including buying and selling! 80% of the top banks and 96% of the top credit card companies use Social Security numbers for people to access their accounts. I.E. "the financial system." And it's about to get even worse! The Social Security Card was just the beginning!

Believe it or not, as far back as 2005, President Bush signed The Real ID Act as a part of a military spending bill that mandates an electronic ID chipped card, a microchip card, for every American to help fight terrorism, of course, once again the same excuse. The final rollout is supposed to be in full force soon, whereupon you will not be able to, "board a plane or access governmental services" without this microchip card. Even the news is telling us it's coming soon.

ABC News Reports:

In 2005 Congress passed the Real ID Act which required enhancements to state issued identification. It's a measure that goes into effect later this year. Real ID is a federally mandated new higher security ID which has a star in the upper right-hand corner of the card and will be added to the Real ID compliant Driver's License issued in Washington DC and you will need one to enter Federal Buildings this fall and by 2016 they will be required to board an airplane.

Nevada was one of the first states to offer these Real ID cards and they have been doing that since November of this year even though it's not Federally mandated until 2016. To apply for the Read ID, you will be required to produce the original copy of your proof of identity, passport, or birth certificate along with proof of residency and your social security card.[4]

Oops! There's that card again that was never to be used for identity purposes! Looks like we need it to get this new and improved card! But, as you saw, this is not make-believe! Without this card, for the first time in American history, you will not be able to board a plane or get into a Federal Building, and soon, it will even control the Matrix! "A new Online ID system would allow government unprecedented power to control your access to the Internet."

"The White House dream dating back several years ago may soon become a reality: The idea proposed by the Obama administration was of a single, secure online ID that Americans would use to verify their identity across multiple websites, starting with government services. It's already being put into play and it's called the "Driver's license for the internet" or the "National Strategy for Trusted Identities in Cyberspace," and this same ID would work across all government services.

Listen to what you would not be able to access without this card. From food stamps and welfare, to filing tax returns, to registering for a fishing license: essentially running the gamut of all key government agency services, and could work for any website, in an "all-access token" for the internet. In other words, without this card, you can't access the Matrix, you can't "buy and sell," get food, and a whole bunch of other things. And we're not the only ones doing it! The European Union is preparing to give its citizens a universal identification so they can "freely move about from country to country." Japan has "launched a compulsory ID system" called Juki Net that links all citizens to a nationwide computer system. And Germany is doing it too, as well as Mexico, Africa, and even Israel!

And it's being linked specifically to financial institutions. It's a card needed to access "buying and selling." Nigeria has now launched a new Biometric ID Card with backing from MasterCard that's supposed to, "Create a cashless economy for more effective governance." The United Arab Emirates has created a, "Mandatory National ID Card to replace bank cards," for "financial transactions as well as authentication purposes and they are also working with MasterCard and VISA to, "integrate their services for global use making financial transactions anywhere in the world" If you don't think this mandatory ID Card to access the Matrix for "buying and selling" isn't going to go global, think again!

Right now, "Globalists are calling for the entire planet to adopt a "Universal ID System" where a digital identity card is automatically issued to you at birth, to be used when you go to the hospital, do your banking, shopping, or when you vote." So, let me put all this together. You first create this Universal Matrix and get everyone used to that, dependent upon it for everything, including buying and selling, then you grab control of it, then you give it over to a global entity. Then you create a Universal ID to directly connect people to it, and if they don't have this Universal ID, they can't access the system and become a non-citizen, shut out, who can't "buy or sell." What's that sounds like?

If I didn't know better, I'd say that's the same kind of cunningness and deceit the Bible says the Antichrist is going to use to implement the Mark of the Beast! As one guy said, "Do we really want to go down this road? Identity cards can be lost, stolen or forged. What's next? Permanently implant our identity cards." Funny you should ask!

The 3rd **way** we've been deceived by the Antichrist to be willing to take the Mark of the Beast is with a **Universal Mark.**

You see, once again, put yourself in the Antichrist's shoes. I mean, here you have the ultimate goal of controlling what people "buy and sell" all over the planet and you already established the Universal Matrix that provided the platform to control what people buy and sell, and then you instituted a Universal ID system to connect people and control their access to the system. But how are you going to get it into their body parts, right? I mean, **Revelation 13** says it's going into your right hand or forehead.

Revelation 13:16-17 "He also forced everyone, small and great, rich and poor, free and slave, to receive a mark on his right hand or on his forehead, so that no one could buy or sell unless he had the mark, which is the name of the beast or the number of his name."

So, the Bible says, this Universal Mark that's going to connect people to this Universal Matrix that controls what people "buy and sell" on the planet is eventually going to go into their bodies, right? Specifically, right hand or forehead.

But the question is, "How are you going to get people to do that? I mean, I can see people getting duped with a Universal Matrix and ID System, but you'd think of all things they would resist this one, right? Well unfortunately, they've thought of that and they're using the tried and tested tool that has worked every single time, to get us to surrender our freedoms and submit to some sort of authoritarian control? It's called FEAR! You see, there's only one problem with all these external ID cards that they're mandating that we have to carry in order to access the system. They're not secure! In fact, they're so unsecure, they have a new term for it, it's called "Electronic Pickpocketing." Check this out!

Speaking of protecting information, your credit card information could be stolen without you even using your credit card. Hackers are using high tech scanning devices that can grab your personal information as they walk right by you. You can be in a mall and have no idea your credit card information is being stolen all at the same time just by someone walking right by you.

It's called pocket surfing, electronic pickpocketing, crowd hacking. But how is it happening? It's as simple as a scanner, a device to boost the power, and it's all available online. It's the same type of technology that allows you to either wave a credit card at a store with a chip on it and not put in any other information. This chip has all your information stored right on your card but a crook can come along with a back pack with a scanner inside and you're just not safe.

You might as well walk along with a large sign with all your information for everyone to see. How fast does it work? In 15 minutes, the security expert walked through the mall and was able to snatch up credit card numbers from 39 people that we're only showing the last 4 digits but the crooks get it all, account numbers, codes and pin numbers. Security expert says, "It's like putting the bad guy inside your purse or your pocket."

Even smart phones can also be programed to steal the same information. He created an innocent tic, tack, toe game as a disguise for the rogue app which is programmed to look for contactless cards. And that's all he needs to buy stuff. Copying the data onto a hotel room key, he can now us it at a restaurant. If it is so simple, why are these cards allowed? According to the Better Business in Florida, Tom Stevens says he is aware of the electronic thieves, as the banks are as well.[5]

You're aware of this serious flaw, why are you doing this? Why are you pushing these kinds of cards? And for further proof, just to show you how hackable these external microchipped cards really are and they know it, "Companies are cashing in on this security problem and are now offering scan-protected jeans, wallets, backpacks, and even nifty blazers for the ladies!

A lot of people assume that when I close my notebook it goes to sleep but that is not necessarily true and the same thing goes for a smart phone. Even though your smart phone is asleep there are certain tasks that remain in the back ground. Hack Shield can help prevent information from being gleaned unwantedly.

Hack Shield is bringing to market a back pack and a messenger bag in addition to a wallet that all incorporate Hack Shield to protect you and your personal data and information from wireless infiltration. Over 10,000,000 identities will be stolen next year. In 2015 over 70% of all credit cards will be vulnerable to illegal RFID scanning. RFID scanners can steal data from over 30 feet away.

Norton has found a new way to protect data from digital pickpocketing. Introducing, ready active jeans and work-it blazer created by Norton, made with RFID blocking material to stop digital pickpocketing. ID thieves just try to get in these pants, go boldly, not blindly.[6]

Oh yeah, these babies are safe! I'm so glad banks and companies are pushing this! Did you catch that part where it said it can be scanned from 30 feet away? You don't need to be close any more like the news report shares! Maybe it's just me, but if you can go out and buy scan-protected jeans, backpacks, wallets, purses, and nifty blazers for the ladies, and it's being pushed by Norton Security, I'm kind of thinking these external micro-chip cards aren't secure, anybody else?

So again, that's the question, why in the world would these companies, banks, credit card companies, the government, be pushing these external microchip cards when they're not safe at all? Can you say, "create another crisis so you can manage the outcome!" You see, if everybody got used to these external microchipped ID cards to "buy and sell" and then a horrible security flaw was to happen, then you could offer the nifty solution!

How about skipping the whole card thing altogether, and just put that microchip inside of you! Then it would be safe, nobody could steal it and you'd never lose it! Wouldn't that be great? And for those of you who think, that's not the plan, remember, as we saw before, people are already doing this, implanting microchips into their bodies to make financial transactions, but according to a recent survey "90% of citizens surveyed in 6 countries say they would be willing to share their biometric information, their body parts, to make their country's borders more secure, and to travel abroad," and maybe even one day to buy and sell.

In fact, an ex-DARPA Director and Google executive, the same ones pushing the brain chip by the way, is now saying the microchip implants, externally or internally, are going to become the new way to "authenticate yourself" in this new global society!

While we are thinking of a whole variety of options for how you can do better at authentication you can start with things like tokens or cards that may have blue tooth or NFC imbedded in them but can also think of a means of authentication that you can wear on your skin every day for a week at a time, say, an electronic tattoo. I am wearing one here on my arm.

This is a developmental system made by MC10, and it has an antenna and censors embedded in it and what we plan to do is work with them to advance a tattoo that can be used for authentication. (The tattoo is a square looking tattoo on the inside of her arm). Now it may be true that a 10 to 20-year-old might not want to wear a watch on their wrist but you can be sure that they will be far more interested in wearing an electronic tattoo.

The question is asked, "That can have a design, right? They would certainly want some kind of cool design." Options, that is something that you wear and if you can imagine some kind of authentication for just your daily habits. If I take a vitamin every morning, what if I could take a vitamin authentication. I have one here that has a small chip inside of it with a switch.

It also has what amounts to an inside out potato battery. When you swallow it, the acids of your stomach serve as the electrolyte and they power it up and the switch goes on and off. It creates an 18-byte ECG like signal in your body and essentially your entire body becomes your authentication token. It means that my arms are like wires, my hands are like alligator clips when I touch my phone, my computer, my door, my car, I'm authenticated in. First super power, like I want that.[7]

I'm sure this whole new younger generation who's being promoted with this stuff, is going to want one too! So, let me get this straight. You first create this Universal Matrix and get everybody dependent upon that for everything including buying and selling, and then you grab control of it, then you give it over to a global entity, then you create a Universal ID Card to access the system BUT you purposely built in it a security flaw so you can offer your goal of, "How about taking a Mark into your body to access the system." You know, if I didn't know better, I'd say that's the same kind of cunningness and deceit the Bible says the Antichrist is going to use to implement the actual Mark of the Beast! And it's all happening right now, which means we're getting close!

That leads us to **the 4th way** people are being deceived into receiving the Mark of the Beast and that is the **Biometric Proof.**

The Bible is clear. You not only have to be connected to this global Matrix System of the Mark of the Beast system in the last days, but you have to be connected to it with your body. And believe it or not, that's happening right now! But don't take my word for it. Let's listen to God's.

Revelation 20:1-4 "And I saw an angel coming down out of heaven, having the key to the Abyss and holding in his hand a great chain. He seized the dragon, that ancient serpent, who is the devil, or Satan, and bound him for a thousand years. He threw him into the Abyss, and locked and sealed it over him, to keep him from deceiving the nations anymore until the thousand years were ended. After that, he must be set free for a short time. I saw thrones on which were seated those who had been given authority to judge. And I saw the souls of those who had been beheaded because of their testimony for Jesus and because of the word of God. They had not worshiped the beast or his image and had not received his mark on their foreheads or their hands. They came to life and reigned with Christ a thousand years."

According to our text, I think it's pretty obvious, there's a great payoff for those who refuse to receive the Mark of the Beast, right? It says they are rewarded with what? They get to rule and reign with Jesus Christ, personally, for 1,000 years! Is that cool or what? And how many of you would say that's much better than going to hell for all eternity for receiving the Mark of the Beast? Now, first of all, you should've got saved before the 7-year Tribulation started, i.e. today, right now, don't delay, and avoided the whole thing but how many of you would say, there's a good incentive in the Bible for not taking the Mark of the Beast?

And so, the question then is, "Well, how does the Antichrist get people to risk this horrible destiny by receiving his mark? How does he get them to compromise? How does he do it?" First of all, notice where the Mark is. The Bible says it's on their foreheads or their hands, right? So, this tells us, that the Antichrist, at some point, has to condition the world into not only being linked to this global Matrix System that controls all the buying and selling on the planet but he has to get them used to being linked to this system using a body part, right? Specifically, the right hand, or the forehead, right? It says it right there.

I don't know about you guys but it's a good thing we see no signs of that happening any time soon, people using a body part to pay for things! Yeah, right! As we saw, it's already happening! In fact, it's got a name. It's called Biometrics. And whether people realize it or not, for the first time in man's history, we now have the ability to biometrically identify people anywhere on the planet and link them to a global Matrix System that controls all of our buying and selling. It's here now! That's how close we are folks, to the actual Mark of the Beast.

The 1st way that Modern Biometrics are conditioning people to receive the actual Mark of the Beast is the **Database Proof.**

Once again, put yourself in the Antichrist's shoes and it makes sense. If you're going to monitor and control the whole planet with this Mark of the Beast system, you not only need to track people wherever they go but you have to have some sort of database to identify who they are and what they're buying and selling in the first place, right? It's common sense! We saw earlier in our study, that they've already got those kinds of databases. They're so big they're called mega-databases.

And as we saw, just one company in the U.S. called Acxiom operates one of the world's largest databases on 95% of all American households. 24 hours a day, they gather and store information on you and me from credit card transactions, magazine subscriptions, telephone numbers, real estate records, car registrations, and even fishing licenses, to name a few. They can provide a full profile of each one of us, right down to whether we own a dog or cat, enjoy camping or gourmet cooking, read the Bible or other books, what our occupation is, what car we drive, what videos we watch, where our favorite vacations spots are & even how much food and gas we buy. They already know what we buy & sell!

Which means, for the first time in mankind's history, the ability for the Antichrist to know everything about everyone on the whole planet, including who you are, where you are, what you buy and sell, is already here! So, here's the point. Databases are just step one. We know, biblically speaking, at some point, we have to be linked to these databases biometrically, or with our body parts, right? That's what the Bible says. That too is already here! Not just databases, but a push for biometric databases. You need to be tied in with a body part. Let's take a look at just how far these biometric databases have progressed.

Biometric databases are not just being pushed, but as we saw before the previous administration was already pushing for a National Biometric ID Card for all Americans, and the FBI has already spent $1 Billion to build the world's largest computer database of peoples' biometrics which will allow them to identify individuals in the United States and abroad biometrically. We also have the Pentagon who spent $5 billion in three years to develop biometric systems that can identify who you are, wherever you are without you ever knowing it, all with your biometrics. In fact, the biometric programs they're building can identify you in a multitude of ways.

The Ear: In 2010, a group of British researchers used a process called "Image Ray Transform" to shoot light rays at your ear and then convert those images into a series of numbers marking the image as your own. It is said that if the trend continues, it may even be possible to develop ear-scanning in a way that makes it more reliable than fingerprints.

Odor: In the early 2000's, DARPA worked on a project called the "Unique Signature Detection Project" which sought to explore ways to detect people by their smell, to spot and identify individuals based on their distinct scent. It's called their "primary odor" and it's believed to be linked to their genetics. Then in 2007, the government's Counter-Terror Technical Support Working Group started a program aimed at collecting and storing human odors for military dog handlers. Dogs have been used to track people by smell for decades, and it's believed they can do that based on our genetic markers. In fact, they're even working on tracking you by your sweat. In 2010, the Army awarded a contract to a California security firm to develop software that can use sensors to recognize "abnormal perspiration and changes in body temperature" to determine "harmful intent." This would be used at border patrol points, stand-off interrogation scenarios, surveillance scenarios, and even commercial applications including surveillance at businesses and shopping areas. The sensors can read sweat from a distance of nearly 150 feet and as one guy said, "If you're freaked out about the idea of sweat-scanners, now might be time for a cold shower."

Heartbeat: Researchers have now developed radars that are sensitive enough to detect minuscule chest movements from hundreds of yards away. In fact, reinforced concrete walls and electromagnetic shielding will not stop these radars, according to defense contractor VAWD Engineering, who works for DARPA's "Biometrics from a Distance Program."

Voice: Speech-Pro is a company in the U.S. that has a technology called Voice-Grid, that automatically recognizes a person's voice as their own on a "Large City, County, State, or National System." It's already being used in Mexico where "It's being used by law enforcement to collect, store, and search for hundreds of thousands of voice prints." And you'll be happy to know that the NSA here in America has also taken an interest in similar technology.

Gait: After 9/11, DARPA made Gait Recognition, or how you walk, one of their cornerstones of its infamous Total Information Awareness Counterterror Program. And one of the devices helping them pull this off is with cell phones. Androids and iPhones all have accelerometers or sensors that measure how far, how fast, and with how much force an object moves. By using the accelerometer sensor in the cell phone, they are now able to capture a person's walking pattern, and as it turns out, these patterns are very good biometric traits for identifying people, and can, "Even be captured without him or her knowing." As one guy said, "You can run...but with a phone in your pocket, it's going to be harder to hide."

DNA: DNA testing used to take months to perform, but now there are machines, one called RapidHIT, that can do it in less than 90 minutes, and the Pentagon wants them. Rapid DNA testing systems can analyze molecules taken off everything from clothing to cigarette butts. So, the question is, "Why do they want our DNA?" Why, to stop terrorism, of course, and other criminal activity! Ever since the missing Malaysian Airlines Flight 370, experts are now saying, "Biometric Passports need to be used now!" Why? Because with everyone's DNA we could reconstruct the actual image of the person committing the crime!

Fox News Reports:

A new technique using DNA that might give scientist the power to solve cases that have gone cold, cases like a double murder of a South Carolina mother and her 3-year-old daughter that happened 4 years ago, still a mystery. Some scientists believe that a suspect's physical trace can be recreated from a speck of blood or a strand of hair and it's called Snap Shot Technology.

Lance Ulanoff of Mashable.com says, "The Parabon Company says they can look a part a of the DNA sample, just like tiny bits of it, to identify traits that are from any person, like hair, eye color, freckles, skin color, ethnicity, things that would build a profile for a person. They actually take this and they turn it into an image of a person.[8]

In fact, this ability to recreate the image of any criminal or terrorist is now going worldwide. Russia is right now building the world's first DNA Databank of All Living Things. It's being called a "Noah's Ark of Biometrics" and is set to be completed by 2018. "It will enable us to cryogenically freeze and store various cellular materials which can then reproduce."[9]

So first we have Bill Gates and his mysterious Seed Vault storing all of the seeds in the world, and now we've got Russia storing all the DNA of humans and animals all over the world. Not looking good folks! In fact, speaking of things not looking so good, all this retrieval of our biometric information from our voice, head, ears, odors, sweat, DNA, you name it, gives the powers that be not only the ability to track, monitor, locate, and recreate you wherever you go, but it can also be used to commit the perfect crime and have you do things you never did, like this:

"Alongside our normal life, we all have online lives. May I introduce my newest friend, Tom DeGroote. Tom is on Facebook since 2010. He has almost 700 friends, now including me. He's 35 and lives in Bruges. That's where he met Sophie. Aren't they adorable? We sent him a 'phishing' mail, from his 'real' bank to confirm certain details.

Afterwards, all it takes is one fake call to empty his account. But I have other plans. I'm not just going to take over his account...but his life, literally. "He proceeds to make a plaster of Toms face and with surgeries starts to look like Tom. *"See you soon, Tom. I am feeling really at home in his shoes. Time for a little test...Let's say hi to 'Krikke', the boss of his favorite pub. There's Tom as a kid at home...Hey Krikke! 'Hi Tom' replies the boss. How are you? 'Good' How will he react when he sees 'himself' on Facebook?*

Tom's phone rings, "Tom here" " *Good afternoon sir, sorry to bother you, this is Jimmy from the Harp hotel in London,"* the caller says. "Yes?" Tom asks. *"We got your online reservation for 4 rooms..."* the hotel clerk tells him. "Excuse me, I didn't make a reservation..." *A few days ago, I found a beautiful antique harp. Obviously, I didn't pay for it. That's what friends are for...As he pulls up to the building,* "Hello Mr. DeGroote," says a man in front of the building. "You're back? OK like that?"

The man has brought a package out of the back end of the truck. "What's that?" asked Tom. "It's your harp I just delivered", replied the delivery man. "What?" Tom asked surprised. *The delivery man shows him a paper,* "You just signed right here." Tom asks, "Where's my signature?" "Here," replies the delivery man. *Tom proceeds to tell the delivery man,* "Yesterday someone called from London saying things had been ordered on my Visa card..."

The Delivery man say, "Well, I just delivered this and you've signed for it.". *Tom is beginning to get upset,* "But I didn't sign for anything!" "Are you joking?" *Asks the delivery man.* "No!" *Tom replies. Tom asks,* "What did that man look like?" "It was you." *He answers. Tom laughs in unbelief.* "Yeah right, it was you..." "But I wasn't here." *Tom replies.* "Take it back. I didn't order it." "I can't take it back." *At that time, a car drives by and the driver honks the horn and waves at Tom and smiles.*

But shocked Tom sees himself driving the car. "What?" *Tom says in unbelief. As the car speeds off he tells the delivery man,* "I'll call the police!". "Wait, was *this him?" as the delivery man. They look on the iPad and a picture is there of a man speaking, "Tom here, delighted your whole life's online and before you know it someone like me takes it over." Tom says, "That's freaky."*[10]

That's freaky alright, and that's just what you get about me online as we saw before, now you've got my voice, my odor, how I walk, even my DNA, what else could you have me do that I never did? You talk about the ultimate tool to get rid of somebody with biometrics! You can have people commit all kinds of crimes they never committed, but how do you defend against that? This is the kind of society we're headed for! Looks to me like every single person on the planet can be accurately and specifically identified, tracked, and linked to a database system using their body parts or biometrics, how about you? For the first time in man's history, a body part is linking them to a database that's needed to pull off the Mark of the Beast. That's how close we are!

The 2nd way modern day biometrics are conditioning us to receive the actual Mark of the Beast is the **Head Proof.**

You see, according to the Bible, if you're going to control and monitor the whole planet with The Mark of the Beast system, then you not only need some sort of general biometric database to identify people who they are and link them to the system but at some point, it has to get specific with specific body parts. Let's remind ourselves of what those parts are.

Revelation 14:9-10 "If anyone worships the beast and his image and receives his mark on the forehead or on the hand, he, too, will drink of the wine of God's fury, which has been poured full strength into the cup of His wrath."

Or, in other words, don't do it! But the point is, what was the first body part mentioned there the head, right? I'm so glad we see no signs of people using their heads specifically to buy and sell stuff, how about you? Yeah right! That too is already here. Let's look at that!

Eye Scanning: Eyeball-scanning is a current reality that's already being deployed in schools, airports, banks, government facilities, you name it, it's just about everywhere. In fact, countries around the world are starting to use iris scanning for border crossings and major companies like Google are using them to restrict entry into its data centers and Bank of America is using iris scanning for building access. And the next big wave is your phone. Apple, who is one of the big promoters of biometrics, has already had an app out for a while now for your phone called EyeD Biometric Password Manager and soon this eye scanning could be built directly into your iPhone or iPad. In fact, eye scanners are becoming so popular that you can now buy your very own called "Myris" to secure all kinds of things around the house, not just your phone. It's being called the next best tool to, "Unlock your digital world." Let's take a "look."[11]

There's got to be a better way than this, type in your password and it either says not a good password or your password has expired. A jumble of numbers and letters we memorize and then forget. But we are told that if we want security (maybe now would also be a good time to let you know there has been suspicious activity in your account) to sacrifice convenience, not any more. (did we mention the tips for strengthening your password?)

Introducing Myris by Eye Lock. The iris identifier authenticator that allows you to access your entire digital world, no more user names, no more passwords. Myris converts your individual iris characteristics to an uncryptic code unique only to you. It matches that code to grant you access to your computer, e-commerce sites, networks and data all in less than one second. Finally, there is a better way and it's as easy as looking in a mirror. Myris, instant and secure access to your digital world, no username, no password.[12]

Oh, but that's right, for those of you who still resist this great personal convenience, you might just have to have your eye scanned anyway, that is, if you wanted to board an airplane. Check out the new biometric scanners being installed here in Las Vegas at McCarran Airport. It's called CLEAR and pretty soon you might have to use a body part to get "cleared" to travel.

On behalf of the Clark County Commissioner I would like to, today, present you with this proclamation, welcoming Clear to McCarran International Airport. "At Clear we really use biometric technology to speed you past the lanes. So, what's in it for the travelers?" Charmaine Taylor, Clear VP of Operations, tells us. "Speed through the process of Security Checkpoints and a VIP level of treatment at the airport. So, we call this the ATM of identity. We have fingerprint readers, as well as iris scanners. We take an iris image and we capture a picture of the iris we use that to say you are who you say you are. We match it up with your passport and your driver's license so we can confirm you are who you say you are.[13]

Face Scanning: Thanks to the efforts of Facebook and other social networking sites that encourage us to upload an image of ourselves and others, there's not only already trillions of facial images already in databases throughout the world, but various authorities around the world are using them to find, track, monitor, and trace people around the world with facial recognition software. In fact, Facebook has now launched a new program called "DeepFace" that will allow them to find any person in a crowd with 97% accuracy, and the NSA has tapped into these images to do their own monitoring of people around the world.

RT News Reports:

The National Security Agency, NSA, is collecting a massive trove of images that it intercepts over social media, emails and texts. Some which are so clear that you can use them as facial recognition operations. According to the New York Times, 'NSA collected millions of faces from web images'. Top-secret NSA documents indicate that the spy agencies global facial recognition technology has seen huge growth in the last 4 years.

Millions of images are intercepted per day only adding to the huge database of personal information the government can have on individuals, both American and foreign. Here's what most people want to know. What qualifies as a target and how do average American's know that they aren't getting caught up in it. I've been working this area for years with governmental agencies.

Everybody is a target. If you appear to be an extreme issue and say the wrong thing on Facebook you're going to be watched. But the key here with the facial recognition software, they are going to be able to create 3D images of the human body, even holographic images. They are working with a Google subsidiary called Pit Pat that will help them to analyze the data.

And Facebook, by the way, has a program called Deepface that they say, "when they look at a crowd and they are looking for your face 97.2% of the time they can actually pick you up." Says John Whitehead, president of the Rutherford Institute.[14]

Oh, but that's not all. Police are now being given hand held facial scanners and it's all being tied together with the pre-existing surveillance system cameras, webcams, and computer systems to not just identify people, but even tell, "What you're thinking," or even, "What kind of emotional state you're in."

Channel 7 News Reports:

We might soon need to take the phrase poker face and consign it to history because now there is technology that can tell what you are really thinking from the expression that the camera captures on your face. Reading joy, sadness or surprise or anger or any culmination of emotions. Allowing marketers and businesses to read your mind and see what really makes you buy.

We heard that it was written all over his face, now the technology that reads that story. "We are in the business of what you call facial coding. Using the camera that is on your phone or on your lap top, having the software interpret your emotions. Mapping the movements of your eyes when you smile, your mouth when you gasp, or the furrow of your brow when you are confused. This pink line shows the amount of happiness they are showing".[15]

What? So now you can "predict" my emotions in public with my face? Folks, what kind of a creepy world are we headed for? Man! This is worse than George Orwell's 1984! But you might be thinking, "Well hey, that's just using your eye or face to link yourself to a database system for tracking purposes. That's not buying and selling. The Bible says you have to use your head to specifically buy and sell and make a financial transaction. That's not happening yet." Really? I'm telling you, it's a step by step process! First get the databases, then link people with biometrics, then get specific with their head to link them to this database, and then use that head to make a payment. That too is already here! It's called EAZE and it combines Google Glass which you wear on your head, with Bitcoin, so you can just "nod your head" to make a payment.

The entire world is at our fingertips and we are always close to people we care about. Technology helps us. It's tailored to our wishes and things that are important to us removing friction instead of adding it. So, we can spend less time with things we don't like. And more time with things important to us. EAZE makes it easy to pay for big, every day or those special purchases.

EAZE makes accepting payments just as easy. Enjoy life, take it easy. Use EAZE, we make payments frictionless. Using cutting edge technologies available to us now. Starting with nod to pay using bitcoins and glass enable payments hands free. EAZE looking forward.[16]

Yeah, looking forward to what? The Mark of the Beast? Can you believe that? For the first time in mankind's history, you can now make a payment with your head! It's not coming, it's here! If you don't think "nodding" with your head to make a payment is going to catch on, check this out. "China has already instituted a "facial recognition system," you know, your head, for online purchases that "links their bank accounts or credit cards to their facial data to make purchases".

A British company called "Facebanx" has done the same thing by launching their own version of an online facial recognition system to make purchases to "buy and sell" with your "head." And even Apple is getting in on this with their new app for your head, that will, "With just the tilt or nod of your head, you can trigger a wide range of "inputs" into a device. For instance, head bobbing can be used for text input commands, create a scroll event, or even control your music with just a simple nod of their head."

What young hipster wouldn't be open for that, as well as make payments with your head! This is not coming, it is here! For the first time in mankind's history people can "buy and sell" with their head! I mean, what's next? Some sort of chip in your head, to do the same thing? This is how close we are to the actual implementation of the Mark of the Beast in the last days! It's happening now.

The 3rd way Modern-Day Biometrics is conditioning us to receive the actual Mark of the Beast with the second option, the **Hand Proof.**

Revelation 13:16-17 "He also forced everyone, small and great, rich and poor, free and slave, to receive a mark on his right hand or on his forehead, so that no one could buy or sell unless he had the mark."

Here we see again, the second option for the Mark of the Beast system, is to not only use your head, but what was the second option there? Your hand, right? Specifically, the right hand. I'm so glad we see no signs of people using their hand to buy and sell stuff in a biometric way. Yeah right! That too is already here.

Finger Scanning: Fingerprint scans are not only being used right now across the world from computer access to building access to park access, to phone access up to 20 feet away, but 76% of 16 to 24-year olds polled said, "They would be happy to adopt biometric security when making payments." And once again, Apple is behind the push. Right now, Apple wants you to, "Store your fingerprint in its Cloud System" not only to unlock your phone, but make financial transactions. They've combined their Apple ID system now with their new Apple Pay system to, "Make paying for things as simple as a swipe of the finger." By the way, has anybody ever noticed Apple's logo? As you can see it's an apple with a bite taken out of it, like in the Garden of Eden. And lest you think that's not really what it stands for, here's an early advertisement of Apple for its computers, and as you can clearly see, it's depicting a Garden of Eden scenario. Furthermore, former Apple executive Jean Louis Gassee even admitted the logo was, "The symbol of lust and knowledge." And speaking of making payments with your hands, Apple is already being called the "Kingpin of Electronic Payments" due to its growing stockpile of credit card data to the tune of 800 million accounts through its App Store and iTunes, which are making thousands of transactions everyday around the world. But that's not all, fingerprint payment is not only being promoted by Apple, it's being implemented all over the world. Right now, thousands of cash machines are already being rolled out in Japan, Poland, and other countries like Turkey that read finger patterns to, "Negate the need of a debit card and pin number." And Bank Muscat, (Saudi Arabian Peninsula) has announced a new biometric fingerprint scanning system that also works with the national ID card over there. Oh, so you first get used to the national ID card then you skip the whole card thing and use your hand. Gee, where have I heard that before?

Hand Scanning: Hand scanners are not only being used at businesses, airports, commercial centers, to identify travelers, but even hospitals are getting in on the action with palm scanners to identify patients by name and even retrieve their personal medical records. And just like the Bible predicted, hand scanners have now become a necessity for making payments. One such system being rolled out is called "Pulse Wallet."

A new technology called Pulse Wallet syncs your credit cards to the palm of your hand using a biometric palm reader. This cardless payment service allows you to pay by simply scanning your vein giving a whole new meaning to blood money. Pulse Wallet seems to have the upper hand on other NFC payment systems. For example, unlike Google Wallet where you scan your phone for payment, Pulse Wallet doesn't require you to bring anything to make a transaction other than yourself. Something tells me it will have businesses eating out of the palm of it.[17]

Oh, so first get used to the phone you carry in your hand, then you just skip the whole phone thing and just use your hand. Where have I heard that before? They then go on to say, "If it all goes to plan, the new log-in method could be used for anything from swiping your hand across a scanner to pay for your shopping, logging into your PC, and eliminating the need to carry credit cards, issue receipts, or even carry a wallet" and it's "stored in the cloud ready for access when needed." But that's not all. Hand payment systems like Pulse Wallet are not only the rage here in the U.S. but it's even spreading throughout Europe and Asia and is spawning other hand payment systems like Quixter in Sweden to, "Make paying for things faster and more secure," as well as to, "Forget carrying a wallet because all you could soon need to pay for your goods is your hand."

"I'm about to authorize a credit card payment using one of the most secure methods around. It has an infrared camera that scans the vein pattern in my right hand. The technology brought by Jiujitsu is already in use in cash machines in Japan and Brazil. I got that idea when I was in line at the super market and I saw that to pay was quite a complex process that takes a lot of time. So, I thought there has to be an easier way to pay". Says Fredrik Leifland, Founder, Quixter. "And a quicker way to pay and that was the start of Quixter. Hold your hand above the censor and the transaction takes less than 5 seconds. So, it's a very quick payment solution". One student says, "I think it's really good. It's easy when I don't have my wallet with me. I can use my hand."[18]

I can use my hand! Do you have any idea how chilling that statement is? 2,000 years ago, we were warned about a hand payment system and that lady's using one right now! Sure, looks to me like we're seeing for the first time in man's history how people are starting to use hand payments to "buy and sell," how about you? And specifically, the right hand too! I mean, gee whiz, what's next? Some sort of chip implant in your hand to do the same thing? That's the plan. It's all being implemented right now as we speak, not fifty years down the road, it's happening right now. This is how close we are!

The 5th way people being deceived into receiving the Mark of the Beast is the **Propaganda Proof**.

Just like they used propaganda for years and years and years to get us to surrender and be open to the idea of a One World Government, a One World Economy, and a One World Religion, so it is with the Mark of the Beast! They are promoting this right and left and yet people still have the audacity to say today, "There's no sign we're getting close. You're a wacko! Stop being a conspiracy nut!" And it was this same skepticism and hypocritical behavior that

Jesus confronted at His First Coming. But don't take my word for it. Let's listen to His.

Luke 12:54-56 "He said to the crowd: 'When you see a cloud rising in the west, immediately you say, 'It's going to rain,' and it does. And when the south wind blows, you say, 'It's going to be hot,' and it is. Hypocrites! You know how to interpret the appearance of the earth and the sky. How is it that you don't know how to interpret this present time?"

In other words, Jesus is saying here, "I am standing right in the midst of you and I've already done all these miracles right in front of you guys, I've demonstrated that I really am God in the flesh and I've fulfilled tons of Old Testament prophecies showing I really am the Messiah, and you still don't get it? And then you have the audacity to say you need more proof. What?"

What does Jesus say about these people and their skeptical attitude towards His First Coming? "You hypocrites," right? He says, "You don't need that much information to make a decision about the weather." In fact, He says, "With just a minimal amount of evidence, one simple fact, you make a confident conclusion about the weather. You do it all the time. You don't require a lot of information to make that prediction. You don't need a TV weather guy. You don't need a Doppler radar. You don't need the Internet. You don't even need satellites.

You just look over here and you see a dark cloud coming off the sea and you say, "Hey, it's going to rain." And you know what? You're right. That's how it works. It turns out that way. In other words, with only a minimal amount of evidence you draw a confident conclusion about the weather, but when the actual evidence of the Messiah's actual coming is staring at you right in the face you still don't get it and that tells us the real problem was not a lack of information, it's just they didn't want to get it! And so, Jesus calls them hypocrites!

It is my contention that this same hypocrisy, demonstrated by the people of Jesus' day during His First Coming, is the exact same thing we're seeing today with His Second Coming! People scoff, they mock, they act like there's no proof or hardly any proof that we're living in the last days and Jesus is getting ready to come back! How much more proof do we need? What more does God have to do to get our attention today? How much more information does He have to give to us to show us we're living in the last days?

Jesus Christ is about ready to come back! His Second Coming is approaching! Especially with this sign here of the Mark of the Beast! It's being promoted right and left all around us with various propaganda!

The 1ˢᵗ way that they're using propaganda to condition people to receive the actual Mark of the Beast right now is **The Media.**

The enemy shows his hand if you know what to look for. But that's just it, people aren't being taught about the Mark of the Beast so they are staring at the media that's promoting it but it goes in one ear and out the other. Let me show you just how long they have been preparing people to receive the Mark of the Beast in the media.

CNN Reports:

With technology changing so rapidly it's hard to imagine what will be commonplace a decade from now. We asked some forward thinkers for their technology forecast. Todays' welcome to the future. "Instead of carrying credit cards or money we will probably be implanted with chips that serve as our credit card and debit card". Says, Douglas Rushkoff, Media Theorist. "And when we check out at the grocery store we will be swiping our own arm over the scanner and that will be something that we feel is something we can't live without."

From the movie Demolition Man with Sandra Bullock and Sylvester Stallone she tells him, "While you were sleeping everyone in the city were installed with a bionic microchip sewn into the skin. Censors all over the city can zero in on anyone at any time". Another officer speaks, "I can't even imagine what you police officers did before it was developed." The chief notices Stallone scratching his hand, "What do you think you are scratching? Do you really think we would let you go without control?"

From another TV show, Law and Order SVU, "RFID chip, Radio Frequency Identification, like the ones they put in dogs. It's the same basic technology. In the future, chips will be equipped with GPS but for now they simply carry a 16-digit number unique to each client. How much information can you put in these chips?

The applications are unlimited. In the future, we will be able to track children, the elderly, criminals, immigrants. "Welcome to the New World Order." From Adweek the headline reads, "CBS Intelligence is the season's most-watched premiere." The top new series on TV today is the series Intelligence. About a government agent who has a computer implanted into his brain so he can connect wirelessly to the internet so it makes him a transhumanist super soldier.

Do I have to point out that the CBS' logo is the all-seeing eye? Back in the 1980's animals started being injected with unique RFID chips to help to track and identify farm animals and find lost pets. EN Gilllespie is a digital science researcher that describes the human microchip as the ultimate app, it's a sexy new piece of technology which could allow us to activate devices like phones, tablets, lights, doors, computers and even vehicles with just a wave of our hands.

This procedure is being done at implantation stations which are microchip stalls that can be found at technology festivals. Because implantation is like a routine vaccination, it gives us speedy access to our apps and devices. We could be living in a world where governments won't even make tracking chips mandatory. People will be itching to get their chip installed just so they can shop and communicate quicker. This cashless, cardless utopia might sound like an idealic digital world that we are all after.

The President put in a lot of money into his stimulus package to advance medical records, if you have the chip you can carry the records with you. Stick in the computer and they will know all there is to know about you. The United Kingdom information commissioner claims that by 2017 consumers will be cashless shoppers. A microchip which will hold all credit card and personal information will be implanted into the body connecting to a database that will know who they are, where they live, what they like and what they don't like. Shoppers will have their hand scanned not their credit card.[19]

Nope! There's no sign of Jesus coming back! You're a wacko! You're a conspiracy nut! You're just trying to scare me? Excuse me? You look at the weather, see the clouds, and say it's going to rain, and you're right! But you see all this promoted in the media, and you still say there's no sign of Jesus coming again! That's hypocritical! If you're paying attention, being a wise disciple of Christ, looking for His appearing you'll see this promotion to receive a microchip implant is everywhere! That is, if you're looking for it and not being a hypocrite!

You might be thinking, "Well, come on! Okay, so they're using the media to get us used to the idea of getting a chip. But nobody is going to fall for this baloney! Nobody's going to be willing to do this! This is crazy!" Well actually, the younger generation who has been brought up on this media promotion of the Mark of the Beast thinks it's the greatest thing since sliced bread! The media is working like a charm! Just ask this guy!

Hello, my name is Amal Graafstra, I am the founder of Dangerous Things and I am a double RFID implantee. I got my first implant in my left hand in 2005 and since then I have been working on different technologies and now I have developed the XNT fully NXE type 2 compliant RFID implant tag. The primary use is to be able to program a tag with URL or information you want to share. I use my implants to get access to my house. I will use it for access control solutions to get into my back door every day after I get home, I use it to get access to my car, I can unlock my car and get in. I can also use it to log into my computer. [20]

And the same technology allows you to buy and sell. Looks to me like that media promotion to receive a microchip implant is working like a charm! In fact, he's not the only one. In an article entitled, "Why I Want a Microchip Implant" from the BBC, it said, "If we just adopted such technology our lives would be so much better. Ultimately, implanted microchips offer a way to make your physical body machine-readable for building access to ATMs. You never lose them; therefore, you're never cut off from your bank account, your gym, your ride home, your proof of ID, and much, much, more. An implanted chip could act as our universal identity token for navigating the world." Or what the Bible calls, a universal Mark that allows me to "buy and sell" anywhere in the world. Nope! No signs of Jesus ever coming back! Are you kidding me? If you're paying attention to the media, they're promoting the Mark of the Beast right now! That's how close we are!

The **2nd way** that they're using propaganda to condition people to receive the actual Mark of the Beast is the **Medical Industry.**

You see, another huge massive area The Mark of the Beast is being promoted is in the medical industry. And just like the media, it's being sold as a panacea for all kinds of things for the so-called betterment of society.

The **1st so-called health benefit** the medical industry is promoting for microchip implants is that it **Will Monitor Your Weight**.

Believe it or not, they've found a new way to shave off those extra pounds around the waist. Move over diet pills, scrap those diets, just get a microchip in your arm. Check this out!

FOX News Reports:

Scientist say they may have found a way to help people lose weight by planting a computer chip into their arms. Researchers are developing a device which can scan the blood for fat and other things. When an obese person eats too much it will release hormones that suppress hunger. They say it will stop releasing those hormones once that person reaches a healthy weight. According to the CDC from 2011 - 2012, 78 million adults in the United States suffer from obesity, that is 34.9% while in 2009-2010 12.5 million children suffer from the disease which is 17%.[21]

So, let's microchip them, and everything will work out great! Can you believe that? No wonder they keep pushing all these obesity shows and reports, and scares about obesity. Sounds to me like somebody wants to get "chipped" to "fix" it! Maybe losing weight isn't your problem, maybe it's losing your memory! Believe it or not, they've got a chip for that!

The 2nd so-called health benefit the medical industry is promoting for microchip implants is that **It Will Monitor Your Loved One.**

It will not only help you lose weight, but it will keep track of your loved one, you know, that one with Alzheimer's! I mean, they don't know better. They've got Alzheimer's. If we put a chip inside of them, we could track them and keep them safe, and you don't have to worry about it. Isn't that great? Believe it or not, it's already being done!

ABC News Reports:

5 million Americans are currently living with Alzheimer's. 5 million with an enormous amount of concern by family members about keeping their loved ones safe throughout the illness. Now we told you before about a high-tech microchip that could be implanted in the arm.

Critical medical details could be accessed, and people are wondering if this could eventually lead to being able to track the people. Well, it isn't without controversy. But some people are ready and lining up to get this chip. John Berman, "That right, one of the greatest fears for someone caring for someone with Alzheimer's, is that their loved one will get lost, show up at a hospital and no one will know who they are or what's wrong with them.

We have reported on this tiny new microchip that might be able to help. Now for the first time, with great controversy, patients are lining up to get them. The chip is the size of a grain of rice. It has a 16-digit identification number which gets scanned at the hospital.

When the number gets put into the database it can provide crucial medical information. The doctor tells the patient, "If you get lost or have any medical problems, we will be able to get the information about you". It's the latest type of high tech gear used to care for the elderly. It's the same technology used to track wayward pets.[22]

Oh, I get it! First get us used to tracking our pets with the chip, then we'll do it to people! But hey, if it'll help you lose weight, find Fido, and track that loved one with Alzheimer's, it's all for our good!

The 3rd so-called health benefit the medical industry is promoting for microchip implants is that **It Will Monitor Your Births.**

Hey, if microchips are good for helping us to lose weight, find missing pets, and keep an eye on those loved ones when they get older, how about controlling when the younger get born, or not! Believe it or not, they've now come out with a remote control birth control via the microchip. Check this out!

CBS News Reports:

This really could be a birth control revolution. Local researchers are working on a microchip that could control a woman's hormones with help from a remote control. Dr. Mallika Marshall, of Health Watch, says, "Sounds crazy, right, a remote control. Well, a biomedical company has teamed up with MIT. Right now, they are testing a contraceptive with wireless capabilities and it could prevent pregnancy for up to 16 years."

Dr. Bob Langer, of the Massachusetts Institute of Technology, says, "This kind of technology could have a major effect in revolutionized aspects in medicine, including birth control." Some experts point out that women already have implantable birth control options, like the IUD. Researchers are now working on the remote to make sure it can't be hacked.[23]

Yeah, that would be horrible, wouldn't it? Some guy controlling all the births around the world. Oh, and by the way, the ones who are pushing this are the Bill and Linda Gates Foundation. The same folks who are for population control. But as you saw, Oh, I get it! First you get ladies used to those other short-lived implants, and then later get them to switch to the longer ones, that just happen to be remote controlled. What kind of a freaky future are we headed for? Oh, but it's for your good! Just get the microchip implant!

The 4th so-called health benefit the medical industry is promoting for microchip implants is that **It Will Monitor Your Diseases.**

That's right! If these microchips are good for losing weight, finding Fido, tracking your loved one with Alzheimer's and controlling those who get born, you know, those "unwanted kids", then how about getting rid of diseases? I mean, wouldn't that be great? And believe it or not, they've got that too in a microchip! They can actually sniff out diseases to create that perfect healthy society!

Nick Glass of Make Create Innovate Reports:

With the help of scientists, we have been catching up with our 4-legged friends, but an extraordinary censor has been developed to help us humans sniff the air around us for anything dangerous, including disease. We have invented a microchip to detect chemicals in the air. It's essentially a microchip with a sense of smell. Combining expertise and chemistry and electronics and nanotechnology, the microchip has been developed in a research lab in Cambridge.

That technology is already used by BP and Shell in the food industry by Coca Cola and Nestles. For the next big market, health care, they hope it could help detect disease. There have already been a number of research papers published suggesting that we can do these sorts of things. Detection of Cancer, the detection of Tuberculosis, and the detection of Asthma, for instance.[24]

If we would all just get a microchip, we could get rid of all kinds of diseases, and live so healthy and, but wait a second. What if they misdiagnosed you? "Hey, we smell cancer on you! It's terminal. Come on in and we'll put you out of your misery." We all know the medical industry never makes a misdiagnosis, talk about another ultimate tool to get rid of people. What about the impaired or infirmed, or those suffering from paralysis? How will their lives improve? Well, funny you should ask!

The 5th so-called health benefit the medical industry is promoting for microchip implants is that **It Will Monitor Your Brain.**

That's right, believe it or not, the medical industry is not only promoting microchip implants in the arms and hands for so-called better health, but they are also promoting it to restore your health. But you have to put it into your brain.

RT News Reports:

There's an old expression for overcoming less than desirable situations, mind over matter, and for 23-year-old quadriplegic, Ian Burkheart, it was exactly what had to be done. He became paralyzed after a 2010 diving accident but now Ohio State University, Wexner Medical Center, has just had a breakthrough discovery that may help many quadriplegics across the globe.

They were able to get Ian Burkheart to move his hand with the power of thought. Doctors, neuroscientists, and engineers, from Betal were about to implement cutting edge technology by installing a chip directly into Ian's brain. The signals are then taken from the chip, bypass the injury in the spinal cord and linking the signal directly to the muscle in the arm.[25]

Wow! If only we would get these chips in our hands or as you saw, even in our heads, what kind of utopia could this world be? Nope! There's no sign of Jesus coming back! You're a wacko! You're a conspiracy nut! You're just trying to scare me! Excuse me? You look at the weather, see the clouds, and say it's going to rain, and you're right! The medical industry is promoting the Mark of the Beast right now. That's how close we are.

The 3rd way that they're using propaganda to condition people to receive the actual Mark of the Beast is **My Employment.**

The Bible is clear, ultimately this choice to go along with this Mark of the Beast technology is going to be taken away. It's being promoted right now all over the place for people to voluntarily accept as you saw but for those resisters out there, you will be forced to do it anyway!

Revelation 13:12,14,15,16-17 "He made the earth and its inhabitants worship the first beast, whose fatal wound had been healed. He ordered them to set up an image in honor of the beast who was wounded by the sword and yet lived. He caused all who refused to worship the image to be killed. He also forced everyone, small and great, rich and poor, free and slave, to receive a mark on his right hand or on his forehead, so that no one could buy or sell unless he had the mark."

So again, we see the option to "opt out" of this system is taken away! The Antichrist is going to make, order, cause, and force people to take this Mark or you are dead meat! I'm telling you, the same kind of pressure tactics are being used right now to implement the Mark of the Beast! Right now, it's voluntary and being promoted by the media and medical industry.

But if you're also paying attention to other signs, that choice is about to go right out the window! People are being forced to get the microchip. Whether as we saw before, soldiers, prisoners, sex offenders, dignitaries, and even police officers just to name a few, but there's now signs that it's even going to come to your job, which you need to get the money to buy and sell.

Whether it's for getting on a bus or getting to the office, many of us these days, are used to swiping an electronic card. But how would you feel if the microchip wasn't in the card but in your hand instead. Not holding in your hand but under the skin. One company in Sweden is doing just that.

It offers its staff to have the chip inserted. Our technology correspondent, Rory James, is finding out how it works. Stockholm, at a non-descript, building has been converted into a high-tech office space. But look under the skin to find something really futuristic. The employee doesn't need a pass to get in. One swipe of his hand gets him in and another swipe to get into his office. What's going on? He's got the chip implant.

So that's why the doors open. Where's the chip? Right inside his hand. The new offices will soon host a shifting population of 700 employees and will all be given the opportunity to be chipped. Rory James even got the chip while doing the report. "It's not a painless process but it doesn't last too long. A small surgical procedure that basically involves a little chip, something like a grain of rice being inserted under your skin. And you can then go off and get it programmed and do various things inside the building. Let's go have a look.

The new offices will allow them to use the photo copiers, and eventually log on to computers, or pay for food in the café. The man behind the scheme, whose business card can be accessed by his chip says the aim is to learn lessons. "We want to be able to understand this technology before big corporations or big governments come to us and say everyone should be chipped." The Google chip, The Facebook chip.[26]

What? Now wait a second. Didn't we already see how Sweden is getting ready to go cashless, and last time we saw they just came out with this new hand payment system called Quixter and now they are pushing this in the workplace. Anybody seeing a pattern here? And notice you can buy and sell with this chip! But they wouldn't mandate it, would they? Get a microchip for the workplace let alone function in society?

Well if you're paying attention to other signs out there, they're about to take the volunteering aspect right out of this. Notice the guy just said, "They are getting used to this before it's mandated! Before the Tax Authority or the Government or Google or whoever says you have to!" And it's getting even more blatant than that! Listen to this, a liberal candidate right now in Australia is proposing to, "Microchip suspects by Sniper Rifle." "Ray King is proposing a radical new policing system in which criminal suspects would be injected with satellite-trackable microchip shot from a high-powered sniper rifle to improve productivity in the Australian Police Force." "What I propose and will endeavor to convince others of is the implementation of microchip technology similar to that being used in controlling the activity of domestic animals and put criminals behind bars."

Oh, but that's not all. Another guy is advocating, "The government should use microchips to deny births to the unworthy." One philosopher noted that, the idea first crossed his mind when he heard a nurse say, "With 10,000 kids dying every day around the world from starvation, you'd think we'd put birth control in the water." After careful thought, in an effort to "give hundreds of millions of future kids a better life, I cautiously endorse the idea of licensing parents." The process, he said, "would be little different than getting a driver's license." Parents must "pass a series of basic tests" in order to "get the green light to get pregnant and raise children." "Those applicants who are deemed unworthy for a variety of reasons – he lists homelessness, criminal history, and poverty among his examples – "would not be allowed until they could demonstrate they were suitable parents."

So how do you regulate it? "He says he's found "near-term hope" in a contraceptive technology funded by Bill and Melinda Gates Foundation, a remote controlled injectable microchip that could effectively sterilize someone for up to 16 years. Still don't see a pattern in this? Oh, but that's still not all. Speaking of Bill Gates, there's also talk of putting this technology in vaccines!

"In recent years, vaccines have meshed with the world of nanobot medicine in the form of a lump of particles injected below the skin, one that would manipulate cells as well as release biological and chemical drug components and can permeate every area of the body, including placenta." And so now you've got a nanobot in the vaccine that can act as a birth control. And by the way, "It is reported that the Bill and Melinda Gates Foundation are also working on developing nano vaccines."

Oh, I get it! If I don't volunteer for your remote-control birth control, you'll get me through a vaccine! Hey, isn't that the rage right now in the media they're talking over this Measles Crisis? Mandatory vaccines? You don't think they'd be that sneaky, listen to this. "India is Holding Bill Gates Accountable for His Vaccine Crimes." "The India Supreme Court has brought a lawsuit against the Bill & Melinda Gates Foundation for multiple deaths and illness from their vaccines and in many cases administered without parental knowledge. And other countries like Pakistan are now blaming him for the deaths of at least 10,000 children caused by their vaccines."

If that wasn't bad enough, right now in Venezuela, people are being forced to "register" in order to buy groceries! Why? Because of the ongoing

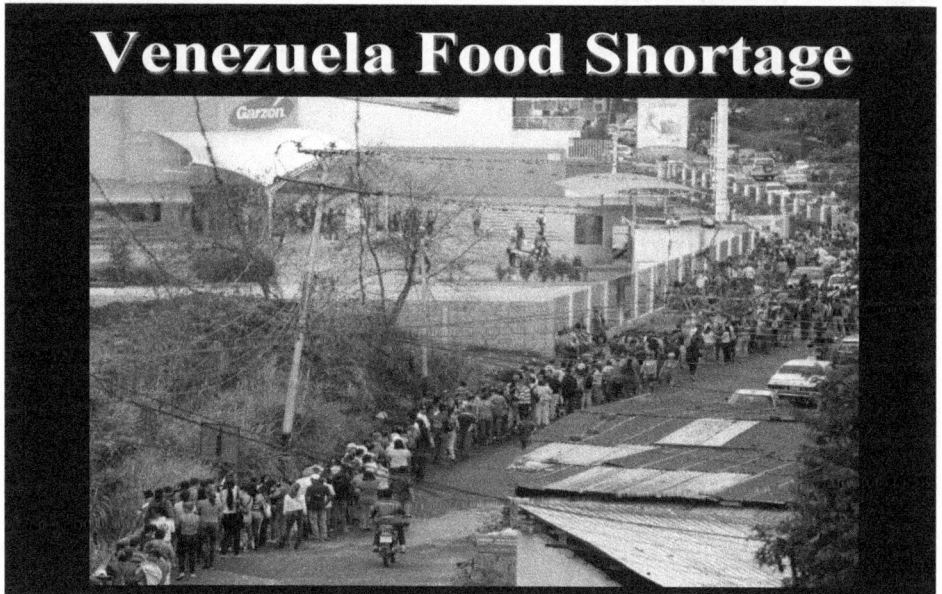

economic crisis caused by falling oil prices, "Venezuela's food distribution is under military protection." To prevent "food hoarding" the Government is marking people with numbers on their arms.

And mandating ID Cards to get those groceries and soon they're going to have to, "Scan their fingers to buy food." And according to this article, this is our soon coming future!

"It's only a matter of time before human-embedded microchips achieve widespread acceptance."

Your initial reaction to this idea may be one of disbelief. There's no way society would accept such a device. Why would anyone want an implant in their body?

But consider where we are right now. For decades Americans rejected the notion that they would submit to being tracked and recorded. Yet, just about every American now carries a mobile phone and embedded in every one of these phones is a microchip that can track our every movement.

And eventually this new technology will be non-voluntary.

To gain access to official services, you'll need to be a verified human. Without verification, you won't even be able to purchase a six pack of beer, let alone get medical care or a driver's license.

And one day, this kind of technology will likely be so pervasive that you won't be able to open a bank account, get a credit card or even buy anything without having either your hand or your face scanned first.

Whether we like it or not this is the future."[27]

Nope! There's no sign of Jesus coming back! You're a wacko! You're a conspiracy nut! You're just trying to scare me? Excuse me? You look at the weather, see the clouds, and say it's going to rain, and you're right! But you see all this promoted in the media and medical industry and now starting to be mandated, and you still say there's no sign of Jesus coming again! That's hypocritical! It's all happening before our very eyes, that is, if you're looking for it!

The 6th way people are being deceived into receiving the Mark of the Beast is the **Willingness Proof.**

You see, the Bible is clear. If you're going to pull off this Mark of the Beast system that the Antichrist is going to do, you not only have to encourage the people on the planet repeatedly over and over again in a multitude of ways, year after year after year, to warm them up to the idea to get an implant as we've been seeing with the propaganda, but at some point, your propaganda has to work, right? It has to get them to the point where they're willing to try it, right? Well, guess what? It has!

For the first time in man's history, people are willing to take the Mark of the Beast! They're not just being conditioned, they're actually willing to take it right now, even though the penalty for doing so is pretty bad!
But don't take my word for it. Let's listen to God's.

Revelation 14:6-11 "Then I saw another angel flying in midair, and he had the eternal gospel to proclaim to those who live on the earth – to every nation, tribe, language and people. He said in a loud voice, 'Fear God and give Him glory, because the hour of His judgment has come. Worship Him Who made the heavens, the earth, the sea and the springs of water.' A second angel followed and said, 'Fallen! Fallen is Babylon the Great, which made all the nations drink the maddening wine of her adulteries.' A third angel followed them and said in a loud voice: 'If anyone worships the beast and his image and receives his mark on the forehead or on the hand, he, too, will drink of the wine of God's fury, which has been poured full strength into the cup of his wrath. He will be tormented with burning sulfur in the presence of the holy angels and of the Lamb. And the smoke of their torment rises for ever and ever. There is no rest day or night for those who worship the beast and his image, or for anyone who receives the mark of his name."

Now, according to our text, I think the Bible is clear on this. If there's one thing you never want to do it's what? Don't take the Mark of the Beast, right? Why? Because you go straight into hell, right? Says it right there! Forever and ever and ever and you are not getting out! So, the question then is this. How does the Antichrist get people to risk this horrible destiny by receiving his mark? We know they will do it. But how does he get them to do it? Well, first of all, he does what he always does. He lies, and he twists the truth, and he makes the bad look good!

The 1st way he's twisting the truth making people willing to receive the Mark of the Beast is by what I call the **Cool Factor**.

I mean, come on, don't you want to be cool? Haven't you heard, if you get a microchip implant, you're cool, you're a part of the in-crowd! Believe it or not, one of the biggest promoters of this so-called "coolness" of getting a microchip implant is in the tattoo and body piercing industry.

I mean, in my generation, tattoos weren't that big of deal, but now, they're everywhere! There's shows about them, reality shows, they're all over the place being promoted. And they're always pushing the envelope getting more wild and weird! Check out the latest rage called 3-D tattoos!

As tattoos continue to evolve, tattoo artists must step up their game. Reporter: Mother of three is about to spend the next 6 to 7 hours getting a tattoo. She says, "I am finishing the sleeve that I started several years ago." She's not the only one. There are more than two hundred tattoo shops listed in the San Antonio area alone. One patron, "I'm getting a tattoo on my leg."

Another says, "I'm getting a tattoo on my foot." Conventions to reality shows, young, old, rich, poor, tattoos are seemingly more mainstream than ever and they are increasingly elaborate. One artist says, "You got to hang with the big boys swimming in the shark tank, you understand." He says, "A big thing right now is photo realism, color portraits, 3D tattoos. It changes the game of tattooing. It's really pushing the limits of our, it's really pushing the envelope, to the next level. A pencil behind your ear, shoe laces on your foot, a terminator arm. Tattooers are just blowing people out of the water. The sky is the limit."

Reporter: With time, shading, and a willing and able artist, you too can have a butterfly resting on your shoulder, a slice of pizza on your stomach, or a snake burrowing into your flesh.[28]

Oh yeah! How many of you want that one? Wouldn't that be cool! What's wrong, don't you guys know style? You're never going to be cool if you keep that up! Normal tattoos aren't good enough anymore. You have got to have something newer, better, crazier, something that will push the envelope even further. And that's precisely what's happened. All this tattooing craze has now led, of course, to body piercings in the tongue, in the nose, in the eyebrow, in the forehead and even body implants in the head. Let me now show you how far people are going to look even cooler than that.

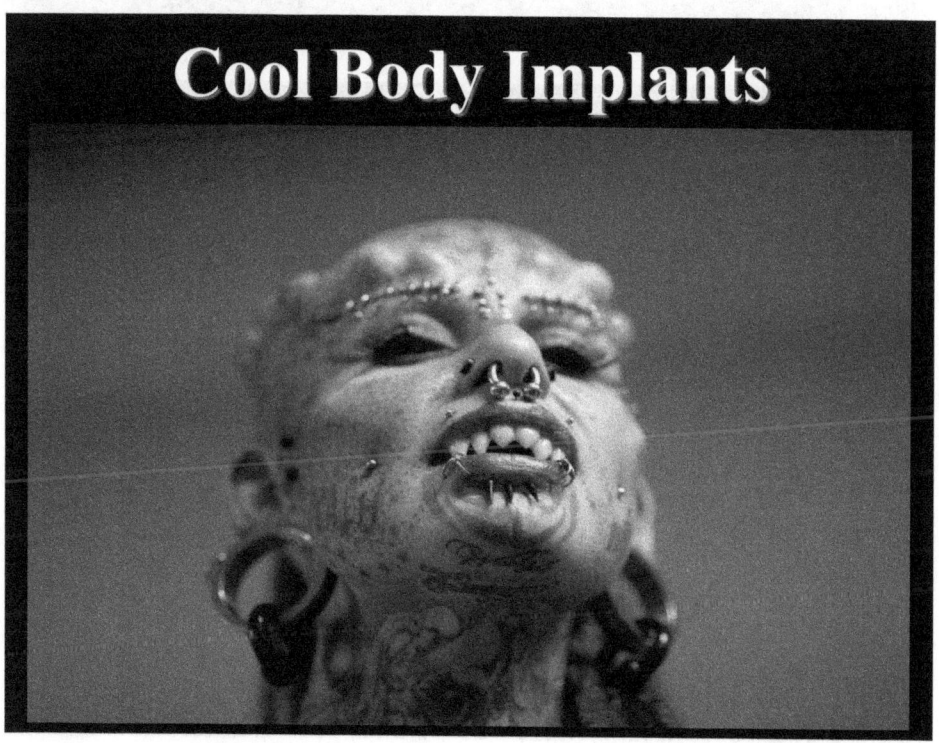

Cool Body Implants

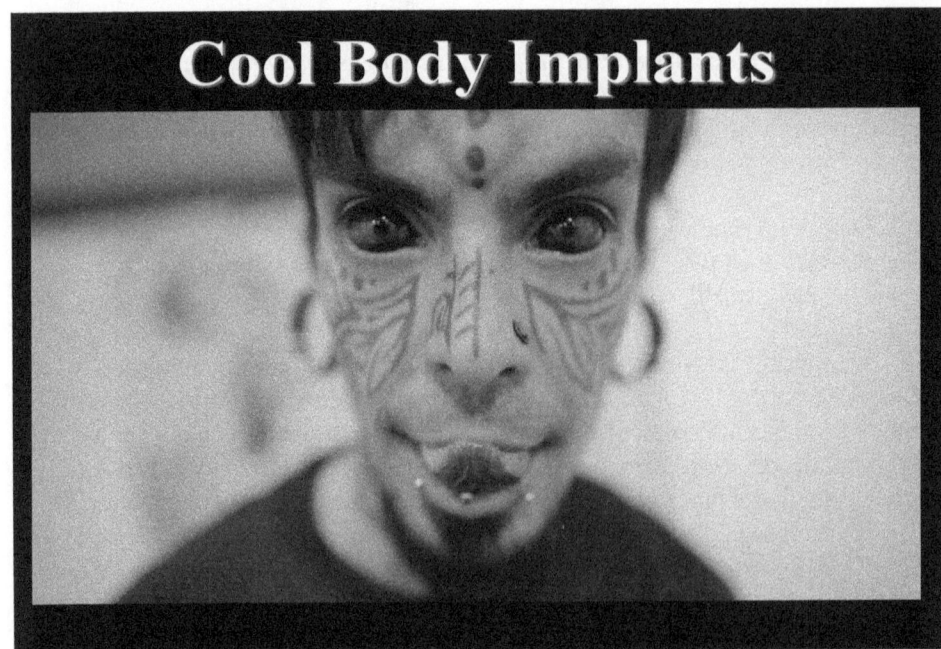

Cool Body Implants

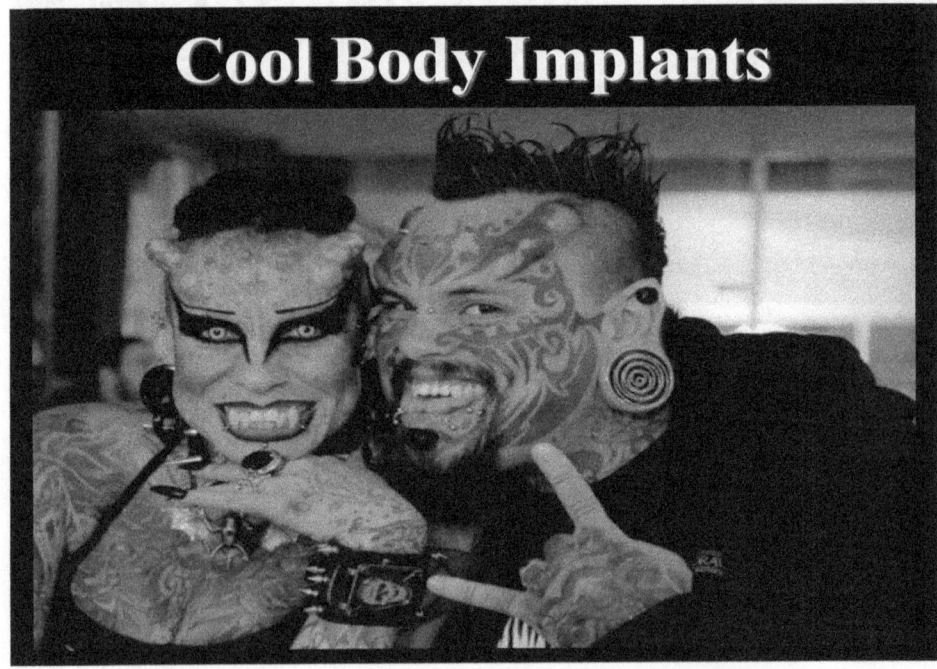

Cool Body Implants

Cool Body Implants

Oh, by the way, those are pictures from the Venezuela Tattoo Expo of 2015. And it just so happens there's something else going on in Venezuela right now. Food shortages. And because of this, listen to what people are having to do.

They are being forced to "register" with the government in order to buy groceries! Why? Because of the ongoing economic crisis caused by falling oil prices, "Venezuela's food distribution is now under military protection." To prevent "food hoarding" the government is marking people with numbers on their arms. But I'm sure this will never turn into getting a microchip implant. Well, first of all, they're already talking about having to use your finger to make a payment, but do you think the people there will resist a microchip implant? You'll implant these into your body in Venezuela to look cool, but you'll balk at this inside your body.

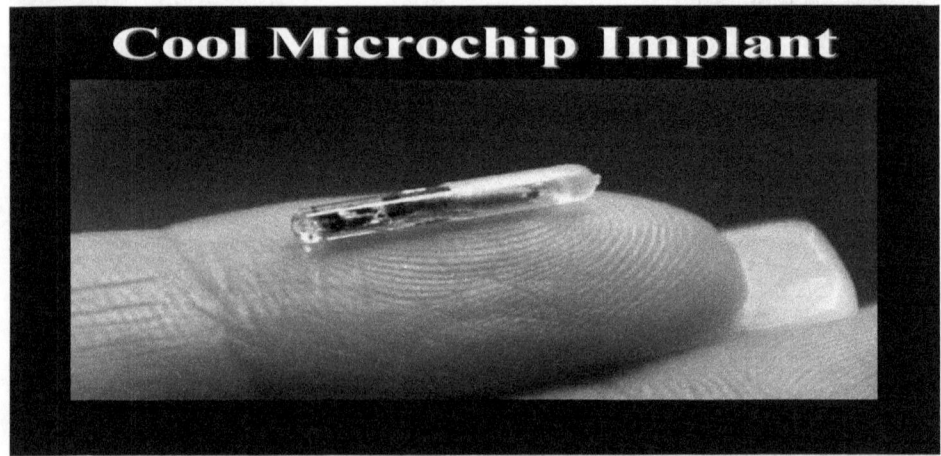

Piece of cake! I don't even think they'd sneeze at the idea! In fact, they're not the only ones. There's now a global phenomenon of people going straight to the microchip!

Here's a recent photo of some folks in Sweden calling themselves "The Rise of the Swedish Cyborgs" who have implanted themselves with microchips and now

they're even having what's called "implant parties".

And remember, this is Sweden, where we already saw they're about to go to a cashless society, and they just came out with a new hand payment system called Quixter, and then they started promoting microchip implants in the workplace and now you're having implant parties for individuals to get a microchip implant. Can anyone see a pattern here? Oh, and they're not only encouraging these parties for individuals, but they soon hope to have this number up to 10,000 people real soon, including this girl.

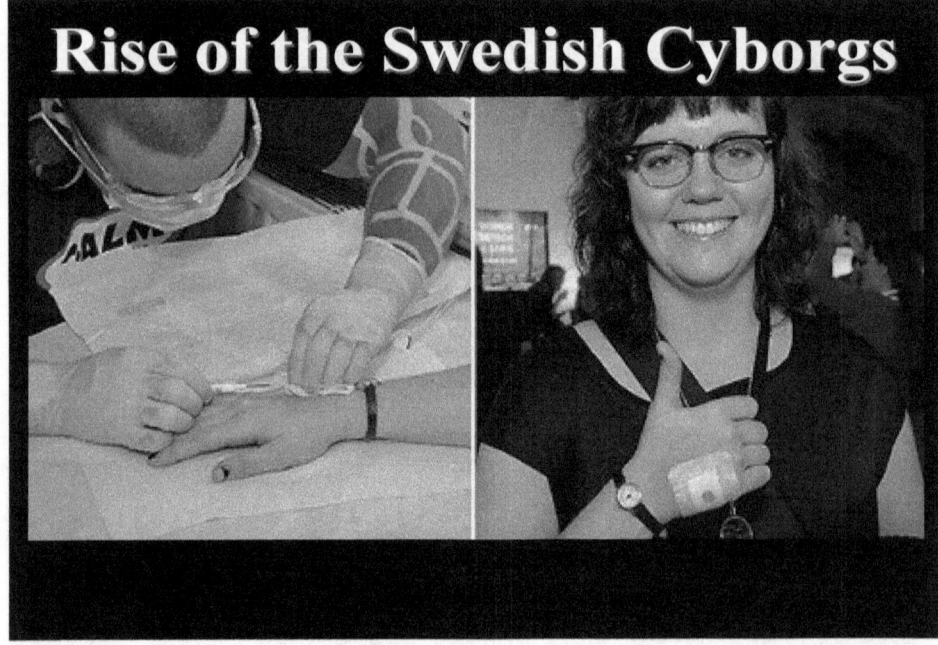

She was so excited she said, "I'm among the first Swedes with a microchip." Don't you see how cool this is! Don't you want to be cool like her? The term they're using in this industry is called, "Bio-hacking." So, pay attention to that in the media. It means Mark of the Beast. There's a pattern here. First tattoos, then body piercings, then bio-hacking microchip implants!

But wait a second. How are you going to power these microchip implants? Well, talk about being cool! One lady in Israel of all places has designed new jewelry to be inserted into your veins.

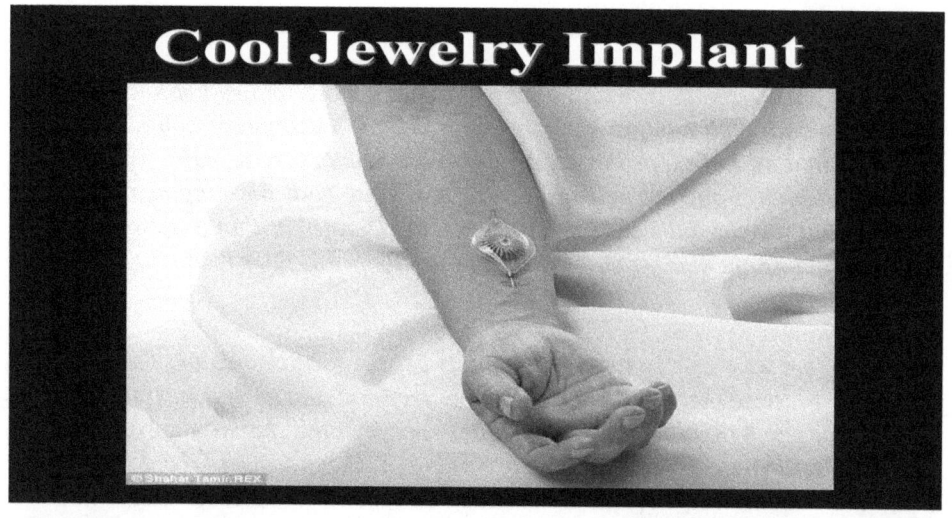

And it actually connects with your blood to turn your blood flow into electricity. You know, just in case you need to power a chip or something, for some reason. I thought somebody in Israel would know better than to promote a marking system in the body. For those of you who still can't see the connection that all this tattooing and body piercing is warming people up to receiving an actual microchip implant for the Mark of the Beast system, let's look now at the latest service tattoo shops have just started to do for you the customer. Can you say microchip implant!

From Dangerousthings.com, they tell us:

So, you might be asking yourself, ok, I want one of these things, but how do I get one in my hand. Well Dangerousthings has partnered with professionals around the world and we have a professional, Dana Bruner, to give us more information. "Dangerousthings partner network is a professional body piercing and body modification service and referral service for the Dangerousthings network to help you find a safe and reputable practitioner to install their technological modification."

The place that we chose to install the chip is between the thumb and the forefinger because the middle of the hand is very soft and easily accessible. There's not much there to cause any trouble between the skin or muscle. It's a safe place and you can see what you are doing and keep track of the device. It's important to be in a safe clean environment and if we have a professional near you that's great, but if we don't, definitely then approach your local piercing place. We will give them piercing guides. We will give them examples of the implant procedure. And talk to them on the phone to bring them up to speed.[29]

In other words, we'll train them on this new trend to make people look even cooler! First tattoos, then body piercings, then a microchip implant. We do it all for you! And you still don't see a pattern here? But you might be thinking, "Well that's just those young whipper snappers! They don't know any better! No adult is going to do this just to look cool!" Really? Well, call it a mid-life crisis or whatever, but apparently even adults want to be cool too, just like the kids, with their own microchip implant. In fact, this adult man is all excited about it!

The man getting the implant tells us, "So, he's going to use a large gauge needle that will install this subcutaneously". The fellow with the needle asks him if he is ready. He's not looking at the needle and is smiling at the guy standing next to him. Meanwhile his hand is being rubbed and the needle is being put into his hand between his thumb and his finger. He still has a smile on his face, "OK, that's in," He looks at his hand, still smiling, "It did not really hurt very much at all." And then the audience claps that the job was completed".[30]

Isn't that great to know? When you as an adult get your own cool microchip implant, it doesn't even hurt! You can be like the kids! Oh, and by the way, that man's name is Raymond McCauley and he was doing this while he was giving a talk in Europe on bio-technology and he stated, "Chip implants are as easy as piercings." You know, the new trend! He said, "Incorporating technology into our bodies may seem repellent or unnatural to some people. But many of us are already cyborgs. For example, vaccination is a kind of technological augmentation." His business partner Peter Diamandis also went up on stage and got an implant and said, "Implants could create the Internet of Things. We could use our hands to unlock doors, start the car, or pay for coffee."

You know, buy and sell! But, as you can see, don't you want to be a part of the in-crowd? Don't you want to be cool with a microchip implant? Don't you want to be hip with the chip? And that's precisely the selling point.

The 2nd way people are being made willing to receive the Mark of the Beast implant is by what I call the **Convenience Factor.**

If only you'd get a microchip implant, you'd not only be cool and a part of the in-crowd, and hip, but you talk about convenience! Why, we could usher in the greatest time of consumer convenience ever! We could get a lot more done, our lives would be much simpler, and we could breeze through lines with a microchip implant, and save so much time! It's this exact same deception the Bible warns about, how the enemy is going to get people to receive the Mark of the Beast. But don't take my word for it. Let's listen to Jesus!

Matthew 24:4-5,10-11,23-25 Jesus answered: "Watch out that no one deceives you. For many will come in My Name, claiming, 'I am the Christ,' and will deceive many. At that time many will turn away from the faith and will betray and hate each other, and many false prophets will appear and deceive many people. At that time if anyone says to you, 'Look, here is the Christ!' or, 'There he is!' do not believe it. For false Christs and false prophets will appear and perform great signs and miracles to deceive even the elect – if that were possible. See, I have told you ahead of time."

In other words, there's no excuse for you to get caught off guard, i.e. don't be deceived! According to our text, Jesus said one of the biggest characteristics in the last days is it's going to be a time of great massive deception, right? All throughout the text, deceit, deceit, deceit! Therefore, Jesus said, "I've told you ahead of time!" Don't get caught off guard!

I'm telling you, this is exactly what's happening with getting people prepared to receive the Mark of the Beast. The enemy's using deceit, deceit, deceit! Just like with the external tattoos and body piercings are being used to warm people up to receiving a microchip implant as the next step under the guise of being cool. So, it is with another trend out there with these implants and that's that they're so incredibly convenient.

The first step they're using to get us used to the idea of an implant is with these new devices out there called Wearables! For those of you who don't know, they are those electronic devices you wear on your hand! They're everywhere! And they're being sold as a panacea for all kinds of creature comforts that will make your life so much more convenient in a multitude of ways.

CNET Reports:

It's time to merge hi-tech with hi-fashion. Intel is showing off a new luxury smart bracelet called the MICA. It's created in partnership with a company called 'Opening Ceremony'. It's essentially jewelry with its own phone number. That means you need a data plan. It receives text messages that are played on the sapphire screen on the wrist and it also will be able to show other notifications.

The smart ring by Mota, the natural, low key, a convenient way to stay on top of what is important in your life. Who is trying to reach you and what you need to do next. Include the people you want, exclude the calls and text you don't. Forget about constantly checking your phone. Stay in sync with what matters using what is right in front of you. The smart ring is the very natural way to see who is trying to reach you.

With the Cicret Bracelet, do what you use to do with a tablet...but directly on your skin and without any smartphone. Let's have a look on Cicret Bracelet's possibilities. It works underwater, your arm can look like your cell phone or it can look like your laptop. You can use it like your phone or your laptop. You can read your emails and your texts right on your arm. You can answer your phone.

You can search Google, count your calories, count the minutes to work, whatever you need to know, right on your wrist. Scan your ticket at the airport and get your football scores.[31]

Don't you see? Look at all the convenience we would have if we would all get these electronic wearables on our hand! I can keep track of my calories, see how far I ran, what my health score is, get a map, play games, even in the bathtub, stay connected to social media, and not have to get off the couch in case the phone rings! Talk about convenient! Who wouldn't want that, right? Just get this device to put on the outside of your hand, and it opens up a whole new world of convenience! If you can't see where this is headed, guess what else these wearables can do? Shocker! They can buy and sell! You can make a payment with one of these devices on your hand. Step by step folks, the plans unfolding!

PayPal is the first payment provider on the Samsung Gear Two Smartwatch. The app lets you check in and pay at the local store, pay, redeem offers and receive payment notifications. With the technology of a wireless payment system, it will replace your wallet as well as your apartment and car keys. And what's more it will assist in keeping tabs on your finances.

Helping to control your expenses, it will keep an accounting of your nutritional input by tallying up the calories of food that you buy at the store and deduct the calories you would spend doing physical activity. In addition, it will not only keep track of your weight but also the nutritional value of your diet indicating to you in a timely manner any deficiencies or overabundance of vitamins and trace minerals that you require according to your chosen diet.

The Ipourit is a system that allows customers to pour their own beer. With an RFID wristband, a valve controls beer flowing through the tap while a meter records the amount of beer the customer pours, accurate to more than 1/100 of an oz. At Ipourit, every ounce of beer is metered and charged to the customer as they are pouring it. Meters can be set per day, per hour or per pour. Once the limit is reached the customer can visit with the host again who can make the decision to allow more ounces to be consumed or cut them off.

Pay for coffee and other smaller transaction with a wave. "Please swipe your wristband for your coffee, $4.00 for coffee, take your receipt, thank you." All by the swipe of your wrist. Pay for parking without taking your wallet out. "Please swipe your wristband, thank you." And in he goes to park his car. Walking by a glass window you can donate to your local charity.

Through the glass of the storefront window he swipes his wrist and his money is donated. In Canada, Mexico, Belgium, USA, United Kingdom, Czech Republic, Netherlands, Norway, Switzerland, over 40 events in 10 countries, over 2.5 million have activated RFID tags. When so many people are used to using this system when it doesn't work they are in quite a pickle. One guy goes to buy coffee and the lady at the counter says "$4.26 please." He swipes his hand and says thank you. She looks at him funny and he swipes it again.

Again, he says thank you and she looks at him funny. Oh, she must want a tip, so he swipes the tip jar and smiles at her. Again, she looks at him funny and he realizes he actually has to pay for the coffee. Then we see a lady and her daughter going to the door to her house. She swipes her chip and proceeds to plunge through the door, but the door doesn't open and she smashes her face into the door. Another lady is in a department store, her purchases have been rung up. She waves her arm at the clerk but the clerk stares at her, "What is that?" she asks.

Next a gentleman is in another department store, his purchases have been rung up, he swipes his chip, the clerk says, "Thank you." And he is on his way to another store. How easy was that. Once you experience 'My Magic Plus at Walt Disney World Resort, you will want to use it everywhere. It opens the door of your room, it makes the purchases, pays for dining, photos, and even your tickets.[32]

      Don't you see it? It's going to be so awesome when all we have to do is make a payment with a wave of my hand using these external wearables, and now Disney World is conditioning us to it! But there's only one problem. What if you lose your wearable? Or what if somebody steals it? Then how are you going to access all this convenience? Well, funny you should ask. Let me see if I can state the obvious pattern.

      First let me get used to a wearable for general convenience, then later switch it to payment convenience, and then maybe one day just skip the whole wearable thing altogether and go straight into the hand? That way you wouldn't lose it, right? Well, guess what? That's exactly what they're saying is coming next! Very soon! It's called Project Underskin! Get that wearable under your skin, and it's really secure!

From Smart phones to Google Glass, this past decade has brought forth a new wave of technology and technological advances and in the next five years those advances are expected to go beneath the surface, literally. The next big thing in wearable technology may be a tattoo implanted into the skin according to Fast Company.

The folks at New Deal Design, the San Francisco based design company behind the Fit/Wellness Watch, drafted a mockup of a tattoo for Fast Company's wearables week. They call it Project Under Skin. The foundation of under skin would be a visible tattoo implanted in the knuckle of the thumb.

Invisible tattoo is implanted in the palm. According to Fast Company the tattoo would interact with everything the consumer touches and would recognize the consumers location as well as the movements of the body.[33]

Interesting, so let me get this straight. First you get me get used to a wearable on my hand for personal convenience, then later you switch it to personal payment, then one day you skip the whole wearable thing altogether and just go straight into the hand? And you're saying it's going to come in the next few years? Anybody seeing a pattern here? A pattern of deceit just like Jesus said would happen when you're living in the last days! And that's why He also said this!

Luke 21:28 "When these things begin to take place, stand up and lift up your heads, because your redemption is drawing near."

If you are reading this and you're not a Christian, then I beg you, please, heed the signs, heed the warnings, give your life to Jesus today because you don't want to be left behind! Everything's going down the tubes, including the Church, and you don't want to be here! It's going to be the worst time in the history of mankind! But if you are a Christian, then what in the world are you doing for Jesus? Are you a fake? Are you an Apostate? Or are you a True Christian? Let's get busy working together fulfilling the Great Commission doing something splendid for Jesus, amen? The reason is, this is urgent! People's lives are really on the line and how much suffering and pain could they avoid if we'd just get serious about what's most important in life, and that's not us, it's about sharing the Gospel, like this man learned.

A letter came to me some years ago from the mission field. My wife brought it to me and said, "Would you please read this?" I was sitting in my office in Dallas…on my comfortable chair. I finished reading the letter, and I was weeping on my knees. The letter came from a dear friend, a missionary who worked in Haridwar, by the River Ganges.

During that couple of weeks' time, thirty-five million Hindus walk and travel by trains, and bullock-carts and buses…from all over the country to go into these dirty, polluted waters of the River Ganges, washing themselves for the forgiveness of sins. This one missionary was working amongst these people, telling them about Jesus.

One evening he was coming home, and now in the letter, he writes the experience of what happened that evening. He said, I saw this young woman, sitting by the bank of the river, weeping uncontrollably, and pounding upon her chest.

Knowing something so terrible happened, I went to her and asked." Why are you weeping? What happened?" She replied, "My husband is sick, he cannot work anymore. My sins are so many that nobody knows about. To find the forgiveness for my sins and solutions to the problems of my home, I have given the best offering I can give to Goddess Ganges-my only son. My six-month-old baby boy, I just threw him into the river".

I sat beside her and explained to her the gospel. Her sins are forgiven 2000 years ago, I explained to her. God is not angry with her, God didn't make them poor. Suddenly, she wiped her tears, and looked straight into my eyes, and said these words: But why? Why didn't you come to me half hour sooner? I didn't have to kill my child. I never heard this before. But why didn't you come to me half hour sooner?[34]

    How many people today would say the same thing to us? "Why, why didn't you come to me half hour sooner Christian co-worker, Christian neighbor, Christian family member? Why didn't you tell me? I didn't have to lose my job. I didn't have to get divorced. I didn't have to ruin my body with drugs or immorality, I didn't have to go to the 7-year Tribulation, I didn't have to go to hell! Why didn't you come half hour sooner?

    You think it's bad now? You haven't seen anything yet! The Antichrist is going to take all this wickedness and put it on steroids! And it's going to become the worst time in the history of mankind and you don't want to be there! This is urgent folks! People's lives really are on the line and how much suffering and pain and hardship could they avoid if we'd just get serious about what's most important in life, sharing the Good News of the Gospel. This is not a game. People's eternal destinies are on the line. Let's be that Christian that makes it there on time with the Gospel, amen?

    But if you're reading this and you're still not saved, I beg you, please get saved now! Call upon the Name of Jesus Christ, ask Him to forgive you of all your sins, believe in your heart that God raised Him from the grave, and the Bible says you will be saved. Do it now before it's too late! Don't be left behind!

How to Receive Jesus Christ:

1. Admit your need (I am a sinner).

2. Be willing to turn from your sins (repent).

3. Believe that Jesus Christ died for you on the Cross and rose from the grave.

4. Through prayer, invite Jesus Christ to come in and control your life through the Holy Spirit. (Receive Him as Lord and Savior.)

What to pray:

Dear Lord Jesus,

I know that I am a sinner and need Your forgiveness. I believe that You died for my sins. I want to turn from my sins. I now invite You to come into my heart and life. I want to trust and follow You as Lord and Savior.

In Jesus' name. Amen.

Notes

Chapter One

1. *Joke About Man Having a Bad Day*
   (Email story) – Source Unknown
2. *Welcome to the Temple Institute*
   https://www.youtube.com/watch?v=nyXAAm7K_3U
3. *Ethiopian Jew Suing Israel*
   http://www.israeltoday.co.il/NewsItem/tabid/178/nid/24614/Default.aspx
4. *Temple Commercial*
   https://www.youtube.com/watch?v=LPmViwmJSJE
5. *Modern Antisemitism 1/4th World*
   https://www.huffingtonpost.com/abraham-h-foxman/rising-anti-semitism-in-e_b_7835610.html
6. *Children's Program to kill Jews*
   https://www.youtube.com/watch?v=0ORAM-usqhQ
7. *Michael Jackson Hologram*
   https://www.youtube.com/watch?v=B70ZSt5lKJ4
8. *Turkish Leader Hologram*
   https://www.theatlantic.com/international/archive/2014/01/giant-hologram-of-turkish-prime-minister-delivers-speech/283374/
9. *Pope Francis 3D Broadcast*
   https://www.youtube.com/watch?v=o6jjGMA8-ZQ
10. *Socibot Face Image*
    https://www.engineeredarts.co.uk/socibot
11. *The Few*
    https://www.youtube.com/watch?v=HkLLOH7qXPg

Chapter Two

1. *Don't Mess with Women*
   (Email story) Author unknown.

2. *Google Driverless Car*
   https://www.youtube.com/watch?v=qtApzKnGU94
3. *Virgin Galactic Test Flight*
   https://www.youtube.com/watch?v=ycq7jmv6-Wo
4. *Vasimr Rocket*
   https://www.google.com/search?q=vasimr+rocket+speed&rlz=1C1CHBF enUS727US727&oq=vasimr+ro&aqs=chrome.2.0j69i57j0l4.11763j0j8 &sourceid =chrome&ie=UTF-8
5. *Amazon Prime Air*
   https://www.recode.net/2017/3/24/15054884/amazon-prime-air-public-us-drone-delivery
6. *3D Printers Material*
   https://www.makerbot.com/replicator/
7. *Singularity*
   https://en.wikipedia.org/wiki/Technological_singularity
8. *3D Printers Body Parts*
   https://www.ted.com/talks/anthony_atala_printing_a_human_kidney
9. *New Trans human Era*
   http://thetranshumanist.news/2017/01/30/top-ten-futuristic-transhumanist-technologies/
10. *Transhumanists will kill you*
    https://www.youtube.com/watch?v=KADSZ8YHtXQS

Chapter Three

1. *Don't Mess with Men*
   (Email story) Source Unknown
2. *Joel Rosenberg Gog and Magog*
   http://www.joelrosenberg.com/ezekiel-38-39-faq/
3. *Luxury Bunkers*
   https://www.youtube.com/watch?v=cLy6AXjwQK8
4. *Big Dog*
   https://www.youtube.com/watch?v=NtU9p1VYtcQ
5. *Various Robotic Animals*
   https://www.youtube.com/watch?v=P7s4DqWn-Xk
6. *Cheetah Robotic Animal*
   https://www.youtube.com/watch?v=d2D71CveQwo
7. *HULC for Soldiers*

    https://www.youtube.com/watch?v=-Hh3C8Fq_SM
8. *TALOS for Soldiers*
    https://www.youtube.com/watch?v=e9BHCaXqdkQ
9. *Super Hero Soldiers*
    https://www.youtube.com/watch?v=07-OZFEAJAo
10. *Avengers Save the Day*
    https://www.youtube.com/watch?v=3LEmNgZvUYg
11. *Sudan Somalia Famine*
    https://www.youtube.com/watch?v=WB7jUMJGycw
12. *Dust Storm in Lubbock Texas*
    https://www.youtube.com/watch?v=tauoBRoRlzU
13. *Texas Town Drinks Toilet Water*
    https://www.youtube.com/watch?v=lOwHEXzVcb4
14. *California Drought*
    https://www.youtube.com/watch?v=rHWHuP91c7Y
15. *California Ground is Sinking*
    https://www.youtube.com/watch?v=4oAFyilGJXc
16. *What California Produces in Food*
    http://www.slate.com/articles/health_and_science/explainer/2013/07/california_grows_all_of_our_fruits_and_vegetables_what_would_we_eat_without.html
17. *World Water Crisis*
    http://www.huffingtonpost.com/entry/water-scarcity-study_us_56c1ebc5e4b0b40245c72f5e
18. *Earthquake Activity*
    https://www.google.com/search?q=USGS+graph+of+earthquake+frequency+2006-008&rlz=1C1CHBF_enUS727US727&tbm=isch&tbo=u&source=univ&sa=X&ved=0ahUKEwjspPSElubVAhUY9mMKHTvwAjkQsAQIKw&biw=868&bih=503
19. *Oklahoma Earthquakes on the Rise*
    https://en.wikipedia.org/wiki/2009%E2%80%9317_Oklahoma_earthquake_swarms
20. *New Madrid Earthquake*
    https://www.youtube.com/watch?v=Fab2nITtlRg
21. *Whooping Cough*
    https://www.youtube.com/watch?v=D8irypzIr2Y
22. *Cholera Outbreak in 1854*
    https://www.youtube.com/watch?v=lNjrAXGRda4

23. Chikungunya Virus
https://www.youtube.com/watch?v=3eSCF3LTqg4
24. Border *Crossings bring Disease*
http://www.wnd.com/2014/06/deadly-diseases-crossing-border-with-illegals/
25. *Mers is Spreading*
https://www.youtube.com/watch?v=V44biQno_F0
26. *Ebola Virus Out of Control*
https://www.youtube.com/watch?v=rDMcPt-tQXo
27. *Recreating the Black Plague*
https://www.youtube.com/watch?v=4PdiA5QQnr0
28. *Plagues Released in Laboratories*
https://www.theatlantic.com/health/archive/2014/05/when-viruses-escape-the-lab/371202/
29. *Overuse of Antibiotics*
https://www.youtube.com/watch?v=HlTb3gRyzcQ
30. *Signs the Sun is Heating Up*
https://briankoberlein.com/2016/01/03/end-of-days/
31. *Sun Destroying the Earth*
https://www.youtube.com/watch?v=vN1SyaSdCeM
32. *Asteroid Strike is close*
https://www.express.co.uk/news/science/819593/asteroid-strike-meteor-chelyabinsk-tunguska
33. *Last Days Volcano*
https://www.express.co.uk/news/science/768778/Yellowstone-eruption-Supervolcano-BRINK-of-erupting-increased-activity
34. *Derecho Land Hurricane*
https://www.youtube.com/watch?v=K61qGvKltL8
35. *Locust on Radar*
http://thevane.gawker.com/radar-shows-millions-of-locusts-a-mile-deep-in-the-air-1585215529
36. *Frog Invasion*
http://metro.co.uk/2010/05/27/millions-of-frogs-close-road-in-greece-348417/

Chapter Four

1. *Obama Joke*
   (Email story) – Source Unknown
2. *Maitreyan signs*
   https://www.youtube.com/watch?v=9JihYJhfAs4&list=PLrY2Ib7dYkF2UDSP09fVG3GlW9RY1Aog
3. *Bills Maher exposes Miranda*
   https://www.youtube.com/watch?v=vwyFvIsoAnw
4. *Miranda coming back*
   http://www.houstonpress.com/news/this-man-thinks-hes-jesus-h-christ-6600307
5. *INRI Cristo Scooter Ride*
   https://www.youtube.com/watch?v=mj2oZyc4yr4
6. *Todd Bentley Kicks People*
   https://www.youtube.com/watch?v=lCO5htE9BJs
7. *Jessa Bentley Elephant Vision*
   https://www.youtube.com/watch?v=XjMYqDHbYtg
8. *Jesus on Different Things*
   http://www.huffingtonpost.com/2013/09/05/jesus-sightings-in-the-news-compilation_n_3874174.html
9. *Visions of Mary*
   https://www.youtube.com/watch?v=u5uWjv9CSb5E&list=PLF8E939D51C38331F
10. *Global Visions of Mary*
    https://www.youtube.com/watch?v=NSRrcBIgvT4
11. *Trances Produce Mary Visions*
    https://www.youtube.com/watch?v=-KFir-f6uEI
12. *Kristine's and Bud's Testimony*
    Video no longer available
13. *Josh Enos Testimony*
    Video no longer available
14. *False Message from Mary*
    https://www.youtube.com/watch?v=vF_zRkVA3BU
15. *Blimps to Mars*
    https://www.express.co.uk/news/weird/589775/leaked-UFO-photos-US-submarine-1971-prove-aliens-Antarctic-Navy-stealth-airship-spy-plane
16. *Aliens and UFO Teachings*
    http://www.openminds.tv/lucifer-is-helping-vatican-astronomers-look-for-extraterrestrials-970/19968
17. *Demon & Aliens Smell like Sulphur*

https://exemplore.com/ufos-aliens/10-reasons-why-aliens-are-actually-fallen-angelsdemons
18. *Testimonies of Rebuking Aliens*
http://www.alienresistance.org/ce4testimonies.htm
19. *UFO's Explain away the Rapture*
http://www.redmoonrising.com/newage.htm
20. *Bill Clinton on UFO Landing*
https://www.youtube.com/results?search_query=bill+clinton+kimmel+ufo
21. *Vatican & UFO's*
https://www.youtube.com/watch?v=4Uu4zX8S2Kc
22. *Vatican Behavior*
https://www.youtube.com/watch?v=V0Y1Qg10pys
23. *Pope Francis to Baptize Aliens*
https://www.youtube.com/watch?v=rObvz3U_pTo
https://www.youtube.com/watch?v=pCjPJlc4ds0
24. *The Last Card*
https://www.youtube.com/watch?v=sknwywK74x4

Chapter Five

1. *Don't Sell the Cow*
   (Email Story) Source Unknown
2. *Leave it to Beaver*
   (Email Story) Source Unknown
3. *Rise in Society Wickedness*
   Video no longer available
4. *Quote Humanists*
   https://borne.wordpress.com/2011/10/25/the-secular-humanist-conspiracy/
5. *Stats of the Rise of Immorality*
   http://www.christianpost.com/news/americans-acceptance-of-wide-range-of-sexual-immorality-growing-gallup-finds-139748
6. *Quote Modern Lady*
   http://tomohalloran.com/2014/07/15/hidden-weakness-pornogogues-running-childrens-schools/
7. *Video Paint Balls per Wicked Word*
   https://www.youtube.com/watch?v=B7t85SESTXI

8. *Ashley Madison*
   https://www.youtube.com/watch?v=VQp9mkuCYBM
9. *Rise of Immorality*
   http://graytotebox.com/the-immorality-in-america-the-statistics/
10. *Brutal Wickedness*
    https://www.jeremiahproject.com/last-days/signs-last-days-increase-wickedness/
11. *Rise in Atheism*
    https://www.youtube.com/watch?v=HIiPDDlwCm0
12. *Average American Church*
    Video no longer available
13. *England's Atheist Church*
    https://www.youtube.com/watch?v=uNn-9hw2YCc
14. *America's Atheist Church*
    https://www.youtube.com/results?search_query=Jerry+Dewitt+Atheist+church+
15. *Stats on Abortion*
    https://www.youtube.com/watch?v=rY-bQ6UzhNI
16. *Planned Parenthood Demonstration*
    https://www.youtube.com/watch?v=RzheWjPnDOg
17. *Comment RE: Abortion*
    https://www.youtube.com/watch?v=PlarG0aTUTc
18. *Examples of Hybrids*
    https://www.youtube.com/watch?v=TJu8sWZDhU4
    https://www.youtube.com/watch?v=7QlWBnL0zjU
19. *US Creates Super Soldiers*
    https://www.youtube.com/watch?v=0rvS1vbc4Nc
20. *US Hurries to Make Hybrids*
    https://www.youtube.com/watch?v=MAK2Mtce9gw
21. Marijuana Traffic Deaths
    https://www.youtube.com/watch?v=6hu9jlNoX8YNO LINK
22. *Marijuana Vending Machines*
    https://www.youtube.com/watch?v=ADVHW_SP9lE
23. *Rise in Drug Use*
    https://www.youtube.com/watch?v=KpvAVhXyq1M
24. *Drug Statistics*
    https://www.youtube.com/watch?v=ntVZ1Ivap6w
25. *Prescription Drugs Cause Killings*
    https://www.youtube.com/watch?v=nVdYQBqr4aA

26. *Psychiatry Industry of Death*
    https://www.youtube.com/watch?v=gvdBSSUviys
27. *Witchcraft Military Service*
    – YouTube Video – Source Unknown)
28. *Vampire Lady*
    https://www.youtube.com/watch?v=Z127wKKWfXg
29. *Vampire Injections*
    https://www.youtube.com/watch?v=vDZgN56_yYA
30. *Harvard Black Mass*
    https://www.youtube.com/watch?v=XcwdvOfL8Vo
31. *Statute of Satan in Oklahoma*
    https://www.youtube.com/watch?v=XcwdvOfL8Vo
32. *Pentagon Zombie Apocalypse*
    https://www.youtube.com/watch?v=pSX-Zg3MCa4

Chapter Six

1. *Bill's Bad Day*
   (Email Story) Source Unknown
2. *Rise of Apostasy*
   https://1s712.americanbible.org/cdn-www-ws03/uploads/content/State_of_the_Bible_2016.pdf
3. *Atheist Pastor*
   https://www.youtube.com/watch?v=4iTznYniqkE
4. *Nude Church*
   https://www.youtube.com/watch?v=1J21fPo40do
5. *McChurch*
   (Email Story) Source Unknown
6. *Child Evangelism Fellowship*
   https://www.youtube.com/watch?v=7ze0skAW7DA
7. *Victoria Osteen Teaches Satanism*
   https://www.youtube.com/watch?v=Y42tZZjQuRA
8. *Pastors Silent on Biblical Issues*
   https://www.youtube.com/watch?v=FGWdAQcL2FY
9. *Salad Bar Religion*
   https://www.youtube.com/watch?v=bVeG6oIs4EY
10. *Apostate Noah Movie*

    https://www.youtube.com/watch?v=-36Cs-B5iG4
11. *Apostate Media*
    Video no Longer available
12. *Apostate Musician*
    https://www.youtube.com/watch?v=8xTtF4Tad-gNO LINK
13. *China is Becoming More Christian*
    https://www.youtube.com/watch?v=AOmcwHZ8TbM
14. *Quote Jeffrey Baker*
    Video no longer available
15. *SheZow Cartoon*
    https://www.youtube.com/watch?v=NcU5QEVJo-U…
16. *Homosexual World Pressure*
    https://www.youtube.com/watch?v=3dhHvBIMh0U
    https://www.youtube.com/results?search_query=homosexual+world+pressure
17. *Burger King Proud Worker*
    https://www.youtube.com/watch?v=zU5NWc78kOQ
18. *Schools Promoting Homosexuality*
    https://www.youtube.com/watch?v=puI4pfRB0w0
    https://www.youtube.com/watch?v=8DUQ1tR9Mpg
19. *Homosexuality in the Church*
    https://www.youtube.com/results?search_query=danny+cortez+same+sex+third+way+church
20. *Gary Hall*
    https://www.youtube.com/results?search_query=gary+hall+homophobia+is+a+sin

Chapter Seven

1. *Orson on a Moped*
   (Email Story) Source Unknown
2. *Hate Crime Pressure*
   https://www.youtube.com/watch?v=r2Hbf2FIkJg
   https://www.youtube.com/watch?v=6Slv2mpxEQg
   https://www.youtube.com/watch?v=2DlvjqzNq3M
   https://www.youtube.com/watch?v=CVzO6qQ0bFk
3. *Hate Crime Persecution*

https://www.youtube.com/watch?v=plCK_4tiFA8
4. *Homosexual Behavior Worsens*
https://www.youtube.com/watch?v=f8rThG0JjV0
https://www.youtube.com/watch?v=Db2BRfP7K80
https://www.youtube.com/watch?v=TsJRp8vU8VI
5. *Russia Says no to Homosexuality*
https://www.youtube.com/watch?v=eF_Ht0ml5Pk
6. *House of One*
https://house-of-one.org/de
7. *We are no Longer a Christian Nation*
https://www.youtube.com/watch?v=zOOrSAbU9z8
8. *World Pluralism*
https://www.youtube.com/watch?v=bue0ighqIwA
9. *Irish Pastor Hate Crime*
https://www.youtube.com/watch?v=6zZum61jkWw
10. *World Persecution*
https://www.youtube.com/watch?v=o9siCE2dFp0
11. *Christian Blood Being Drained and Sold*
https://www.youtube.com/watch?v=fYF3N9bkZAM
12. *Persecution in America*
https://www.youtube.com/watch?v=wsUFG7HY5mY
13. *Paul Washer*
https://www.youtube.com/watch?v=8BtVP37SWqs
14. *Vatican Promoting One World Religion*
https://www.youtube.com/watch?v=cABfvA6-1Lo
15. *Headquarters of World Religions*
http://bigthink.com/ideafeed/pope-francis-speaks-before-un-why-not-a-un-for-religions
https://www.youtube.com/watch?v=e-sFJ3QwsFk
16. *Pope Francis Praying with other Religions*
https://www.youtube.com/watch?v=-0kLLwJGHYU
17. *Vatican Three Festivals in Jerusalem*
http://www.cuttingedge.org/news/n2115.cfm
http://israelmilitary.net/showthread.php?t=12444
18. *All People go to Heaven*
https://www.youtube.com/watch?v=cW6VMt-8WRE
19. *Pope speaks at Kenneth Copelands Church*
https://www.youtube.com/watch?v=S94msQbNFZY
20. *Charismatic Movement and the Pope*

https://www.youtube.com/watch?v=Ge6Ge-WWlIM
21. *Beth Moore*
    https://www.youtube.com/watch?v=IqUiqdGYit8
22. *Joel Osteen Loves the Pope*
    https://www.youtube.com/watch?v=49ItTjxe0ZQ
23. *Rick Warren Loves the Pope*
    https://www.youtube.com/watch?v=igNCUw1adIw
24. *Mother Angelica*
    https://www.youtube.com/watch?v=51CiJ8_P1ZU
25. *Minister Converts to Catholicism*
    https://www.youtube.com/watch?v=-QZTB64-26M

Chapter Eight

1. *Bills Bad Day Part 3*
   (Email Story) Source Unknown
2. *Obama New World Order*
   https://www.youtube.com/watch?v=OLW6eIhuWYk
3. *Biden New World Order*
   https://www.youtube.com/watch?v=fDACY15Jxa0
4. *Chuck Hagel New World Order*
   https://www.youtube.com/watch?v=gId56HQtuYQ
5. *Military Purge*
   https://www.youtube.com/watch?v=3yf98iOdkYY
6. *Paul Henri Spaak*
   Video no longer available
7. *Illuminati Map of the World*
   1952 http://www.cuttingedge.org/news/n1270.cfm
8. *Chinese Military on American Soil*
   https://www.youtube.com/watch?v=uCGZ5gBbrbw
9. *Chinese Police in Paris*
   https://www.youtube.com/watch?v=xWg_dvy1f4E
10. *Henry Kissinger Quote*
    https://www.thenewamerican.com/world-news/item/19030-globalist-henry-Kissinger-outlines-new-world-order
11. *Obama Brain Initiative*
    https://www.youtube.com/watch?v=1yovwtZhyZU

12. *Brain Chip*
    https://www.washingtonpost.com/news/the-switch/wp/2016/08/15/putting-a-computer-in-your-brain-is-no-longer-science-fiction/?utm_term=.40cb27ca6e6b
13. *Super Soldier Brain Chip*
    http://www.dailymail.co.uk/news/article-3252239/Micro-chipped-super-soldiers-reality-book-claims-Implants-combat-PTSD-make-military-resilient-warfare-rolled-couple-years.html
14. *Map of ten Kingdoms*
    https://view.officeapps.live.com/op/view.aspx?src=http://www.laydownlife.net/yedidah/word/Ten%20Kingdoms.doc
15. *Russia Eurasia Economic Union*
    https://www.youtube.com/watch?v=3xHAwpawOv0
16. *Unions Being Formed*
    https://nuclearsuntan.blogspot.com/
17. *Crisis can Create the Amero*
    https://www.youtube.com/watch?v=UVRBMiTzMoo
18. *Marci Kaptur on Super Highway*
    https://www.youtube.com/watch?v=cd29U90s_ik
19. *Superhighway Facts*
    https://www.youtube.com/watch?v=oAHN9rKil_k
20. *Civil Assistance Plan*
    http://www.wnd.com/2008/02/57228/
21. *Border Crisis Chinese Crossing*
    https://www.youtube.com/watch?v=4dbtRF3bWzs
22. *National I.D. Card*
    https://www.youtube.com/watch?v=n9CZ5OUet3s
23. *RFID to Travel*
    https://www.youtube.com/results?search_query=RFID+IMPLANT+start
24. *Take a Stand*
    https://www.youtube.com/watch?v=qPvuYxUxEto
25. *Last Days Weather Report*
    (Email Story) Source Unknown
26. *Mind Reader*
    https://www.youtube.com/watch?v=F7pYHN9iC9I
27. *NSA Running out of Room*
    https://nsa.gov1.info/surveillance/
28. *NSA Utah Data Center*
    https://www.youtube.com/watch?v=jXXSgmIe7dY

20. *Argus Spy Camera*
    https://www.youtube.com/watch?v=BBfSbdAC-3k
30. *Last Days News Report*
    (Email Story) Source Unknown
31. *Police Tracking Darts*
    https://www.youtube.com/watch?v=qmqHrgKI1ak
32. *Zoomback Personal Locator*
    https://www.youtube.com/watch?v=WQ4xLB91Kvk
33. *EZ Pass Tracking*
    https://www.youtube.com/watch?v=Fpq1uGk5QgE
34. *Video License Plate*
    https://www.youtube.com/watch?v=ZjyaB5xBBjs
35. *Car Dealer Tracking*
    https://www.youtube.com/watch?v=guuDUAvEqng
36. *Mandatory Black Boxes*
    https://www.youtube.com/watch?v=JA-TarTVAnA
37. *Camera in Cars*
    http://time.com/3256037/gm-sensors-distracted-driving/
38. *Cities Installing Camera*
    https://www.youtube.com/watch?v=caL2C2rqVGM
39. *Google Glass App*
    https://www.youtube.com/watch?v=1CCx7MpsSsE
40. *Larry Walters Flight*
    https://www.youtube.com/watch?v=CFFVVo9usFY
41. *NSA Collecting Phone Records*
    https://www.youtube.com/watch?v=y6zy01J6cA8
42. *Tracking Lost Phone*
    https://www.youtube.com/watch?v=Y7WDVciEwdQ
43. *Tracking your friends*
    https://www.youtube.com/watch?v=uVL7Inyac78
44. *Tracking your Kids*
    https://www.youtube.com/watch?v=uVL7Inyac78
45. *Tracking by Police*
    https://www.youtube.com/results?search_query=tracking+by+police
46. *Tracking by Government*
    https://www.youtube.com/watch?v=diM4egpjxx8
47. *Tracking by Games*
    http://www.foxnews.com/tech/2014/01/27/nsa-spying-through-angry-birds-google-maps.html

48. Video *Watching & Listening to Cell Phones*
    https://www.youtube.com/watch?v=34oMf5g4h5g
49. *Video Companies*
    https://www.youtube.com/watch?v=O9fp1xoKhOI
50. *NSA Planting Bugs*
    https://www.youtube.com/watch?v=YEcd1EAjXjs
51. *Baby Cam*
    https://www.youtube.com/watch?v=fdG_BDWjLmg
52. *Web Cam get Hacked*
    https://www.youtube.com/watch?v=Gz9uzfrFVxY
53. *Google Chrome Listens*
    https://www.youtube.com/watch?v=AMmEhCke_eE
54. *Google uses Gmail to report to Police*
    https://www.youtube.com/watch?v=PvORBy4hf7A
55. *What NEST Does*
    https://nest.com/thermostat/meet-nest-thermostat/
56. *LED Lights Monitoring US*
    http://www.cbsnews.com/news/technology-in-led-smart-lights-raises-privacy-concerns/
57. *What Does Echo Do*
    https://www.youtube.com/watch?v=xenOYWVwkGY
58. *Lady jailed for Being off Grid*
    https://www.youtube.com/watch?v=y3UalgTRsxE

Chapter Nine

1. *Sound Engineer Fixes Bad Singer*
   (Email Story) Source Unknown
2. *TPP Treaty*
   https://www.youtube.com/watch?v=M9ZFDpuiFUs
3. *Global Currency War*
   http://money.cnn.com/2016/01/07/news/economy/global-currency-war-sparked-by-china/index.html
4. *Libya Becomes Economic Threat*
   https://www.youtube.com/watch?v=ZdjVVIlq-1g
5. *China Threatens Global Currency*
   https://www.youtube.com/watch?v=3bdZwtOxE3w

6. *What is Bitcoin*
   https://www.youtube.com/watch?v=Um63OQz3bjo
7. *Man Implants Bitcoin*
   https://www.youtube.com/watch?v=wbSxC6BfEwk
8. *Cashless Family*
   https://www.youtube.com/watch?v=c_Wi8AxNihc
9. *Cashless People in Europe*
   https://www.youtube.com/watch?v=xCtN4zWCf2M
10. *Cashless Gets Rid of Terrorist*
    https://www.youtube.com/watch?v=bKJ81XxBk04
11. *Cashless Apple Pay*
    https://www.youtube.com/watch?v=KdYB7T_eQsk
12. *Starbucks is Cashless*
    https://www.youtube.com/watch?v=or6U0GeZ4j0
13. *Cell Phone Payment from afar*
    https://www.youtube.com/watch?v=dnPxKJpYOCs
14. *Sweden Cashless Society*
    https://www.youtube.com/watch?v=-ftiaRrB-u4
15. *Motorola Digital Tattoo*
    https://www.youtube.com/watch?v=4owGFqQCHys
16. *Mandatory Microchip Implants*
    https://www.youtube.com/watch?v=5nkNewmMylc

Chapter Ten

1. *You Chop It*
   (Email Story) Source Unknown
2. *Sony Hack to Control Internet*
   https://www.youtube.com/watch?v=8c0OcJD7dcY
3. *Global Entity to control Internet*
   https://www.youtube.com/watch?v=_udJngtDVAQ
4. *Real ID Coming Soon*
   https://www.youtube.com/watch?v=6YyzVKhkx4I
5. *Electronic Pick Pocket*
   https://www.youtube.com/watch?v=bUz6oe6AlFs
6. *Video Scan Protected Clothing*

http://www.azcentral.com/story/money/business/tech/2014/12/27/proactive-fighting-electronic-pickpockets/20933951/
7. *Regina Dugan Pushing Implants*
https://www.youtube.com/watch?v=ZR6Onwg8wyQ
8. *DNA Recreates a Persons Face*
https://www.youtube.com/watch?v=Ln-1-WysCbw
9. *Biometric Database*
https://www.youtube.com/watch?v=sgyhwZKDIRY
10. *Biometrics can Steal Your Identity*
https://www.youtube.com/watch?v=Rn4Rupla11M
11. *Biometric Head*
https://tascent.com/?gclid=EAIaIQobChMIndGGm-HP1gIVRZV-Ch0oqAbiEAAYASAAEgLIvPD_BwE
12. *Myris Personal Eye Scanner*
https://www.youtube.com/watch?v=mJhav4R5rW4
13. *McCarren Eye Scanner*
https://www.youtube.com/watch?v=gN3jTEVgs5M
14. *NSA Images on Facebook*
https://www.youtube.com/watch?v=6jTxiTFeTW4
15. *Read Your Face Read Your Mind*
https://www.cl.cam.ac.uk/research/rainbow/emotions/mrm.html
16. *EAZE Nod to Payment*
https://www.youtube.com/watch?v=Wu7tMD3ufKI
17. *Video Pulse Wallet*
https://www.youtube.com/watch?v=FPvrVHH8xdo
18. *Quixter Hand Payment*
thttps://www.youtube.com/watch?v=9oq_bpDGdB8
19. *Media Promotes Implants*
https://www.youtube.com/watch?v=0pRYMUGv0Bg
20. *Amal Graafstra Promotes Implants*
https://www.youtube.com/watch?v=O0fGf5MAj8s
21. *Microchip to lose Weight*
https://www.youtube.com/watch?v=16Z8umjBqKk
22. *Microchip for Alzheimer's*
https://www.youtube.com/watch?v=fuvI1RH4jMI
23. *Microchip for Birth Control*
https://www.youtube.com/watch?v=GP8QbKUhFVs
24. *Microchip for Disease Control*

http://www.cnn.com/2014/12/19/tech/innovation/digital-nose-disease-breathalyzer/index.html
25. *Microchip for Brain Control*
https://www.youtube.com/watch?v=jryvMQfwaH0
26. *Microchip in Work place*
https://www.youtube.com/watch?v=m-h9BW20_Ws
27. *Future of Microchipping*
https://www.youtube.com/watch?v=eb_aFOhpS8g
28. *3D Tattoos*
https://www.youtube.com/watch?v=MuuTe6IhJ50
29. *Tattoos Lead to Mark of the Beast*
https://www.youtube.com/watch?v=qNwIZRbAWp0
30. *Adult Man gets Implant*
https://www.youtube.com/watch?v=hTBJ6OIGkzc
31. *Wearables for Convenience*
https://www.youtube.com/results?search_query=bracelet+called+the+MICA
32. *Wearables for Payment*
https://www.youtube.com/watch?v=Durkpz3GvVk
33. *Wearables Lead to Implants*
https://www.youtube.com/watch?v=CABlsa5VDzA
34. *Half Hour Sooner*
(Email Story) Source Unknown

www.ingramcontent.com/pod-product-compliance
Lightning Source LLC
Chambersburg PA
CBHW032029150426
43194CB00006B/209